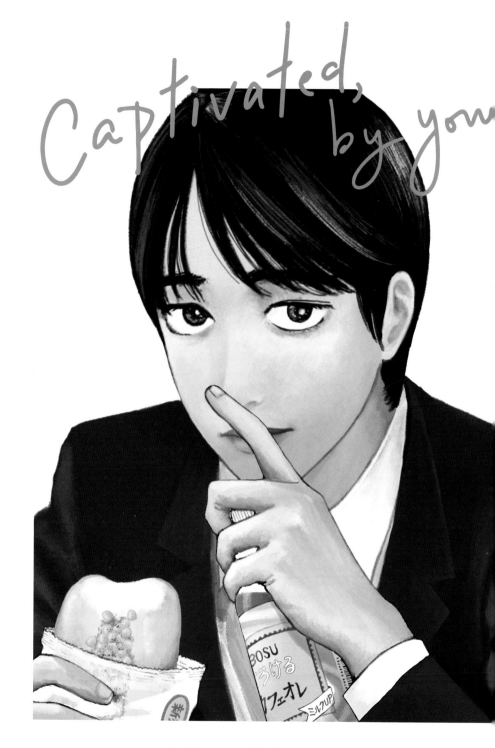

Captivated, by you

Yama Wayama

Contents

[Someone Cute]

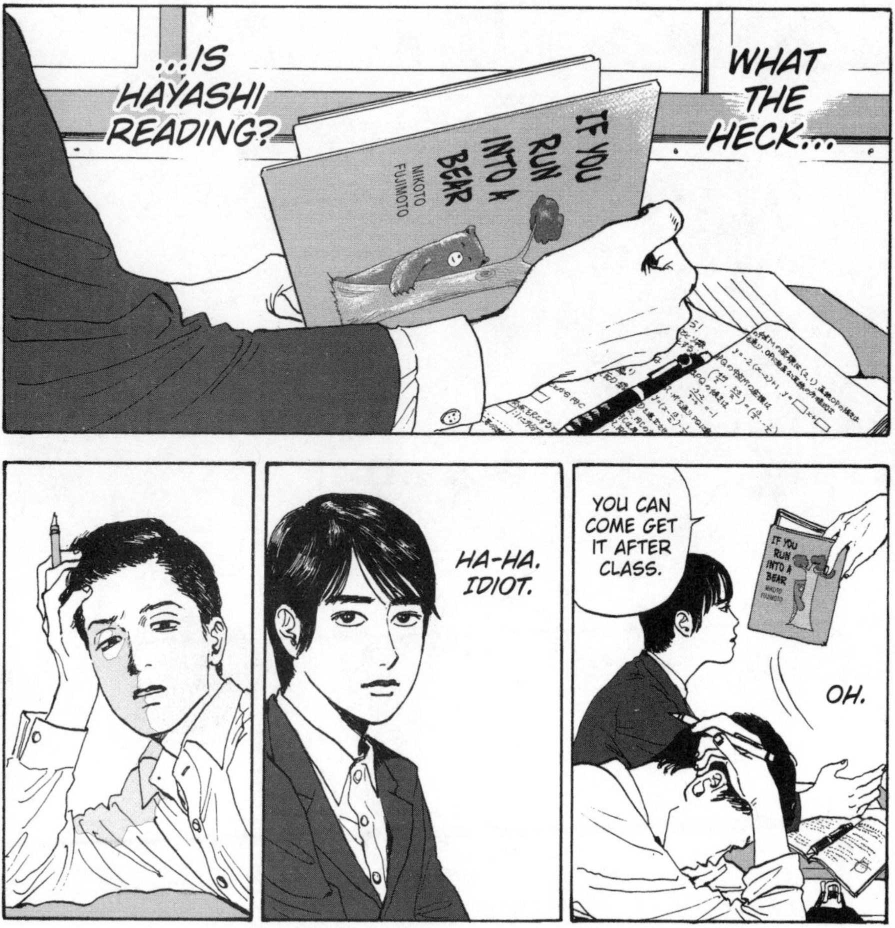
WHAT THE HECK...
...IS HAYASHI READING?
IF YOU RUN INTO A BEAR
MIKOTO FUJIMOTO
YOU CAN COME GET IT AFTER CLASS.
IF YOU RUN INTO A BEAR
OH.
HA-HA. IDIOT.

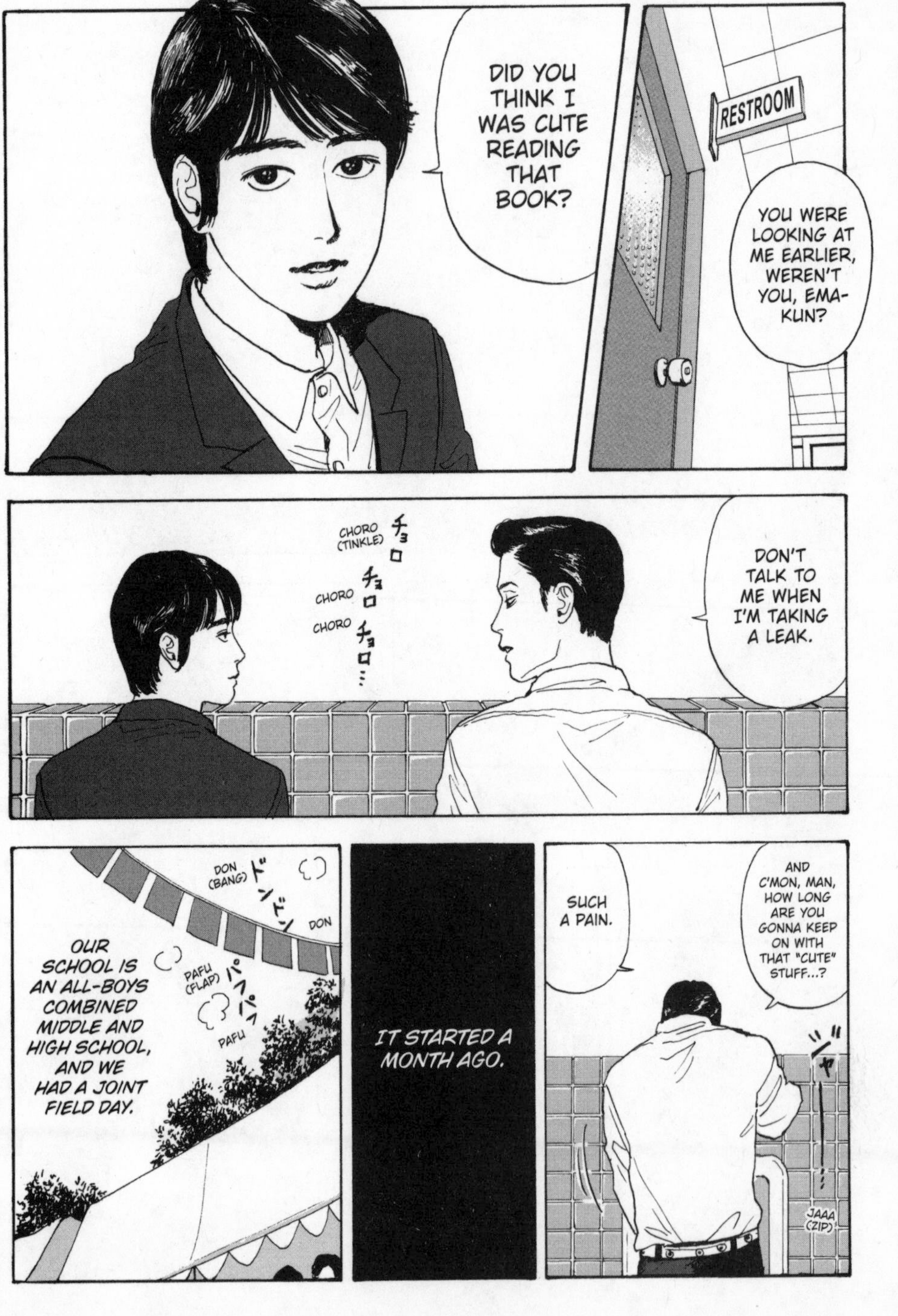

RESTROOM
YOU WERE LOOKING AT ME EARLIER, WEREN'T YOU, EMA-KUN?
DID YOU THINK I WAS CUTE READING THAT BOOK?
DON'T TALK TO ME WHEN I'M TAKING A LEAK.
CHORO (TINKLE) チョロ
CHORO チョロ
CHORO チョロ…
AND C'MON, MAN, HOW LONG ARE YOU GONNA KEEP ON WITH THAT "CUTE" STUFF...?
SUCH A PAIN.
ジャー…
JAAA (ZIP)
IT STARTED A MONTH AGO.
DON (BANG) ドン
ドン
DON
PAFU (FLAP) パフ
パフ
PAFU
OUR SCHOOL IS AN ALL-BOYS COMBINED MIDDLE AND HIGH SCHOOL, AND WE HAD A JOINT FIELD DAY.

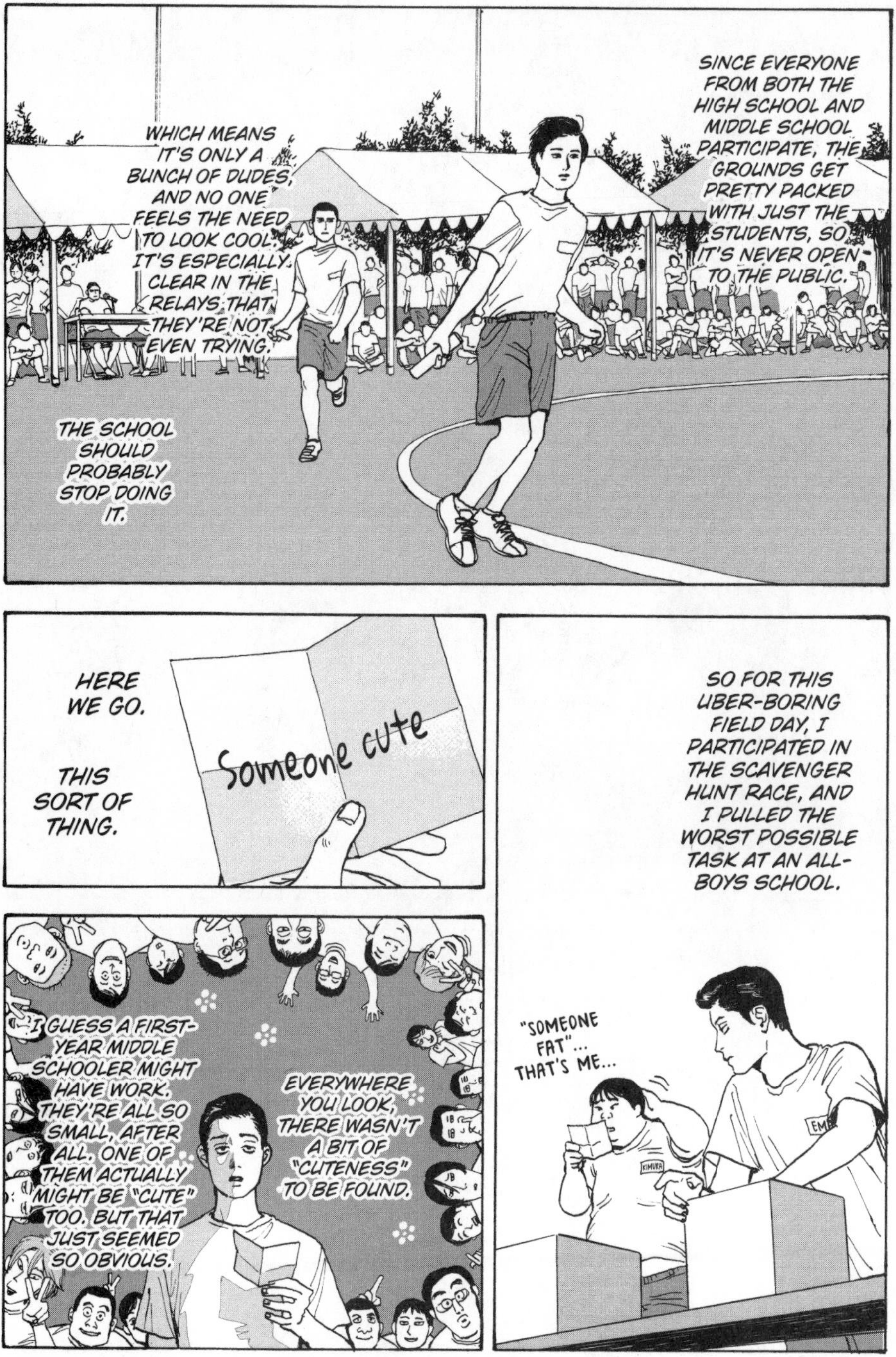
SINCE EVERYONE FROM BOTH THE HIGH SCHOOL AND MIDDLE SCHOOL PARTICIPATE, THE GROUNDS GET PRETTY PACKED WITH JUST THE STUDENTS, SO IT'S NEVER OPEN TO THE PUBLIC.
WHICH MEANS IT'S ONLY A BUNCH OF DUDES, AND NO ONE FEELS THE NEED TO LOOK COOL. IT'S ESPECIALLY CLEAR IN THE RELAYS THAT THEY'RE NOT EVEN TRYING.
THE SCHOOL SHOULD PROBABLY STOP DOING IT.
SO FOR THIS UBER-BORING FIELD DAY, I PARTICIPATED IN THE SCAVENGER HUNT RACE, AND I PULLED THE WORST POSSIBLE TASK AT AN ALL-BOYS SCHOOL.
"SOMEONE FAT"... THAT'S ME...
KIMURA
HERE WE GO.
Someone cute
THIS SORT OF THING.
EVERYWHERE YOU LOOK, THERE WASN'T A BIT OF "CUTENESS" TO BE FOUND.
I GUESS A FIRST-YEAR MIDDLE SCHOOLER MIGHT HAVE WORK. THEY'RE ALL SO SMALL, AFTER ALL. ONE OF THEM ACTUALLY MIGHT BE "CUTE" TOO. BUT THAT JUST SEEMED SO OBVIOUS.

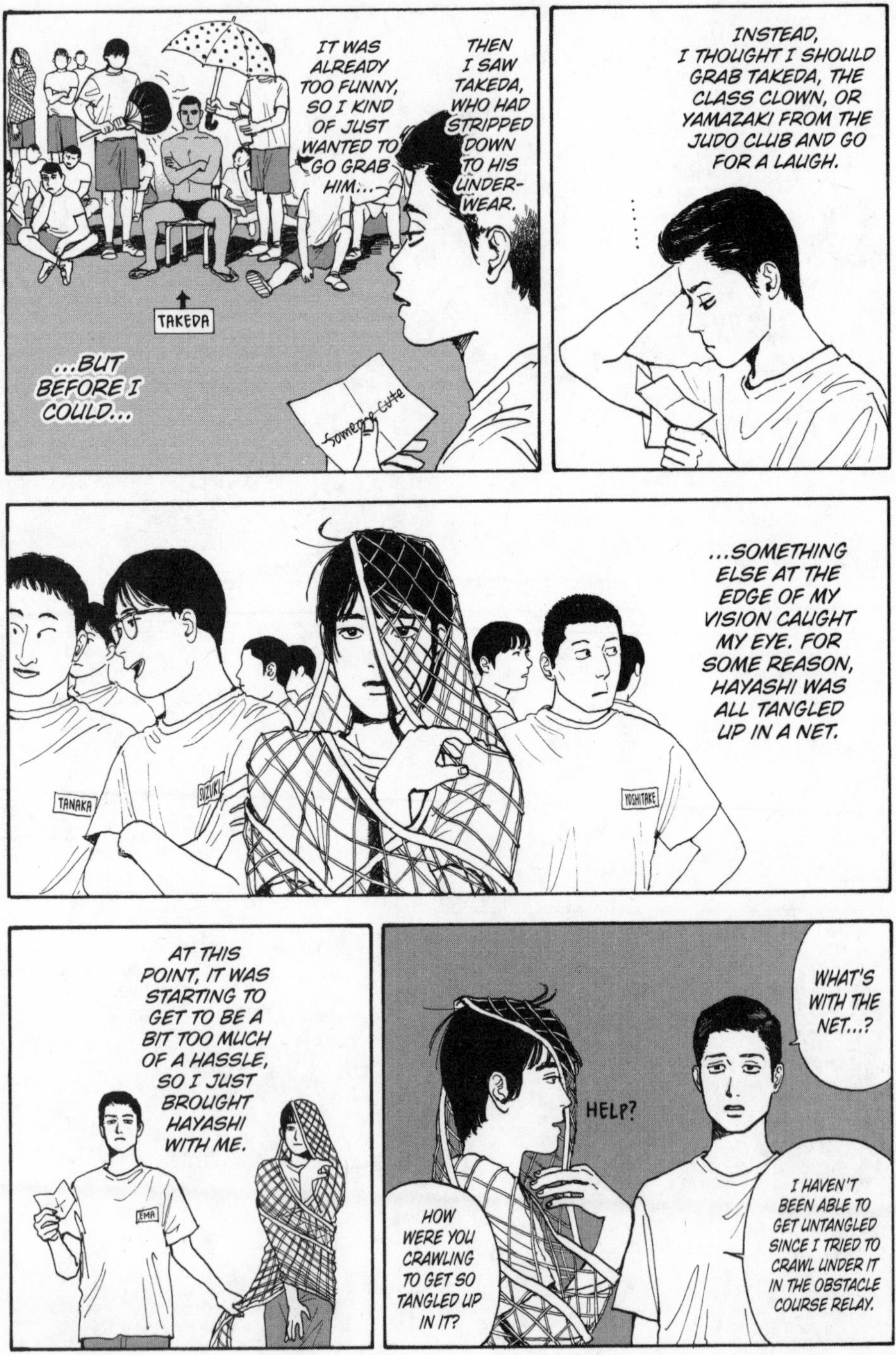
INSTEAD, I THOUGHT I SHOULD GRAB TAKEDA, THE CLASS CLOWN, OR YAMAZAKI FROM THE JUDO CLUB AND GO FOR A LAUGH.
......
THEN I SAW TAKEDA, WHO HAD STRIPPED DOWN TO HIS UNDER-WEAR.
IT WAS ALREADY TOO FUNNY, SO I KIND OF JUST WANTED TO GO GRAB HIM...
TAKEDA
...BUT BEFORE I COULD...
Someone Cute
...SOMETHING ELSE AT THE EDGE OF MY VISION CAUGHT MY EYE. FOR SOME REASON, HAYASHI WAS ALL TANGLED UP IN A NET.
YOSHITAKE
SUZUKI
TANAKA
WHAT'S WITH THE NET...?
HELP?
I HAVEN'T BEEN ABLE TO GET UNTANGLED SINCE I TRIED TO CRAWL UNDER IT IN THE OBSTACLE COURSE RELAY.
HOW WERE YOU CRAWLING TO GET SO TANGLED UP IN IT?
AT THIS POINT, IT WAS STARTING TO GET TO BE A BIT TOO MUCH OF A HASSLE, SO I JUST BROUGHT HAYASHI WITH ME.
EMA

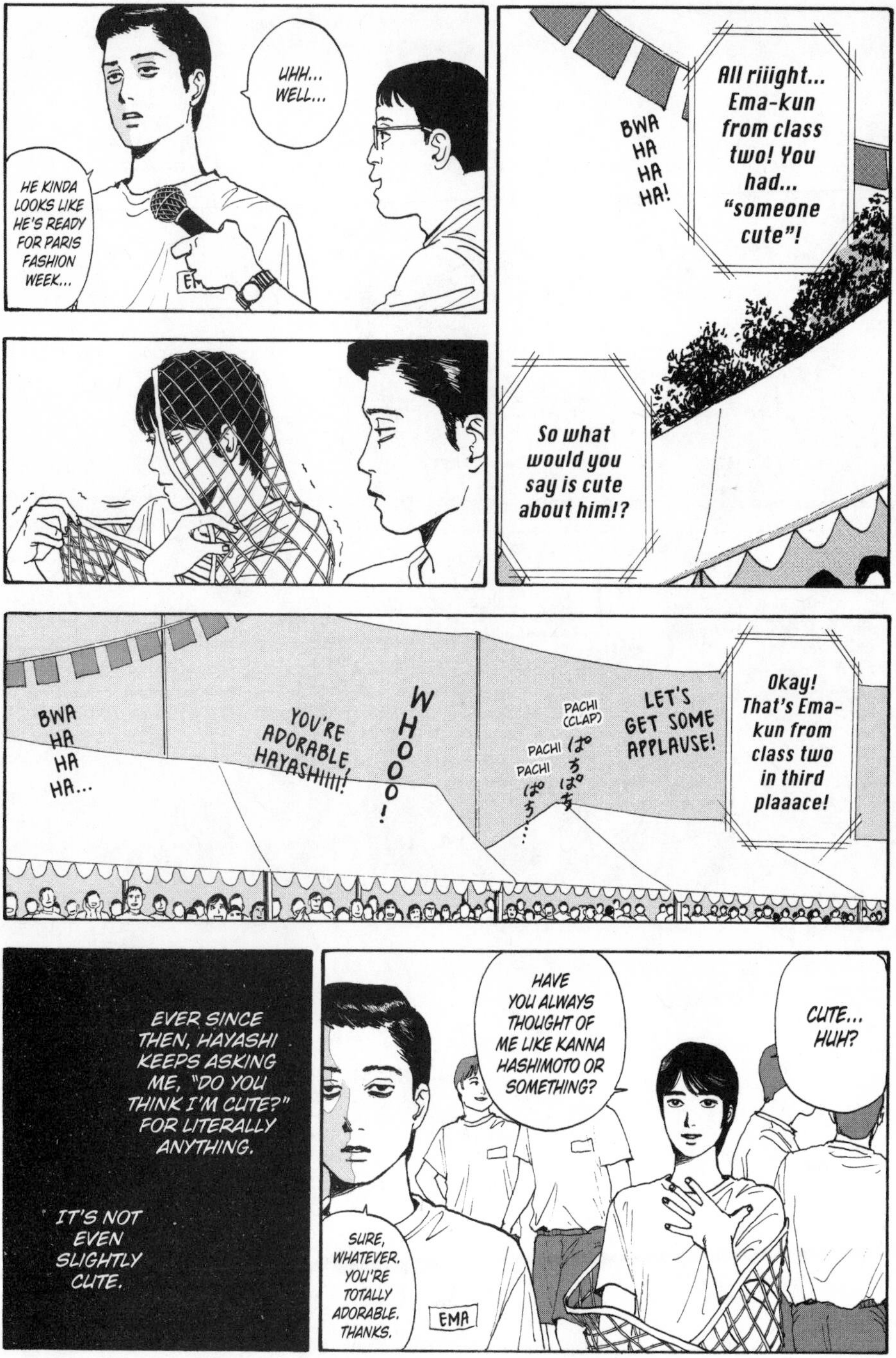
All riiight... Ema-kun from class two! You had... “someone cute”!
BWA HA HA HA!
So what would you say is cute about him!?
UHH... WELL...
HE KINDA LOOKS LIKE HE'S READY FOR PARIS FASHION WEEK...
Okay! That's Ema-kun from class two in third plaaace!
LET'S GET SOME APPLAUSE!
PACHI (CLAP) ぱちぱち
PACHI
PACHI ぱち…
WHOOOO!
YOU'RE ADORABLE, HAYASHIIIII!
BWA HA HA HA...
CUTE... HUH?
HAVE YOU ALWAYS THOUGHT OF ME LIKE KANNA HASHIMOTO OR SOMETHING?
SURE, WHATEVER. YOU'RE TOTALLY ADORABLE. THANKS.
EMA
EVER SINCE THEN, HAYASHI KEEPS ASKING ME, “DO YOU THINK I'M CUTE?” FOR LITERALLY ANYTHING.
IT'S NOT EVEN SLIGHTLY CUTE.

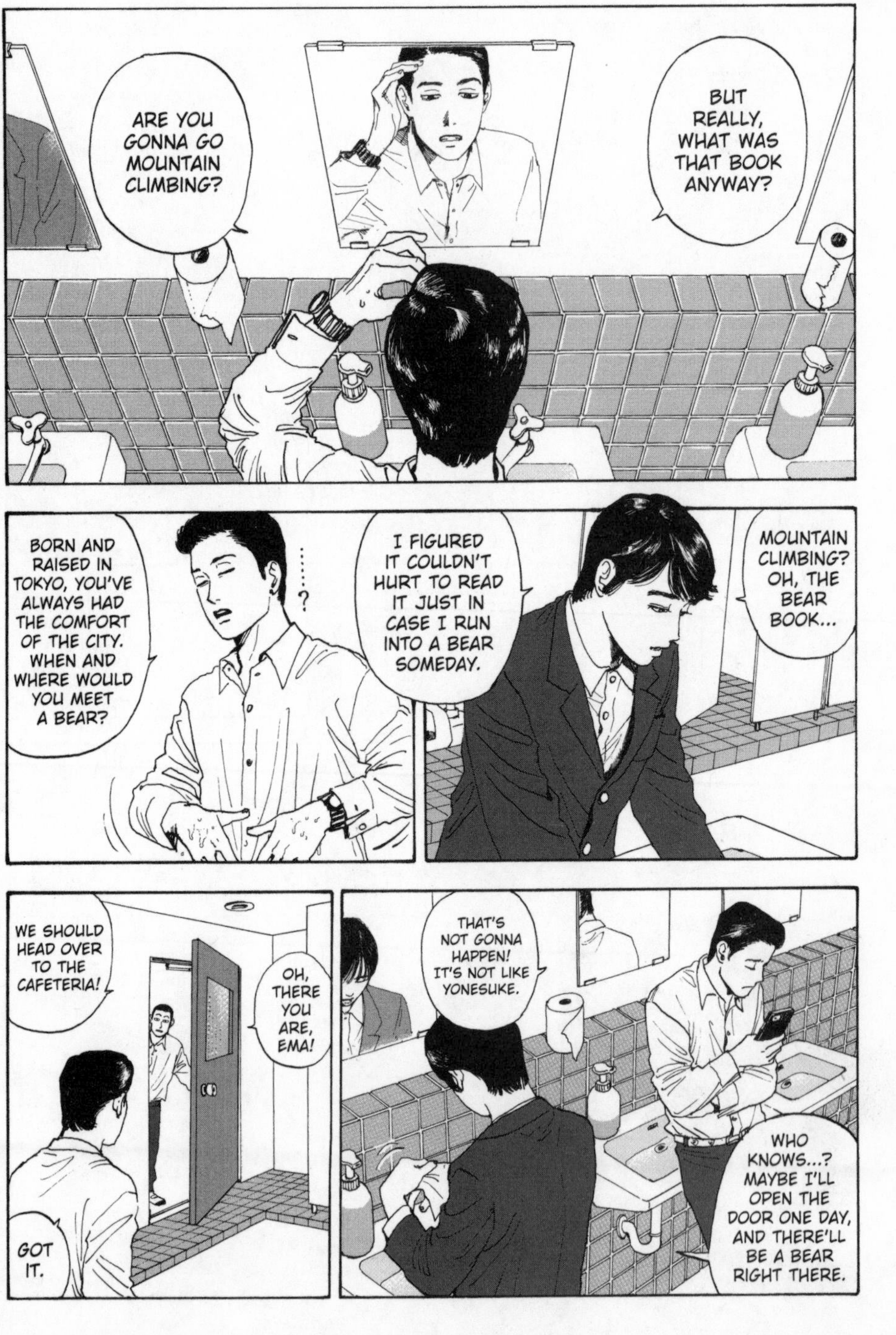
BUT REALLY, WHAT WAS THAT BOOK ANYWAY?
ARE YOU GONNA GO MOUNTAIN CLIMBING?
MOUNTAIN CLIMBING? OH, THE BEAR BOOK...
I FIGURED IT COULDN'T HURT TO READ IT JUST IN CASE I RUN INTO A BEAR SOMEDAY.
.....?
BORN AND RAISED IN TOKYO, YOU'VE ALWAYS HAD THE COMFORT OF THE CITY. WHEN AND WHERE WOULD YOU MEET A BEAR?
THAT'S NOT GONNA HAPPEN! IT'S NOT LIKE YONESUKE.
WHO KNOWS...? MAYBE I'LL OPEN THE DOOR ONE DAY, AND THERE'LL BE A BEAR RIGHT THERE.
OH, THERE YOU ARE, EMA!
WE SHOULD HEAD OVER TO THE CAFETERIA!
GOT IT.

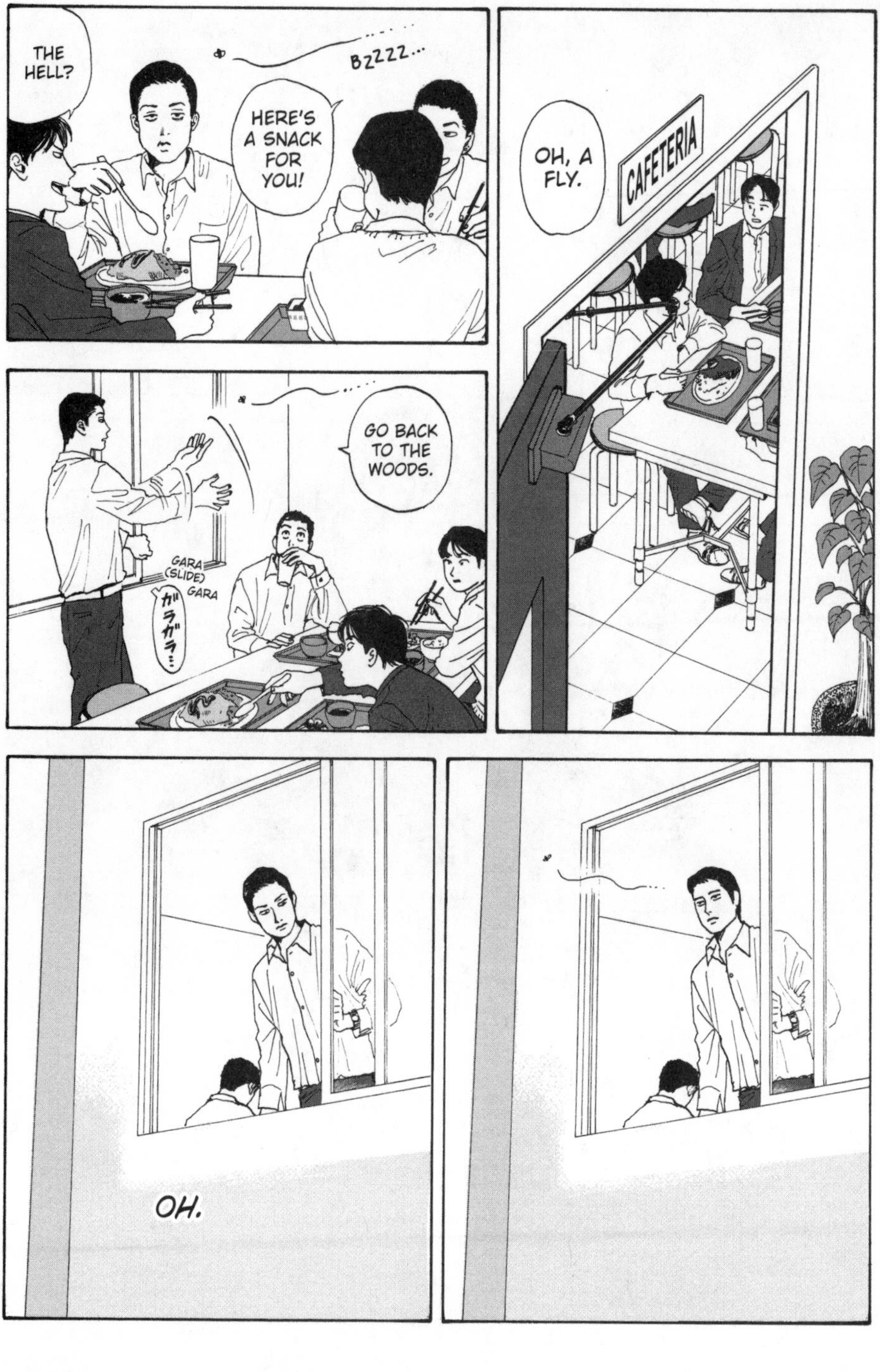
OH, A FLY.
CAFETERIA
BZZZZ...
HERE'S A SNACK FOR YOU!
THE HELL?
GO BACK TO THE WOODS.
GARA (SLIDE) GARA
ガラガラ…
OH.

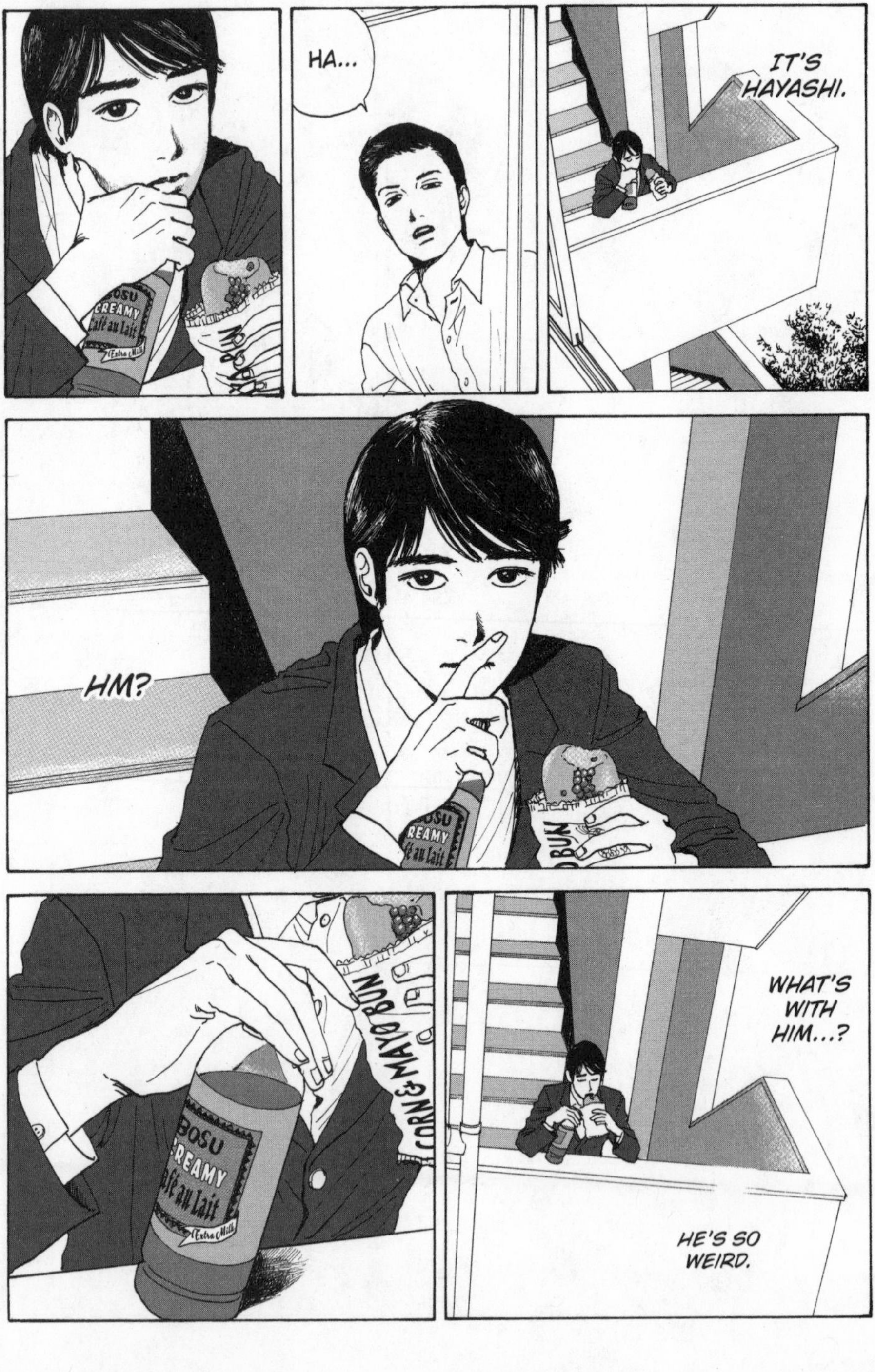
IT'S HAYASHI.
HA...
BOSU CREAMY Café au Lait
Extra Milk
HM?
WHAT'S WITH HIM...?
HE'S SO WEIRD.
CORN & MAYO BUN
Extra Milk

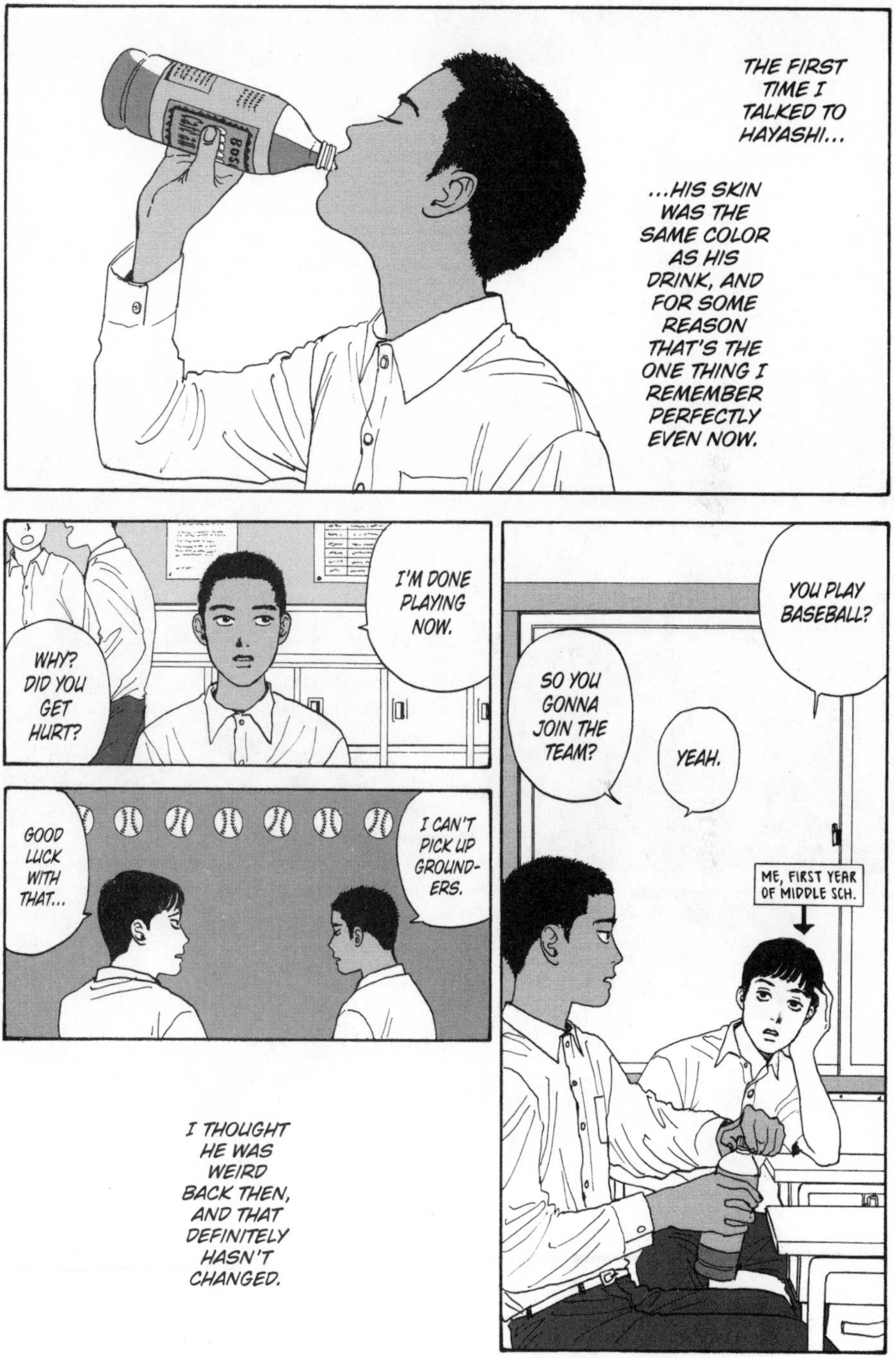
THE FIRST TIME I TALKED TO HAYASHI...
...HIS SKIN WAS THE SAME COLOR AS HIS DRINK, AND FOR SOME REASON THAT'S THE ONE THING I REMEMBER PERFECTLY EVEN NOW.
YOU PLAY BASEBALL?
YEAH.
SO YOU GONNA JOIN THE TEAM?
ME, FIRST YEAR OF MIDDLE SCH.
I'M DONE PLAYING NOW.
WHY? DID YOU GET HURT?
I CAN'T PICK UP GROUNDERS.
GOOD LUCK WITH THAT...
I THOUGHT HE WAS WEIRD BACK THEN, AND THAT DEFINITELY HASN'T CHANGED.

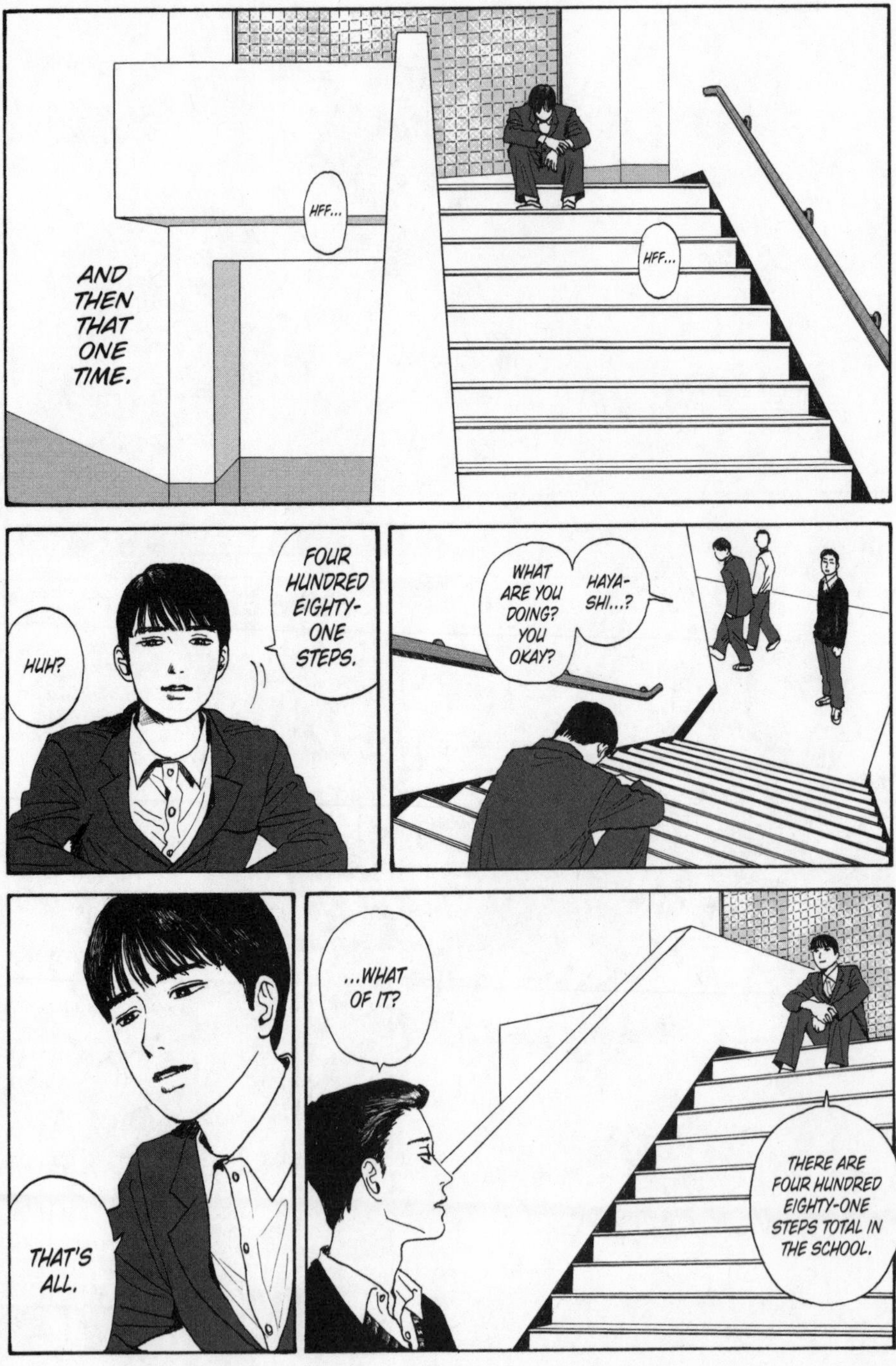
HFF...
HFF...
AND THEN THAT ONE TIME.
HAYA-SHI...?
WHAT ARE YOU DOING? YOU OKAY?
FOUR HUNDRED EIGHTY-ONE STEPS.
HUH?
THERE ARE FOUR HUNDRED EIGHTY-ONE STEPS TOTAL IN THE SCHOOL.
...WHAT OF IT?
THAT'S ALL.

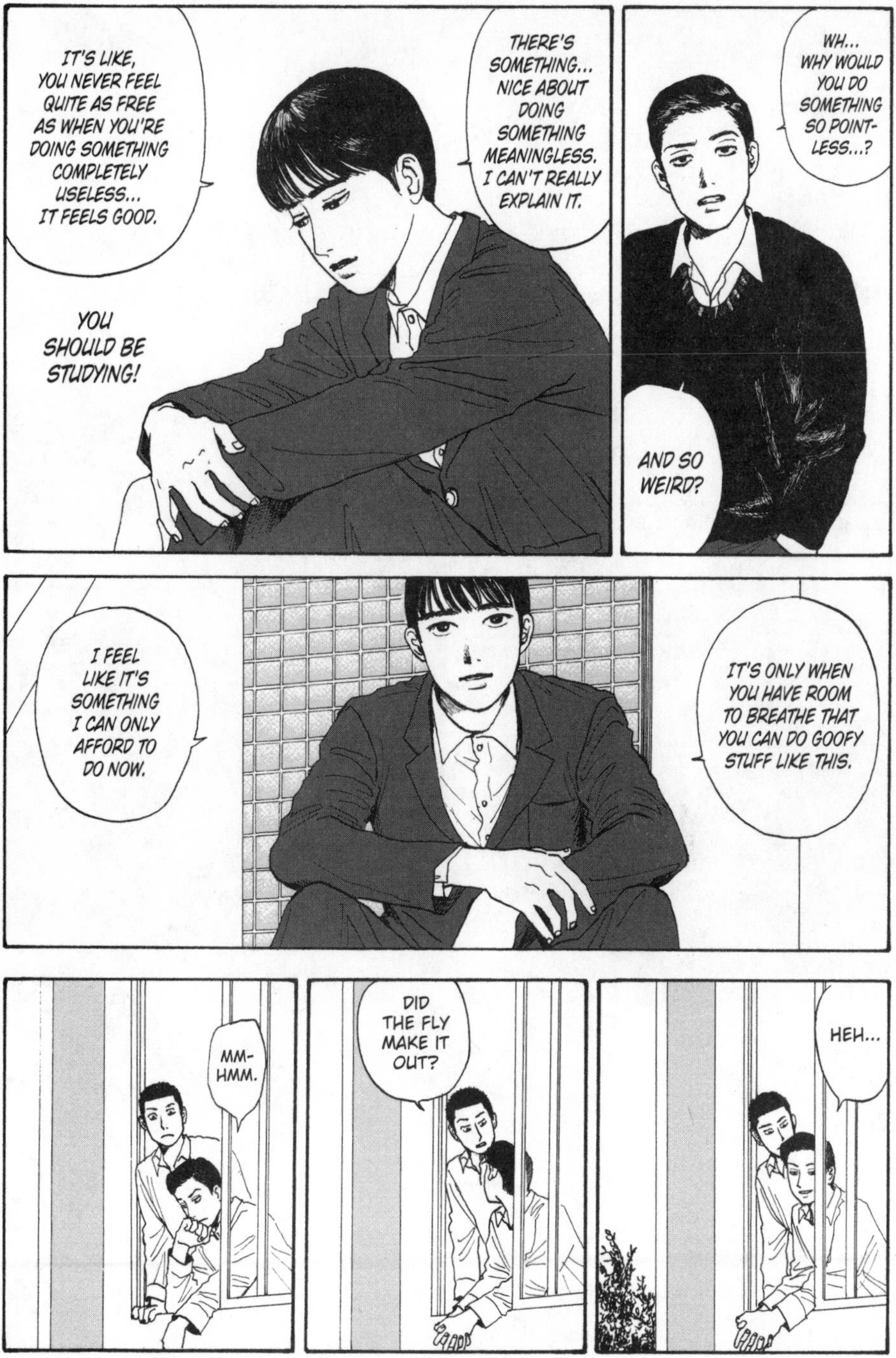
WH... WHY WOULD YOU DO SOMETHING SO POINT-LESS...?
AND SO WEIRD?
THERE'S SOMETHING... NICE ABOUT DOING SOMETHING MEANINGLESS. I CAN'T REALLY EXPLAIN IT.
IT'S LIKE, YOU NEVER FEEL QUITE AS FREE AS WHEN YOU'RE DOING SOMETHING COMPLETELY USELESS... IT FEELS GOOD.
YOU SHOULD BE STUDYING!
IT'S ONLY WHEN YOU HAVE ROOM TO BREATHE THAT YOU CAN DO GOOFY STUFF LIKE THIS.
I FEEL LIKE IT'S SOMETHING I CAN ONLY AFFORD TO DO NOW.
HEH...
DID THE FLY MAKE IT OUT?
MM-HMM.

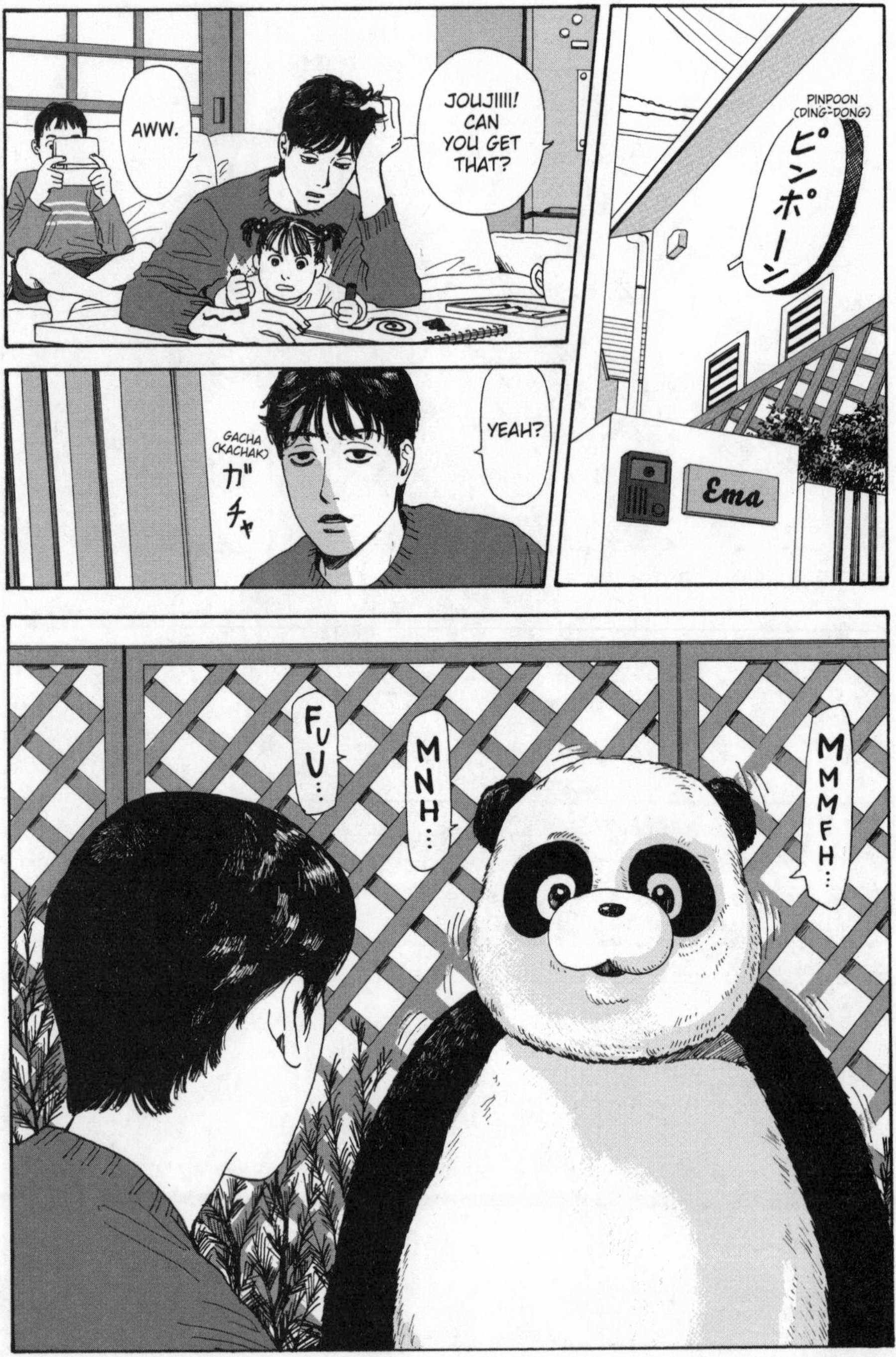
PINPOON (DING-DONG)
ピンポーン
JOUJIIII! CAN YOU GET THAT?
AWW.
YEAH?
GACHA (KACHAK)
ガチャ
MMMFH…
MNH…
FUU…

....
...HUH?
MNH...
WHO...?
...WHA—?
HELLO.
PHEW.
HAYA-SHI!?
WHAT THE? HUH?
WHAT ARE YOU DOING HERE? AND WHAT'S WITH THE GETUP?
MY FAMILY'S CHINESE RESTAURANT IS HAVING ITS THIRTIETH ANNIVERSARY.
SO I'VE BEEN OUT IN FRONT OF THE RESTAURANT IN THIS COSTUME, HANDING OUT COUPONS TO PEOPLE IN THE MARKETPLACE.
I GOT SICK OF LITTLE KIDS PUNCHING ME AND TRYING TO STICK THEIR FINGERS UP MY BUTT, SO I RAN AWAY.
OHH...

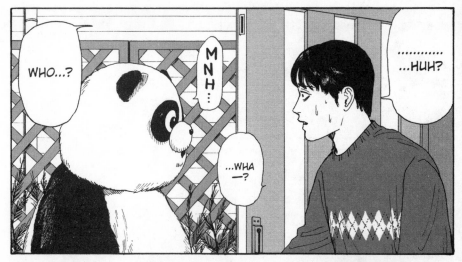

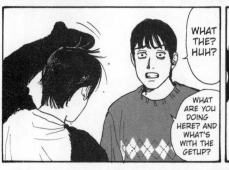

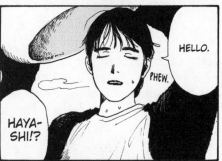

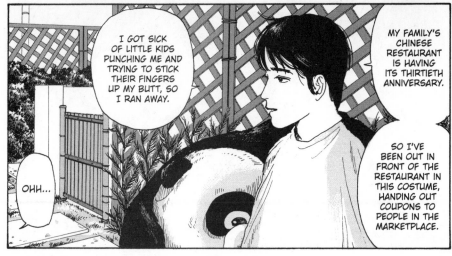

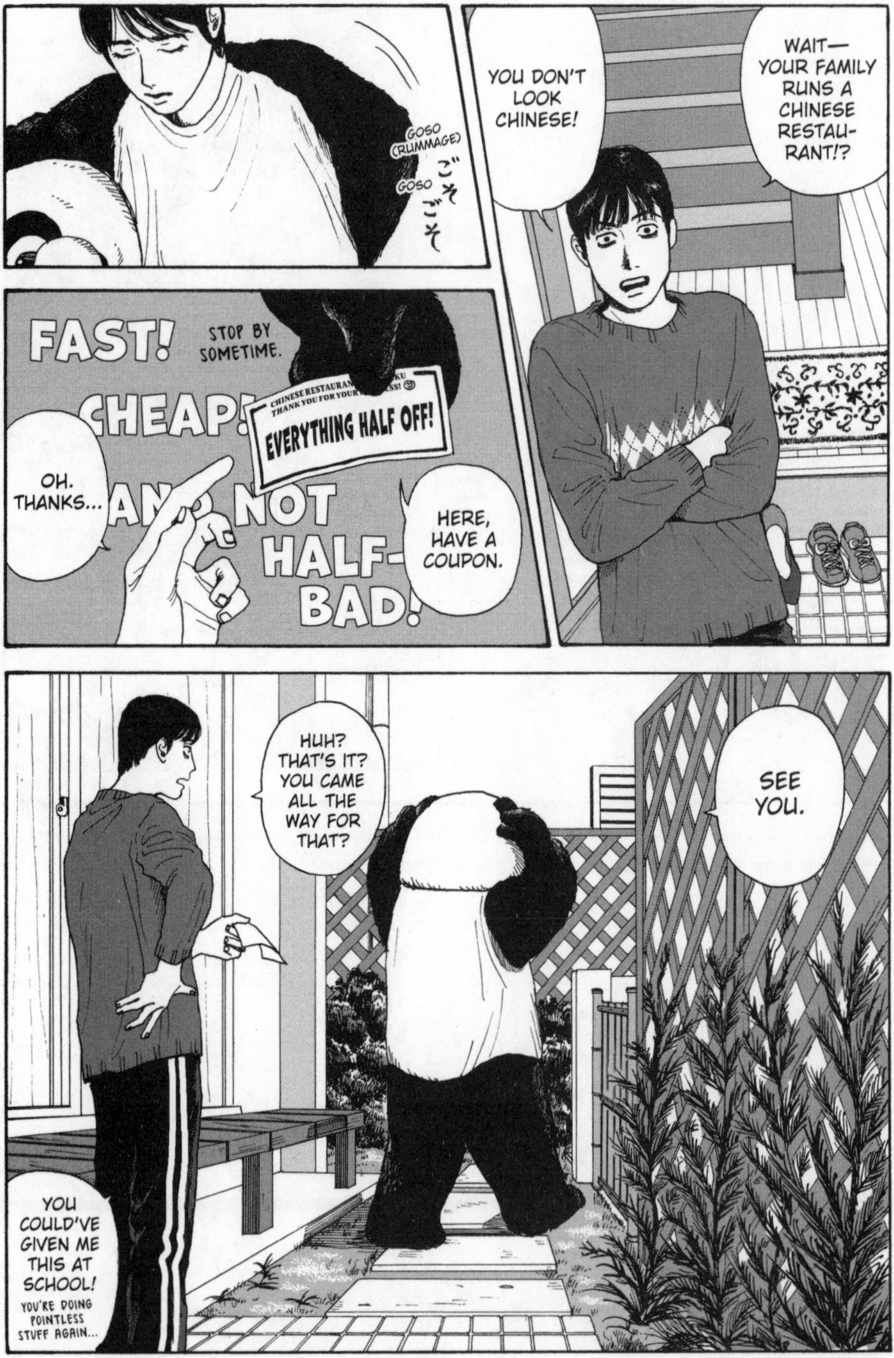

WAIT— YOUR FAMILY RUNS A CHINESE RESTAURANT!?
YOU DON'T LOOK CHINESE!
GOSO (RUMMAGE)
GOSO
ごそごそ
FAST! CHEAP! AND NOT HALF-BAD!
STOP BY SOMETIME.
EVERYTHING HALF OFF!
HERE, HAVE A COUPON.
OH. THANKS...
SEE YOU.
HUH? THAT'S IT? YOU CAME ALL THE WAY FOR THAT?
YOU COULD'VE GIVEN ME THIS AT SCHOOL!
YOU'RE DOING POINTLESS STUFF AGAIN...

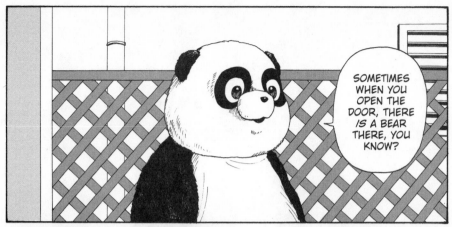

SOMETIMES WHEN YOU OPEN THE DOOR, THERE *IS* A BEAR THERE, YOU KNOW?
UH...
YOU'RE A PANDA.
PANDAS ARE BEARS TOO.
OKAY, WHAT-EVER YOU SAY.
BE CAREFUL OUT THERE.
DON'T GET IN TROUBLE WITH THE COPS.
PETA (PLOD)
ぺた
PETA
ぺた
ALREADY DID, TWICE.
BWA HA!

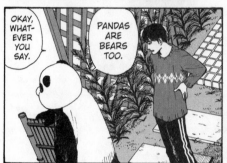

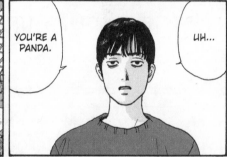

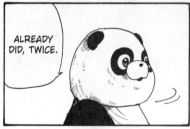

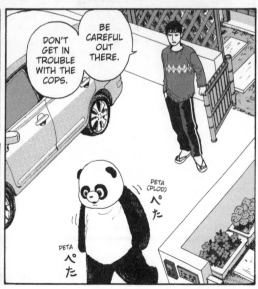

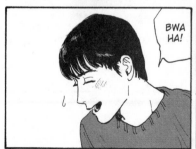

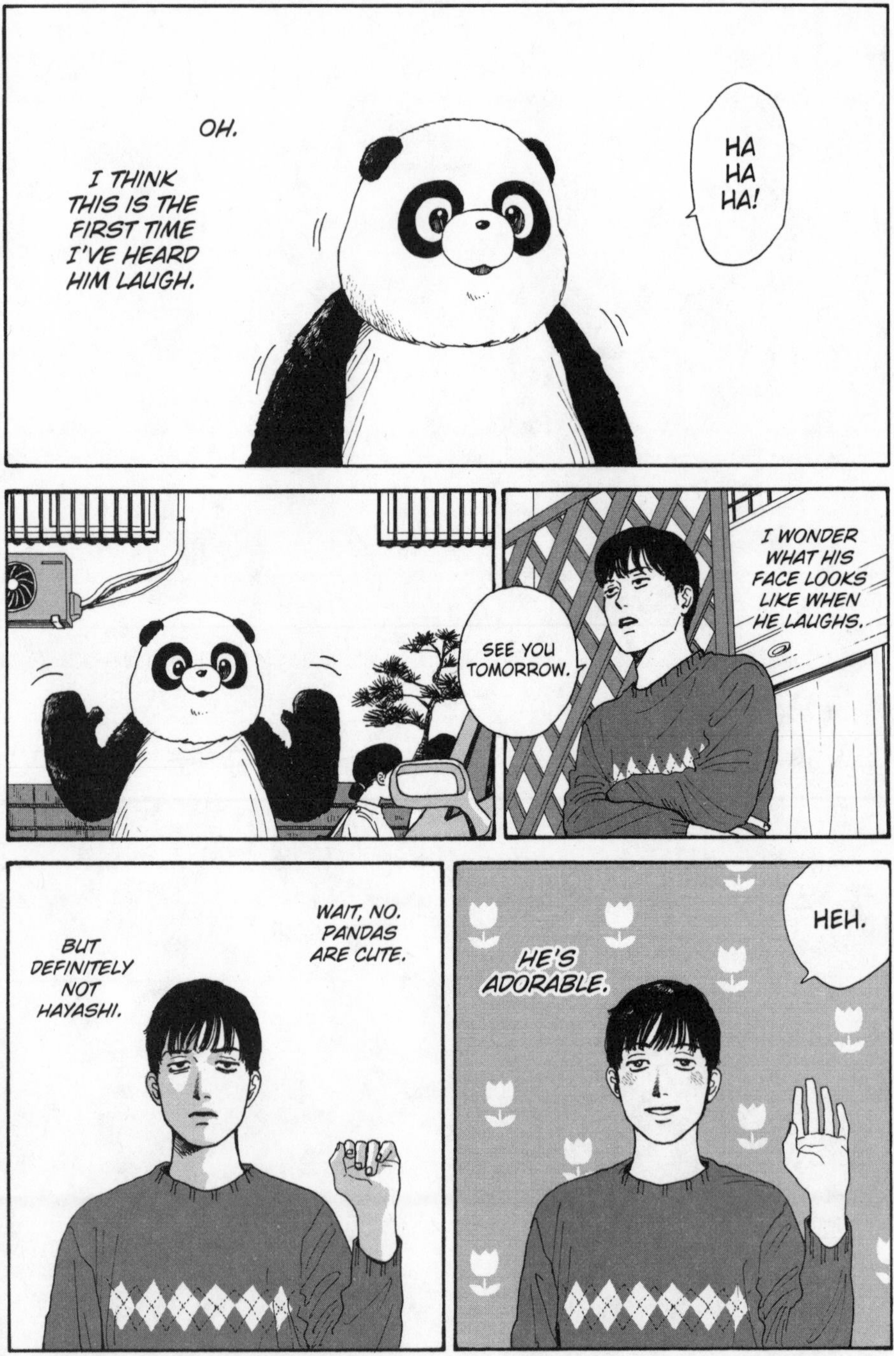
HA HA HA!
OH.
I THINK THIS IS THE FIRST TIME I'VE HEARD HIM LAUGH.
I WONDER WHAT HIS FACE LOOKS LIKE WHEN HE LAUGHS.
SEE YOU TOMORROW.
HEH.
HE'S ADORABLE.
WAIT, NO. PANDAS ARE CUTE.
BUT DEFINITELY NOT HAYASHI.

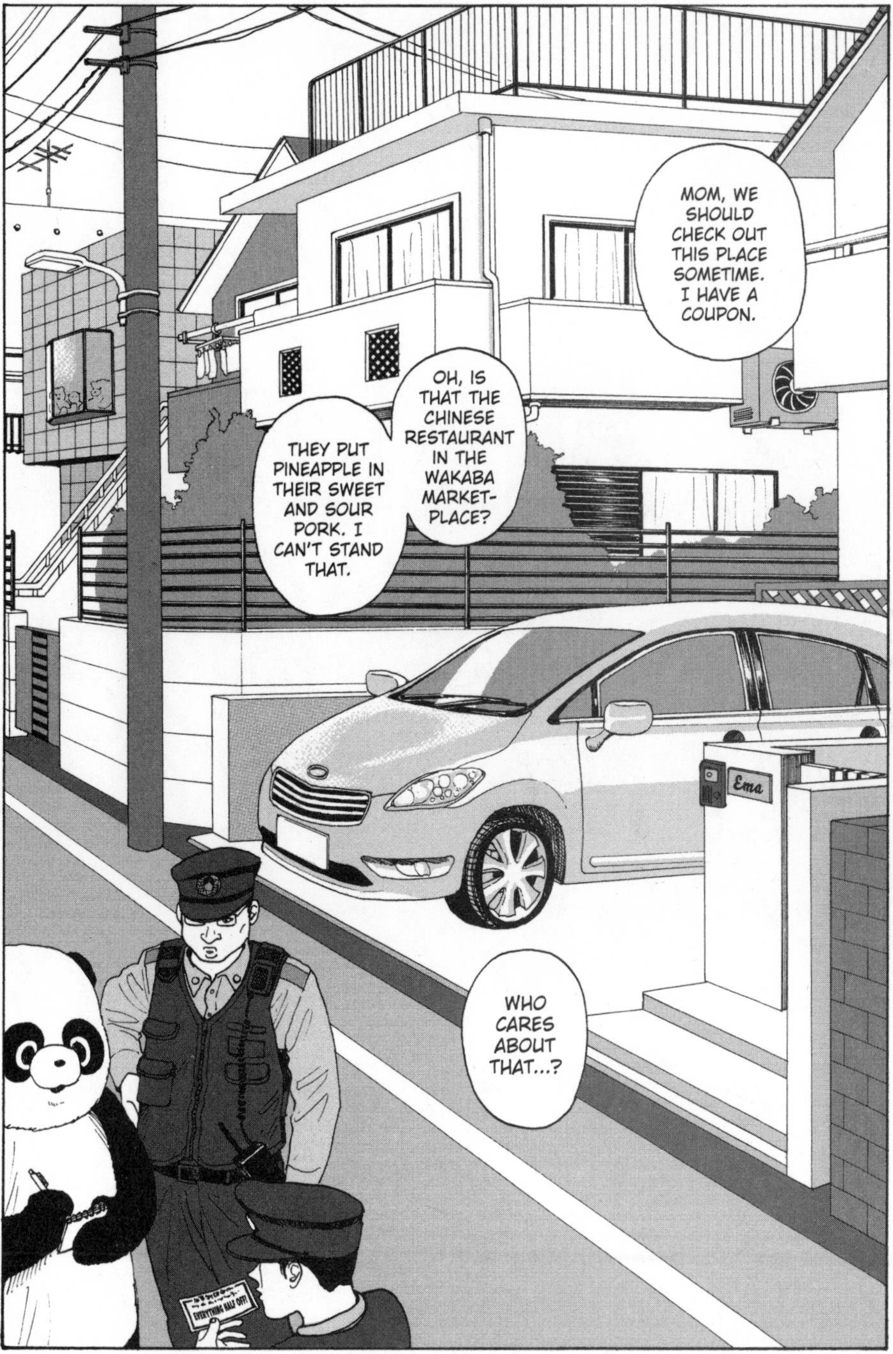
MOM, WE SHOULD CHECK OUT THIS PLACE SOMETIME. I HAVE A COUPON.
OH, IS THAT THE CHINESE RESTAURANT IN THE WAKABA MARKET-PLACE?
THEY PUT PINEAPPLE IN THEIR SWEET AND SOUR PORK. I CAN'T STAND THAT.
Ema
WHO CARES ABOUT THAT...?
EVERYTHING HALF OFF!

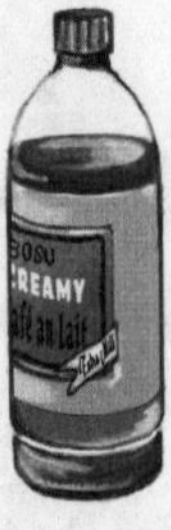
BOSU
CREAMY

[Would You Be My Friend?]

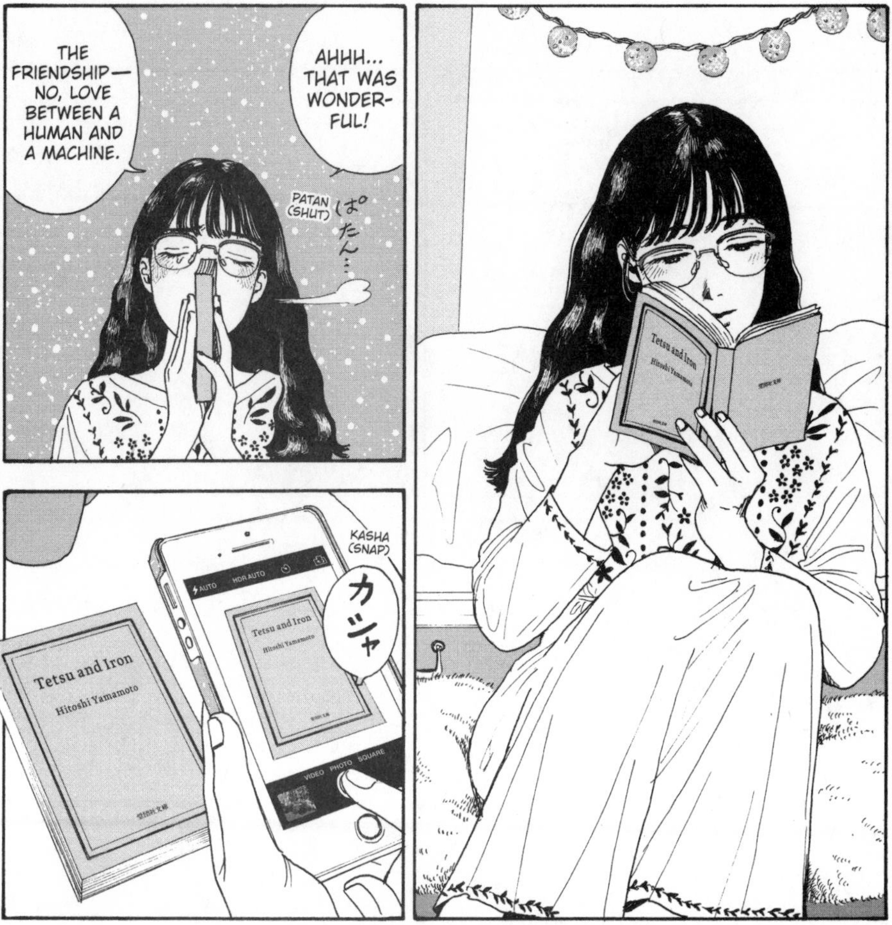
Tetsu and Iron
Hitoshi Yamamoto
AHHH... THAT WAS WONDERFUL!
THE FRIENDSHIP—NO, LOVE BETWEEN A HUMAN AND A MACHINE.
PATAN (SHUT)
ぱたん…
KASHA (SNAP)
カシャ
AUTO
HDR AUTO
Tetsu and Iron
Hitoshi Yamamoto
VIDEO PHOTO SQUARE
Tetsu and Iron
Hitoshi Yamamoto

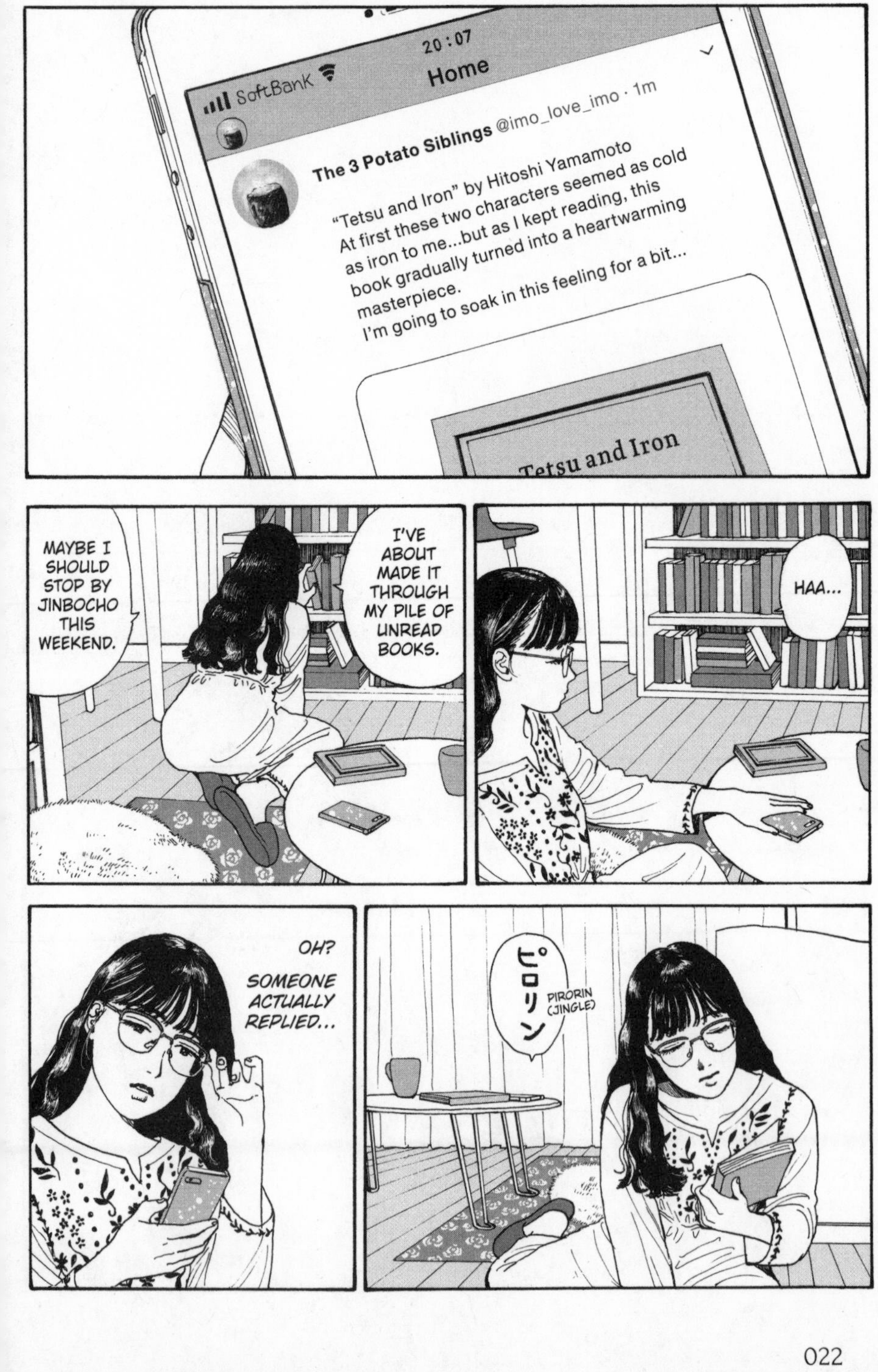

20:07
SoftBank
Home
The 3 Potato Siblings @imo_love_imo · 1m
"Tetsu and Iron" by Hitoshi Yamamoto
At first these two characters seemed as cold as iron to me...but as I kept reading, this book gradually turned into a heartwarming masterpiece.
I'm going to soak in this feeling for a bit...
Tetsu and Iron
HAA...
I'VE ABOUT MADE IT THROUGH MY PILE OF UNREAD BOOKS.
MAYBE I SHOULD STOP BY JINBOCHO THIS WEEKEND.
ピロリン
PIRORIN (JINGLE)
OH?
SOMEONE ACTUALLY REPLIED...

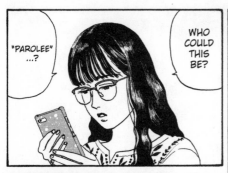

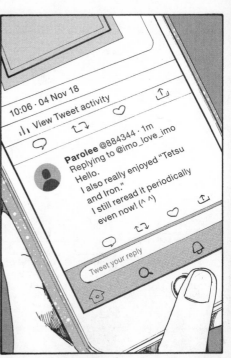

10:06 · 04 Nov 18
View Tweet activity
Parolee @884344 · 1m
Replying to @imo_love_imo
Hello.
I also really enjoyed "Tetsu and Iron."
I still reread it periodically even now! (^ ^)
Tweet your reply
"PAROLEE" ...?
WHO COULD THIS BE?
Follow
Parolee
@884344
10 Followers
"CROMARTIE"...
LIVING
IN
disgrac
1
Parolee @884344 · 13 Sep 18
"LIVING IN DISGRACE"...

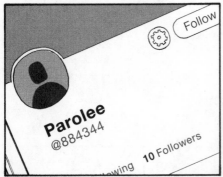

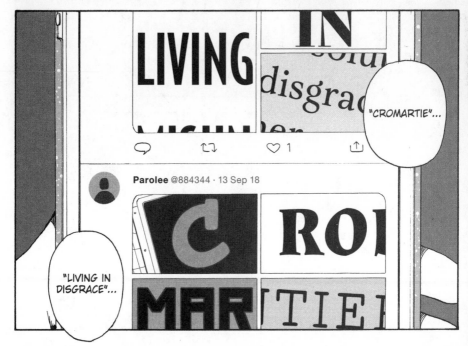

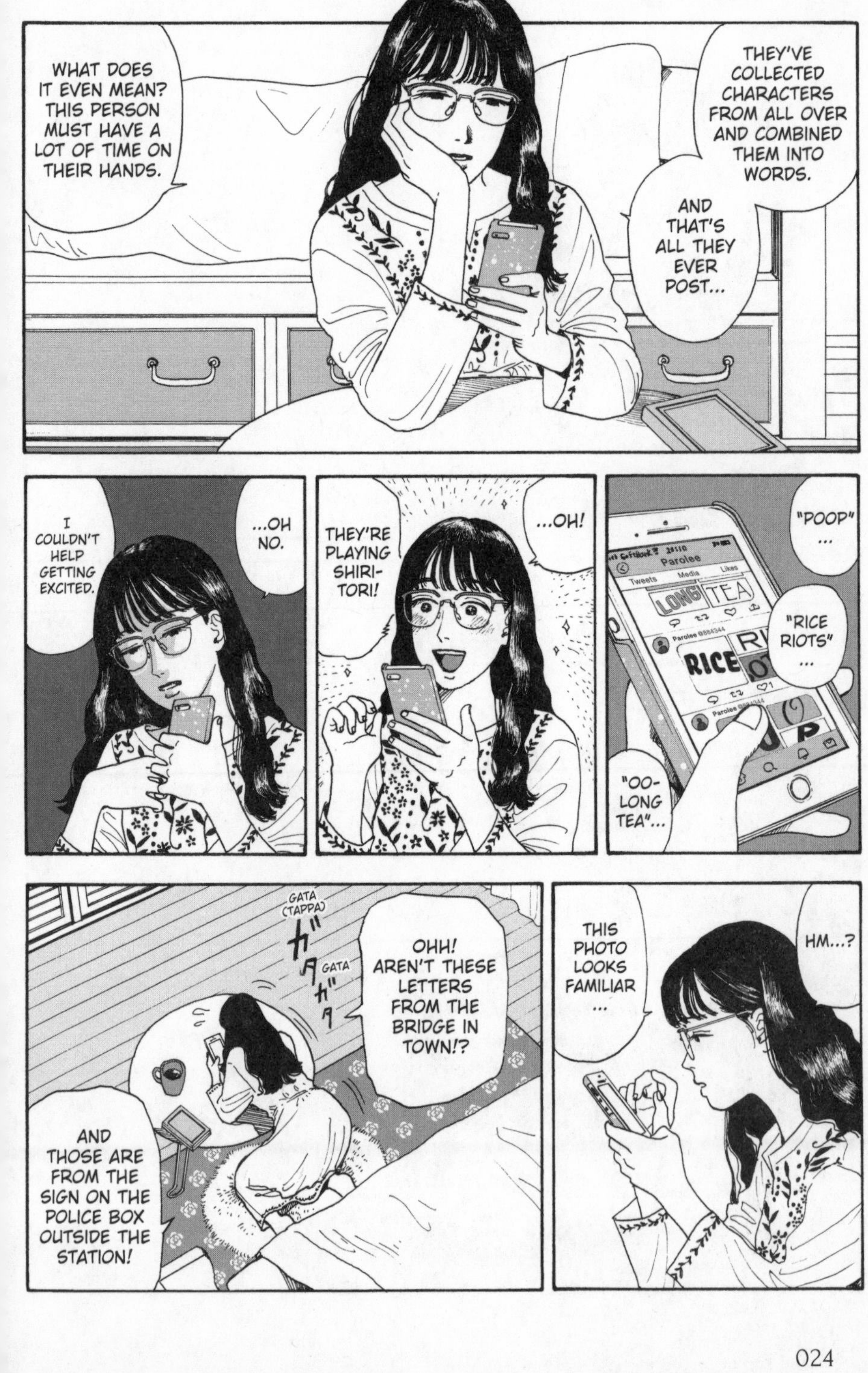
THEY'VE COLLECTED CHARACTERS FROM ALL OVER AND COMBINED THEM INTO WORDS.
AND THAT'S ALL THEY EVER POST...
WHAT DOES IT EVEN MEAN? THIS PERSON MUST HAVE A LOT OF TIME ON THEIR HANDS.
"POOP"...
Parolee
Tweets
Media
Likes
LONG
TEA
RICE
"RICE RIOTS"...
"OO-LONG TEA"...
...OH!
THEY'RE PLAYING SHIRI-TORI!
...OH NO.
I COULDN'T HELP GETTING EXCITED.
HM...?
THIS PHOTO LOOKS FAMILIAR...
OHH! AREN'T THESE LETTERS FROM THE BRIDGE IN TOWN!?
GATA (TAPPA)
ガタ
ガタ
GATA
AND THOSE ARE FROM THE SIGN ON THE POLICE BOX OUTSIDE THE STATION!

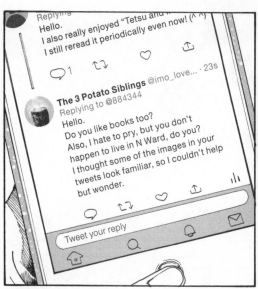

NO WAY...
YOU MEAN, PAROLEE LIVES AROUND HERE...?
Hello.
I also really enjoyed "Tetsu and
I still reread it periodically even now! (^ ^)
1
The 3 Potato Siblings @imo_love... · 23s
Replying to @884344
Hello.
Do you like books too?
Also, I hate to pry, but you don't happen to live in N Ward, do you?
I thought some of the images in your tweets look familiar, so I couldn't help but wonder.
Tweet your reply
MAYBE THAT WAS A LITTLE TOO FORWARD FOR SOMEONE I'VE NEVER MET BEFORE.
PIRORIN (JINGLE)
ピロリーン
!
BA (GRAB)
ばっ
1
Parolee @884344 · 19s
Replying to @imo_love_imo
I absolutely do live in N Ward.
You don't live in the area too, do you? If you do, then we might even end up running into each other around town. (^ ^)
Also, I do a bit of reading.

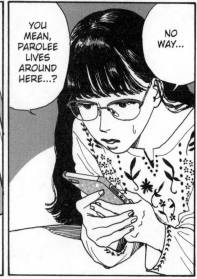

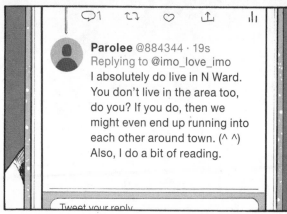

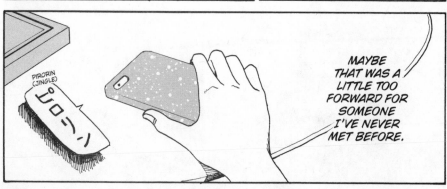

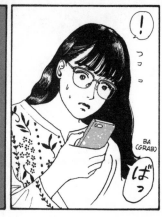

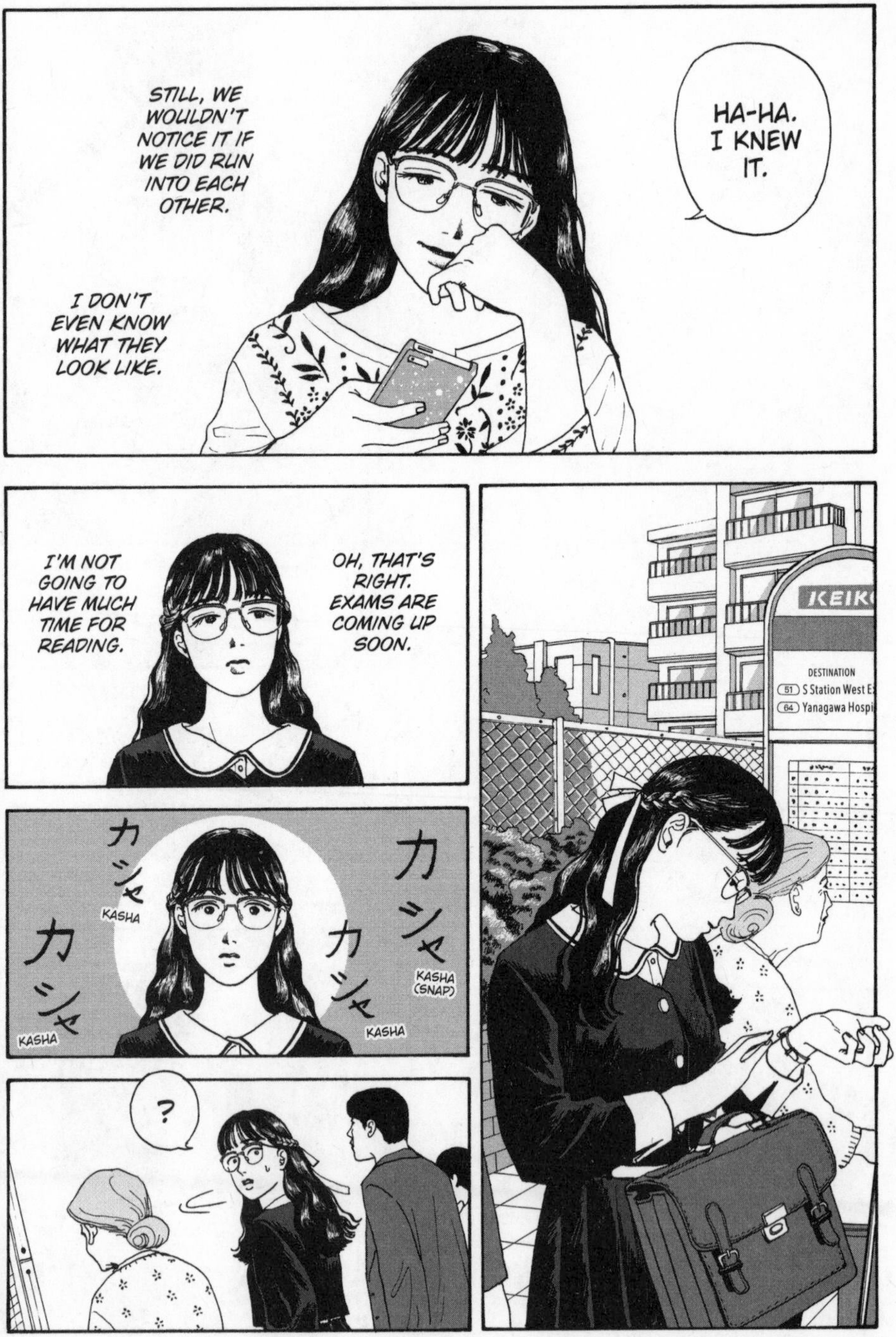
HA-HA. I KNEW IT.
STILL, WE WOULDN'T NOTICE IT IF WE DID RUN INTO EACH OTHER.
I DON'T EVEN KNOW WHAT THEY LOOK LIKE.
KEIK
DESTINATION
51 S Station West E
64 Yanagawa Hospi
OH, THAT'S RIGHT. EXAMS ARE COMING UP SOON.
I'M NOT GOING TO HAVE MUCH TIME FOR READING.
カシャ
KASHA (SNAP)
カシャ
KASHA
カシャ
KASHA
カシャ
KASHA
?

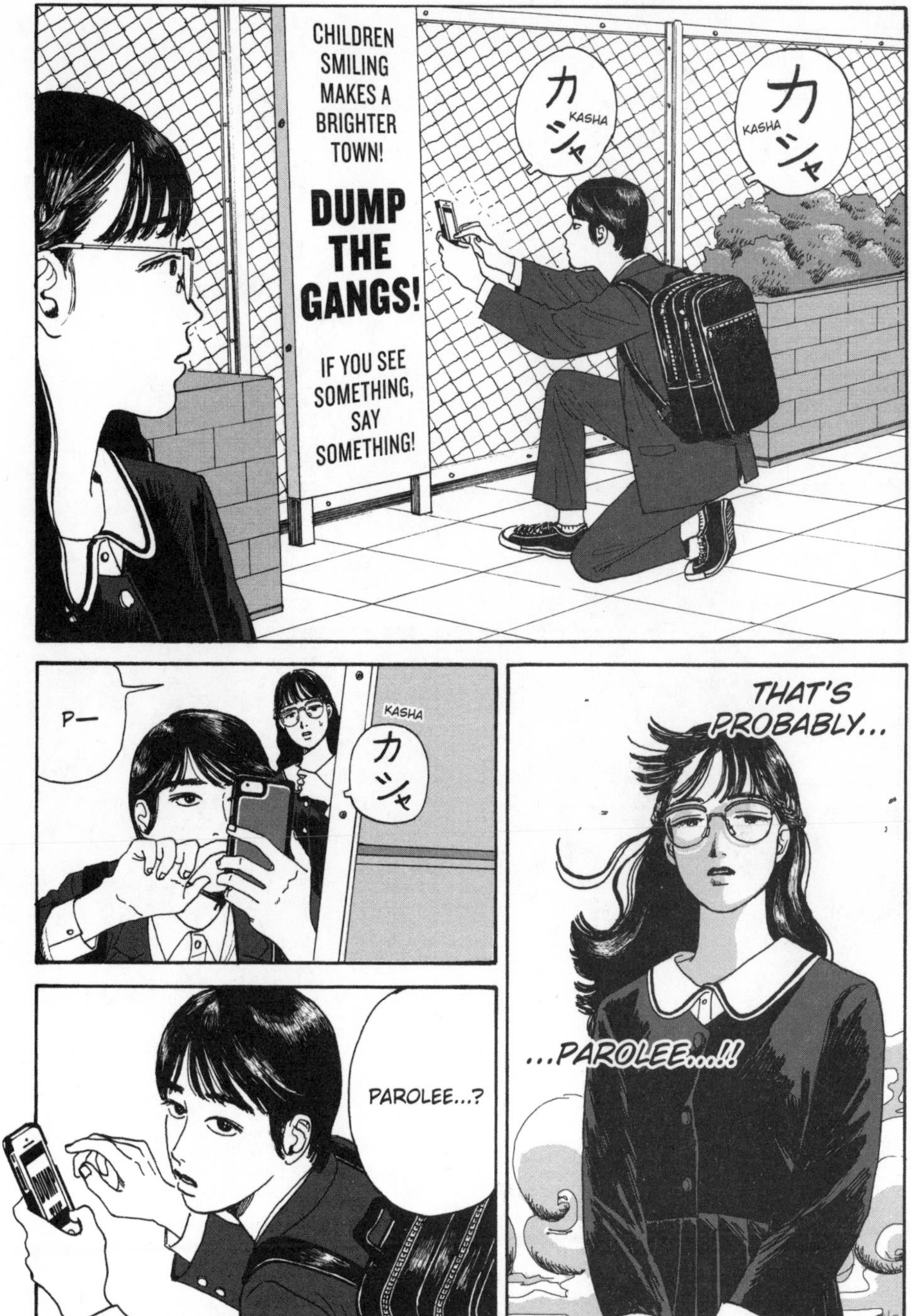
カシャ KASHA
カシャ KASHA
CHILDREN SMILING MAKES A BRIGHTER TOWN!
DUMP THE GANGS!
IF YOU SEE SOMETHING, SAY SOMETHING!
THAT'S PROBABLY...
...PAROLEE...!!
カシャ KASHA
P—
PAROLEE...?

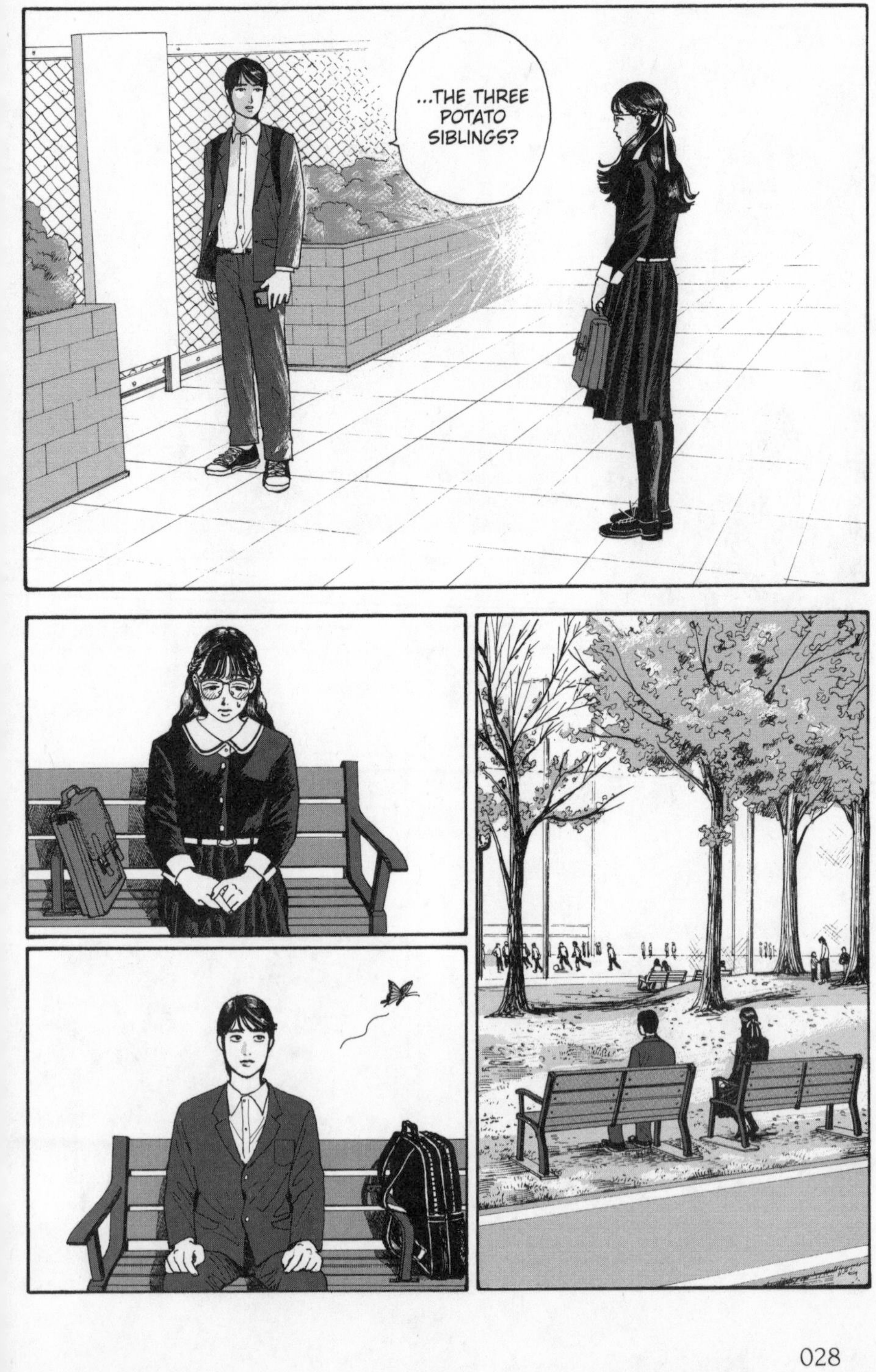
...THE THREE POTATO SIBLINGS?

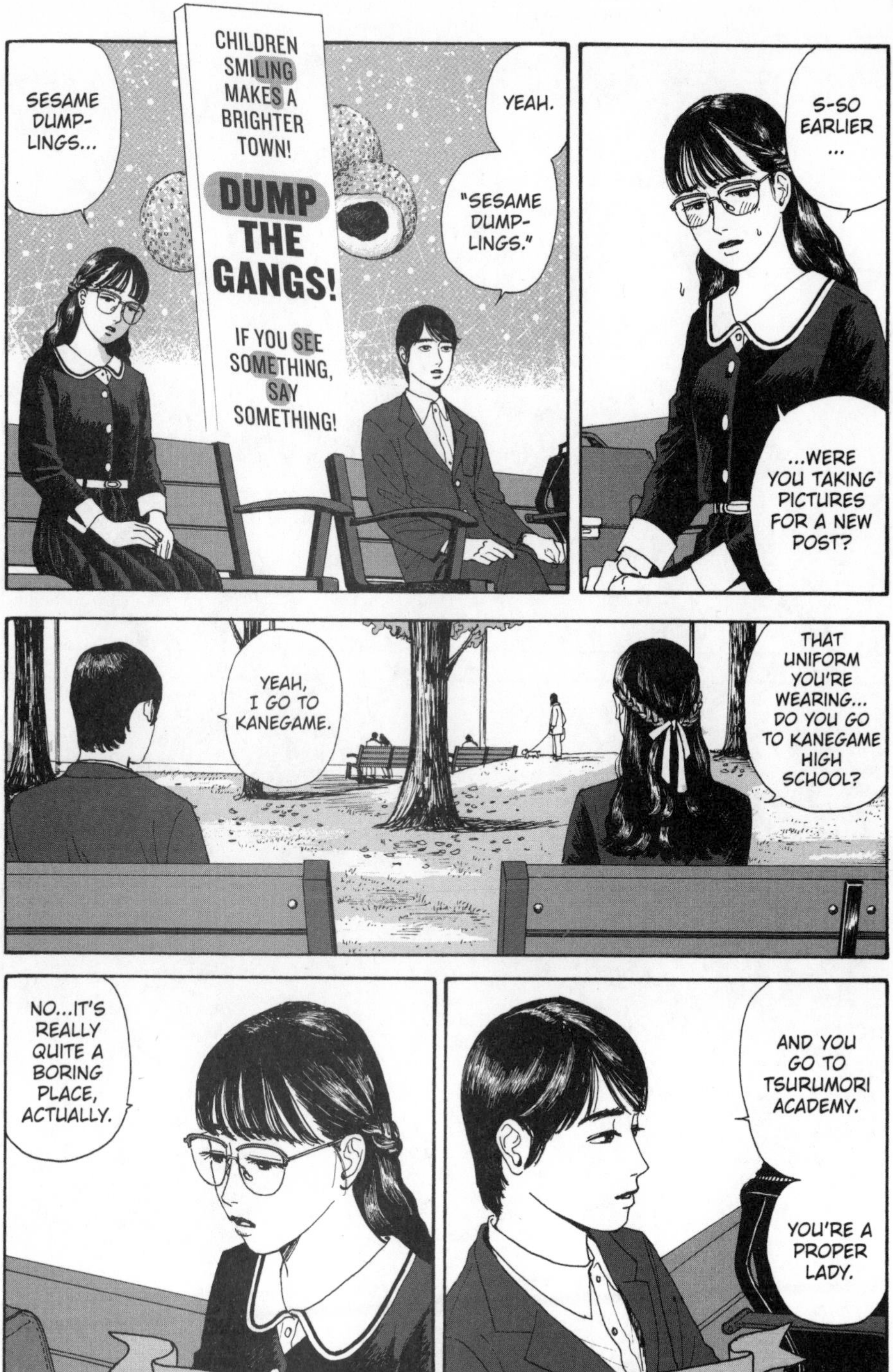
S-SO EARLIER...
...WERE YOU TAKING PICTURES FOR A NEW POST?
YEAH.
"SESAME DUMPLINGS."
CHILDREN SMILING MAKES A BRIGHTER TOWN!
DUMP THE GANGS!
IF YOU SEE SOMETHING, SAY SOMETHING!
SESAME DUMPLINGS...
THAT UNIFORM YOU'RE WEARING... DO YOU GO TO KANEGAME HIGH SCHOOL?
YEAH, I GO TO KANEGAME.
AND YOU GO TO TSURUMORI ACADEMY.
YOU'RE A PROPER LADY.
NO...IT'S REALLY QUITE A BORING PLACE, ACTUALLY.
THEY CAN'T EVEN LOOK EACH OTHER IN THE EYE.

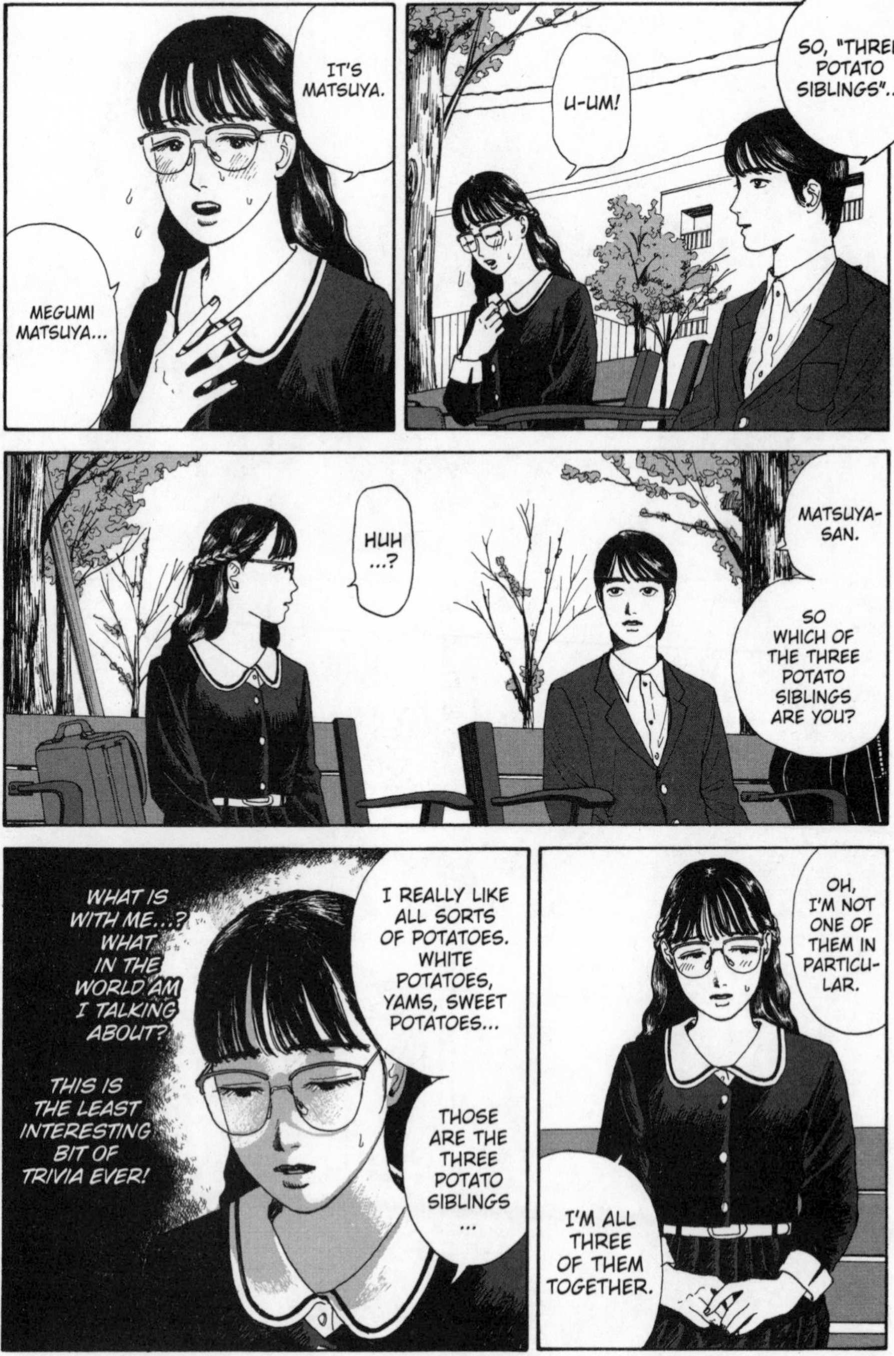
SO, "THREE POTATO SIBLINGS"...
U-UM!
IT'S MATSUYA.
MEGUMI MATSUYA...
MATSUYA-SAN.
SO WHICH OF THE THREE POTATO SIBLINGS ARE YOU?
HUH ...?
OH, I'M NOT ONE OF THEM IN PARTICULAR.
I'M ALL THREE OF THEM TOGETHER.
I REALLY LIKE ALL SORTS OF POTATOES. WHITE POTATOES, YAMS, SWEET POTATOES...
THOSE ARE THE THREE POTATO SIBLINGS ...
WHAT IS WITH ME...? WHAT IN THE WORLD AM I TALKING ABOUT?
THIS IS THE LEAST INTERESTING BIT OF TRIVIA EVER!

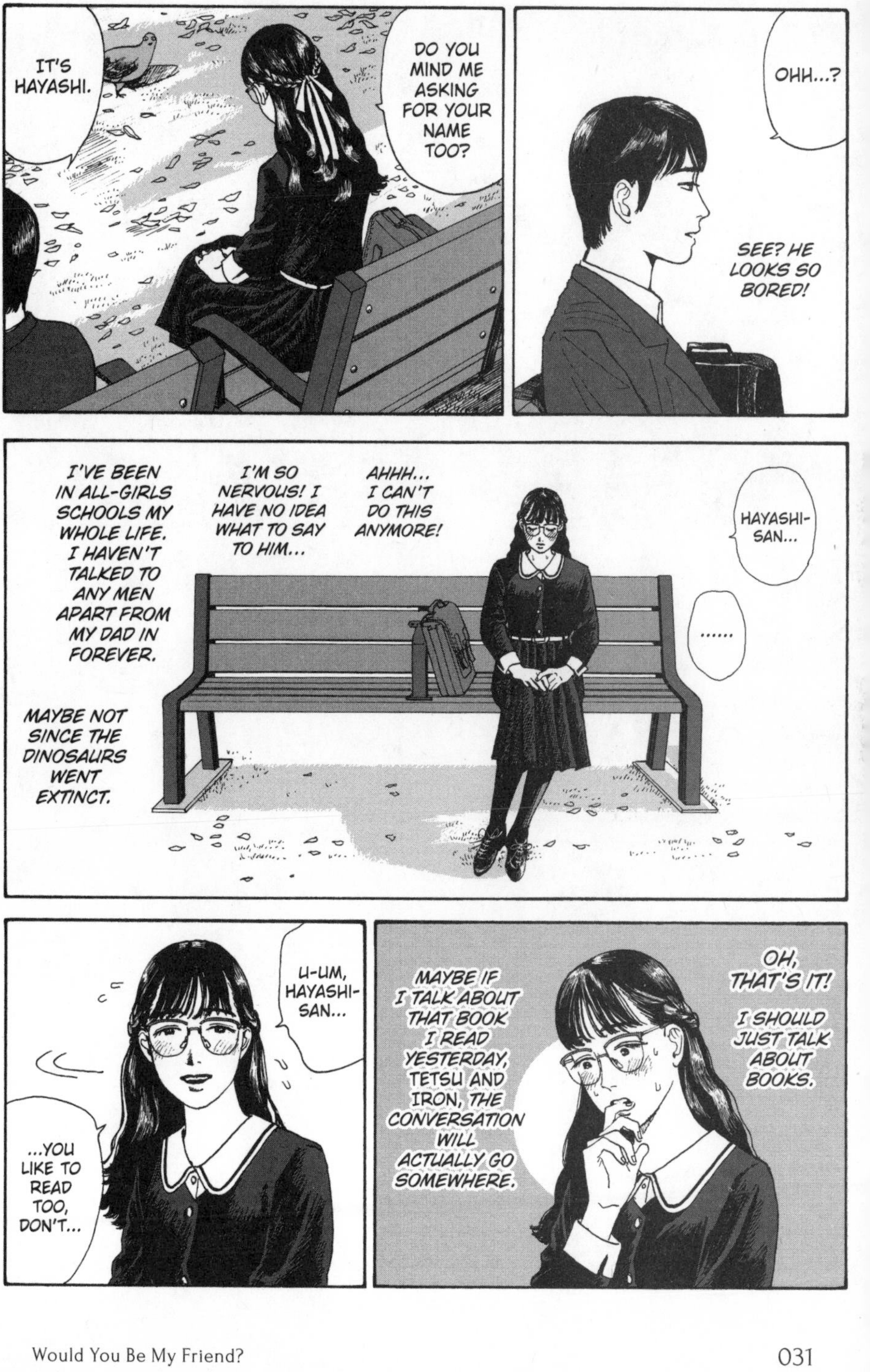
OHH...?
SEE? HE LOOKS SO BORED!
DO YOU MIND ME ASKING FOR YOUR NAME TOO?
IT'S HAYASHI.
HAYASHI-SAN...
......
AHHH... I CAN'T DO THIS ANYMORE!
I'M SO NERVOUS! I HAVE NO IDEA WHAT TO SAY TO HIM...
I'VE BEEN IN ALL-GIRLS SCHOOLS MY WHOLE LIFE. I HAVEN'T TALKED TO ANY MEN APART FROM MY DAD IN FOREVER.
MAYBE NOT SINCE THE DINOSAURS WENT EXTINCT.
OH, THAT'S IT!
I SHOULD JUST TALK ABOUT BOOKS.
MAYBE IF I TALK ABOUT THAT BOOK I READ YESTERDAY, TETSU AND IRON, THE CONVERSATION WILL ACTUALLY GO SOMEWHERE.
U-UM, HAYASHI-SAN...
...YOU LIKE TO READ TOO, DON'T...

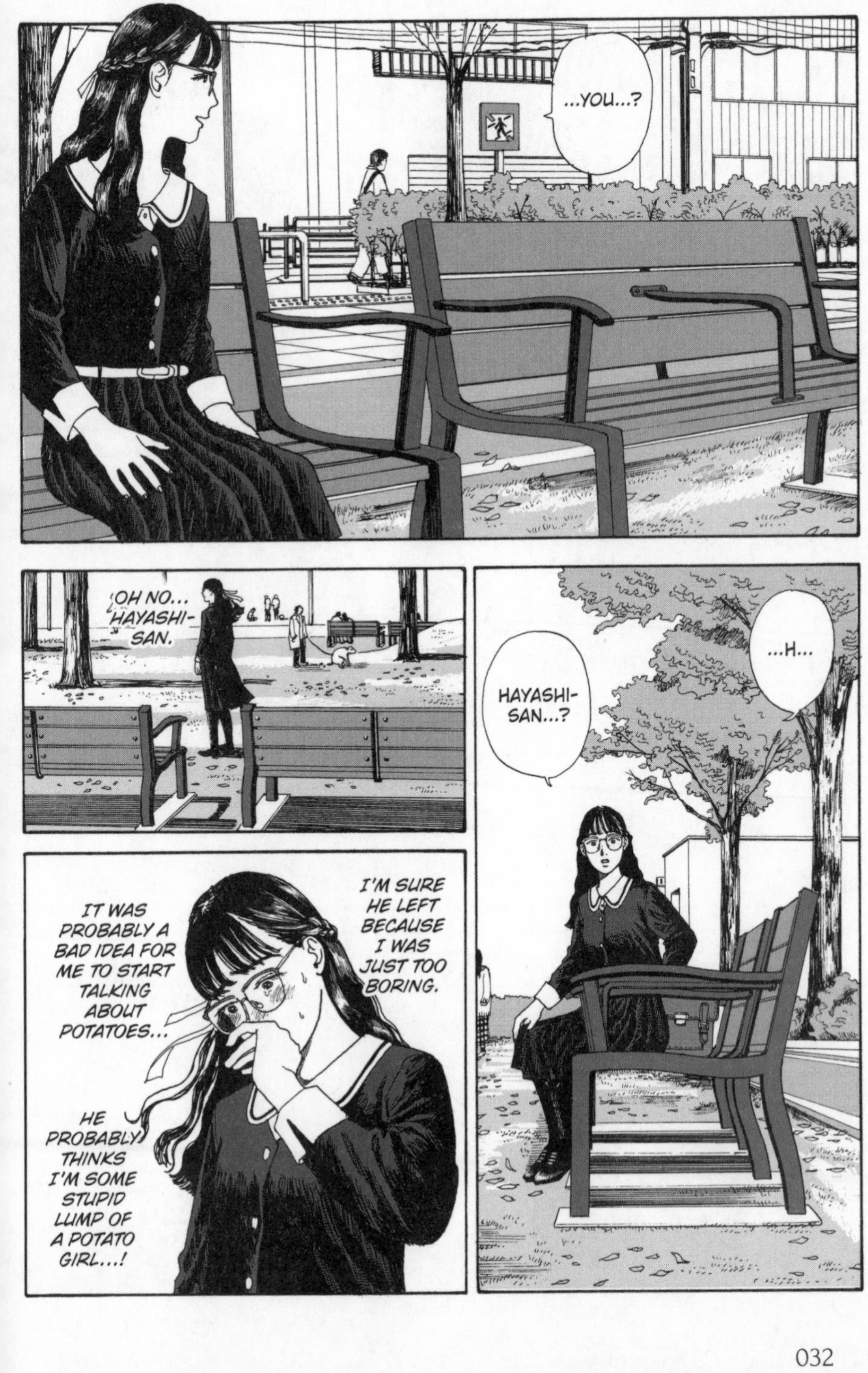
...YOU...?
...H...
HAYASHI-SAN...?
OH NO... HAYASHI-SAN.
I'M SURE HE LEFT BECAUSE I WAS JUST TOO BORING.
IT WAS PROBABLY A BAD IDEA FOR ME TO START TALKING ABOUT POTATOES...
HE PROBABLY THINKS I'M SOME STUPID LUMP OF A POTATO GIRL...!

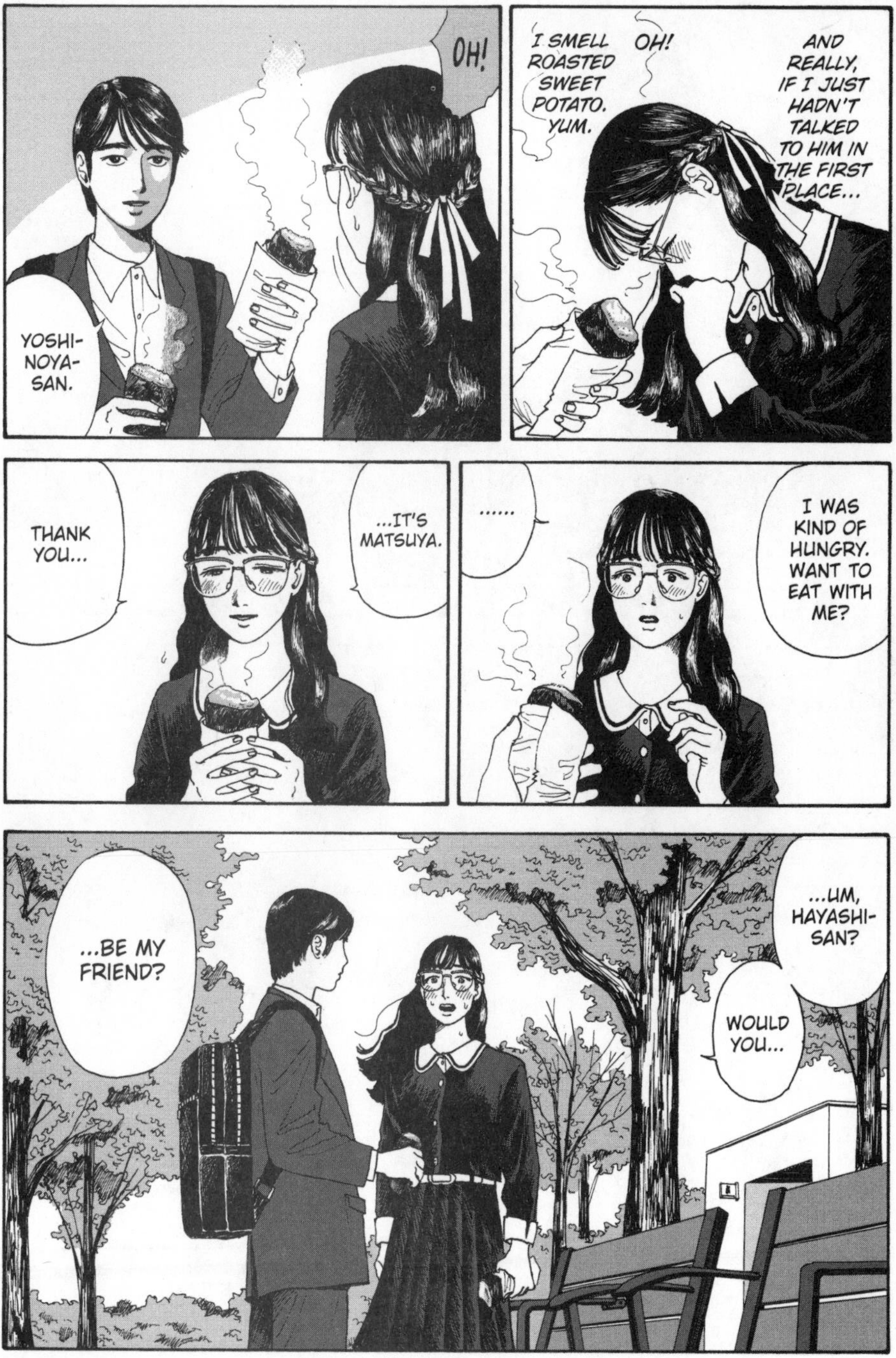
AND REALLY, IF I JUST HADN'T TALKED TO HIM IN THE FIRST PLACE...
OH!
I SMELL ROASTED SWEET POTATO. YUM.
OH!
YOSHI-NOYA-SAN.
I WAS KIND OF HUNGRY. WANT TO EAT WITH ME?
......
...IT'S MATSUYA.
THANK YOU...
...UM, HAYASHI-SAN?
WOULD YOU...
...BE MY FRIEND?

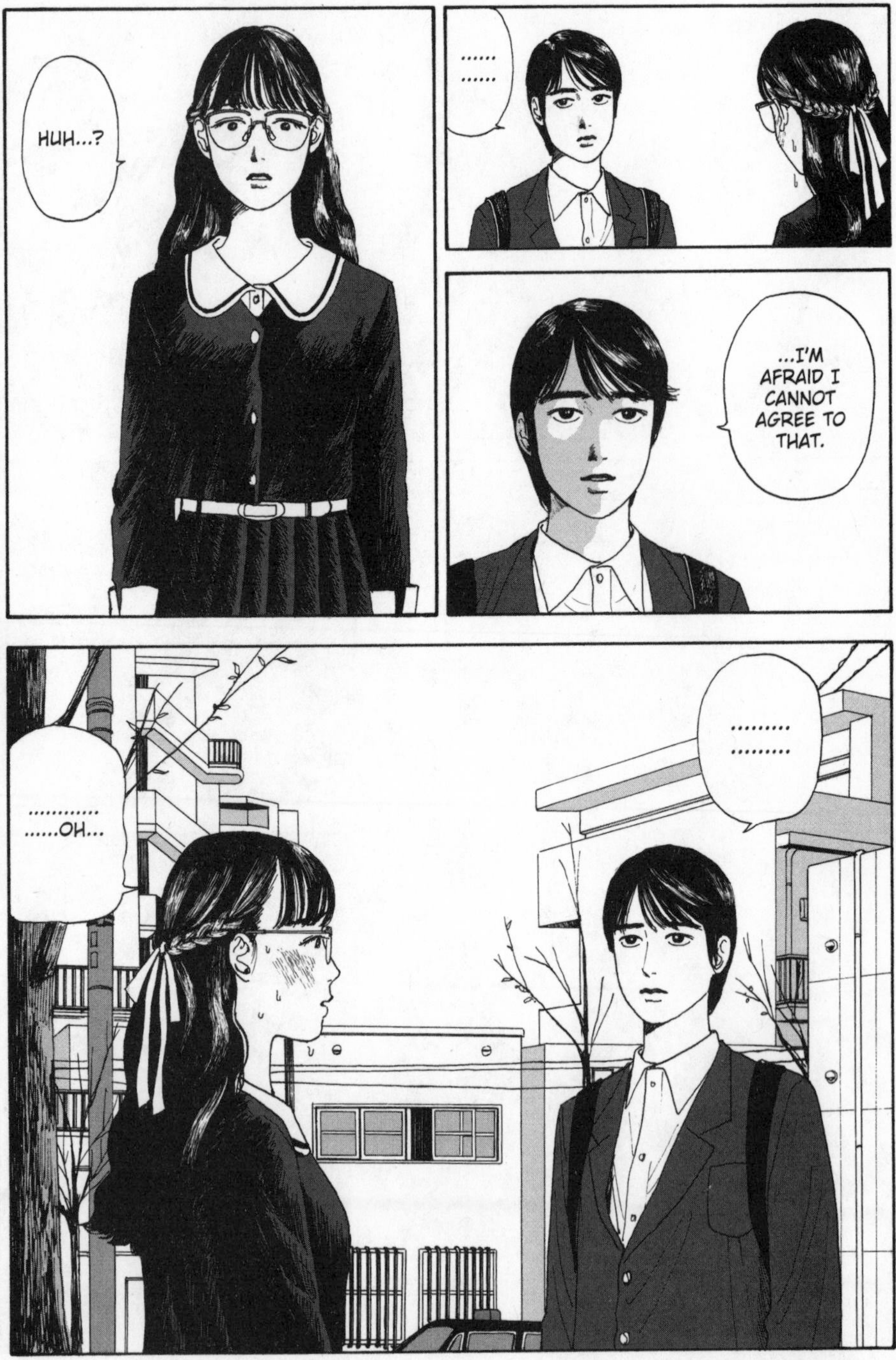
……
……
...I'M AFRAID I CANNOT AGREE TO THAT.
HUH...?
………
………
…………
……OH…

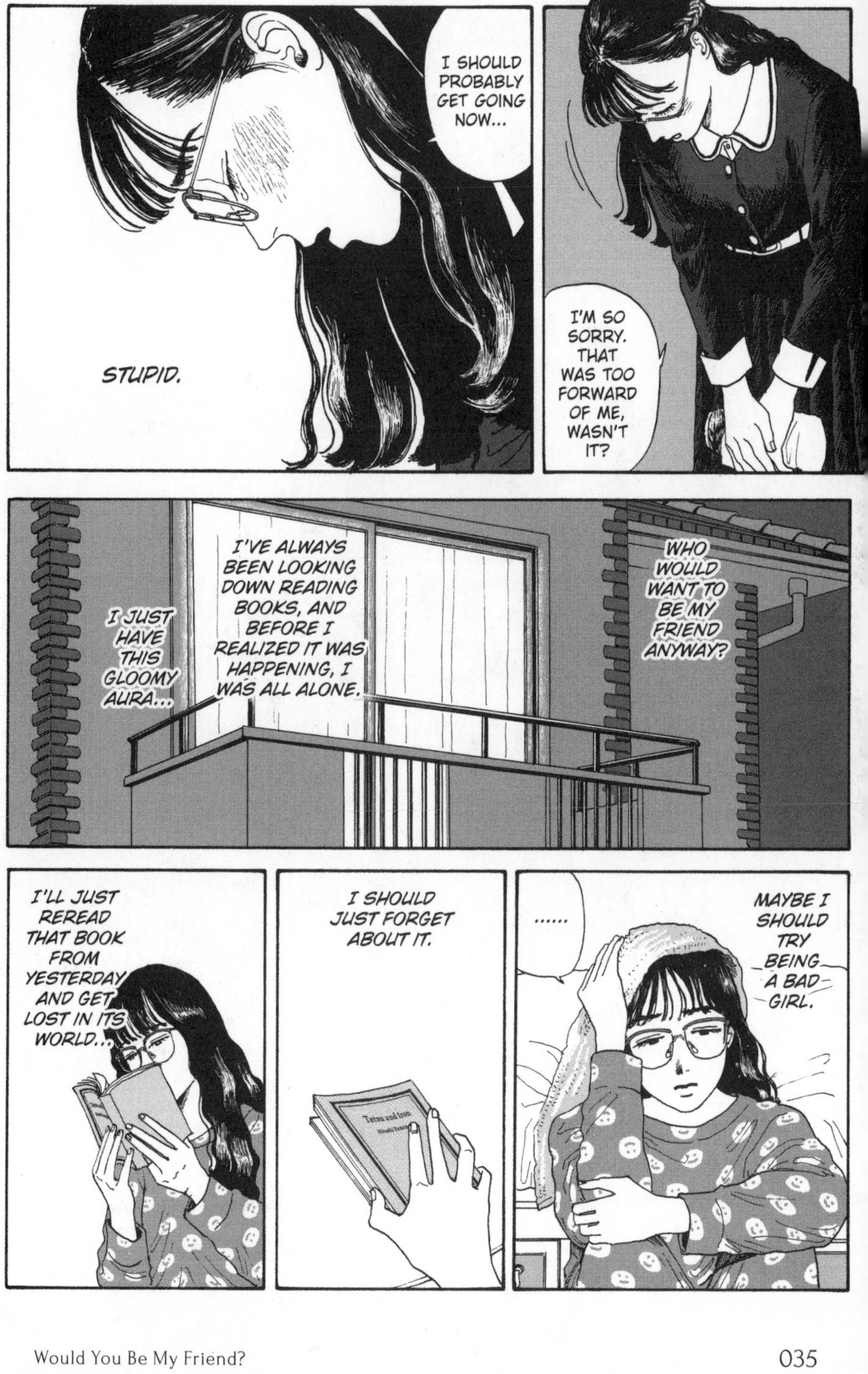
I'M SO SORRY. THAT WAS TOO FORWARD OF ME, WASN'T IT?
I SHOULD PROBABLY GET GOING NOW...
STUPID.
WHO WOULD WANT TO BE MY FRIEND ANYWAY?
I'VE ALWAYS BEEN LOOKING DOWN READING BOOKS, AND BEFORE I REALIZED IT WAS HAPPENING, I WAS ALL ALONE.
I JUST HAVE THIS GLOOMY AURA...
MAYBE I SHOULD TRY BEING A BAD GIRL.
......
I SHOULD JUST FORGET ABOUT IT.
I'LL JUST REREAD THAT BOOK FROM YESTERDAY AND GET LOST IN ITS WORLD...

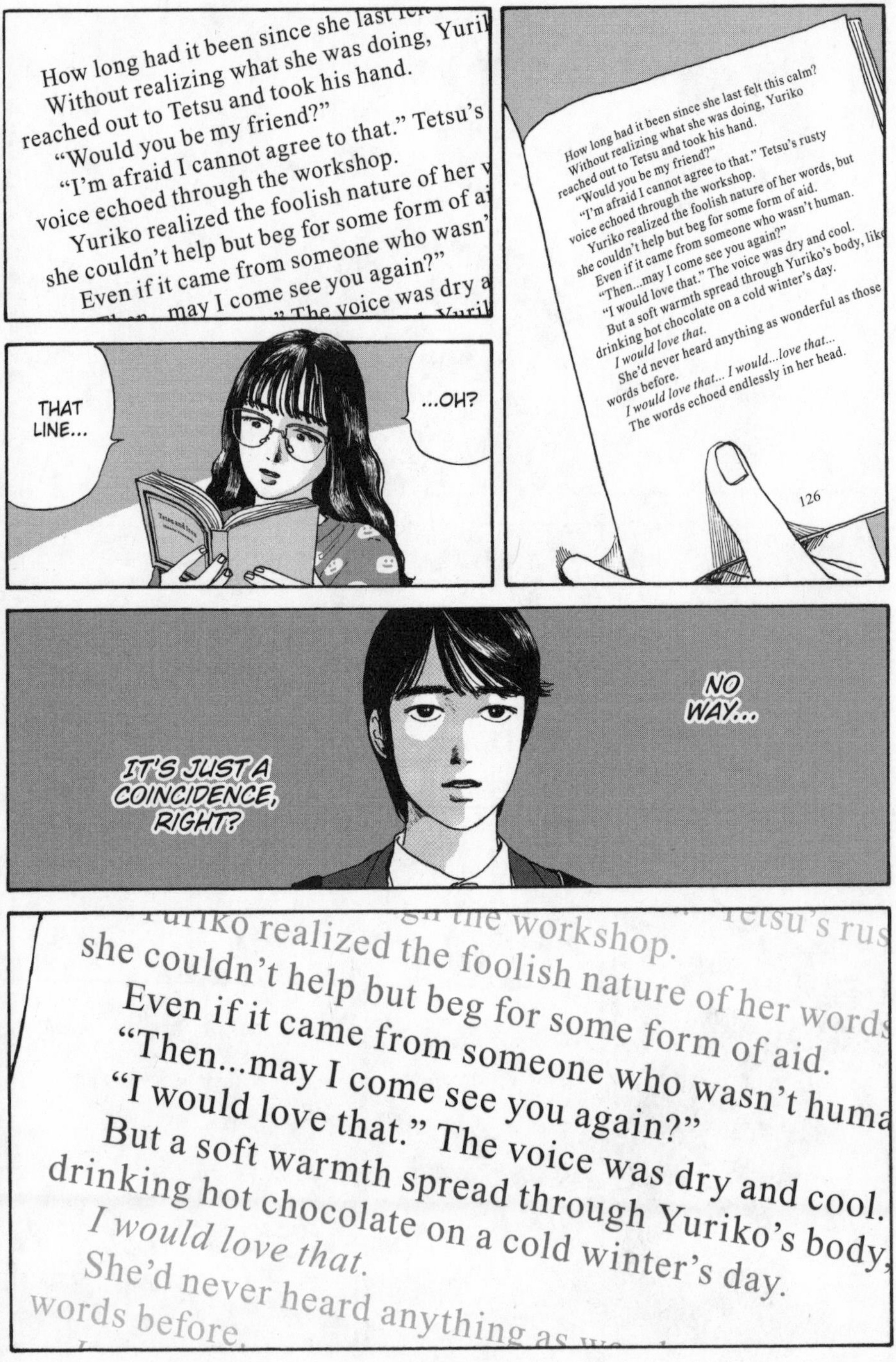

How long had it been since she last felt this calm?
Without realizing what she was doing, Yuriko
reached out to Tetsu and took his hand.
"Would you be my friend?"
"I'm afraid I cannot agree to that." Tetsu's rusty
voice echoed through the workshop.
Yuriko realized the foolish nature of her words, but
she couldn't help but beg for some form of aid.
Even if it came from someone who wasn't human.
"Then...may I come see you again?"
"I would love that." The voice was dry and cool.
But a soft warmth spread through Yuriko's body, like
drinking hot chocolate on a cold winter's day.
I would love that.
She'd never heard anything as wonderful as those
words before.
I would love that... I would...love that...
The words echoed endlessly in her head.
126
How long had it been since she last
Without realizing what she was doing,
reached out to Tetsu and took his hand.
"Would you be my friend?"
"I'm afraid I cannot agree to that." Tetsu's
voice echoed through the workshop.
Yuriko realized the foolish nature of her
she couldn't help but beg for some form of
Even if it came from someone who
...may I come see you again?"
...OH?
THAT LINE...
NO WAY...
IT'S JUST A COINCIDENCE, RIGHT?
Yuriko realized the foolish nature of her words
she couldn't help but beg for some form of aid.
Even if it came from someone who wasn't
"Then...may I come see you again?"
"I would love that." The voice was dry and cool.
But a soft warmth spread through Yuriko's body,
drinking hot chocolate on a cold winter's day.
I would love that.
She'd never heard anything as
words before.

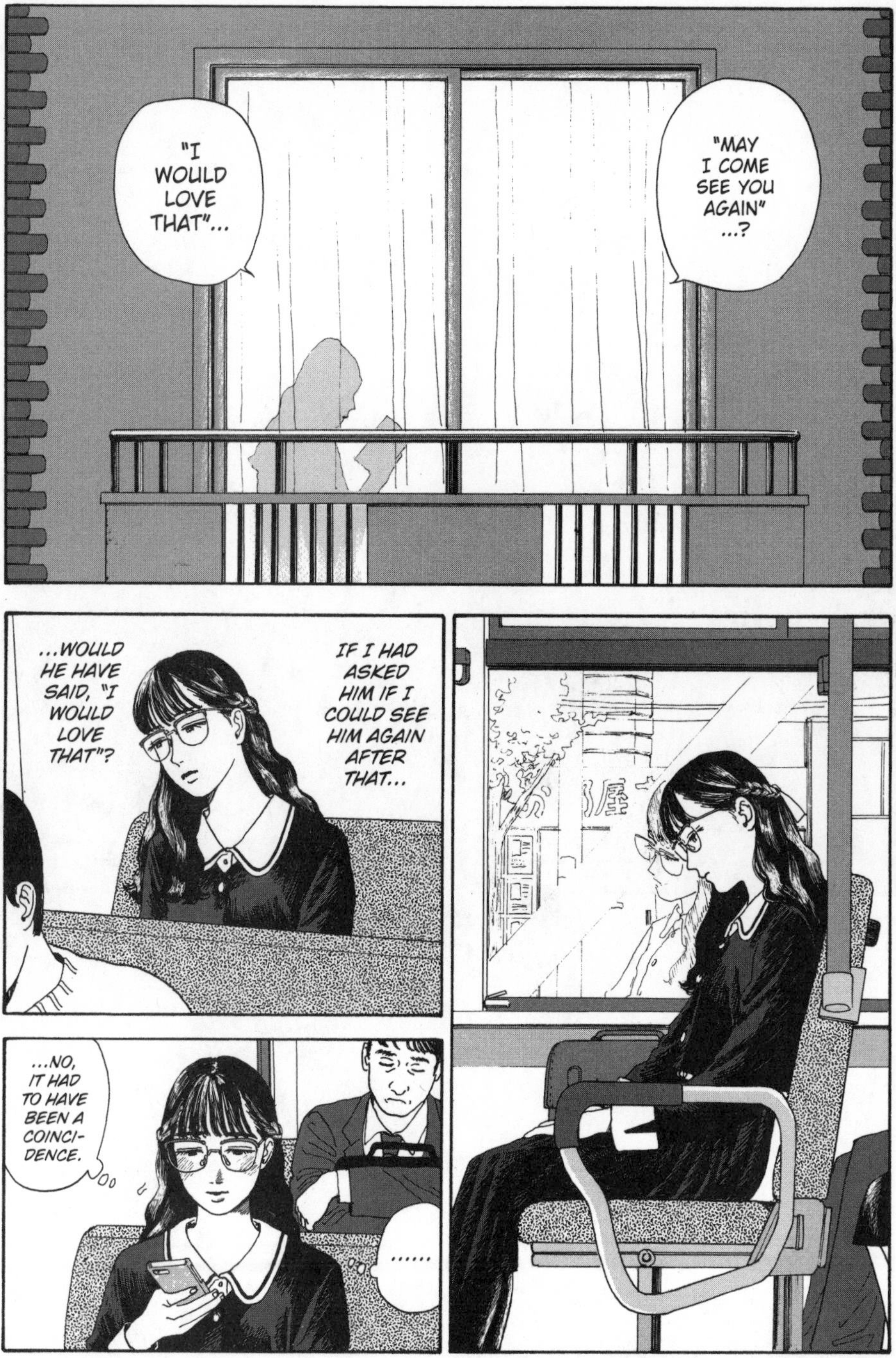
"MAY I COME SEE YOU AGAIN" ...?
"I WOULD LOVE THAT"...
IF I HAD ASKED HIM IF I COULD SEE HIM AGAIN AFTER THAT...
...WOULD HE HAVE SAID, "I WOULD LOVE THAT"?
...NO, IT HAD TO HAVE BEEN A COINCI-DENCE.
......

HE'S PROBABLY OUT LOOKING FOR NEW THINGS TO TWEET.

HAYASHI-SAN...

Parolee
@884344

10 Follower
wing

YOU AGAIN

Parolee @884344 · 32m

YAI

MATSU san

HM...?

"MAY I"...
"COME SEE"...
"YOU"...

"MATSUYA-SAN"...

"AGAIN?"...

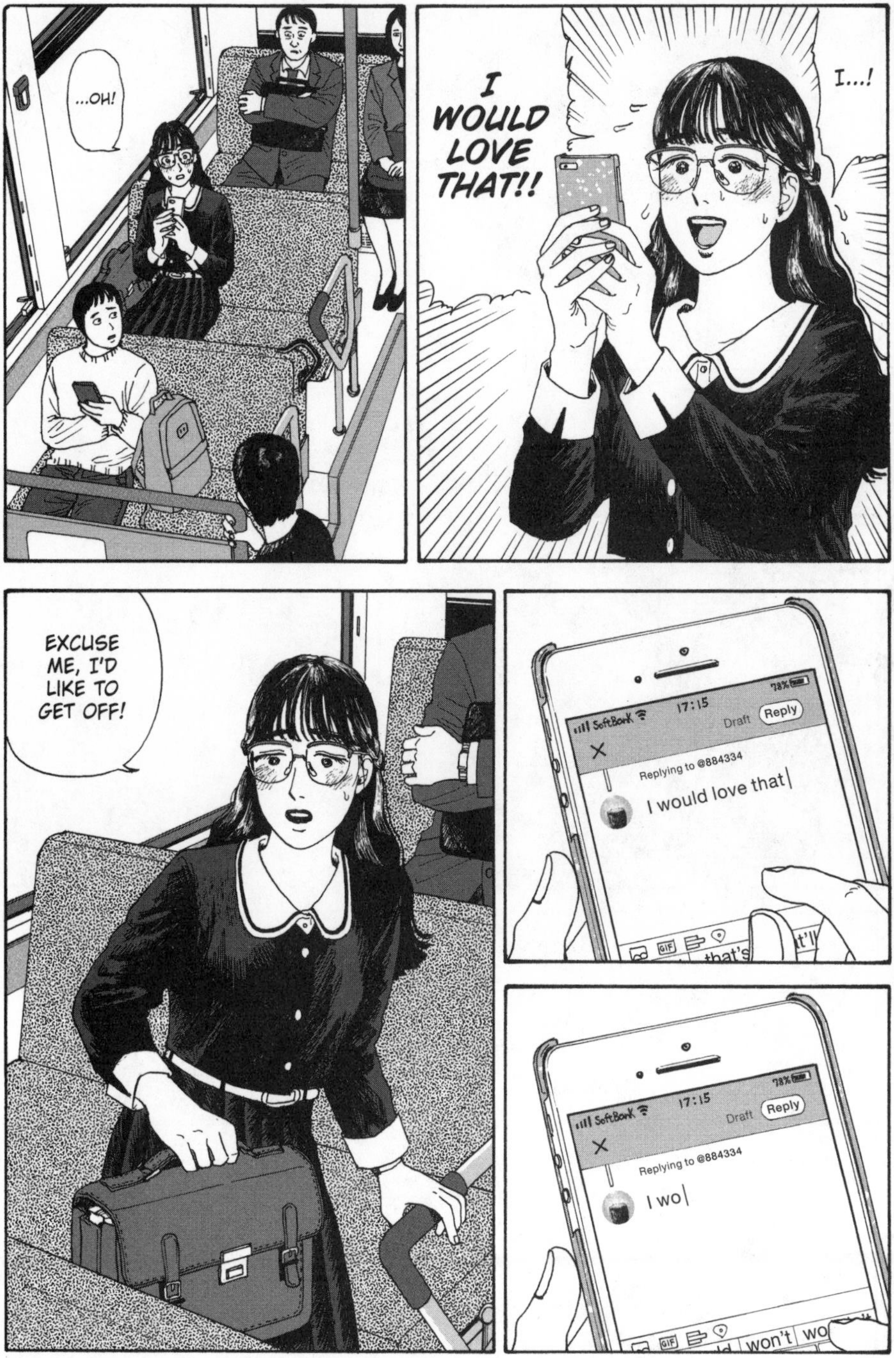
I...!
I WOULD LOVE THAT!!
...OH!
SoftBank
17:15
78%
Draft
Reply
Replying to @884334
I would love that
that's
SoftBank
17:15
78%
Draft
Reply
Replying to @884334
I wo
won't
EXCUSE ME, I'D LIKE TO GET OFF!

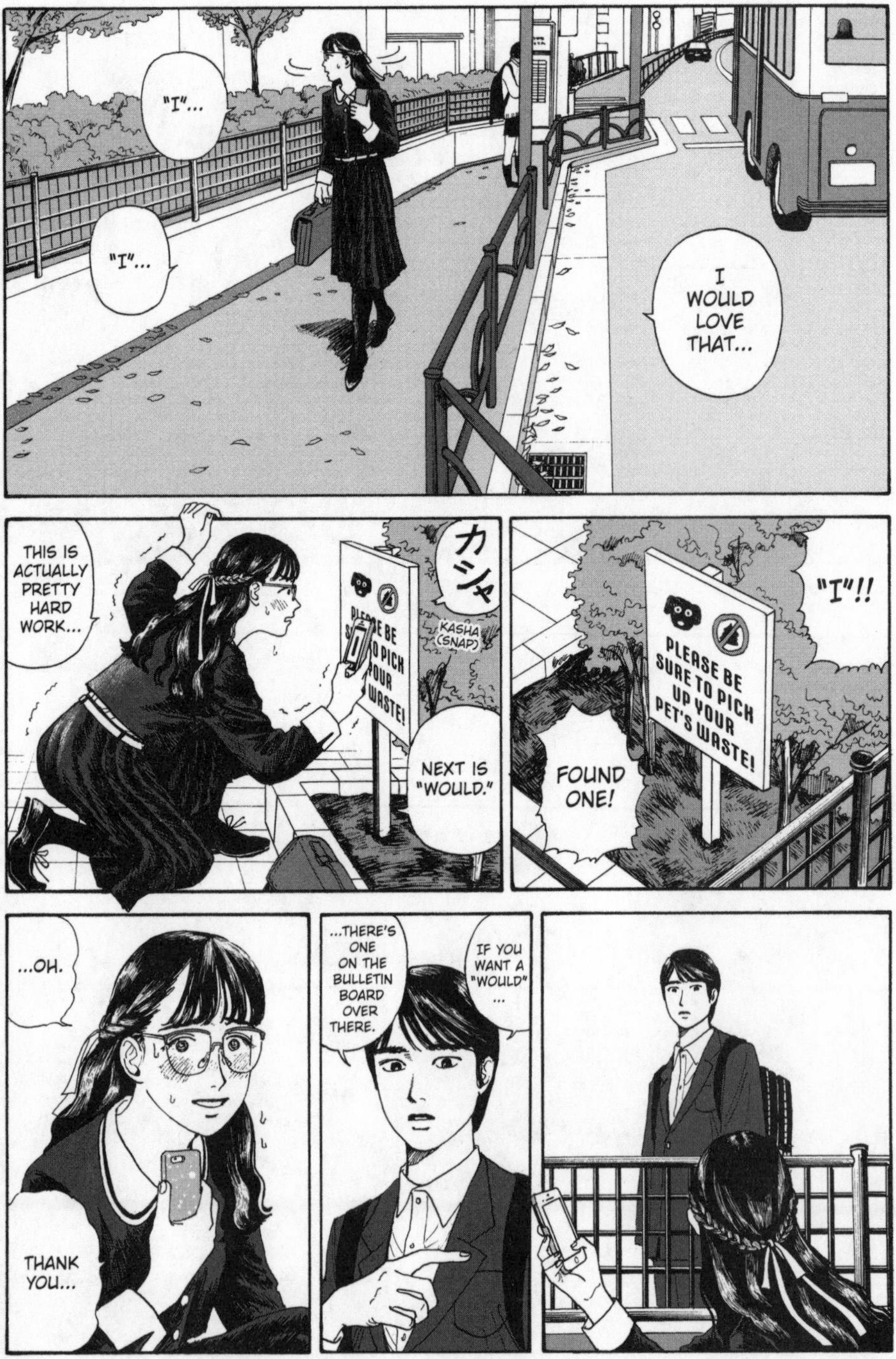
I WOULD LOVE THAT...
"I"...
"I"...
"I"!!
PLEASE BE SURE TO PICK UP YOUR PET'S WASTE!
FOUND ONE!
カシャ
KASHA (SNAP)
THIS IS ACTUALLY PRETTY HARD WORK...
NEXT IS "WOULD."
IF YOU WANT A "WOULD"...
...THERE'S ONE ON THE BULLETIN BOARD OVER THERE.
...OH.
THANK YOU...

I'M SORRY.

HA HA!

HEH.

THERE'S SOMETHING I'VE BEEN WONDERING FOR A BIT NOW. WHY DID YOU CHOOSE "PAROLEE" AS YOUR USERNAME?

IT WAS MY NICKNAME IN MIDDLE SCHOOL.

...WH-WHAT WERE YOU LIKE IN MIDDLE SCHOOL...?

Would You Be My Friend?

[The Artist]

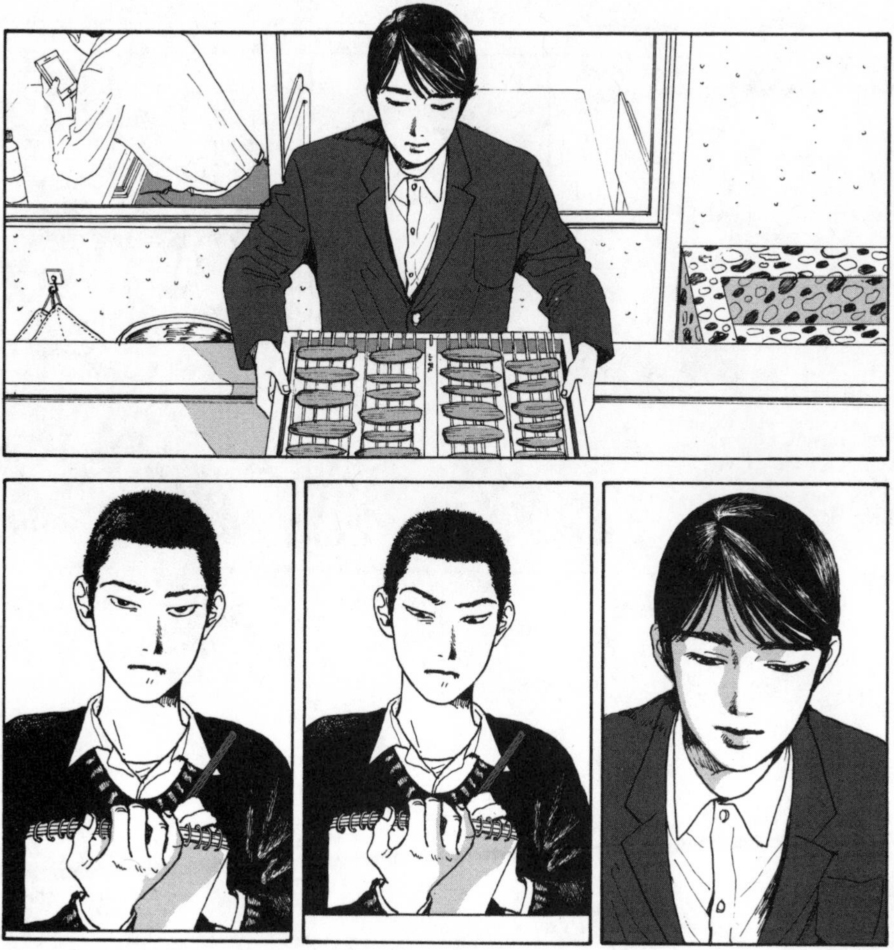

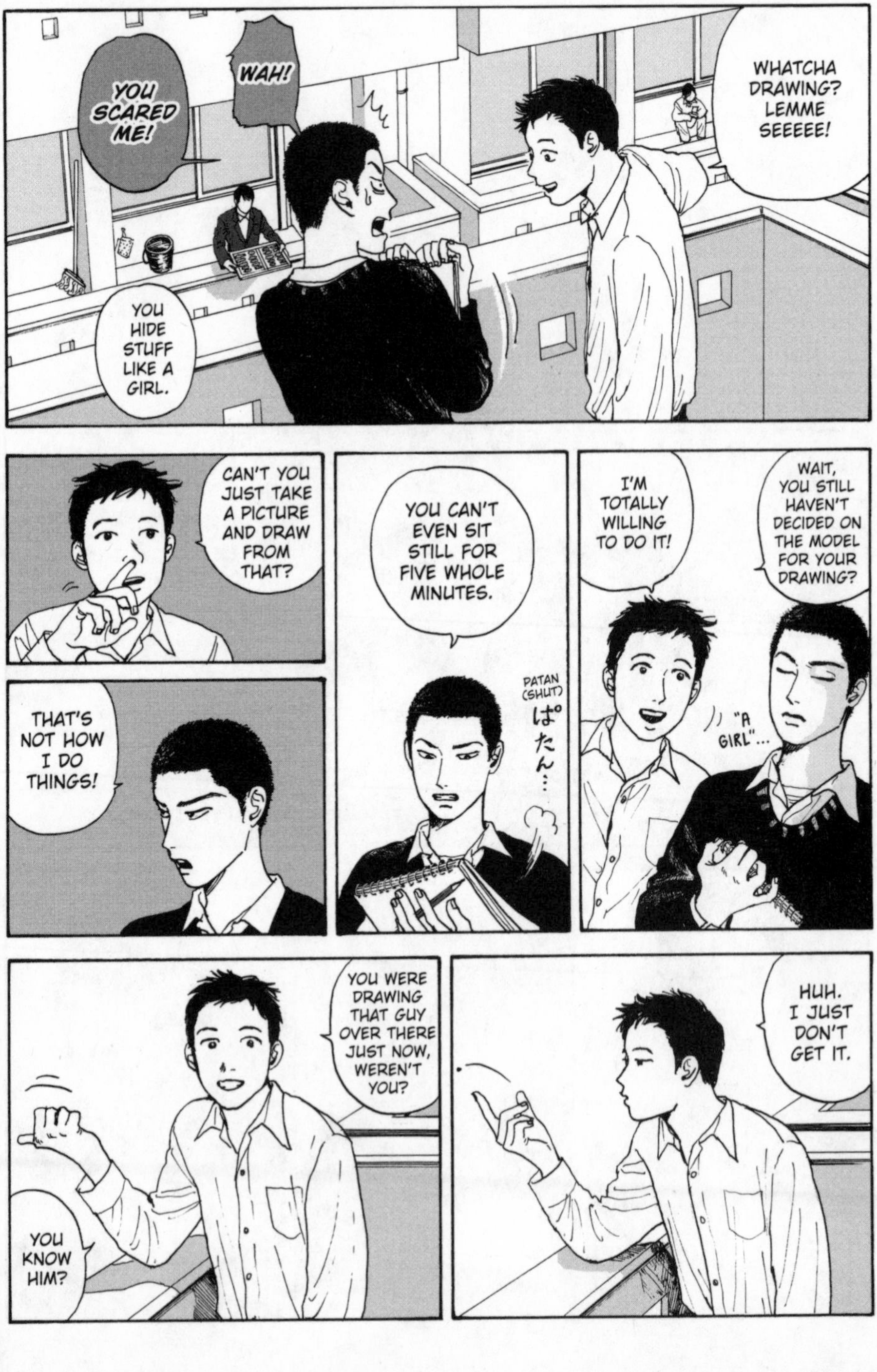
WHATCHA DRAWING? LEMME SEEEEE!
WAH!
YOU SCARED ME!
YOU HIDE STUFF LIKE A GIRL.
WAIT, YOU STILL HAVEN'T DECIDED ON THE MODEL FOR YOUR DRAWING?
I'M TOTALLY WILLING TO DO IT!
"A GIRL"...
YOU CAN'T EVEN SIT STILL FOR FIVE WHOLE MINUTES.
PATAN (SHUT)
ぱたん…
CAN'T YOU JUST TAKE A PICTURE AND DRAW FROM THAT?
THAT'S NOT HOW I DO THINGS!
HUH. I JUST DON'T GET IT.
YOU WERE DRAWING THAT GUY OVER THERE JUST NOW, WEREN'T YOU?
YOU KNOW HIM?

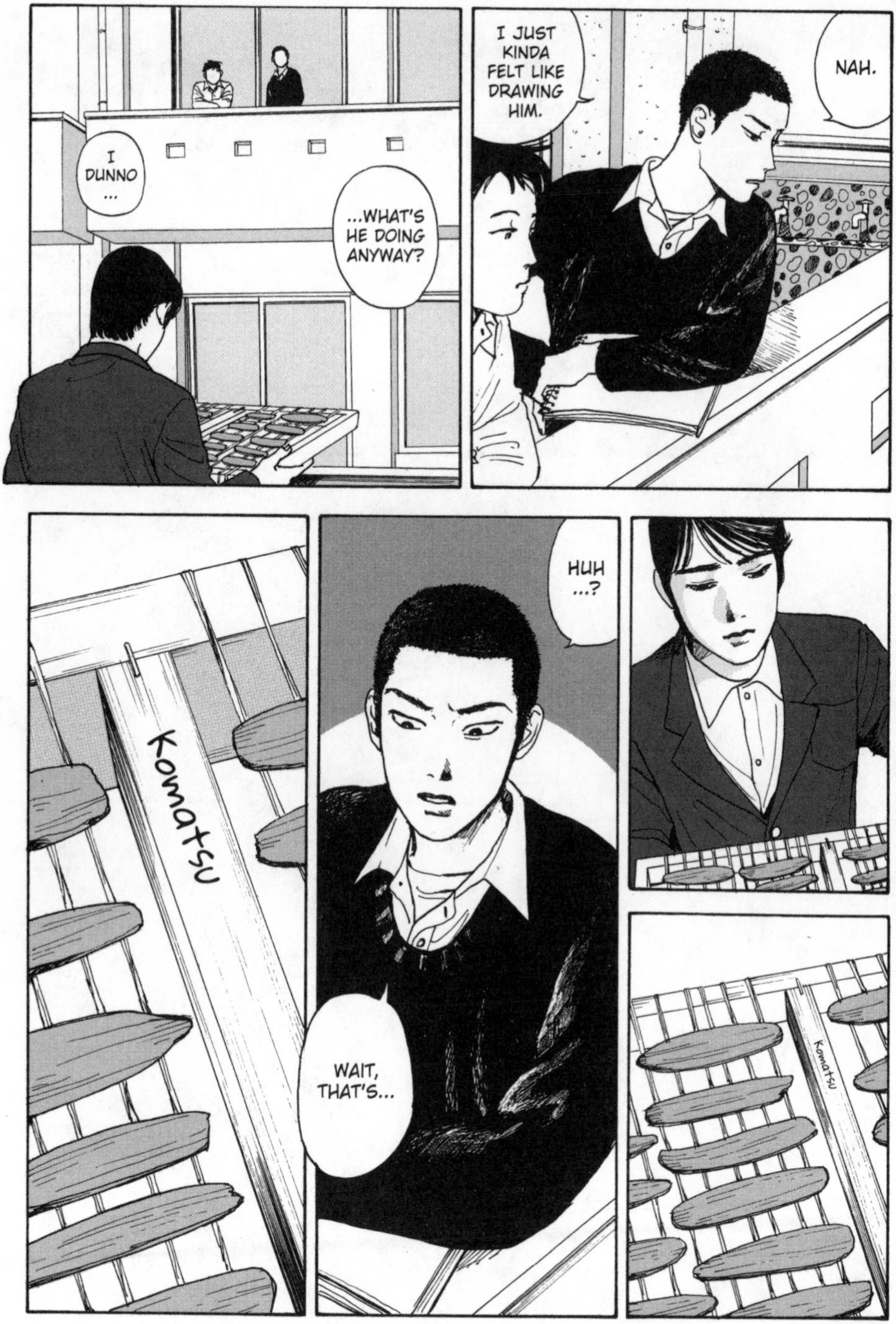
NAH.
I JUST KINDA FELT LIKE DRAWING HIM.
...WHAT'S HE DOING ANYWAY?
I DUNNO ...
Komatsu
HUH ...?
WAIT, THAT'S...
Komatsu

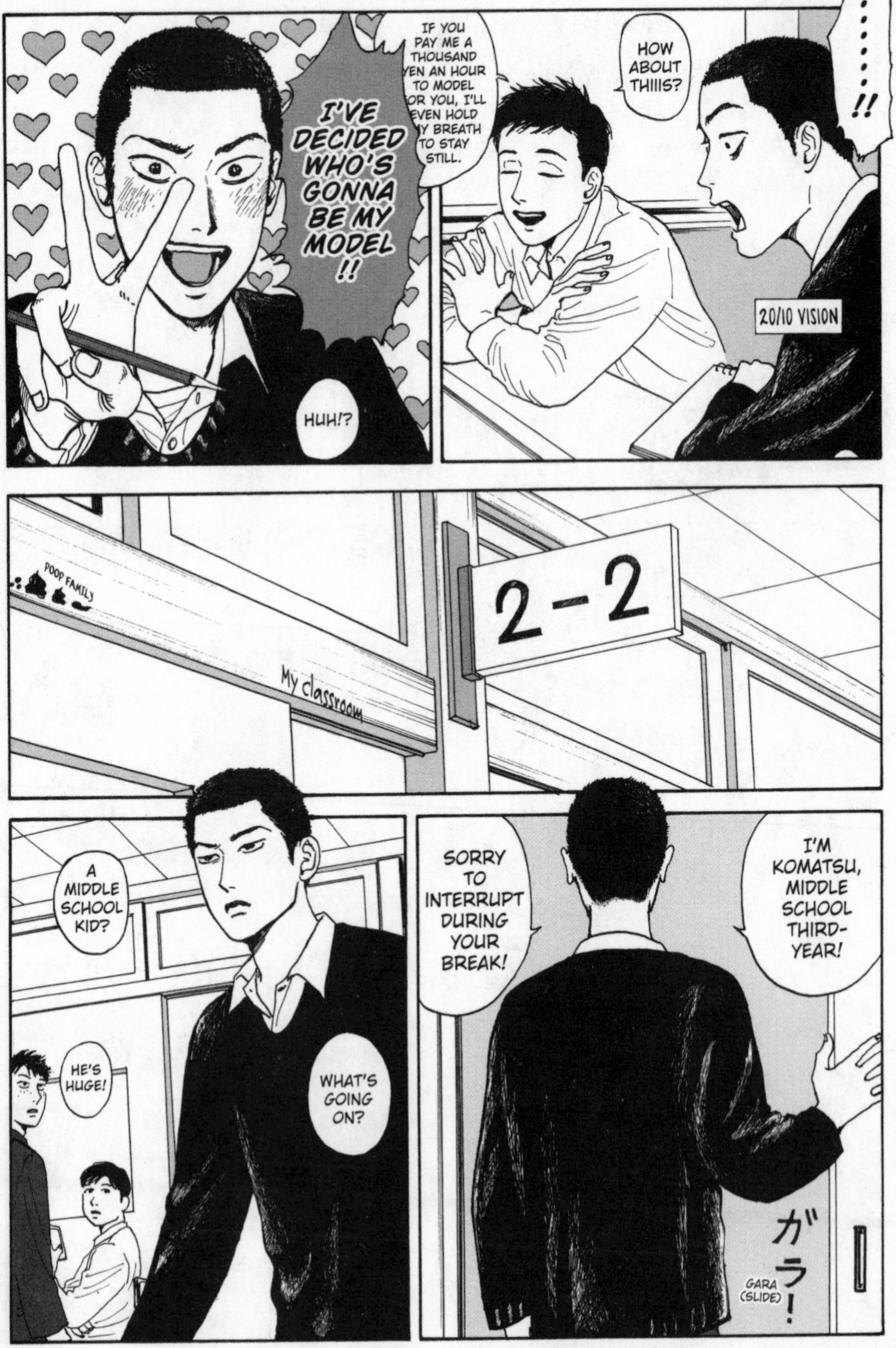

......!!
HOW ABOUT THIIIS?
20/10 VISION
IF YOU PAY ME A THOUSAND YEN AN HOUR TO MODEL FOR YOU, I'LL EVEN HOLD MY BREATH TO STAY STILL.
I'VE DECIDED WHO'S GONNA BE MY MODEL!!
HUH!?
2-2
POOP FAMILY
My classroom
I'M KOMATSU, MIDDLE SCHOOL THIRD-YEAR!
SORRY TO INTERRUPT DURING YOUR BREAK!
ガラ!
GARA (SLIDE)
A MIDDLE SCHOOL KID?
WHAT'S GOING ON?
HE'S HUGE!

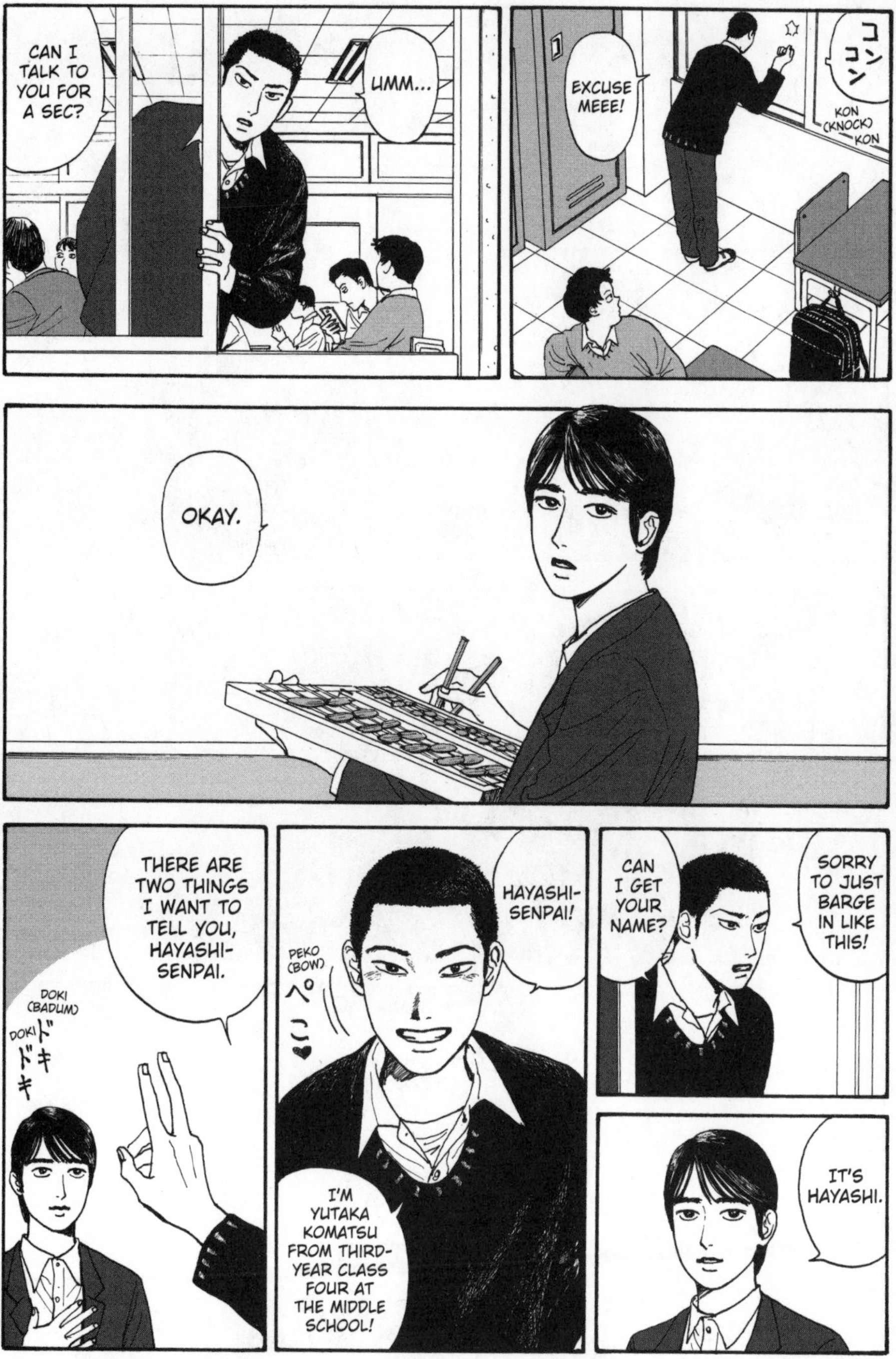
コンコン
KON (KNOCK) KON
EXCUSE MEEE!
UMM...
CAN I TALK TO YOU FOR A SEC?
OKAY.
SORRY TO JUST BARGE IN LIKE THIS!
CAN I GET YOUR NAME?
IT'S HAYASHI.
HAYASHI-SENPAI!
ぺこ
PEKO (BOW)
I'M YUTAKA KOMATSU FROM THIRD-YEAR CLASS FOUR AT THE MIDDLE SCHOOL!
THERE ARE TWO THINGS I WANT TO TELL YOU, HAYASHI-SENPAI.
ドキドキ
DOKI (BADUM) DOKI

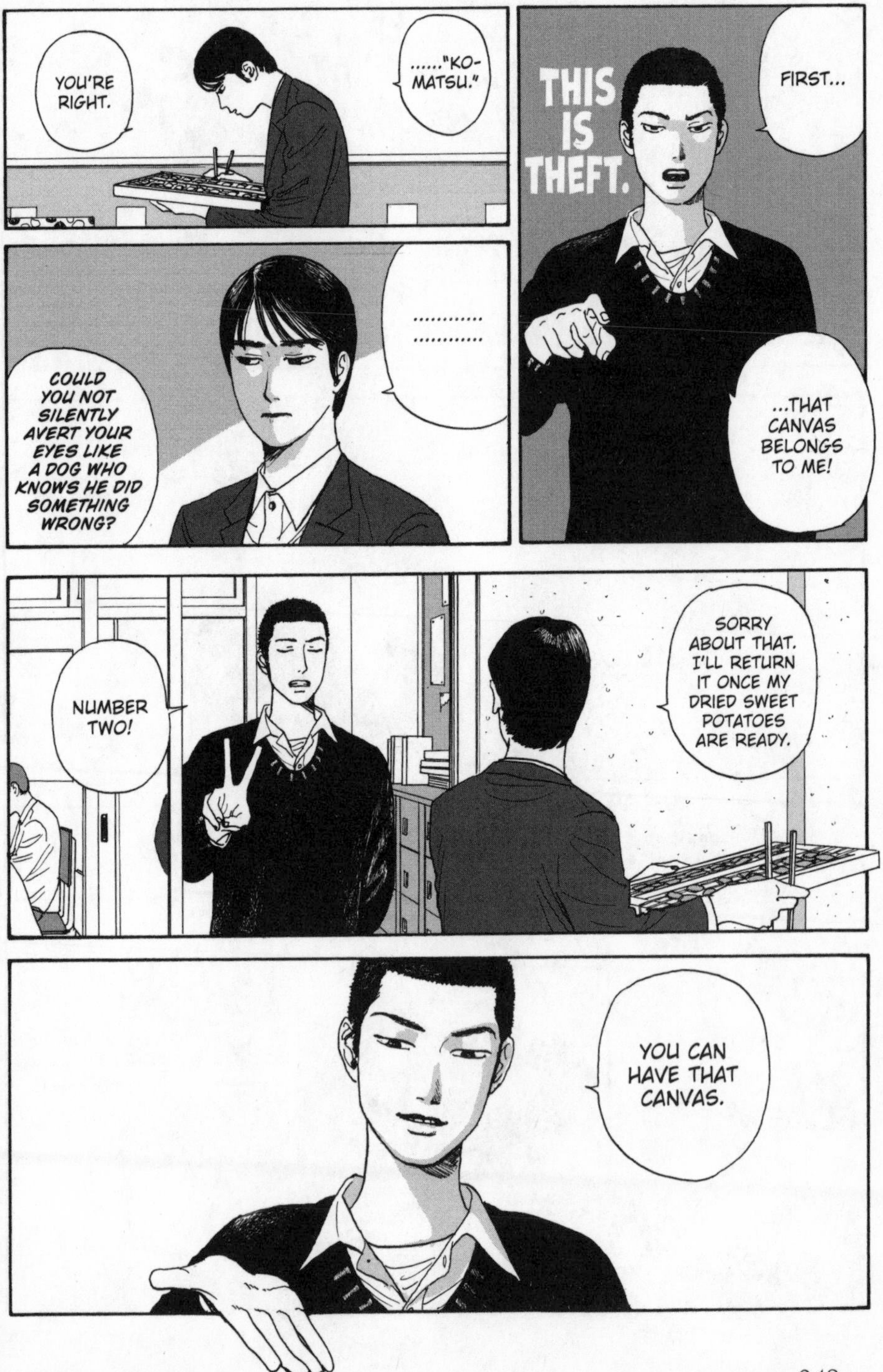
FIRST...
THIS IS THEFT.
...THAT CANVAS BELONGS TO ME!
......"KO-MATSU."
YOU'RE RIGHT.
....
....
COULD YOU NOT SILENTLY AVERT YOUR EYES LIKE A DOG WHO KNOWS HE DID SOMETHING WRONG?
SORRY ABOUT THAT. I'LL RETURN IT ONCE MY DRIED SWEET POTATOES ARE READY.
NUMBER TWO!
YOU CAN HAVE THAT CANVAS.

...WOULD YOU MODEL FOR ME!?

IN EXCHANGE...

THAT'S RIGHT!

MY *DRAWING*!!

HUH?

HUH?

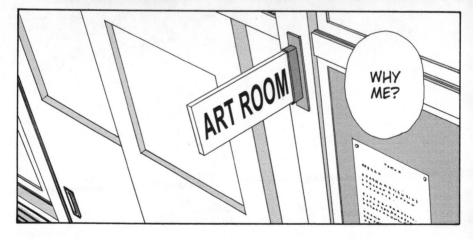

ART ROOM

WHY ME?

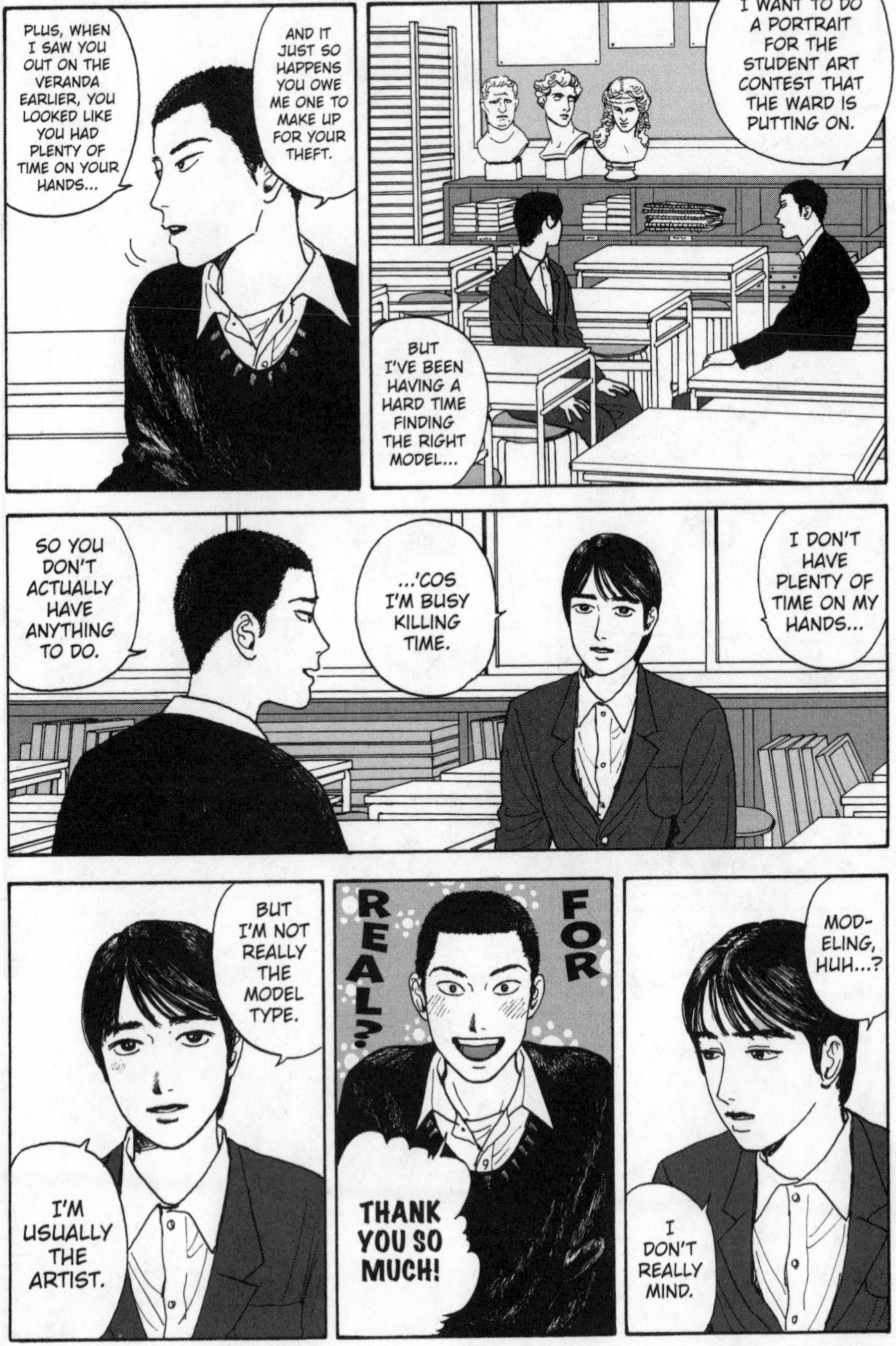
I WANT TO DO A PORTRAIT FOR THE STUDENT ART CONTEST THAT THE WARD IS PUTTING ON.
BUT I'VE BEEN HAVING A HARD TIME FINDING THE RIGHT MODEL...
AND IT JUST SO HAPPENS YOU OWE ME ONE TO MAKE UP FOR YOUR THEFT.
PLUS, WHEN I SAW YOU OUT ON THE VERANDA EARLIER, YOU LOOKED LIKE YOU HAD PLENTY OF TIME ON YOUR HANDS...
I DON'T HAVE PLENTY OF TIME ON MY HANDS...
...'COS I'M BUSY KILLING TIME.
SO YOU DON'T ACTUALLY HAVE ANYTHING TO DO.
MOD-ELING, HUH...?
I DON'T REALLY MIND.
FOR REAL?!
THANK YOU SO MUCH!
BUT I'M NOT REALLY THE MODEL TYPE.
I'M USUALLY THE ARTIST.

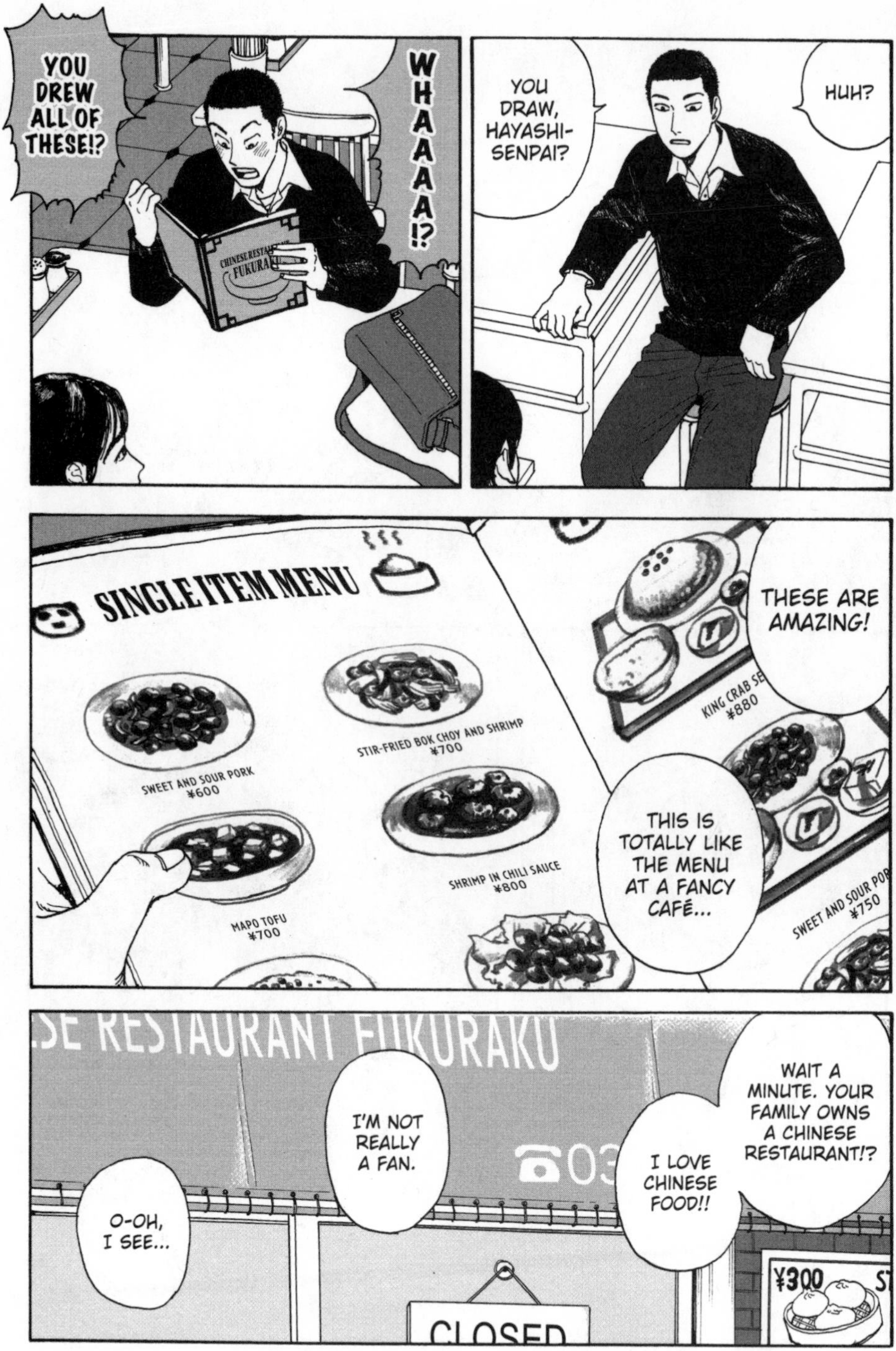
HUH?
YOU DRAW, HAYASHI-SENPAI?
WHAAAAA!?
YOU DREW ALL OF THESE!?
CHINESE RESTAURANT FUKURAKU
THESE ARE AMAZING!
THIS IS TOTALLY LIKE THE MENU AT A FANCY CAFÉ...
SINGLE ITEM MENU
STIR-FRIED BOK CHOY AND SHRIMP ¥700
SWEET AND SOUR PORK ¥600
SHRIMP IN CHILI SAUCE ¥800
MAPO TOFU ¥700
¥880
¥750
WAIT A MINUTE. YOUR FAMILY OWNS A CHINESE RESTAURANT!?
I LOVE CHINESE FOOD!!
I'M NOT REALLY A FAN.
O-OH, I SEE...
¥300

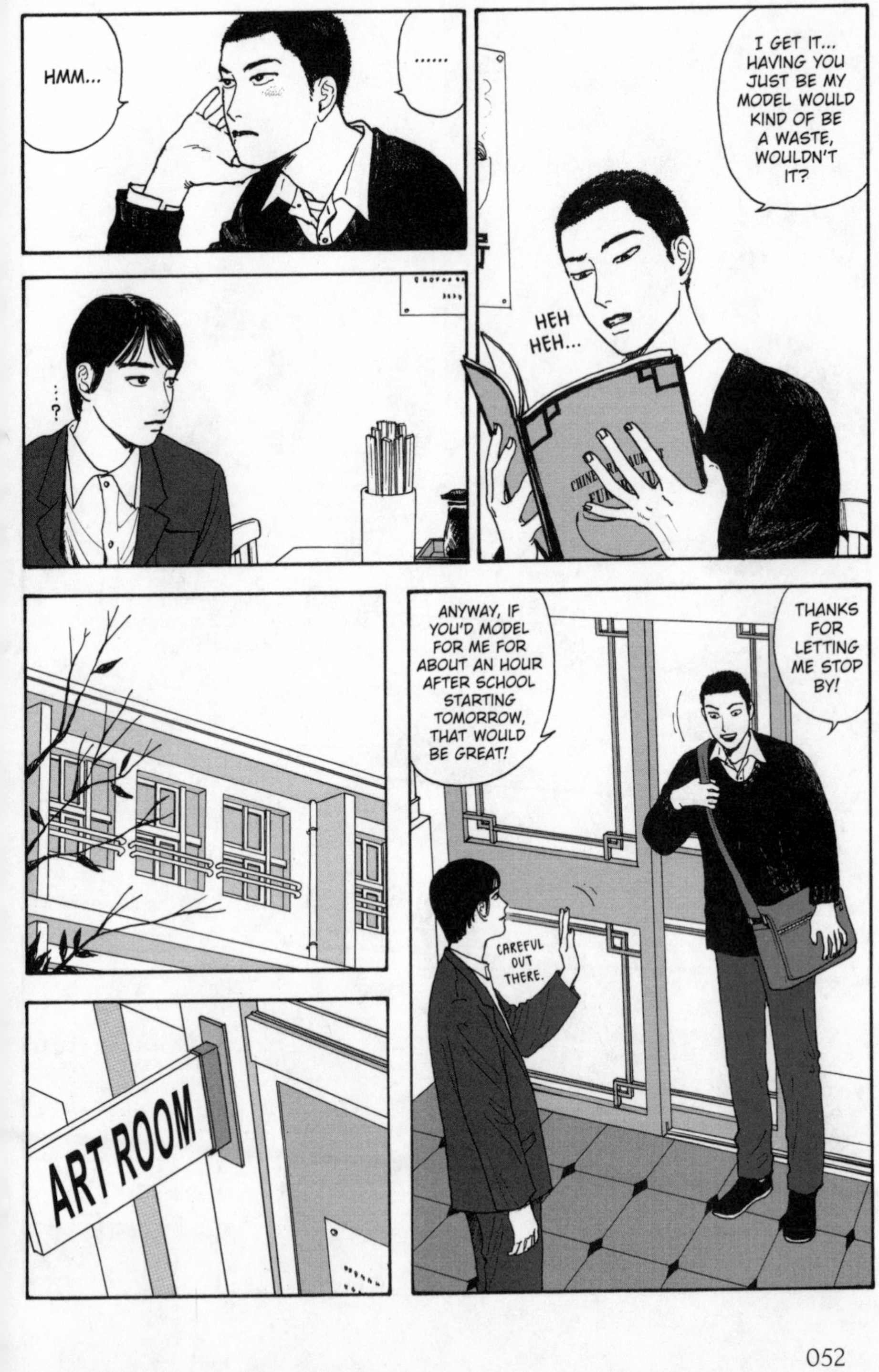
I GET IT... HAVING YOU JUST BE MY MODEL WOULD KIND OF BE A WASTE, WOULDN'T IT?
HEH HEH...
......
HMM...
...?
THANKS FOR LETTING ME STOP BY!
ANYWAY, IF YOU'D MODEL FOR ME FOR ABOUT AN HOUR AFTER SCHOOL STARTING TOMORROW, THAT WOULD BE GREAT!
CAREFUL OUT THERE.
ART ROOM

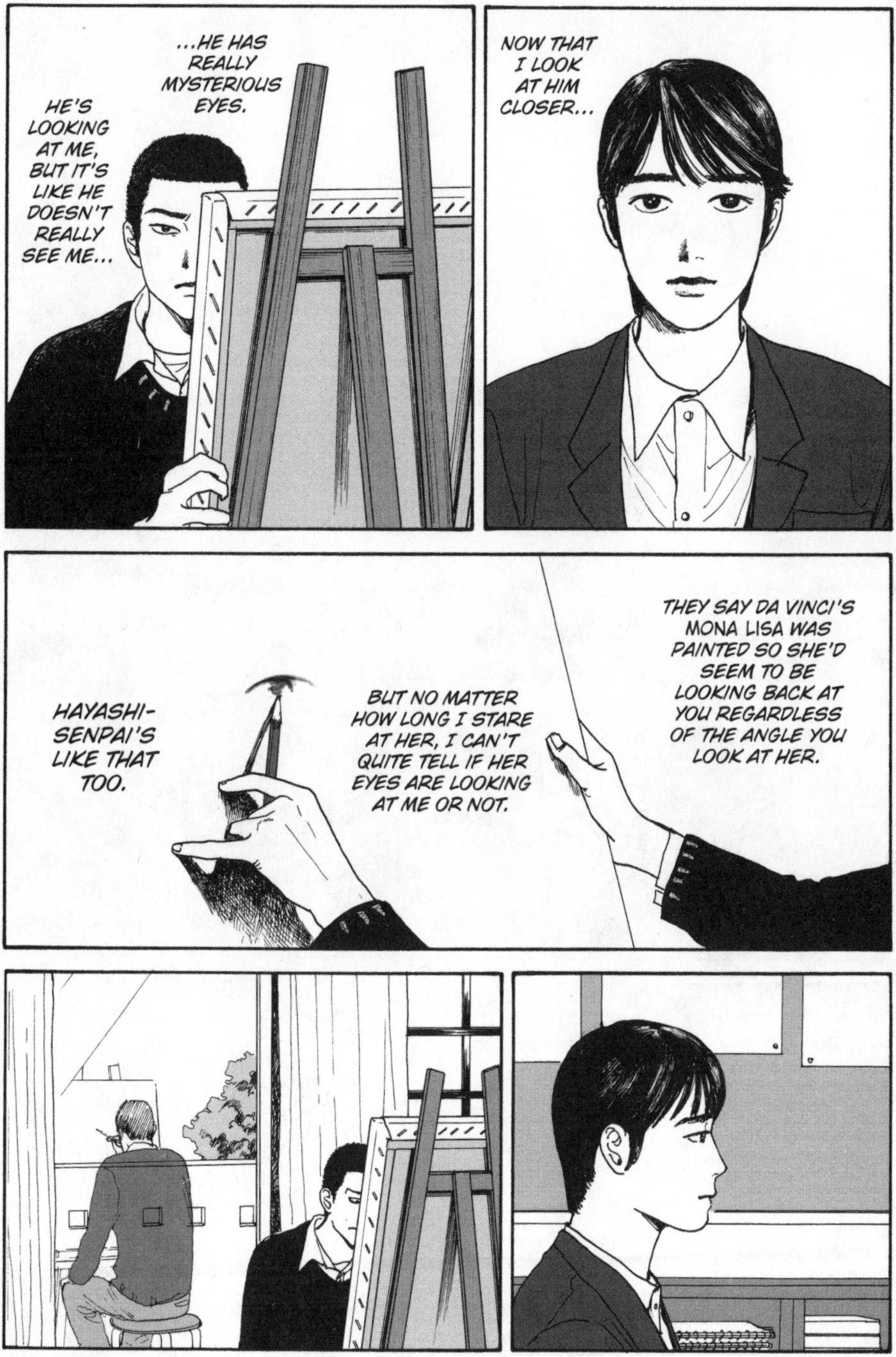
NOW THAT I LOOK AT HIM CLOSER...
...HE HAS REALLY MYSTERIOUS EYES.
HE'S LOOKING AT ME, BUT IT'S LIKE HE DOESN'T REALLY SEE ME...
THEY SAY DA VINCI'S MONA LISA WAS PAINTED SO SHE'D SEEM TO BE LOOKING BACK AT YOU REGARDLESS OF THE ANGLE YOU LOOK AT HER.
BUT NO MATTER HOW LONG I STARE AT HER, I CAN'T QUITE TELL IF HER EYES ARE LOOKING AT ME OR NOT.
HAYASHI-SENPAI'S LIKE THAT TOO.

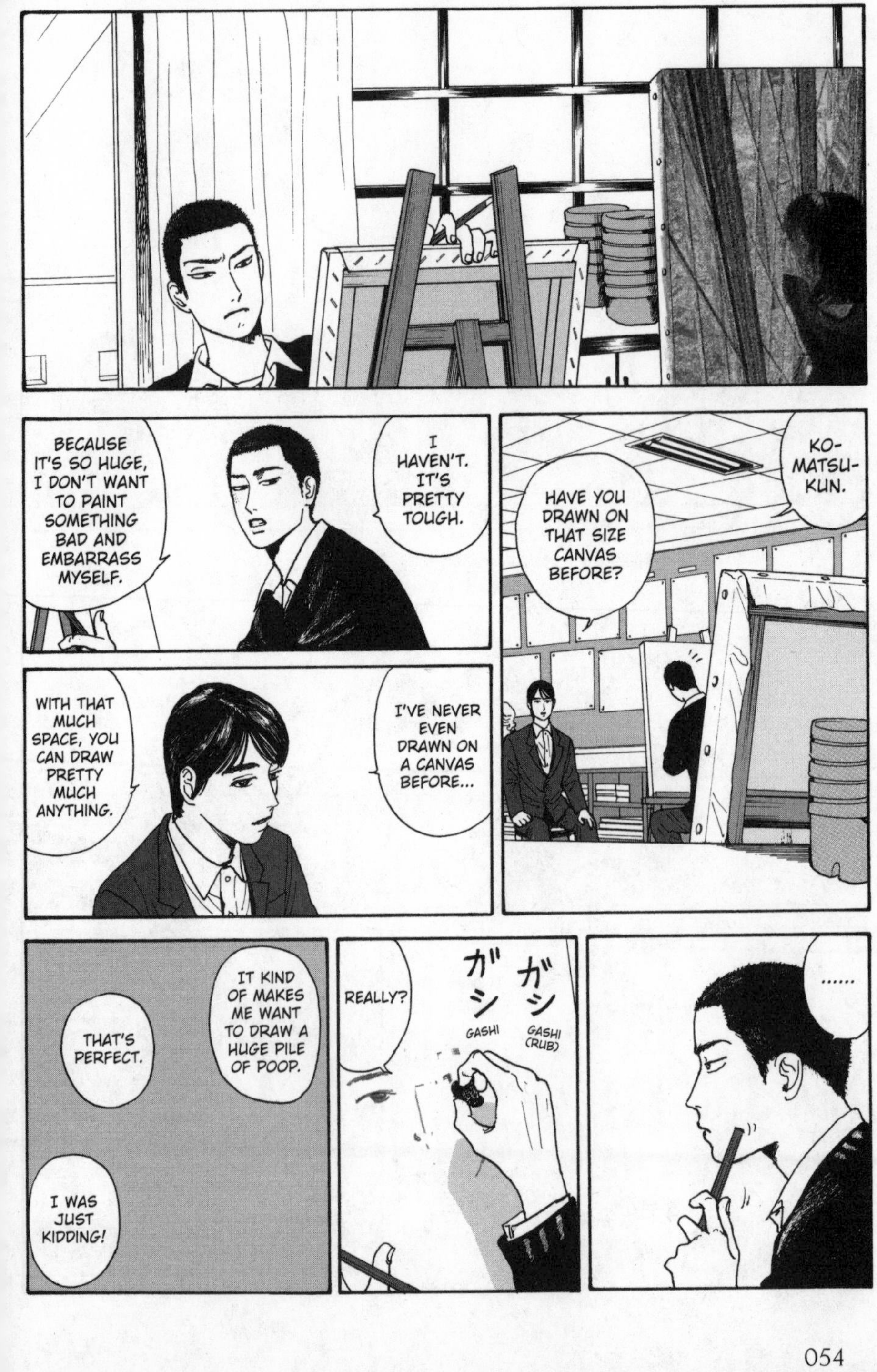
KO-MATSU-KUN.
HAVE YOU DRAWN ON THAT SIZE CANVAS BEFORE?
I HAVEN'T. IT'S PRETTY TOUGH.
BECAUSE IT'S SO HUGE, I DON'T WANT TO PAINT SOMETHING BAD AND EMBARRASS MYSELF.
I'VE NEVER EVEN DRAWN ON A CANVAS BEFORE...
WITH THAT MUCH SPACE, YOU CAN DRAW PRETTY MUCH ANYTHING.
......
ガシ
GASHI (RUB)
ガシ
GASHI
REALLY?
IT KIND OF MAKES ME WANT TO DRAW A HUGE PILE OF POOP.
THAT'S PERFECT.
I WAS JUST KIDDING!

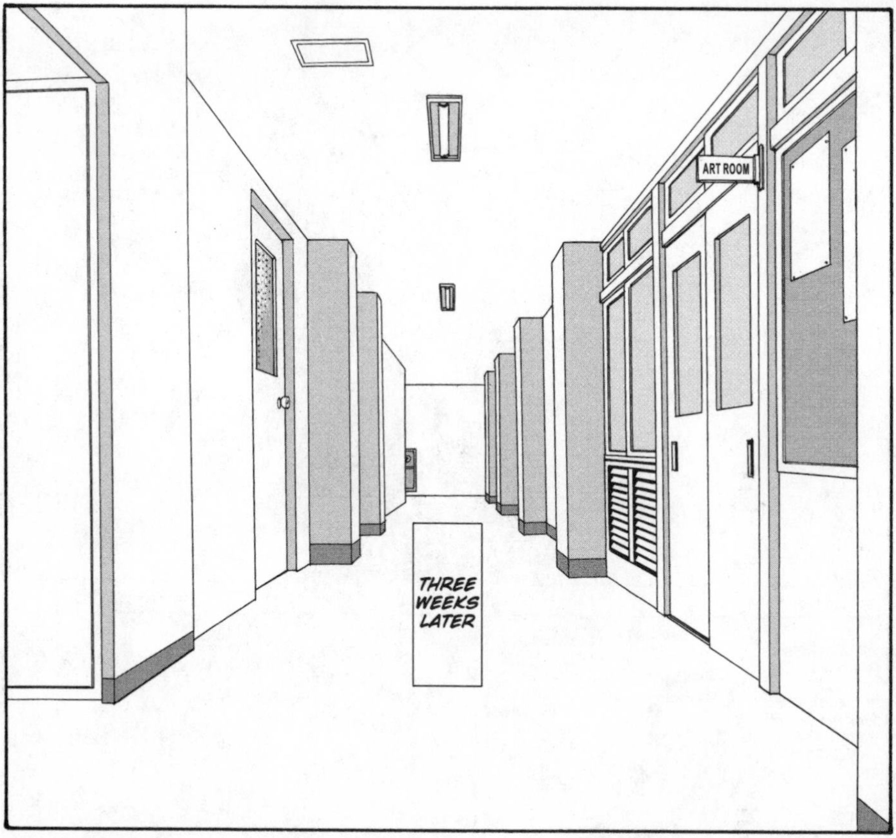
ART ROOM
THREE WEEKS LATER

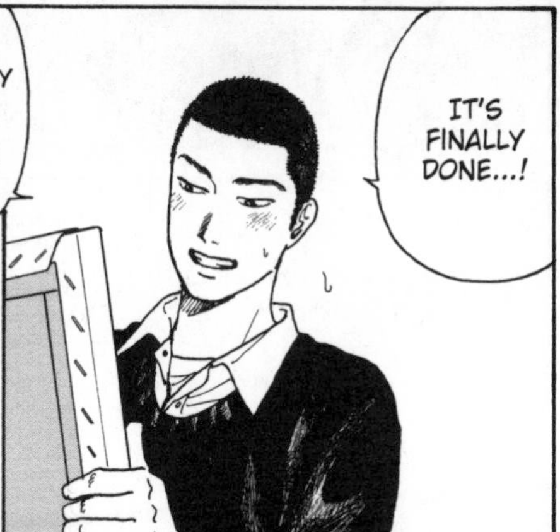
IT'S FINALLY DONE...!

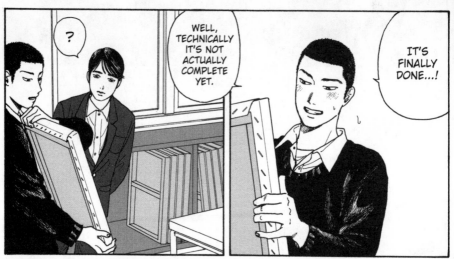

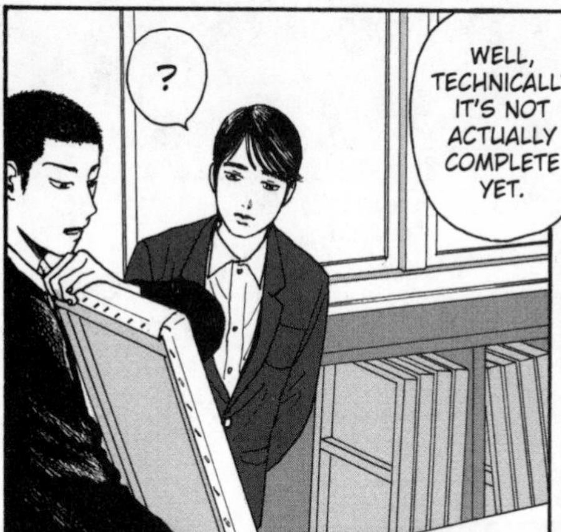
WELL, TECHNICALLY IT'S NOT ACTUALLY COMPLETE YET.
?

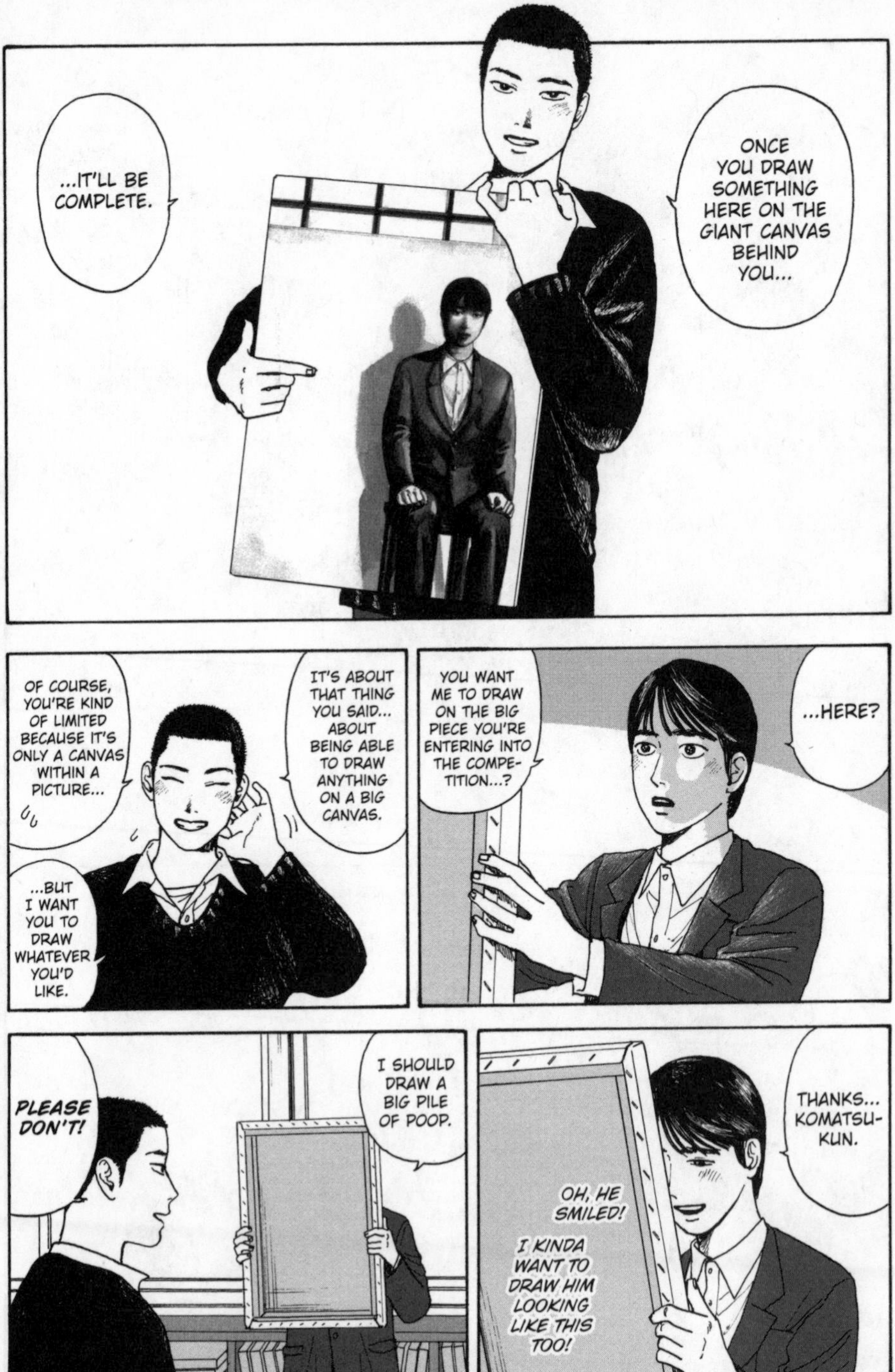
ONCE YOU DRAW SOMETHING HERE ON THE GIANT CANVAS BEHIND YOU...
...IT'LL BE COMPLETE.
...HERE?
YOU WANT ME TO DRAW ON THE BIG PIECE YOU'RE ENTERING INTO THE COMPE-TITION...?
IT'S ABOUT THAT THING YOU SAID... ABOUT BEING ABLE TO DRAW ANYTHING ON A BIG CANVAS.
OF COURSE, YOU'RE KIND OF LIMITED BECAUSE IT'S ONLY A CANVAS WITHIN A PICTURE...
...BUT I WANT YOU TO DRAW WHATEVER YOU'D LIKE.
THANKS... KOMATSU-KUN.
OH, HE SMILED!
I KINDA WANT TO DRAW HIM LOOKING LIKE THIS TOO!
I SHOULD DRAW A BIG PILE OF POOP.
PLEASE DON'T!

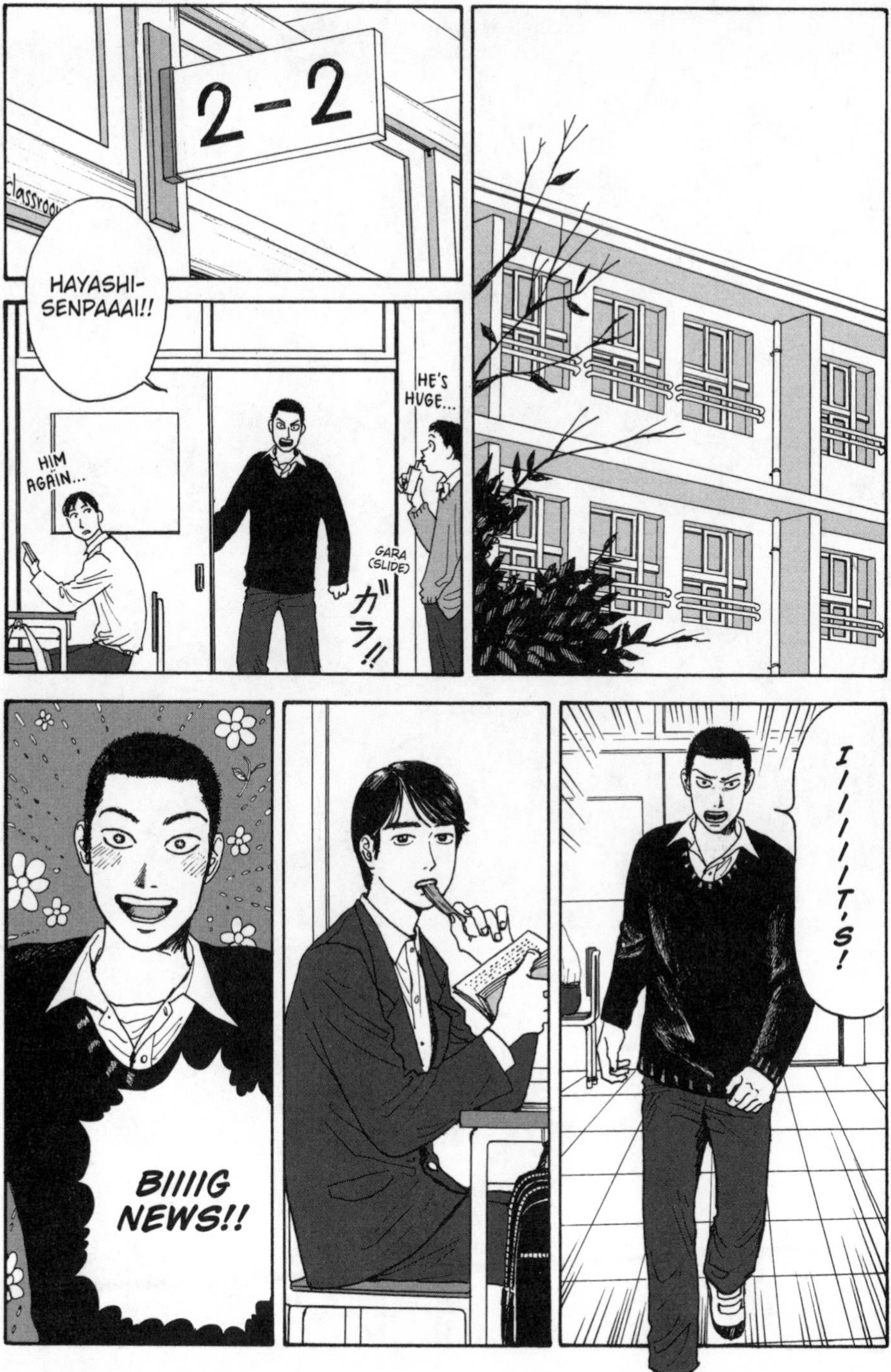
2-2
HAYASHI-SENPAAAI!!
HE'S HUGE...
HIM AGAIN...
GARA (SLIDE)
ガラ!!
I-I-I-I-IT'S!
BIIIG NEWS!!

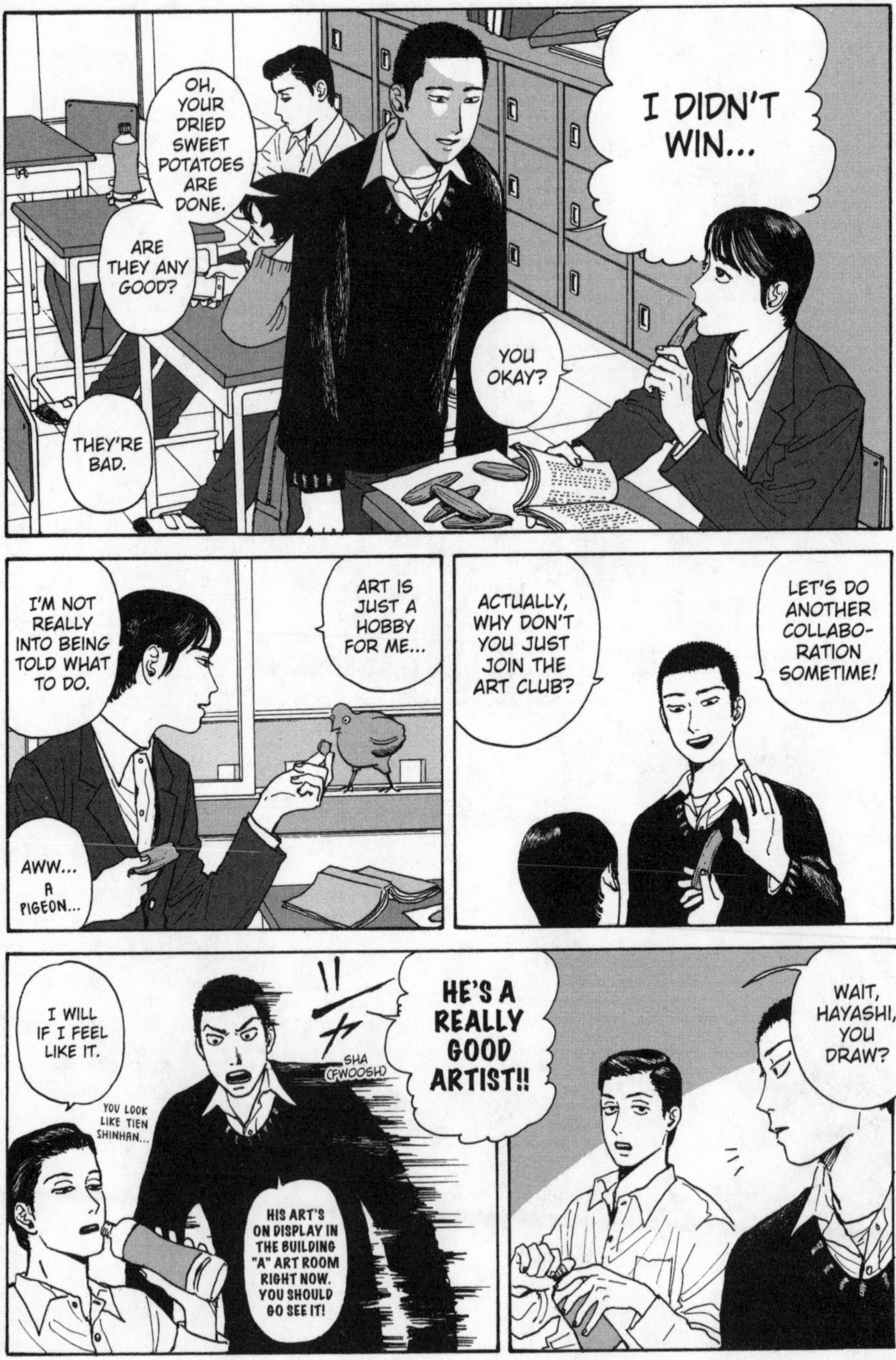
I DIDN'T WIN...
OH, YOUR DRIED SWEET POTATOES ARE DONE.
ARE THEY ANY GOOD?
THEY'RE BAD.
YOU OKAY?
LET'S DO ANOTHER COLLABO-RATION SOMETIME!
ACTUALLY, WHY DON'T YOU JUST JOIN THE ART CLUB?
ART IS JUST A HOBBY FOR ME...
I'M NOT REALLY INTO BEING TOLD WHAT TO DO.
AWW... A PIGEON...
WAIT, HAYASHI, YOU DRAW?
HE'S A REALLY GOOD ARTIST!!
SHA (FWOOSH)
I WILL IF I FEEL LIKE IT.
YOU LOOK LIKE TIEN SHINHAN...
HIS ART'S ON DISPLAY IN THE BUILDING "A" ART ROOM RIGHT NOW. YOU SHOULD GO SEE IT!

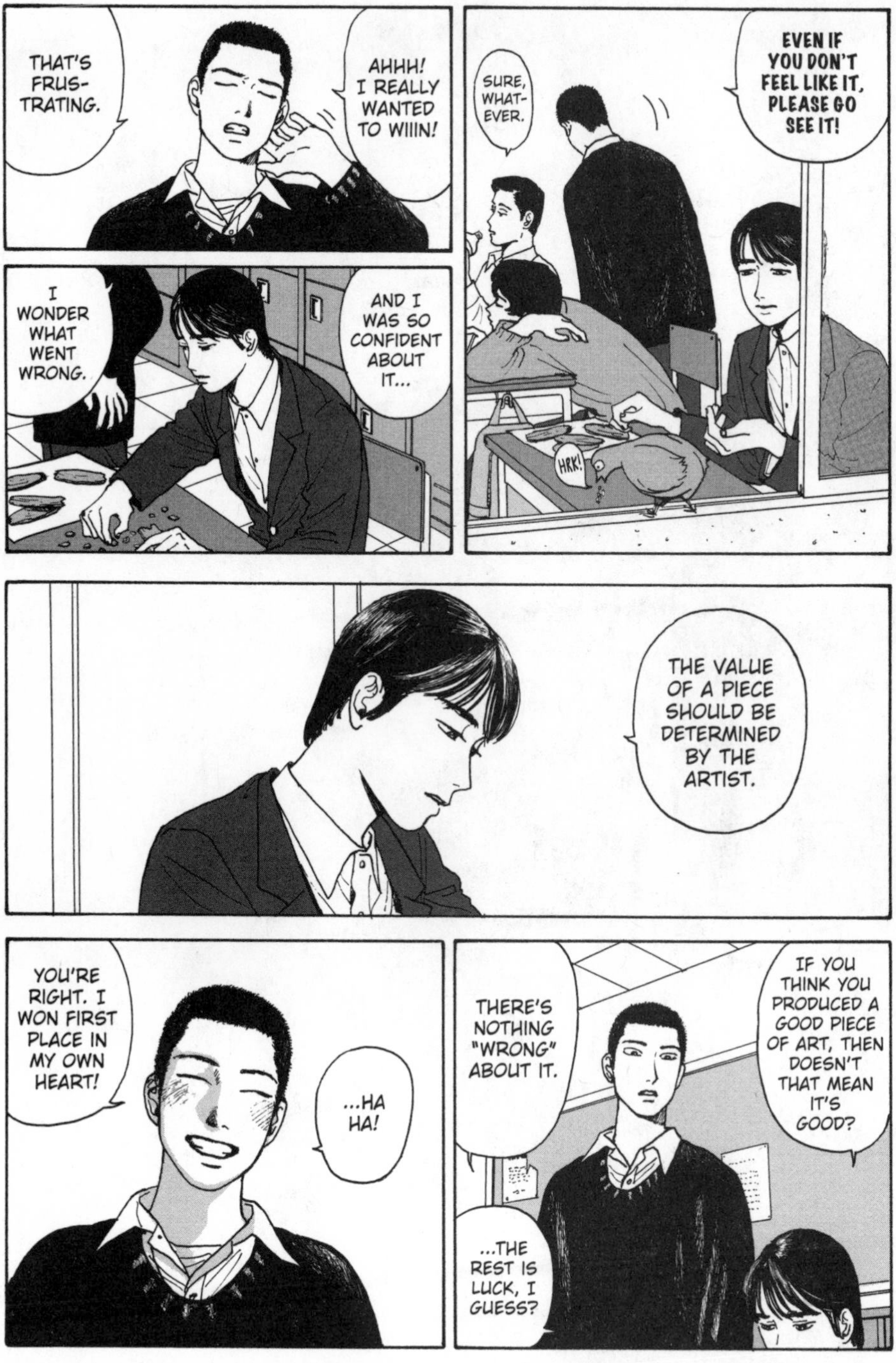
EVEN IF YOU DON'T FEEL LIKE IT, PLEASE GO SEE IT!
SURE, WHAT-EVER.
HRK!
AHHH! I REALLY WANTED TO WIIIN!
THAT'S FRUS-TRATING.
AND I WAS SO CONFIDENT ABOUT IT...
I WONDER WHAT WENT WRONG.
THE VALUE OF A PIECE SHOULD BE DETERMINED BY THE ARTIST.
IF YOU THINK YOU PRODUCED A GOOD PIECE OF ART, THEN DOESN'T THAT MEAN IT'S GOOD?
THERE'S NOTHING "WRONG" ABOUT IT.
...THE REST IS LUCK, I GUESS?
...HA HA!
YOU'RE RIGHT. I WON FIRST PLACE IN MY OWN HEART!

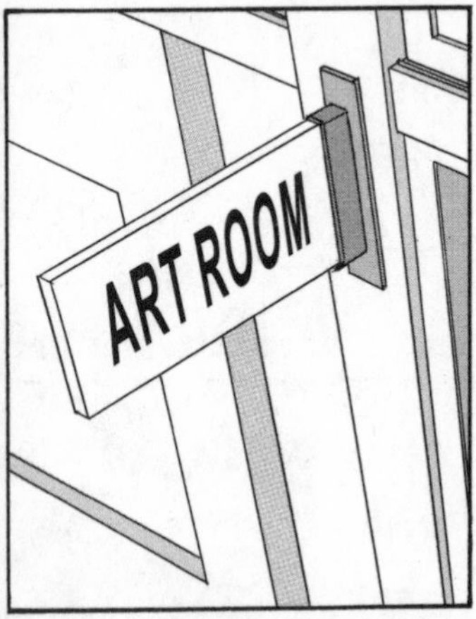
ART ROOM

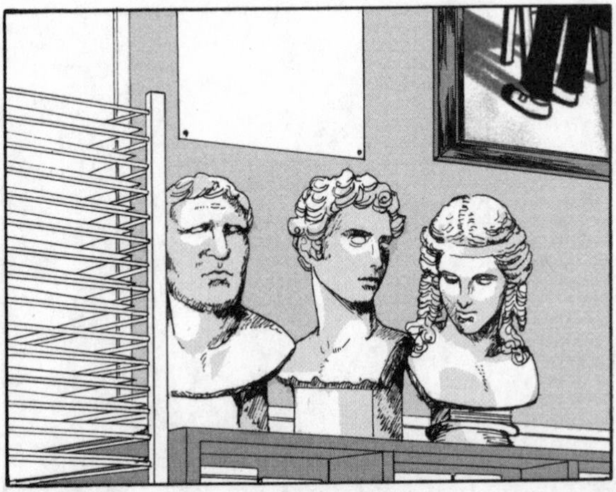

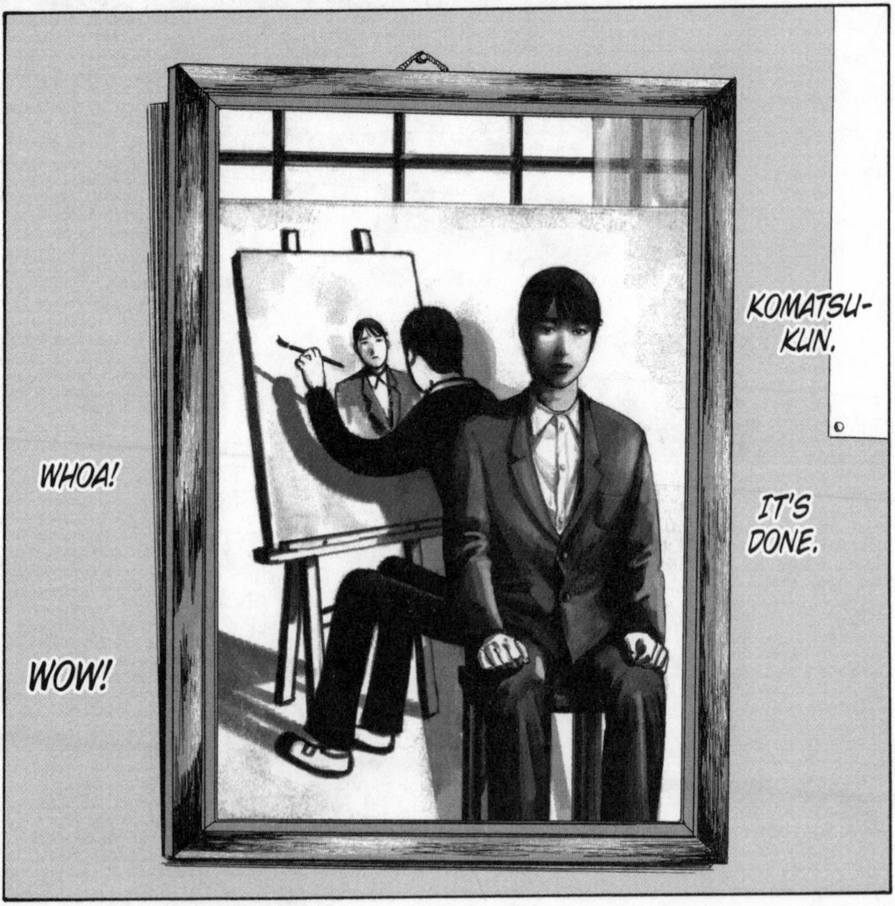
KOMATSU-KUN.
IT'S DONE.
WHOA!
WOW!

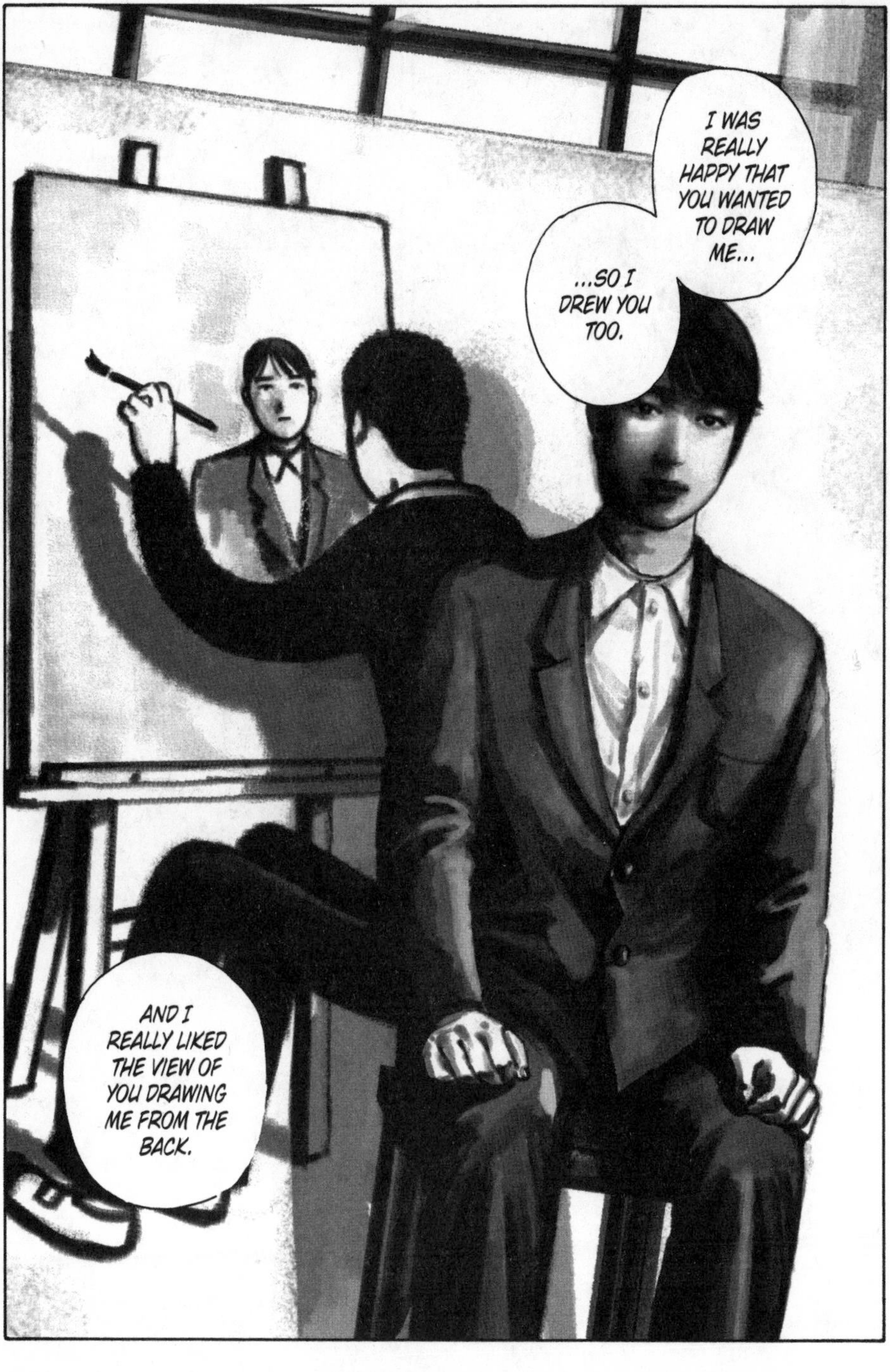
I WAS REALLY HAPPY THAT YOU WANTED TO DRAW ME...
...SO I DREW YOU TOO.
AND I REALLY LIKED THE VIEW OF YOU DRAWING ME FROM THE BACK.

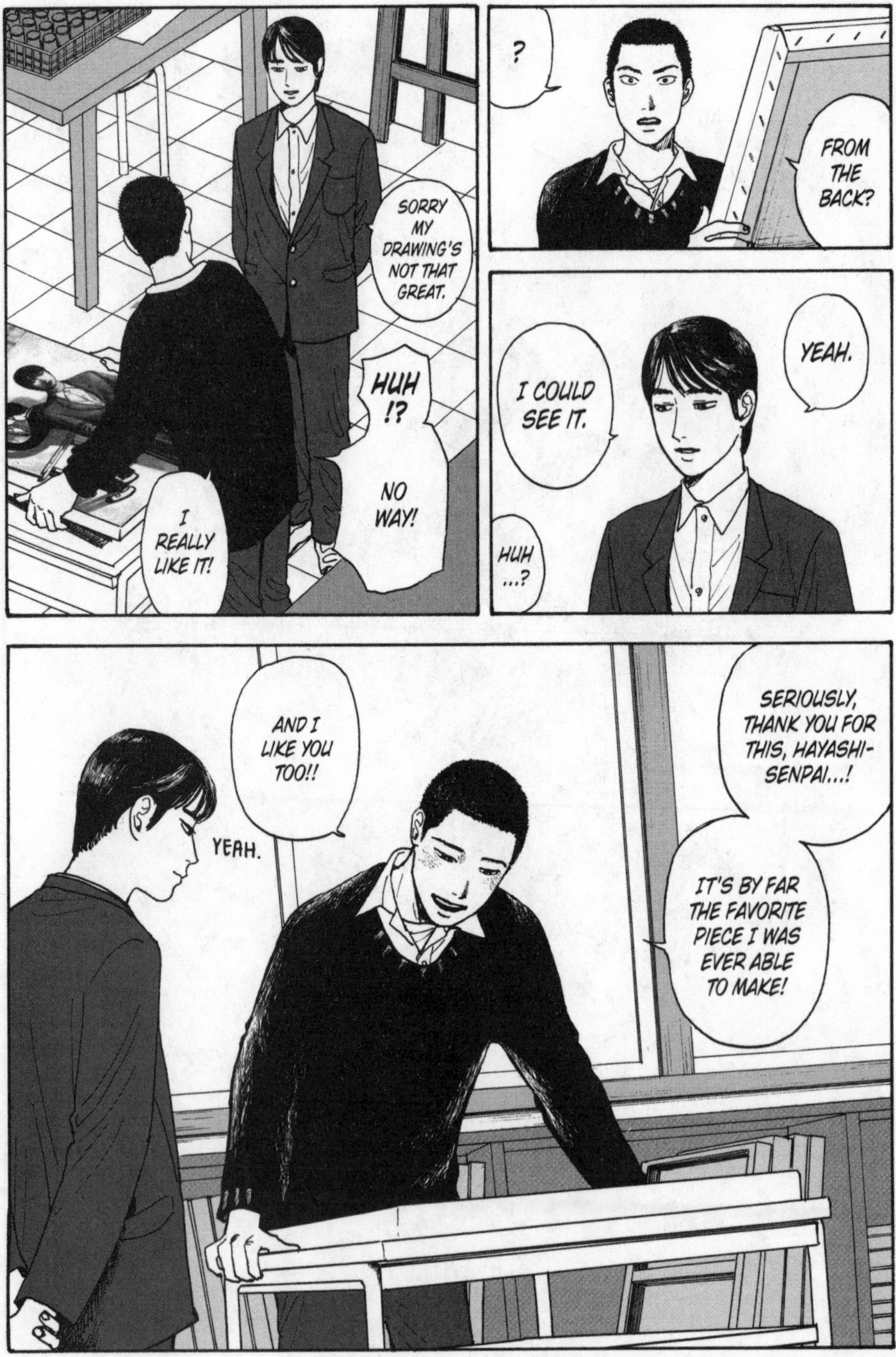
?
FROM THE BACK?
YEAH.
I COULD SEE IT.
HUH ...?
SORRY MY DRAWING'S NOT THAT GREAT.
HUH !?
NO WAY!
I REALLY LIKE IT!
SERIOUSLY, THANK YOU FOR THIS, HAYASHI-SENPAI...!
IT'S BY FAR THE FAVORITE PIECE I WAS EVER ABLE TO MAKE!
AND I LIKE YOU TOO!!
YEAH.

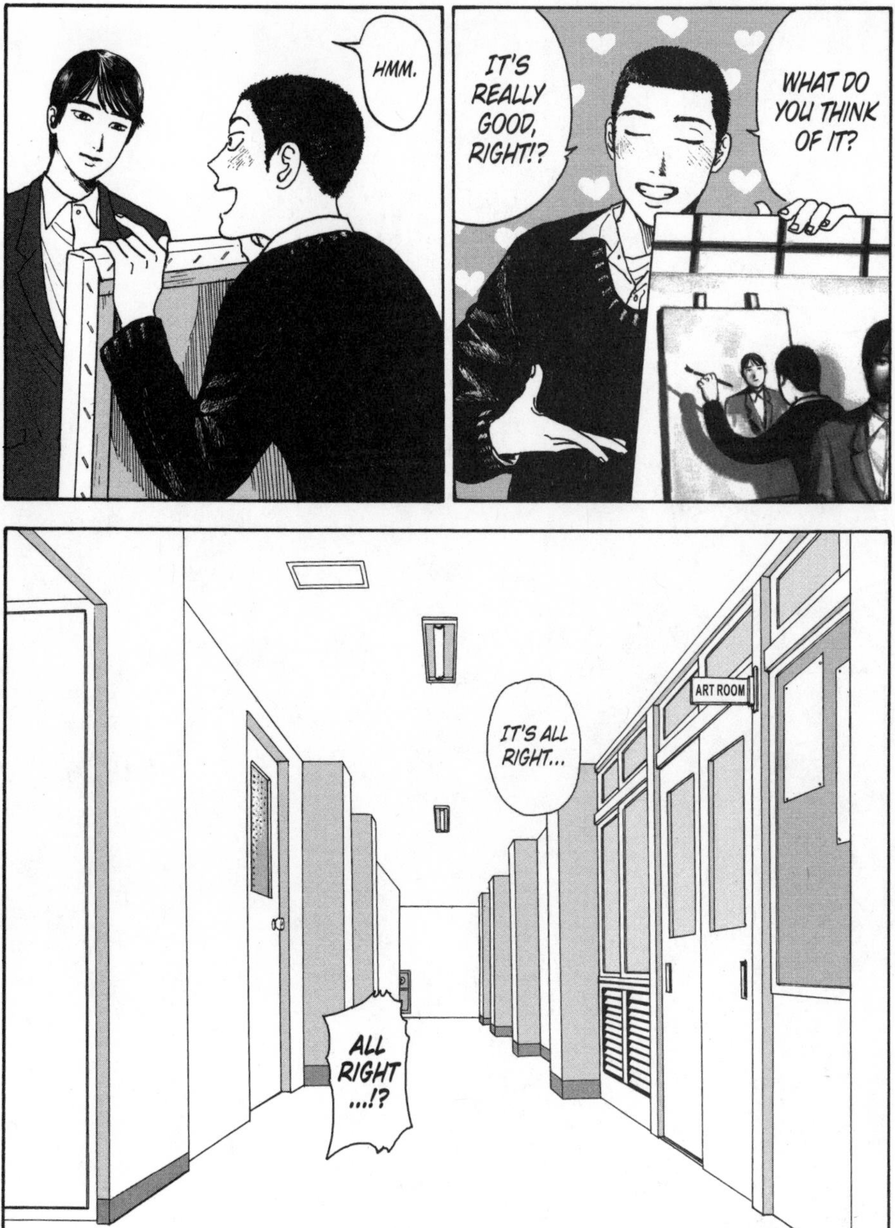
WHAT DO YOU THINK OF IT?
IT'S REALLY GOOD, RIGHT!?
HMM.
ART ROOM
IT'S ALL RIGHT...
ALL RIGHT ...!?

[Run, Yamada!]

HOOOOO...
RUN, YAMADAAAA!!!
...!
GATA (CLATTER)
ガタッ

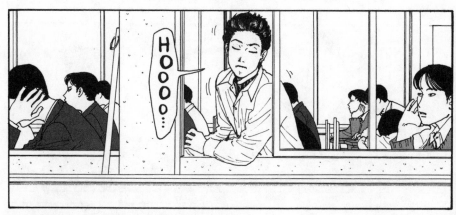

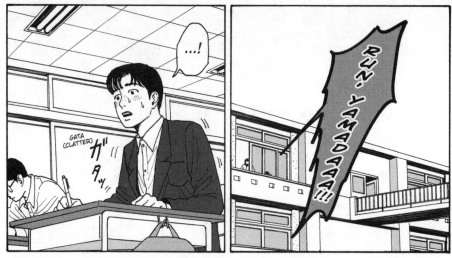

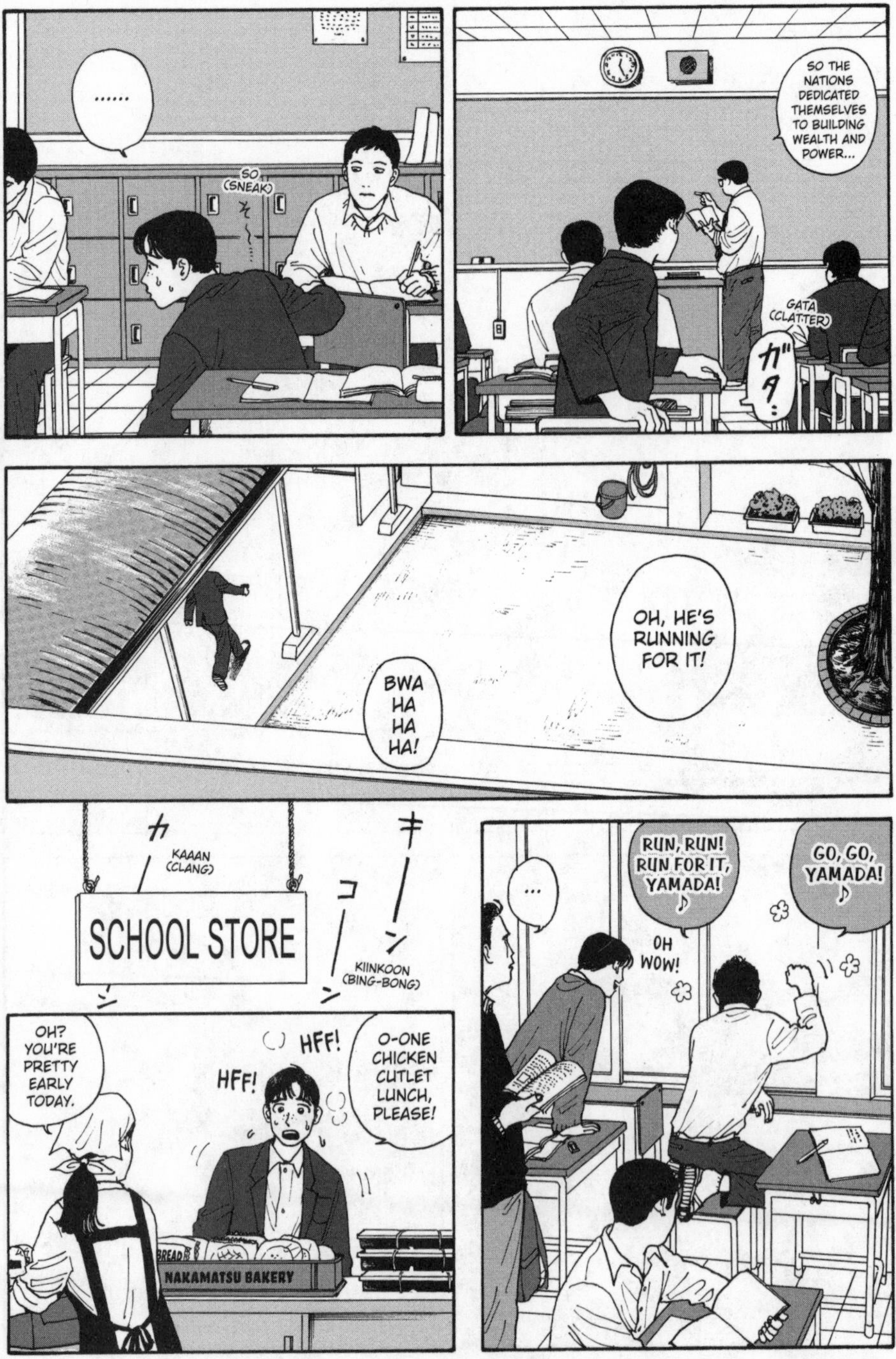
SO THE NATIONS DEDICATED THEMSELVES TO BUILDING WEALTH AND POWER...
GATA (CLATTER)
ガタ
......
SO (SNEAK)
そ～
OH, HE'S RUNNING FOR IT!
BWA HA HA HA!
GO, GO, YAMADA! ♪
RUN, RUN! RUN FOR IT, YAMADA! ♪
OH WOW!
...
キーンコーン
KIINKOON (BING-BONG)
カーン
KAAAN (CLANG)
SCHOOL STORE
O-ONE CHICKEN CUTLET LUNCH, PLEASE!
HFF!
HFF!
OH? YOU'RE PRETTY EARLY TODAY.
BREAD
NAKAMATSU BAKERY

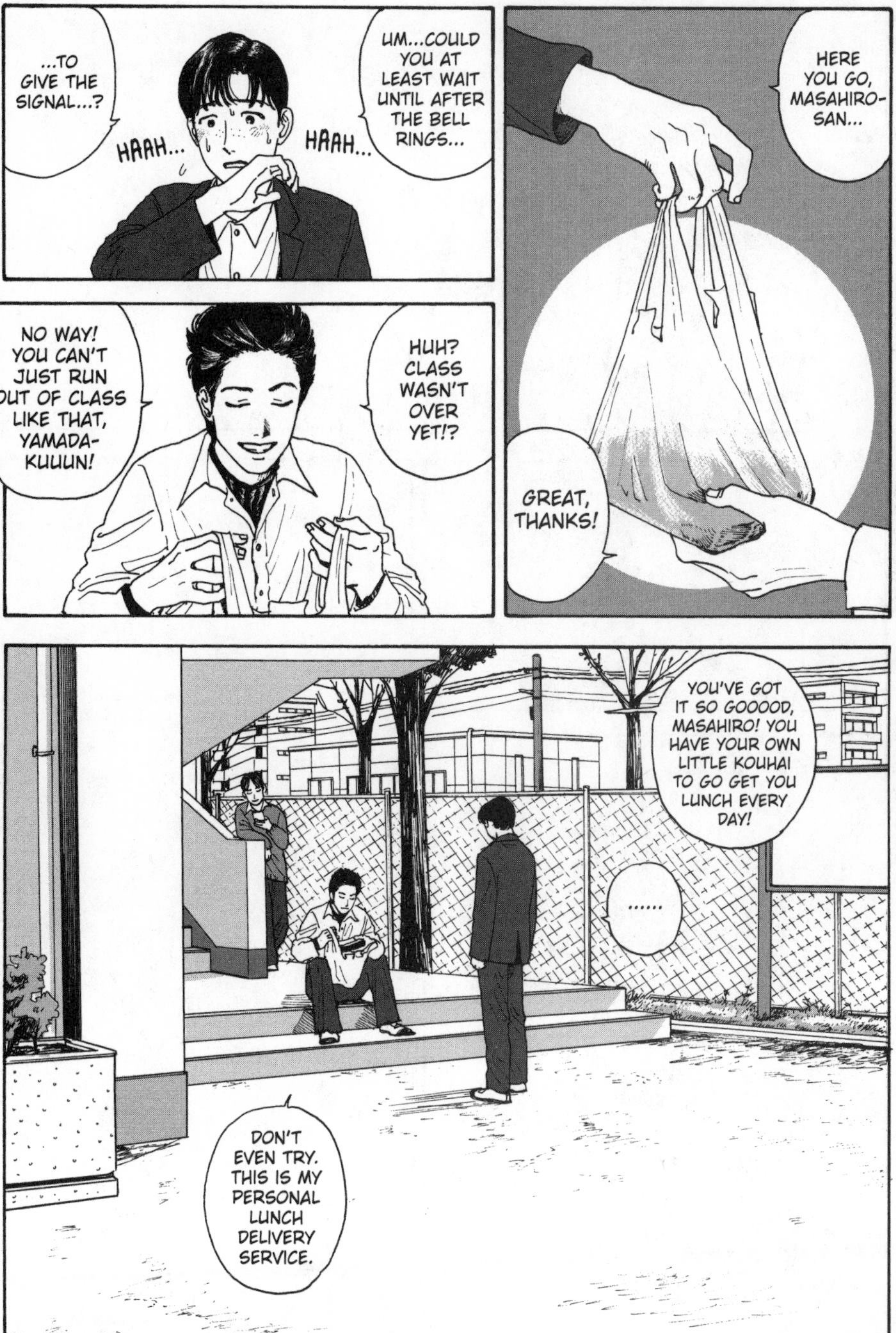
HERE YOU GO, MASAHIRO-SAN...
GREAT, THANKS!
UM...COULD YOU AT LEAST WAIT UNTIL AFTER THE BELL RINGS...
HAAH...
HAAH...
...TO GIVE THE SIGNAL...?
HUH? CLASS WASN'T OVER YET!?
NO WAY! YOU CAN'T JUST RUN OUT OF CLASS LIKE THAT, YAMADA-KUUUN!
YOU'VE GOT IT SO GOOOOD, MASAHIRO! YOU HAVE YOUR OWN LITTLE KOUHAI TO GO GET YOU LUNCH EVERY DAY!
......
DON'T EVEN TRY. THIS IS MY PERSONAL LUNCH DELIVERY SERVICE.

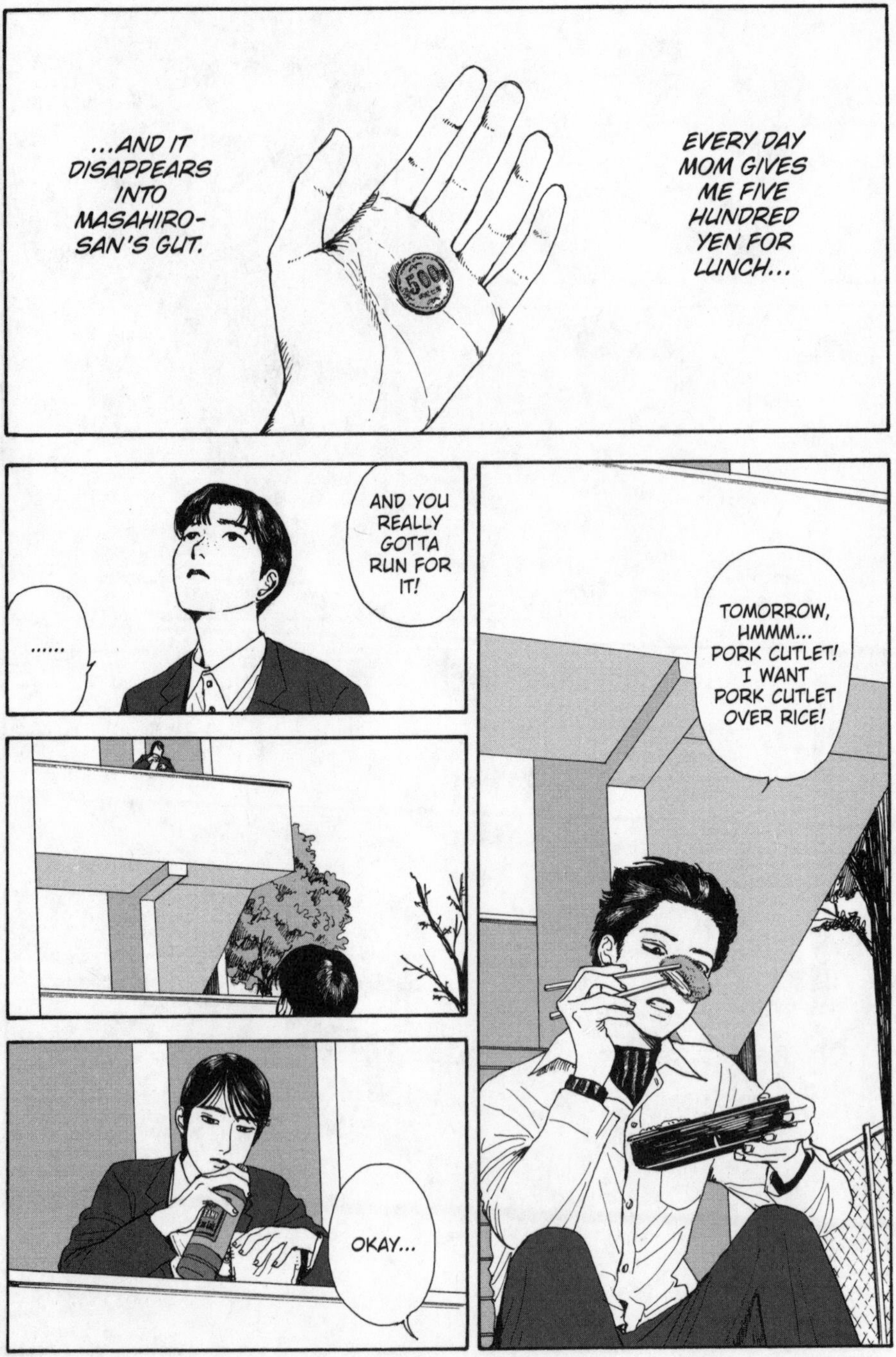
EVERY DAY MOM GIVES ME FIVE HUNDRED YEN FOR LUNCH...
...AND IT DISAPPEARS INTO MASAHIRO-SAN'S GUT.
TOMORROW, HMMM... PORK CUTLET! I WANT PORK CUTLET OVER RICE!
AND YOU REALLY GOTTA RUN FOR IT!
......
OKAY...

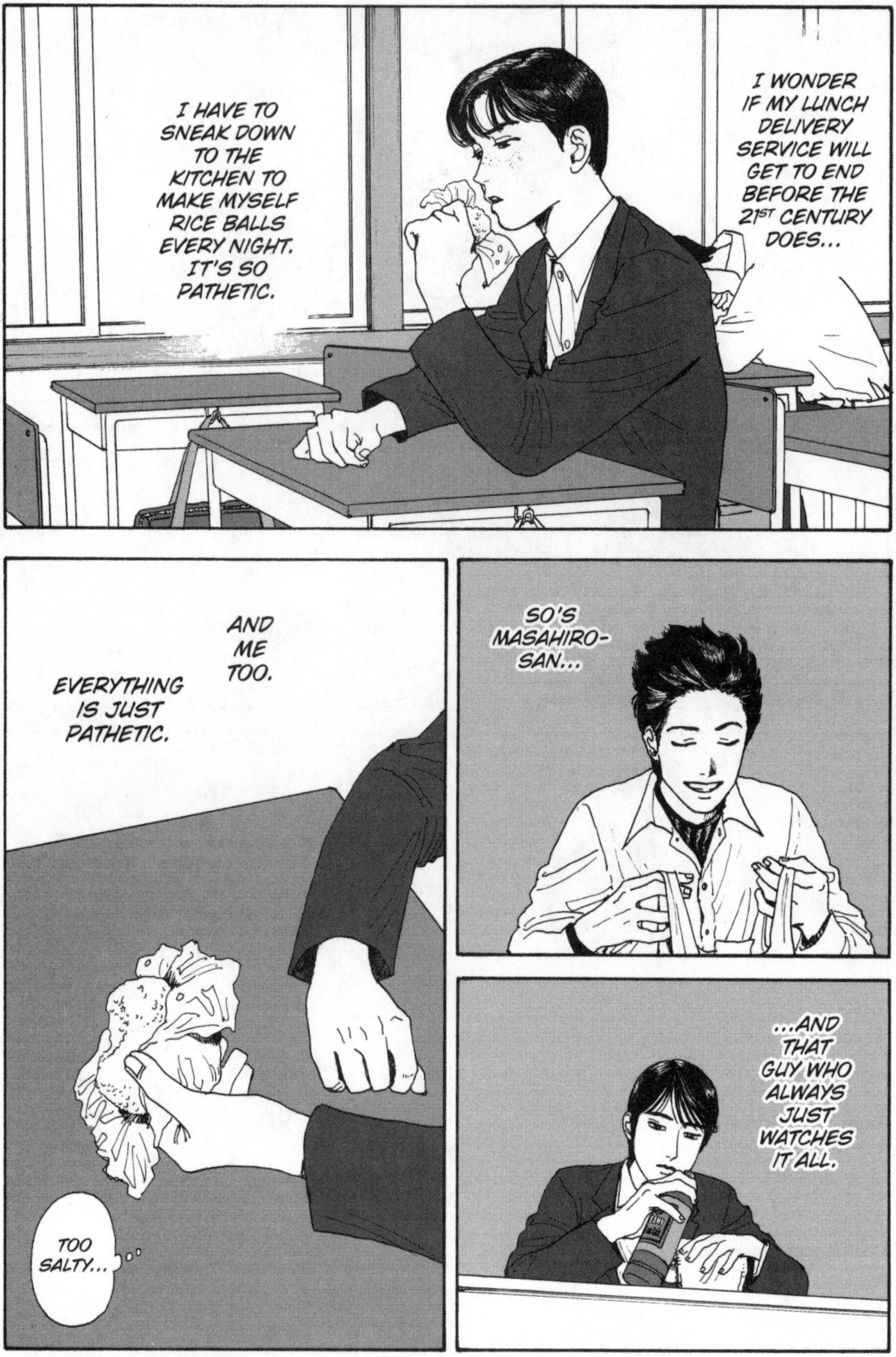
I WONDER IF MY LUNCH DELIVERY SERVICE WILL GET TO END BEFORE THE 21ST CENTURY DOES...
I HAVE TO SNEAK DOWN TO THE KITCHEN TO MAKE MYSELF RICE BALLS EVERY NIGHT. IT'S SO PATHETIC.
SO'S MASAHIRO-SAN...
...AND THAT GUY WHO ALWAYS JUST WATCHES IT ALL.
AND ME TOO.
EVERYTHING IS JUST PATHETIC.
TOO SALTY...

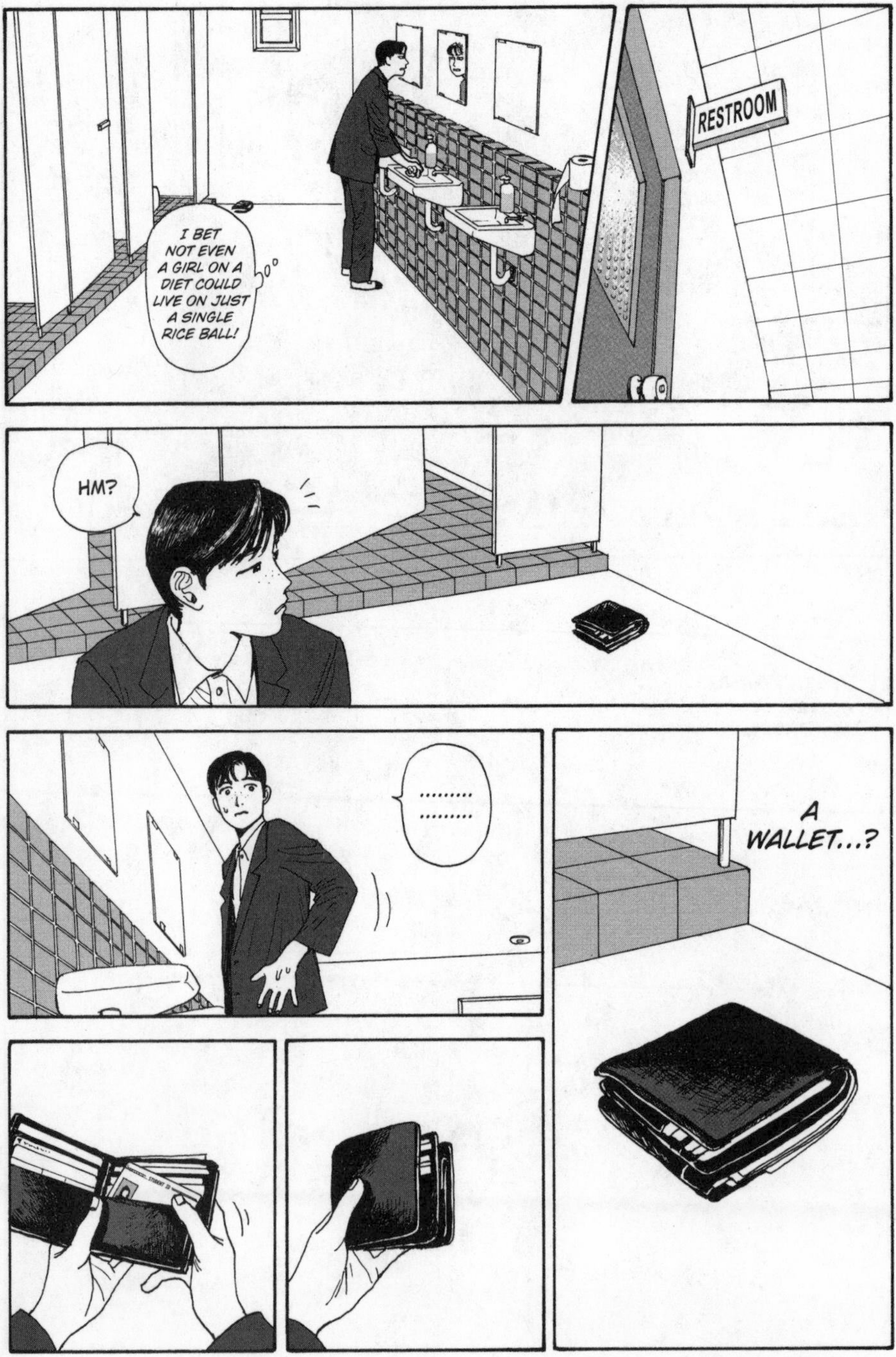
RESTROOM
I BET NOT EVEN A GIRL ON A DIET COULD LIVE ON JUST A SINGLE RICE BALL!
HM?
A WALLET...?
....
....

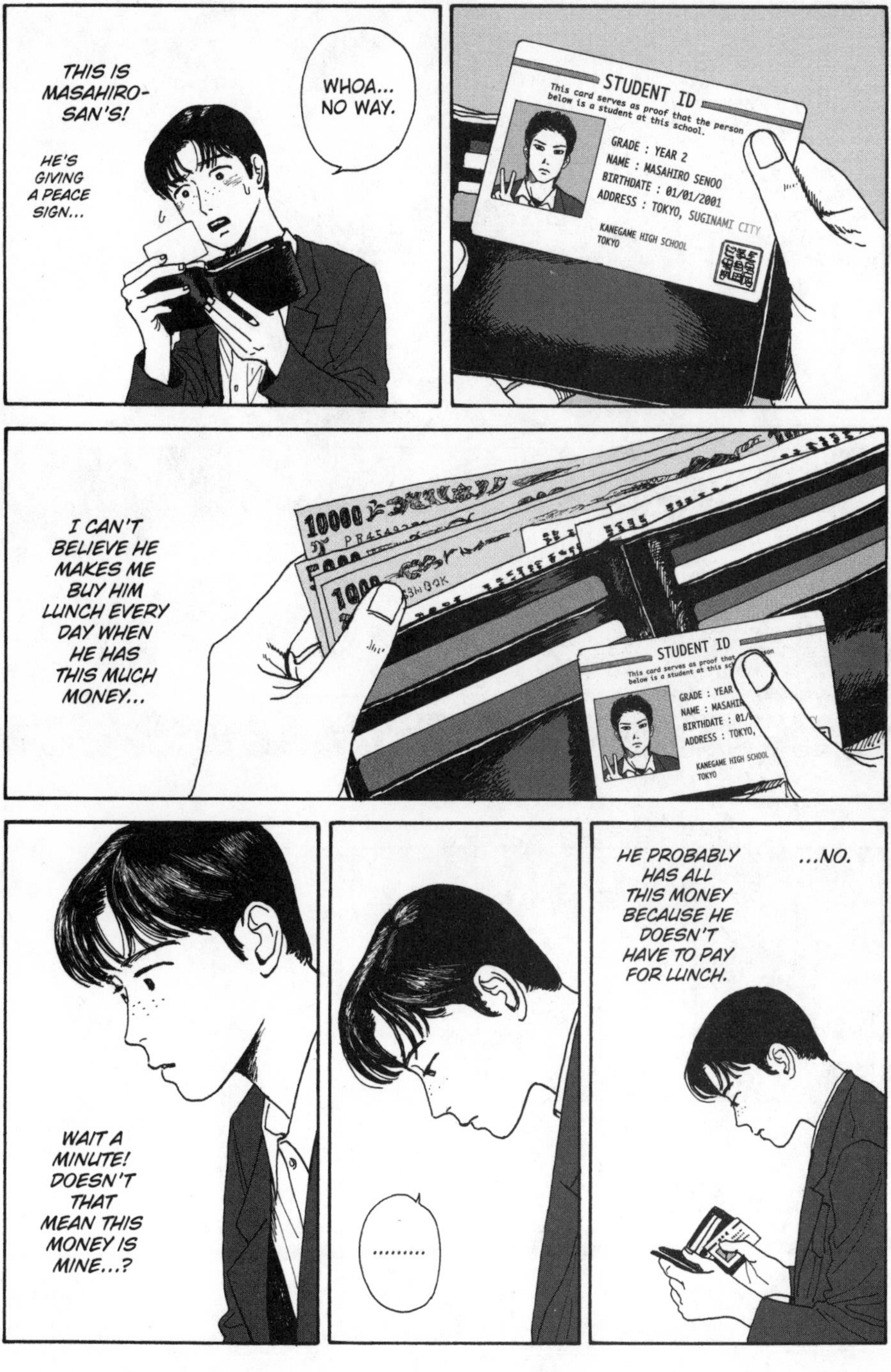
STUDENT ID
This card serves as proof that the person below is a student at this school.
GRADE : YEAR 2
NAME : MASAHIRO SENOO
BIRTHDATE : 01/01/2001
ADDRESS : TOKYO, SUGINAMI CITY
KANEGAME HIGH SCHOOL TOKYO
WHOA... NO WAY.
THIS IS MASAHIRO-SAN'S!
HE'S GIVING A PEACE SIGN...
I CAN'T BELIEVE HE MAKES ME BUY HIM LUNCH EVERY DAY WHEN HE HAS THIS MUCH MONEY...
STUDENT ID
...NO.
HE PROBABLY HAS ALL THIS MONEY BECAUSE HE DOESN'T HAVE TO PAY FOR LUNCH.
....
WAIT A MINUTE! DOESN'T THAT MEAN THIS MONEY IS MINE...?

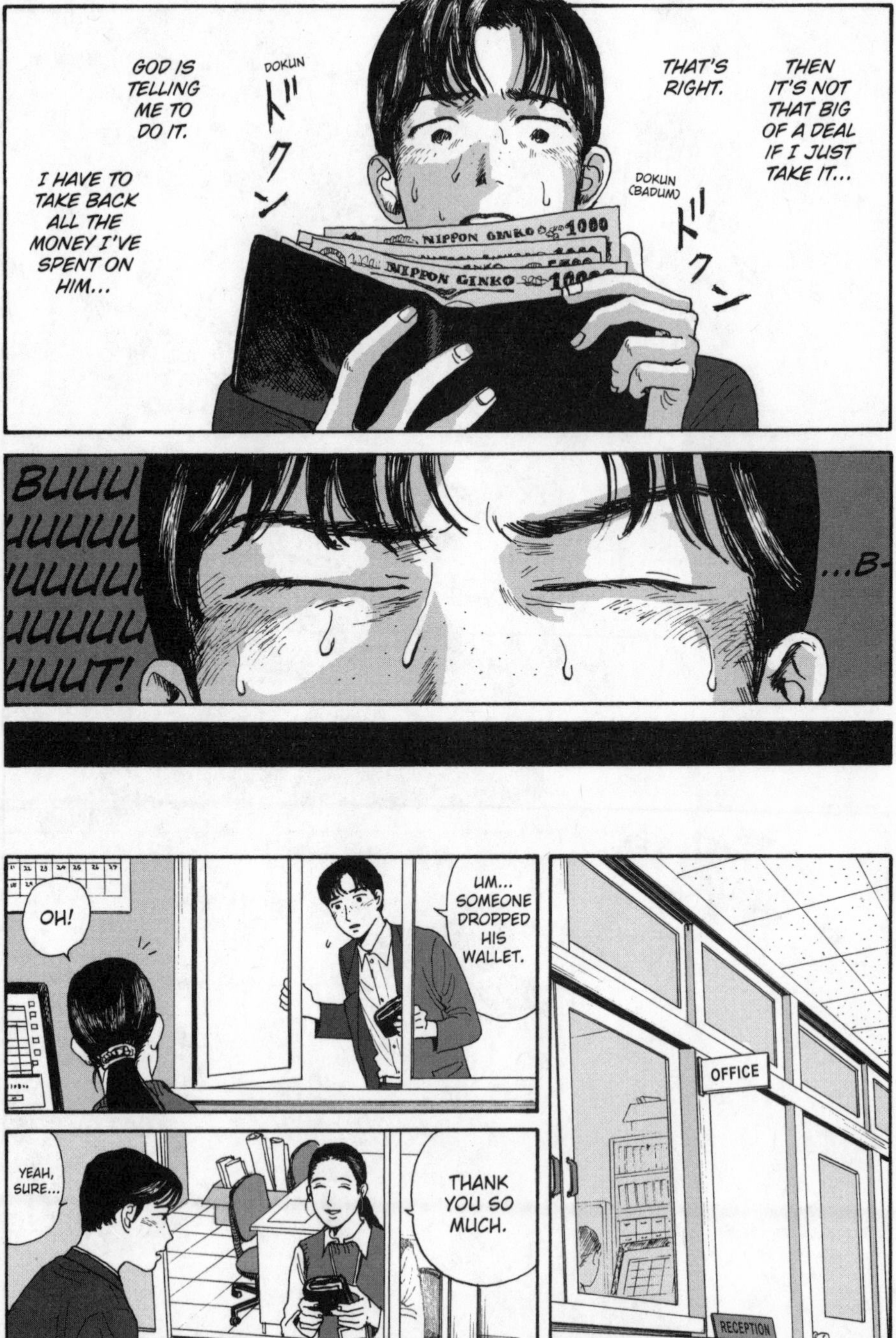
THEN IT'S NOT THAT BIG OF A DEAL IF I JUST TAKE IT...
THAT'S RIGHT.
DOKUN (BADUM)
ドクン
GOD IS TELLING ME TO DO IT.
DOKUN
ドクン
I HAVE TO TAKE BACK ALL THE MONEY I'VE SPENT ON HIM...
NIPPON GINKO 1000
NIPPON GINKO 10000
...B-
BUUUUUUUUUUUUUUUUUUUUUUUUT!
OFFICE
RECEPTION
UM... SOMEONE DROPPED HIS WALLET.
OH!
THANK YOU SO MUCH.
YEAH, SURE...

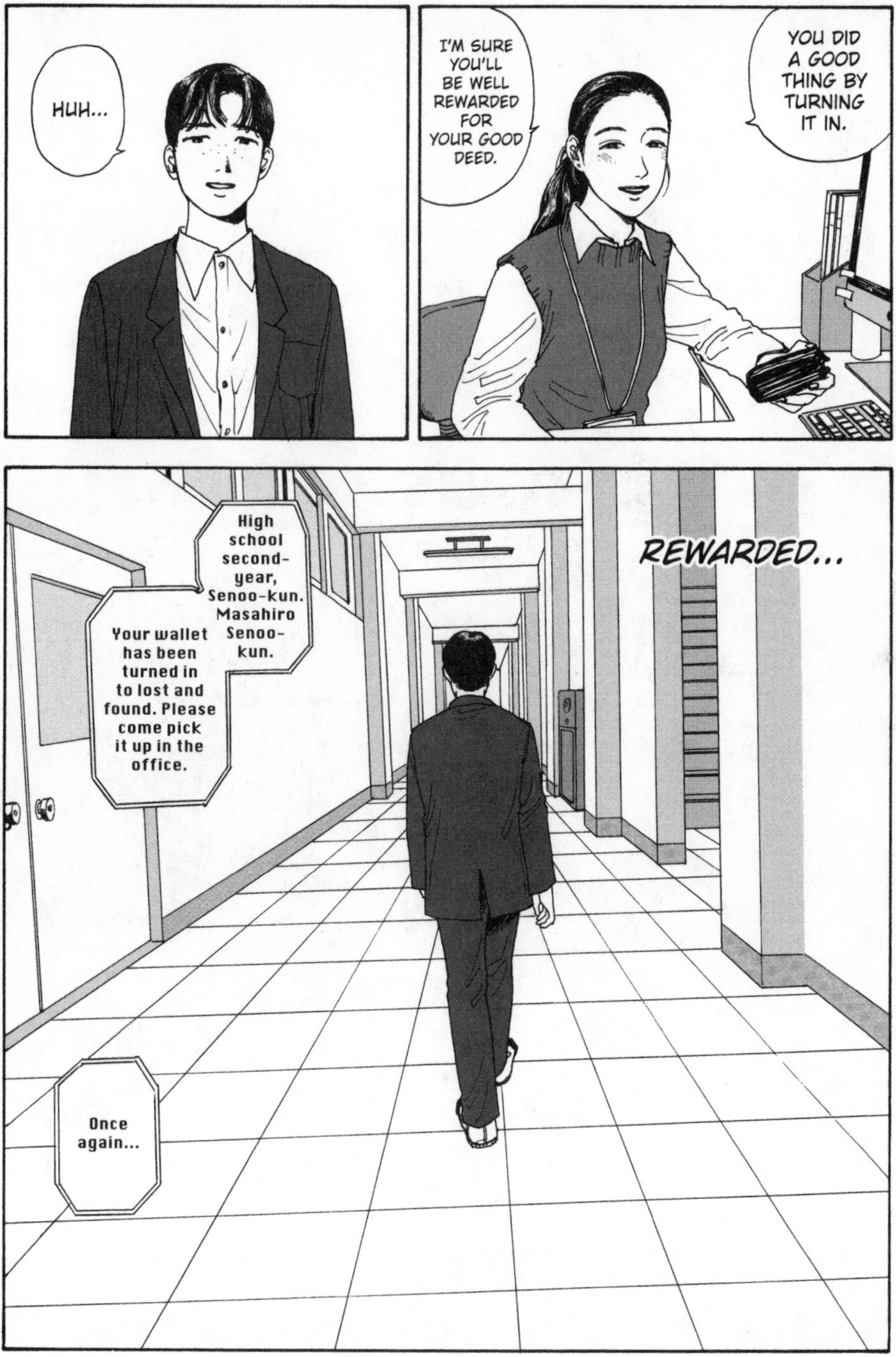
YOU DID A GOOD THING BY TURNING IT IN.
I'M SURE YOU'LL BE WELL REWARDED FOR YOUR GOOD DEED.
HUH...
REWARDED...
High school second-year, Senoo-kun. Masahiro Senoo-kun.
Your wallet has been turned in to lost and found. Please come pick it up in the office.
Once again...

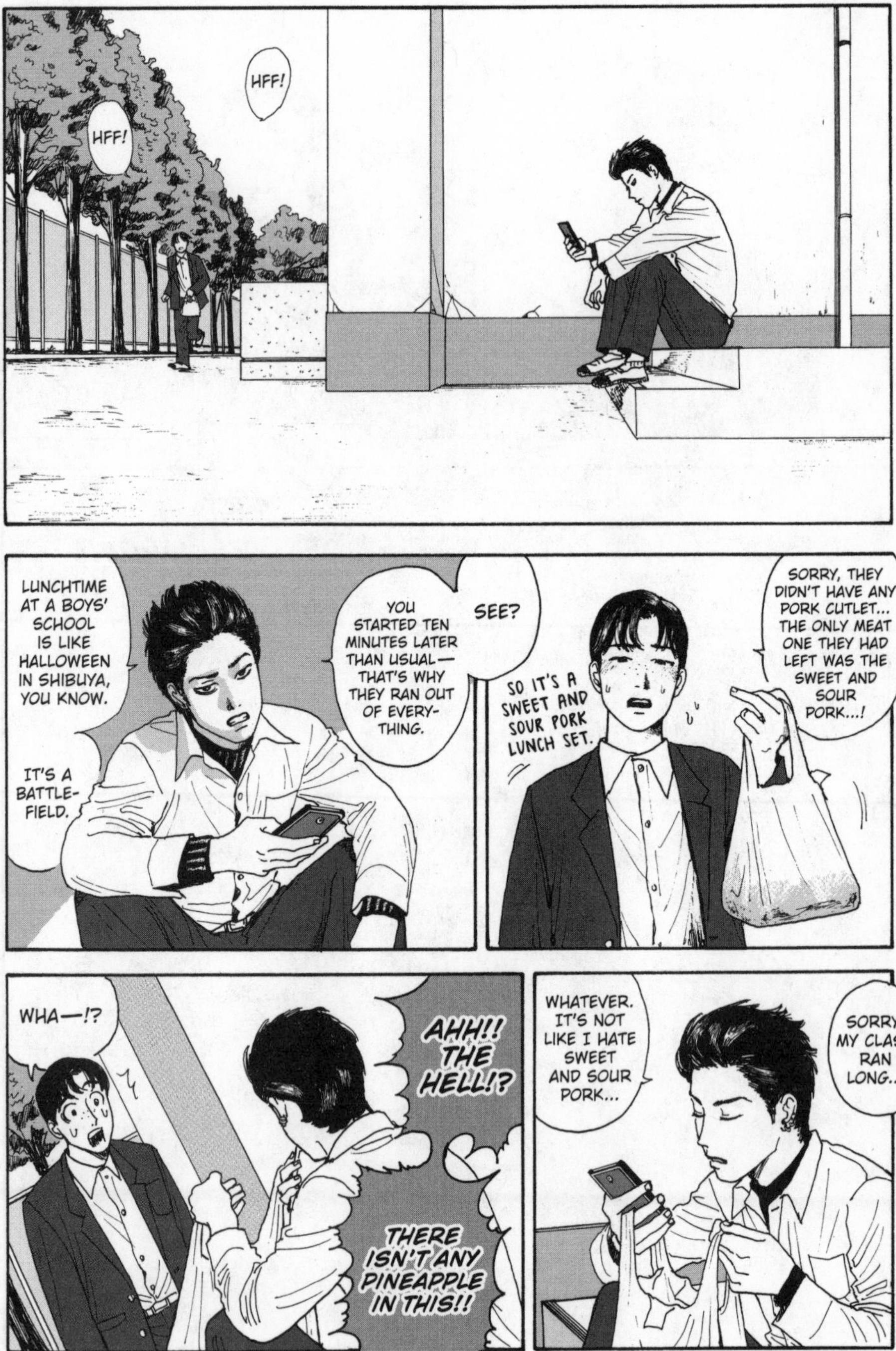
HFF!
HFF!
SORRY, THEY DIDN'T HAVE ANY PORK CUTLET... THE ONLY MEAT ONE THEY HAD LEFT WAS THE SWEET AND SOUR PORK...!
SO IT'S A SWEET AND SOUR PORK LUNCH SET.
SEE?
YOU STARTED TEN MINUTES LATER THAN USUAL—THAT'S WHY THEY RAN OUT OF EVERY-THING.
LUNCHTIME AT A BOYS' SCHOOL IS LIKE HALLOWEEN IN SHIBUYA, YOU KNOW.
IT'S A BATTLE-FIELD.
SORRY. MY CLASS RAN LONG...
WHATEVER. IT'S NOT LIKE I HATE SWEET AND SOUR PORK...
AHH!! THE HELL!?
THERE ISN'T ANY PINEAPPLE IN THIS!!
WHA—!?

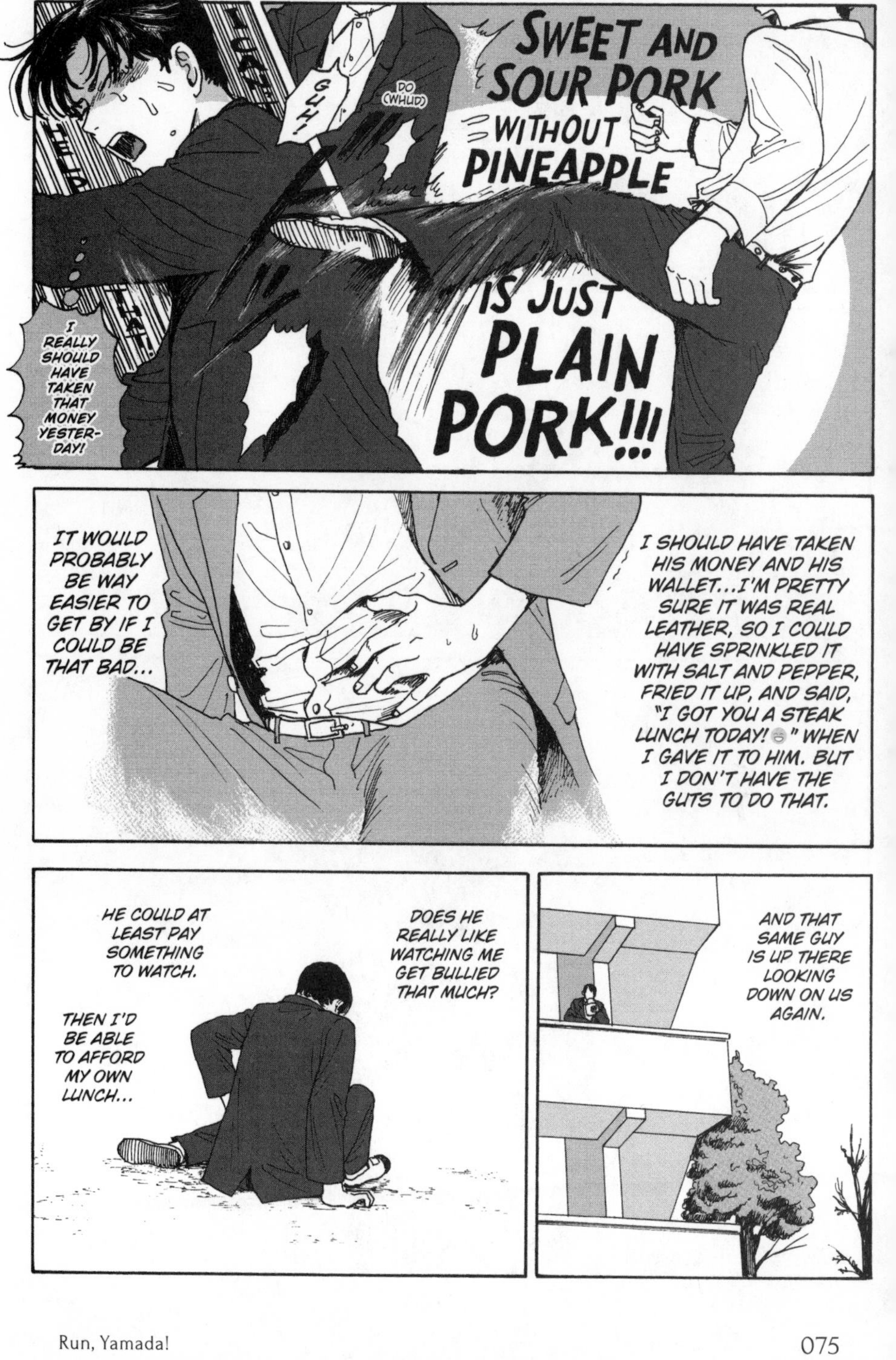
SWEET AND SOUR PORK WITHOUT PINEAPPLE IS JUST PLAIN PORK!!!
DO (WHUD)
GUH!
I REALLY SHOULD HAVE TAKEN THAT MONEY YESTER-DAY!
I SHOULD HAVE TAKEN HIS MONEY AND HIS WALLET...I'M PRETTY SURE IT WAS REAL LEATHER, SO I COULD HAVE SPRINKLED IT WITH SALT AND PEPPER, FRIED IT UP, AND SAID, "I GOT YOU A STEAK LUNCH TODAY!" WHEN I GAVE IT TO HIM. BUT I DON'T HAVE THE GUTS TO DO THAT.
IT WOULD PROBABLY BE WAY EASIER TO GET BY IF I COULD BE THAT BAD...
AND THAT SAME GUY IS UP THERE LOOKING DOWN ON US AGAIN.
DOES HE REALLY LIKE WATCHING ME GET BULLIED THAT MUCH?
HE COULD AT LEAST PAY SOMETHING TO WATCH.
THEN I'D BE ABLE TO AFFORD MY OWN LUNCH...

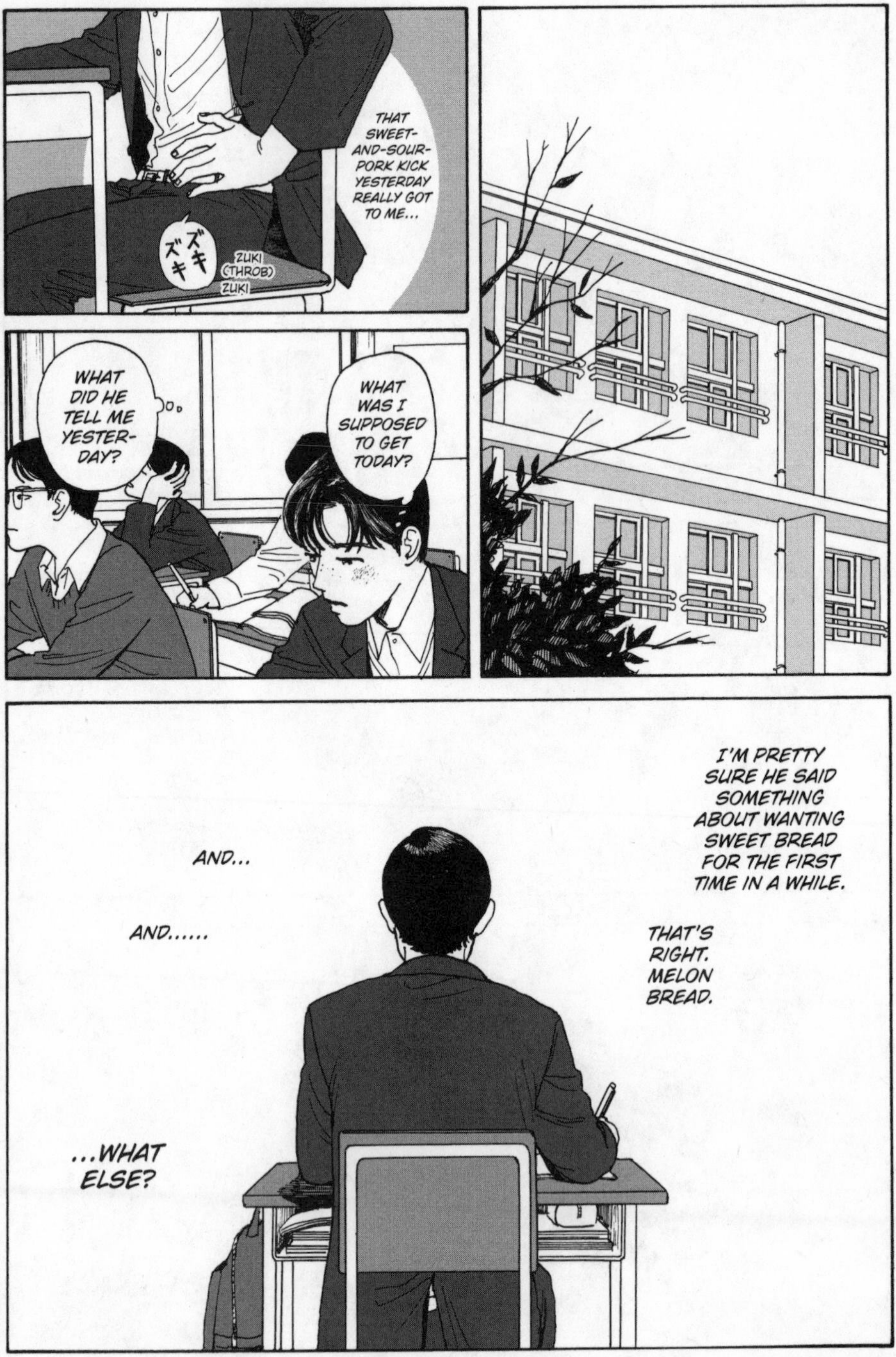
THAT SWEET-AND-SOUR-PORK KICK YESTERDAY REALLY GOT TO ME...
ズキズキ
ZUKI (THROB) ZUKI
WHAT WAS I SUPPOSED TO GET TODAY?
WHAT DID HE TELL ME YESTER-DAY?
I'M PRETTY SURE HE SAID SOMETHING ABOUT WANTING SWEET BREAD FOR THE FIRST TIME IN A WHILE.
THAT'S RIGHT. MELON BREAD.
AND...
AND......
...WHAT ELSE?

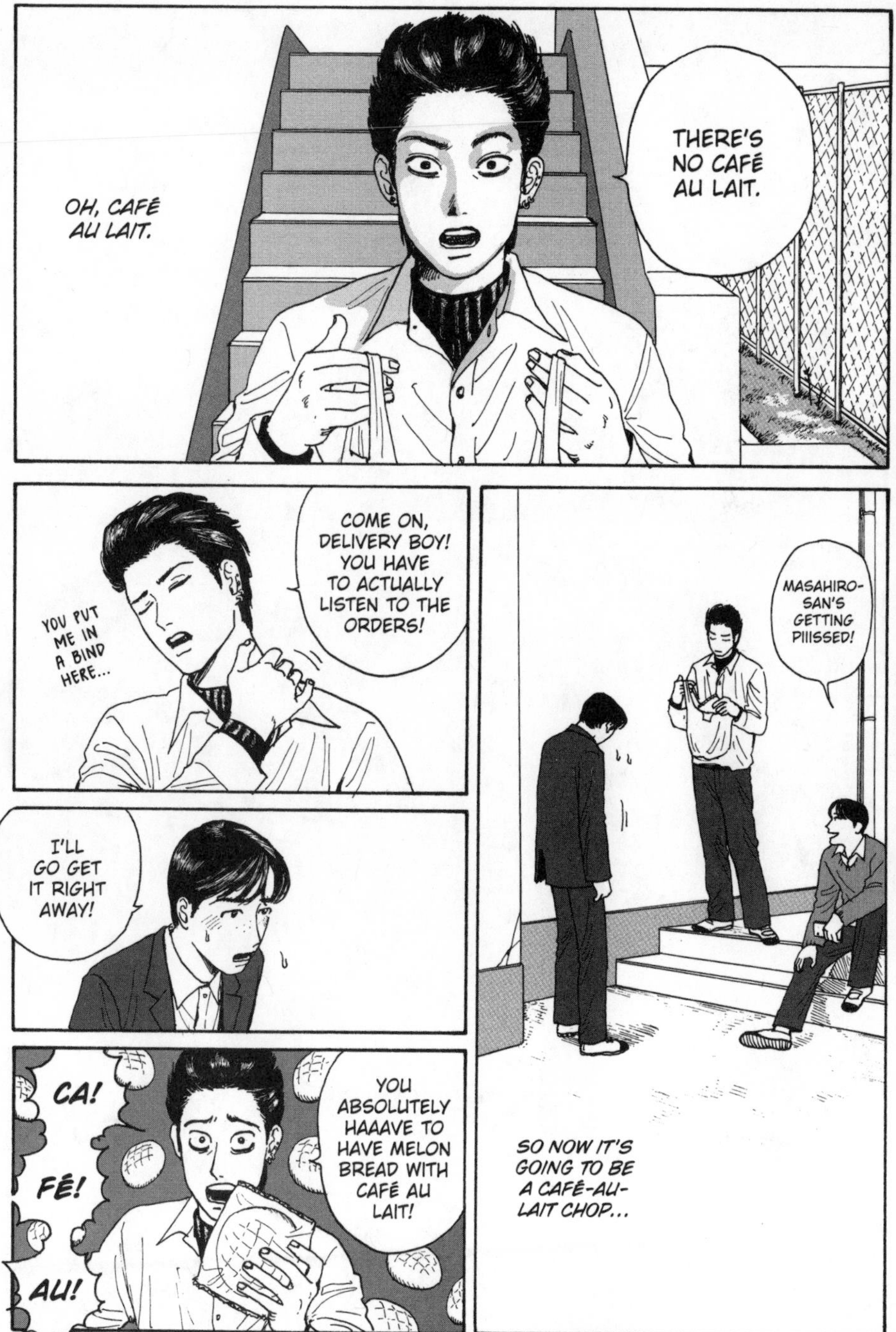
THERE'S NO CAFÉ AU LAIT.
OH, CAFÉ AU LAIT.
MASAHIRO-SAN'S GETTING PIIISSED!
SO NOW IT'S GOING TO BE A CAFÉ-AU-LAIT CHOP...
COME ON, DELIVERY BOY! YOU HAVE TO ACTUALLY LISTEN TO THE ORDERS!
YOU PUT ME IN A BIND HERE...
I'LL GO GET IT RIGHT AWAY!
YOU ABSOLUTELY HAAAVE TO HAVE MELON BREAD WITH CAFÉ AU LAIT!
CA!
FÉ!
AU!

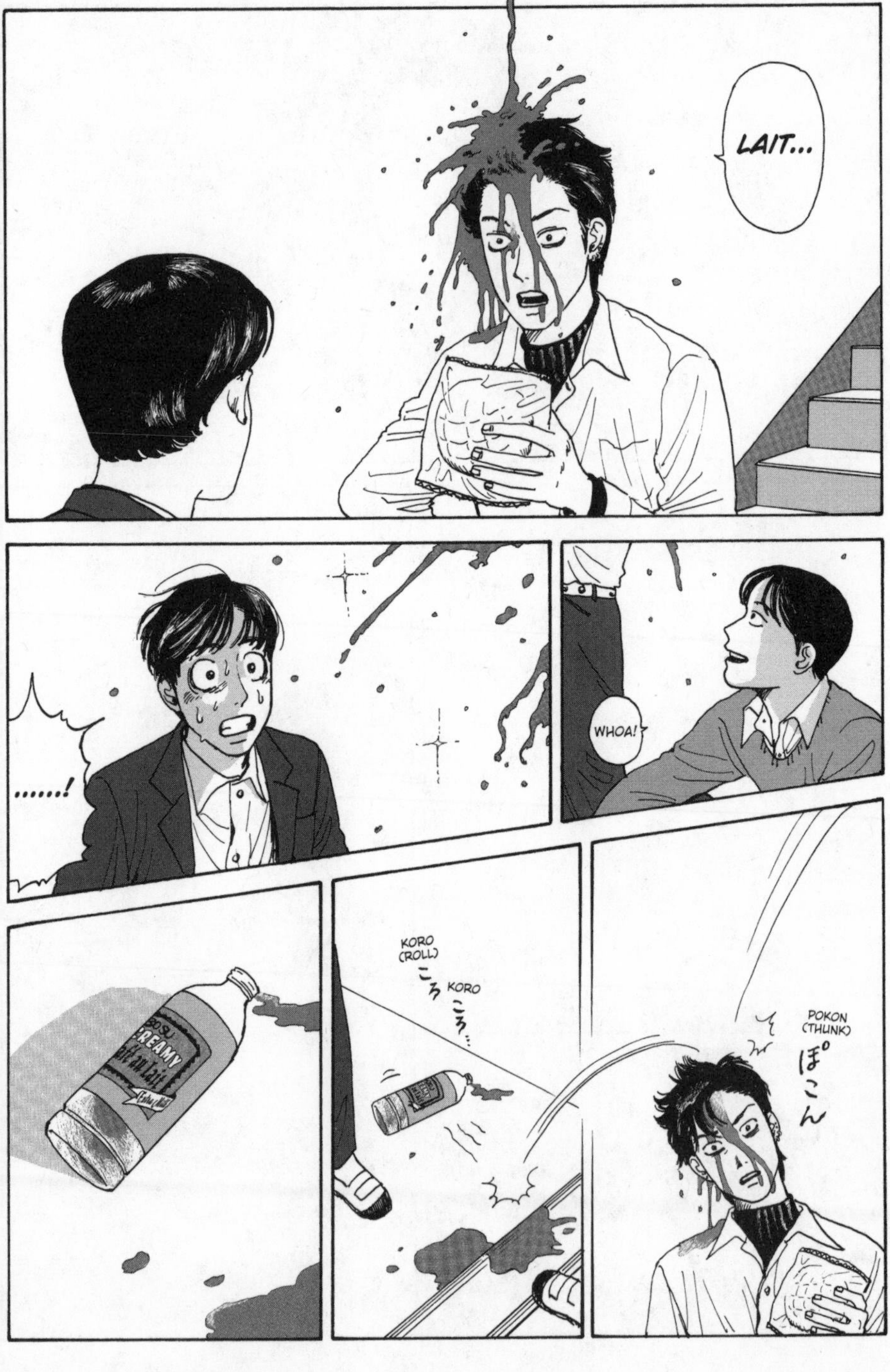
LAIT...
WHOA!
......!
POKON (THUNK)
ぽこん
KORO (ROLL)
ころ
KORO
ころ...
CREAMY
Café au Lait

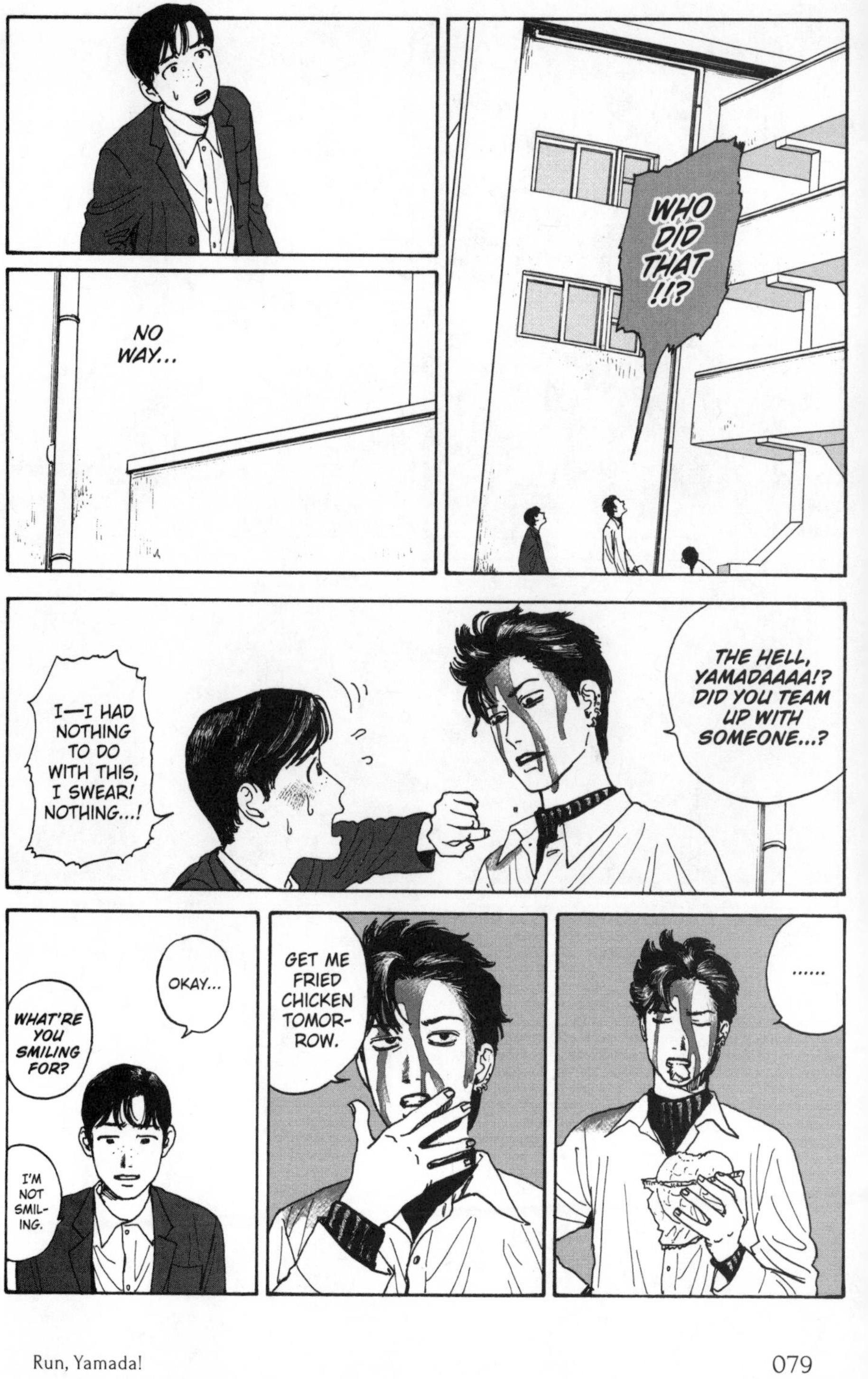
WHO DID THAT!!?
NO WAY...
THE HELL, YAMADAAAA!? DID YOU TEAM UP WITH SOMEONE...?
I—I HAD NOTHING TO DO WITH THIS, I SWEAR! NOTHING...!
......
GET ME FRIED CHICKEN TOMOR-ROW.
OKAY...
WHAT'RE YOU SMILING FOR?
I'M NOT SMIL-ING.

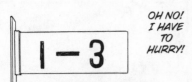

キーンコーン
KIINKOON (BING-BONG)
1-3
OH NO! I HAVE TO HURRY!
FRIED CHICKEN, FRIED CHICKEN!
THAT SELLS OUT QUICK, SO I HAVE TO GET MOVING.
....
HUH? MY WALLET...
IT'S GONE...
DID I LEAVE IT AT HOME?
...NO, I...
DOKIN (BA-THUMP)
ドキ
...GOT SOMETHING TO DRINK FROM THE VENDING MACHINE THIS MORNING.
......

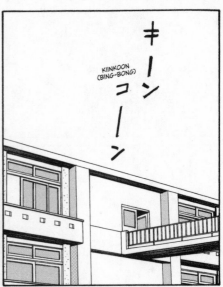

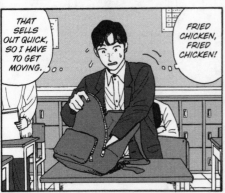

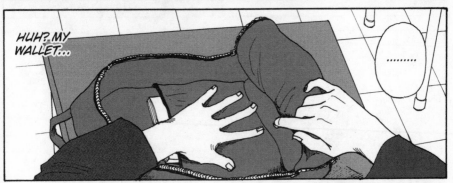

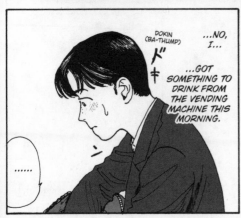

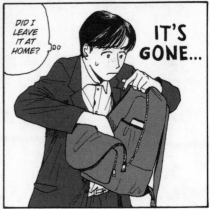

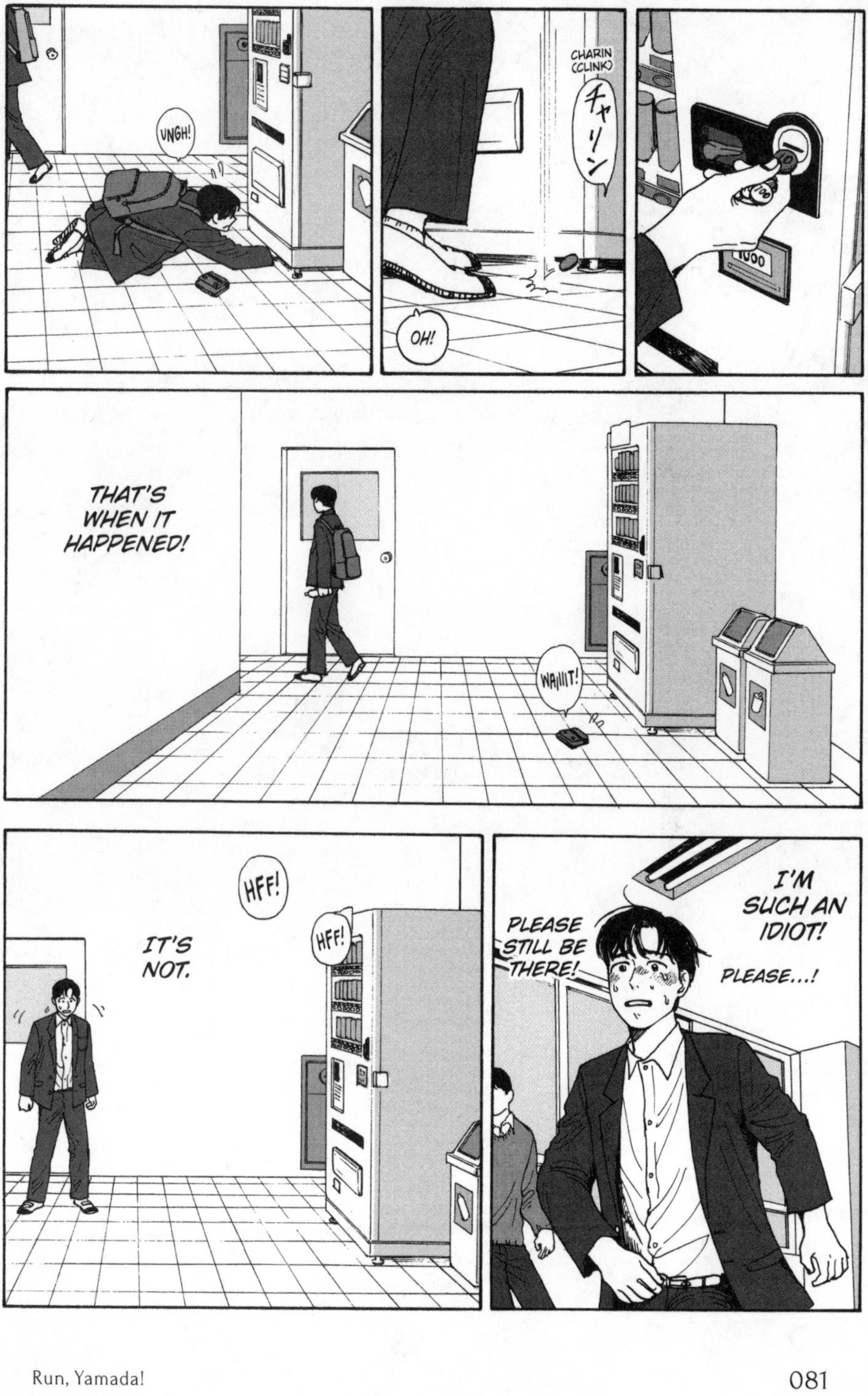
CHARIN (CLINK)
チャリン
OH!
UNGH!
THAT'S WHEN IT HAPPENED!
WAIIIIT!
I'M SUCH AN IDIOT!
PLEASE STILL BE THERE!
PLEASE...!
HFF!
HFF!
IT'S NOT.

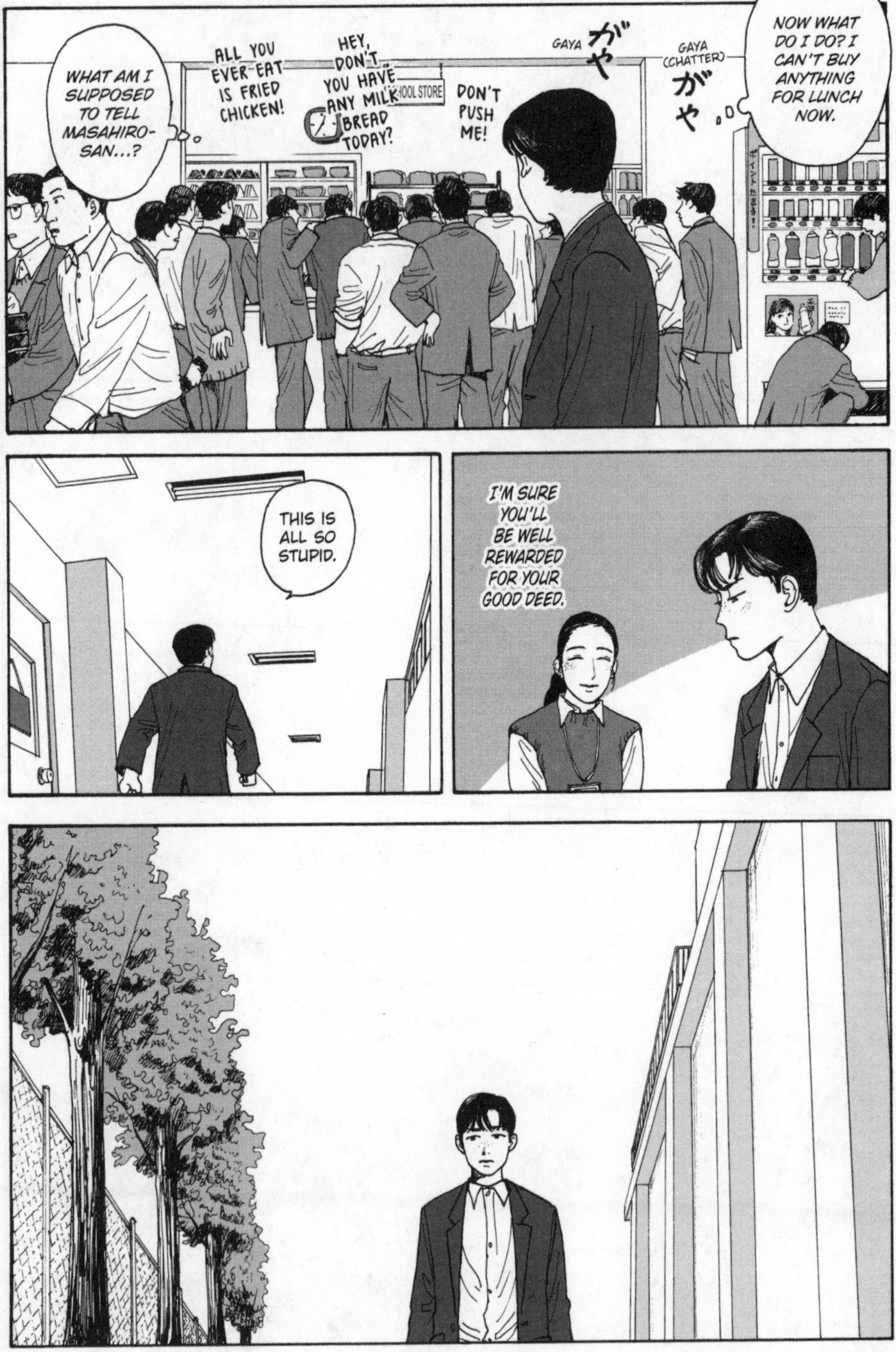
NOW WHAT DO I DO? I CAN'T BUY ANYTHING FOR LUNCH NOW.
GAYA (CHATTER) がや
GAYA がや
DON'T PUSH ME!
HEY, DON'T YOU HAVE ANY MILK BREAD TODAY?
ALL YOU EVER EAT IS FRIED CHICKEN!
WHAT AM I SUPPOSED TO TELL MASAHIRO-SAN...?
I'M SURE YOU'LL BE WELL REWARDED FOR YOUR GOOD DEED.
THIS IS ALL SO STUPID.

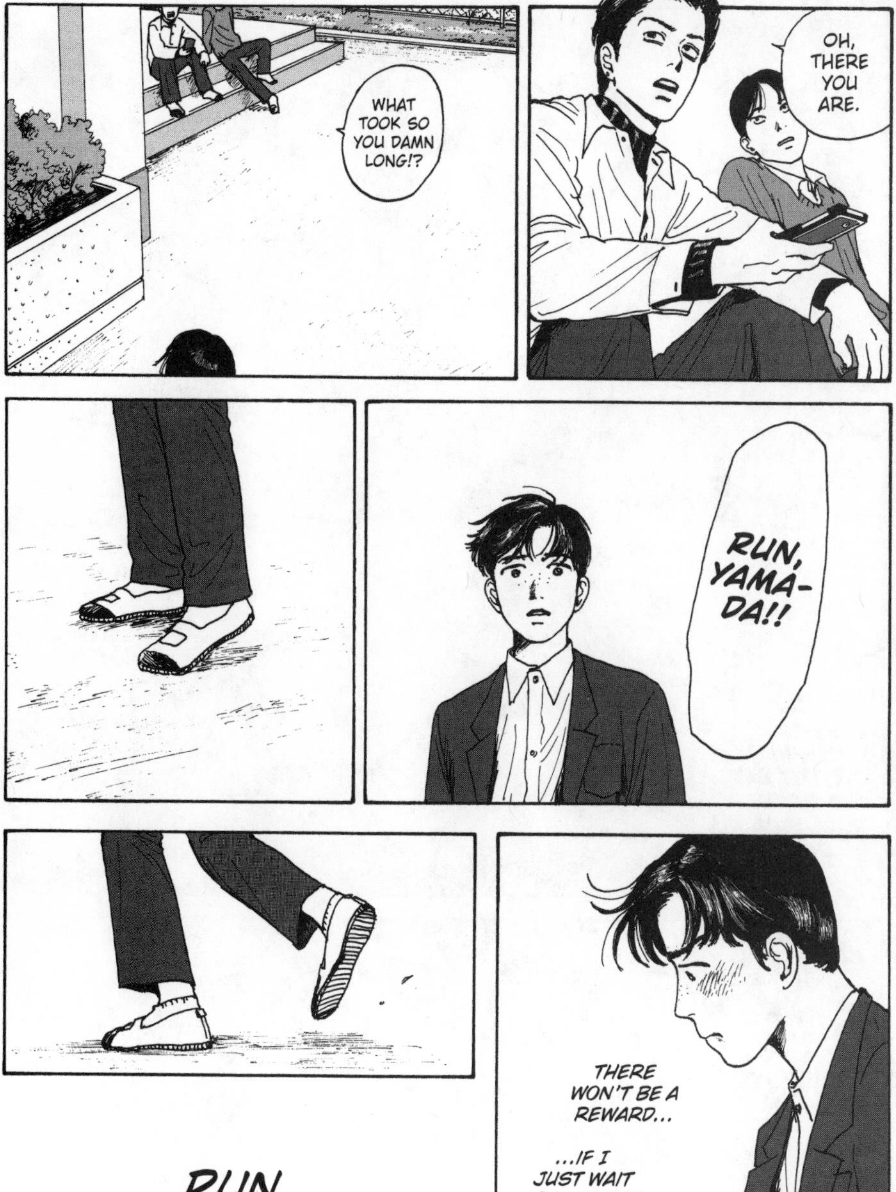
OH, THERE YOU ARE.
WHAT TOOK YOU SO DAMN LONG!?
RUN, YAMA-DA!!
THERE WON'T BE A REWARD...
...IF I JUST WAIT AROUND FOR SOMETHING TO HAPPEN...
RUN, YAMADA!

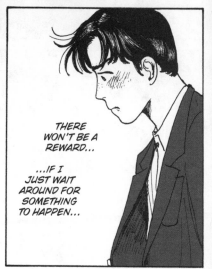

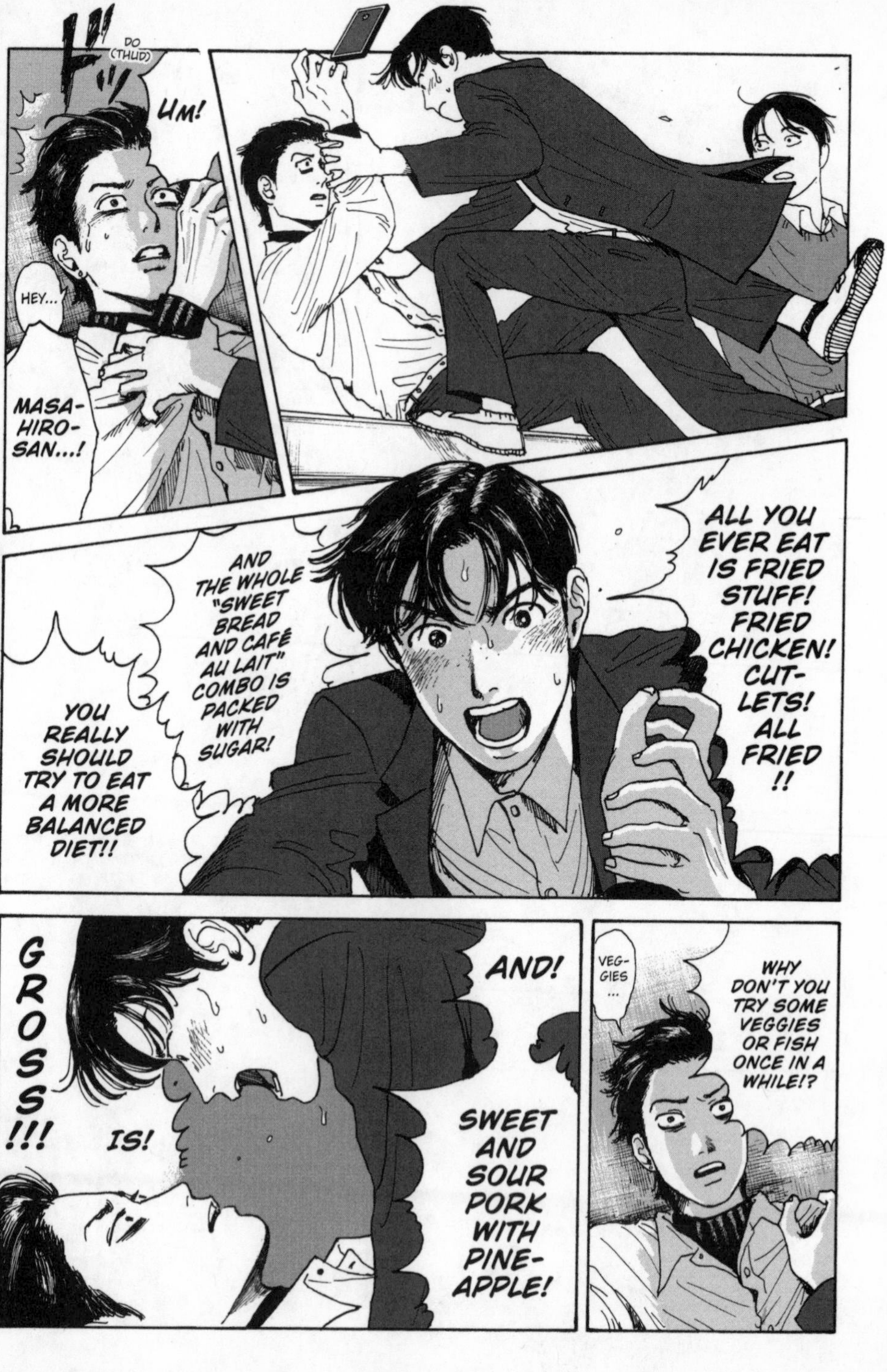
DO (THUD)
UM!
HEY...
MASA-HIRO-SAN...!
ALL YOU EVER EAT IS FRIED STUFF! FRIED CHICKEN! CUT-LETS! ALL FRIED !!
AND THE WHOLE "SWEET BREAD AND CAFÉ AU LAIT" COMBO IS PACKED WITH SUGAR!
YOU REALLY SHOULD TRY TO EAT A MORE BALANCED DIET!!
WHY DON'T YOU TRY SOME VEGGIES OR FISH ONCE IN A WHILE!?
VEG-GIES ...
AND!
SWEET AND SOUR PORK WITH PINE-APPLE!
IS!
GROSS!!!

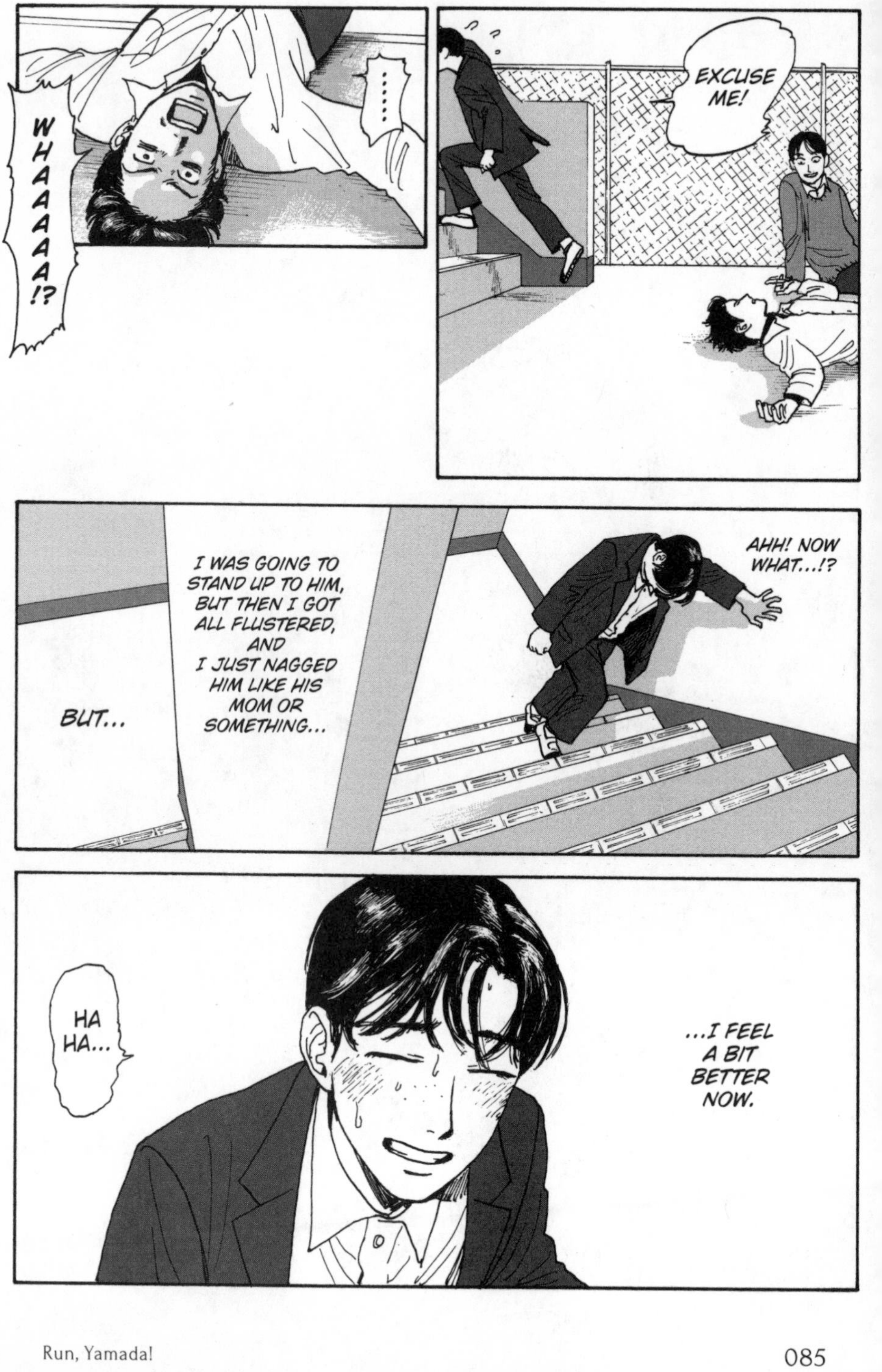
EXCUSE ME!
WHAAAAAA!?
......
AHH! NOW WHAT...!?
I WAS GOING TO STAND UP TO HIM, BUT THEN I GOT ALL FLUSTERED, AND I JUST NAGGED HIM LIKE HIS MOM OR SOMETHING...
BUT...
...I FEEL A BIT BETTER NOW.
HA HA...

AS OF TODAY, THE YAMADA LUNCH DELIVERY SERVICE IS CLOSED.

ギイイ...
GII (CREAK)

OH.

HIM...

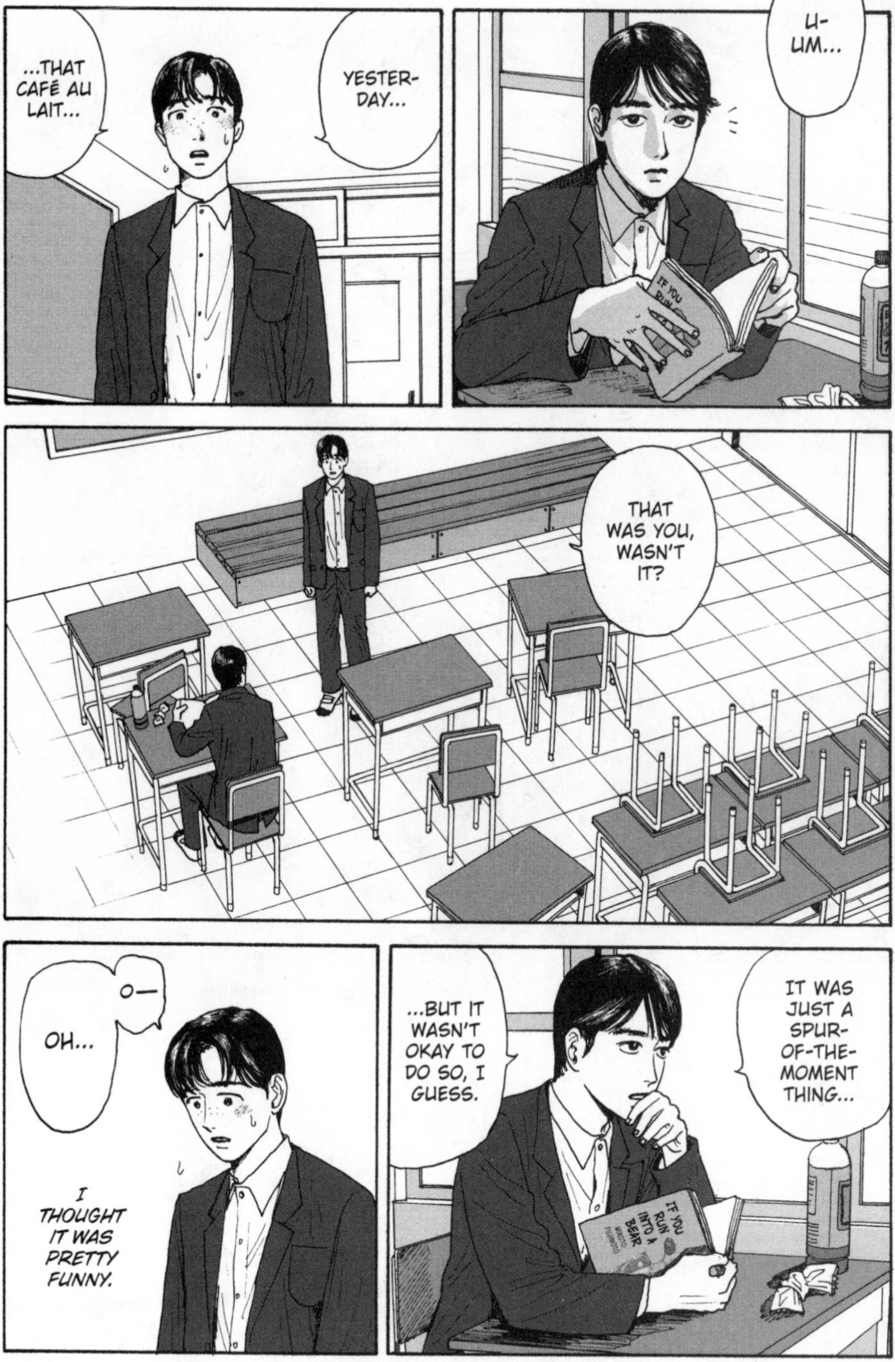
U-UM...
YESTER-DAY...
...THAT CAFÉ AU LAIT...
THAT WAS YOU, WASN'T IT?
IT WAS JUST A SPUR-OF-THE-MOMENT THING...
...BUT IT WASN'T OKAY TO DO SO, I GUESS.
IF YOU RUN INTO A BEAR
O— OH...
I THOUGHT IT WAS PRETTY FUNNY.

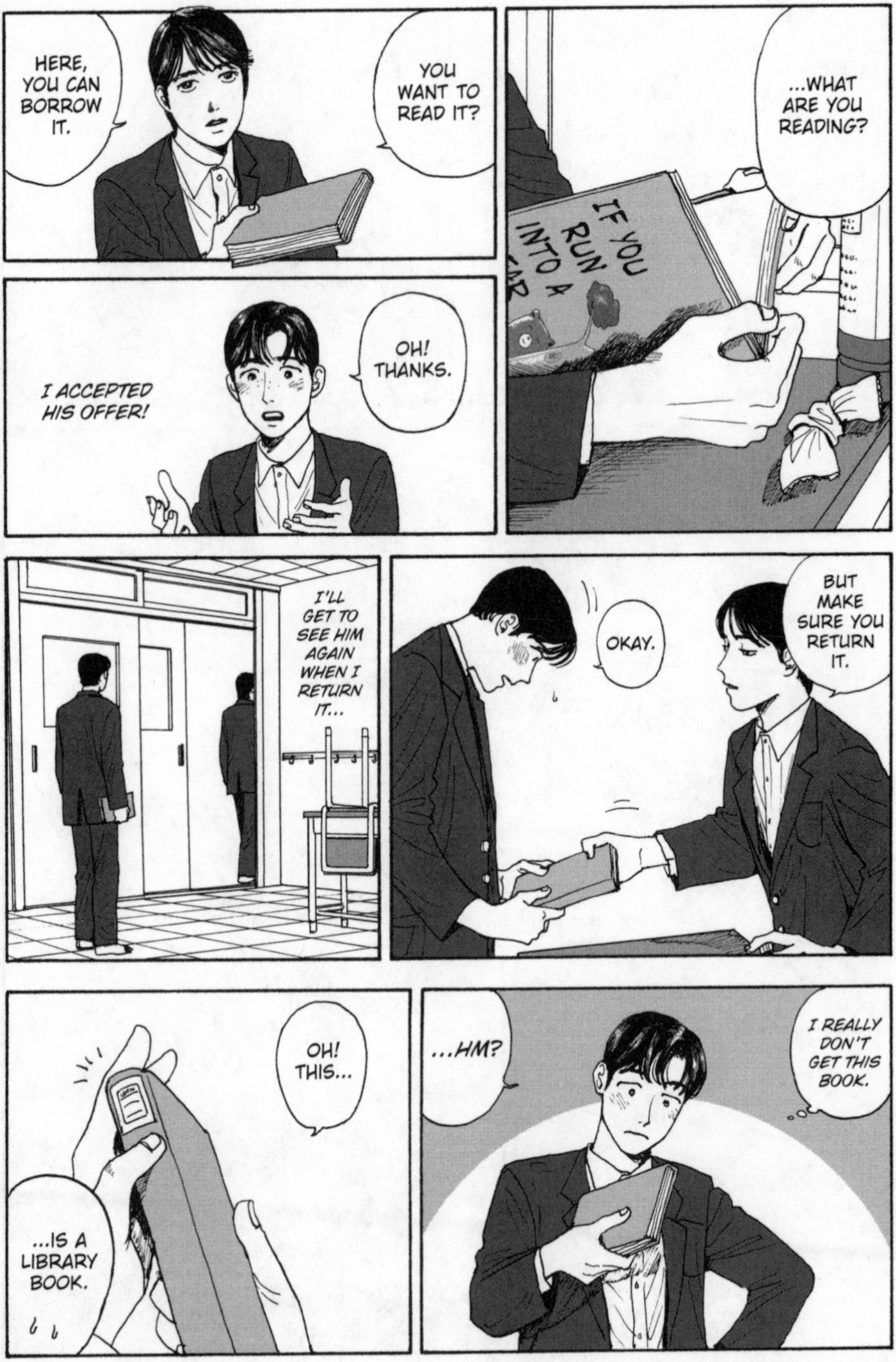
...WHAT ARE YOU READING?
IF YOU RUN INTO A
YOU WANT TO READ IT?
HERE, YOU CAN BORROW IT.
OH! THANKS.
I ACCEPTED HIS OFFER!
BUT MAKE SURE YOU RETURN IT.
OKAY.
I'LL GET TO SEE HIM AGAIN WHEN I RETURN IT...
I REALLY DON'T GET THIS BOOK.
...HM?
OH! THIS...
...IS A LIBRARY BOOK.

Title: If You Run Into a Bear
Author: Mikoto Fujimoto

Grade	Name	Checked Out	Due Date
2	Miyoshi Hayashi	10/18	11/1

MI-YOSHI HA-YASHI.

M-MIYOSHI ...?

PARA (FLIP)

High school first-year, Yamada-kun. Shoutarou Yamada-kun.

AND IT'S DUE BACK TODAY!

HE PLAYED ME...

Your wallet has been turned in to lost and found. Please come pick it up in the office.

Once again...

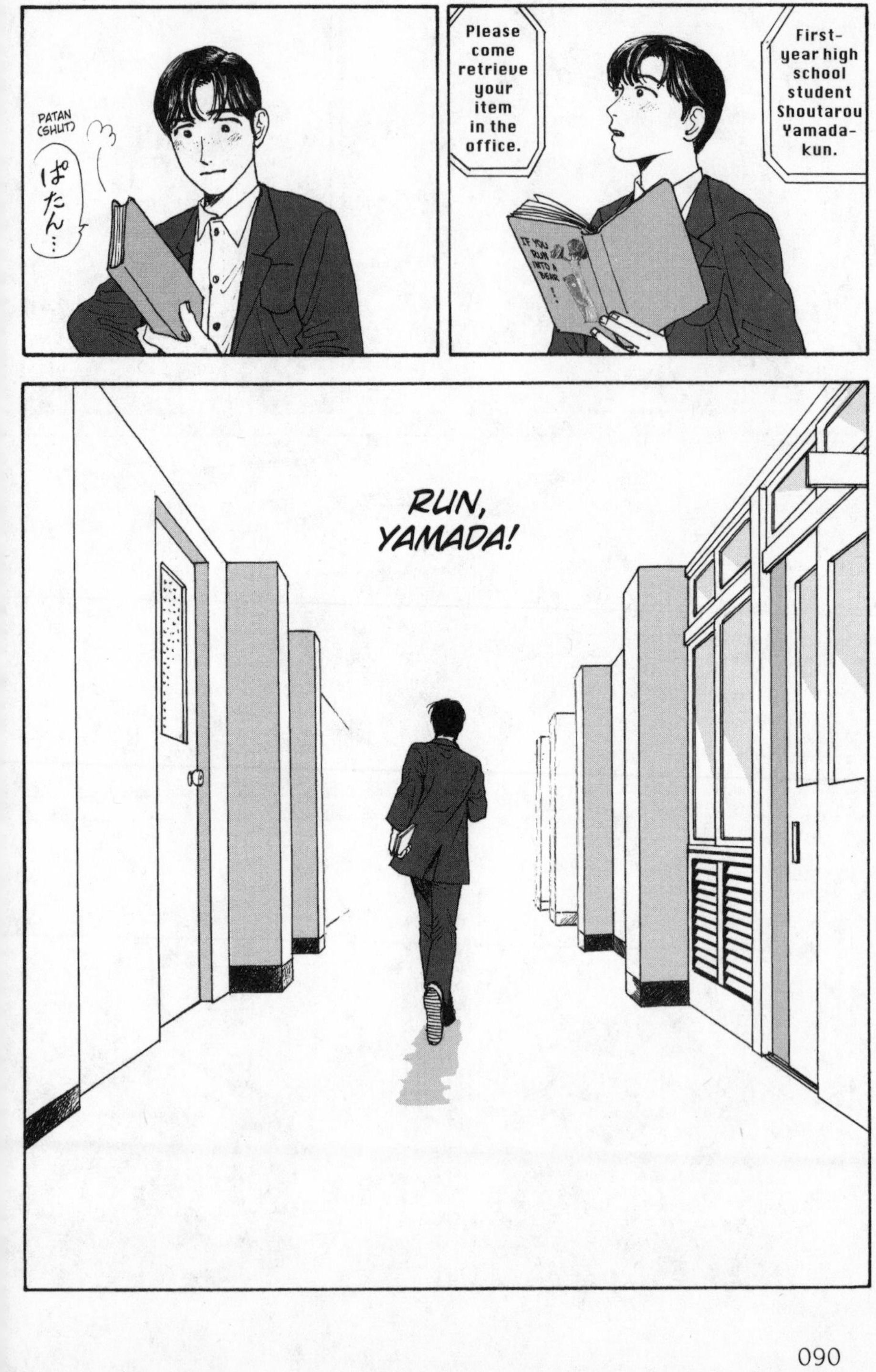
First-year high school student Shoutarou Yamada-kun.
Please come retrieve your item in the office.
IF YOU RUN INTO A BEAR
PATAN (SHUT)
ぱたん…
RUN, YAMADA!

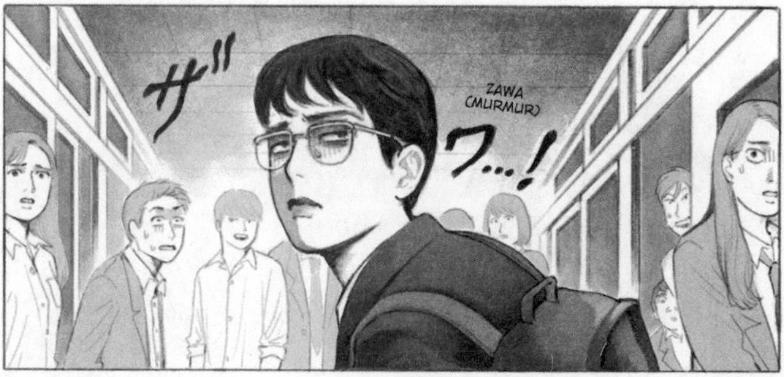
ザ
ZAWA (MURMUR)
ワ…!

[Nikaidou Behind Me]

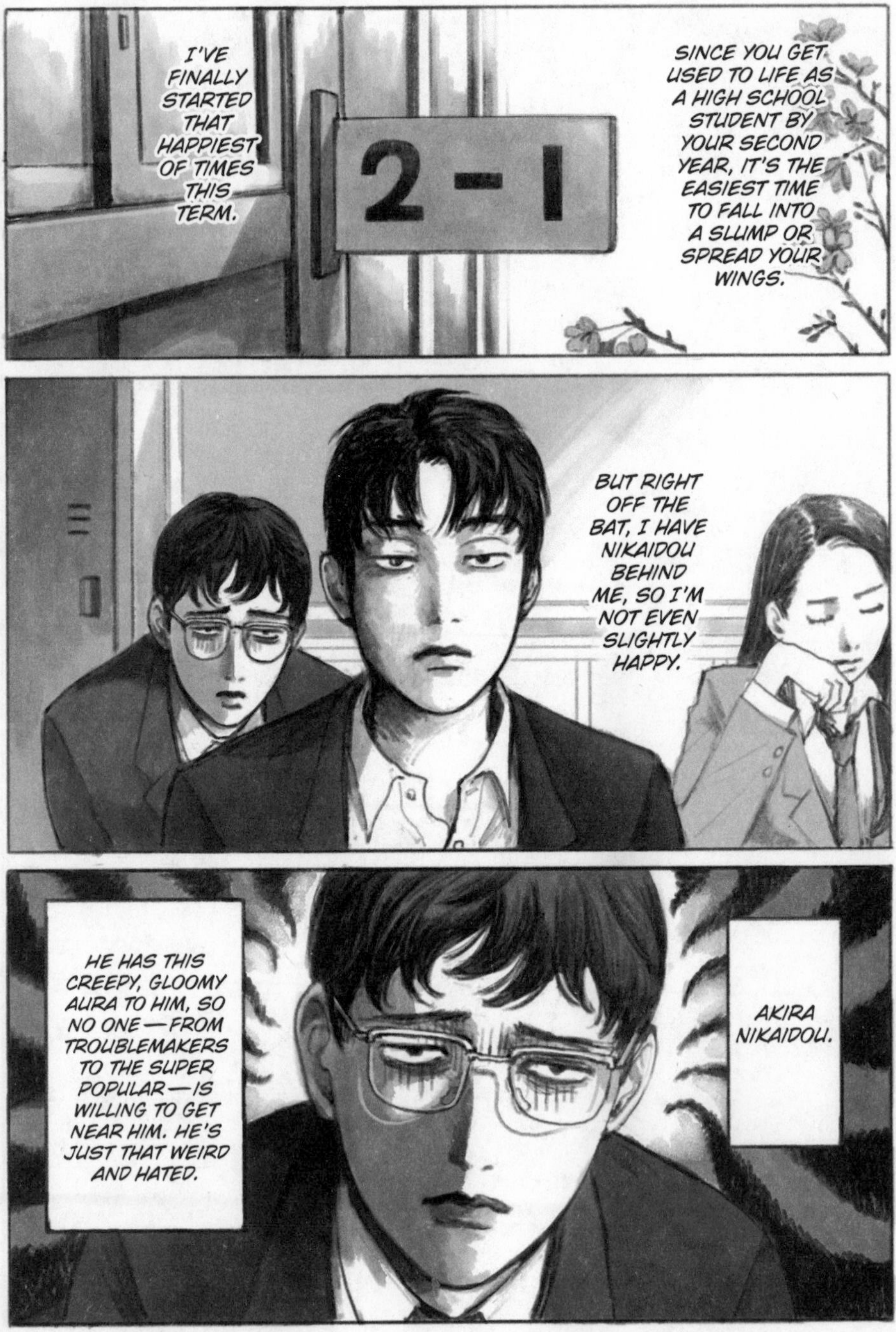
SINCE YOU GET USED TO LIFE AS A HIGH SCHOOL STUDENT BY YOUR SECOND YEAR, IT'S THE EASIEST TIME TO FALL INTO A SLUMP OR SPREAD YOUR WINGS.
2-1
I'VE FINALLY STARTED THAT HAPPIEST OF TIMES THIS TERM.
BUT RIGHT OFF THE BAT, I HAVE NIKAIDOU BEHIND ME, SO I'M NOT EVEN SLIGHTLY HAPPY.
AKIRA NIKAIDOU.
HE HAS THIS CREEPY, GLOOMY AURA TO HIM, SO NO ONE—FROM TROUBLEMAKERS TO THE SUPER POPULAR—IS WILLING TO GET NEAR HIM. HE'S JUST THAT WEIRD AND HATED.

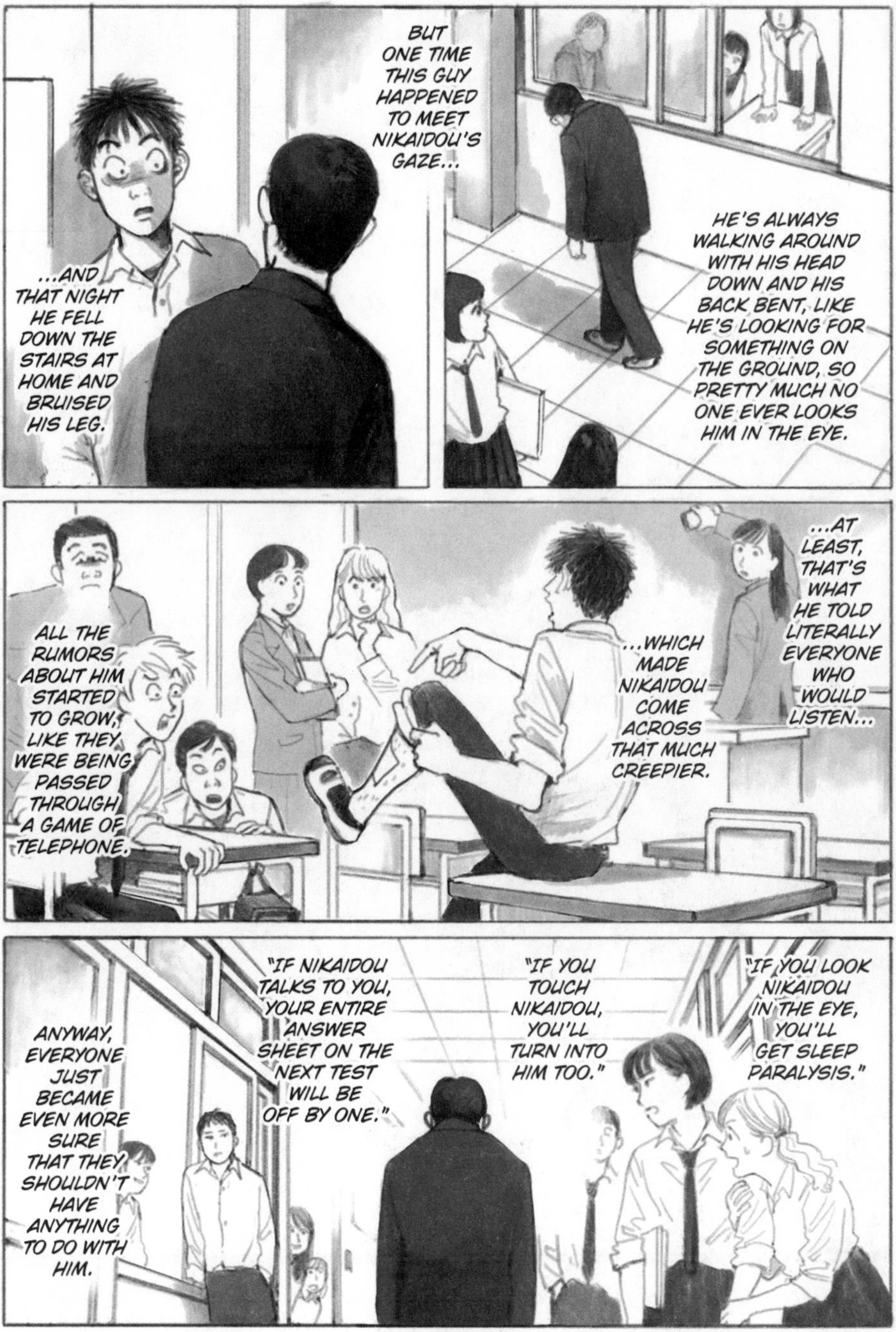
HE'S ALWAYS WALKING AROUND WITH HIS HEAD DOWN AND HIS BACK BENT, LIKE HE'S LOOKING FOR SOMETHING ON THE GROUND, SO PRETTY MUCH NO ONE EVER LOOKS HIM IN THE EYE.
BUT ONE TIME THIS GUY HAPPENED TO MEET NIKAIDOU'S GAZE...
...AND THAT NIGHT HE FELL DOWN THE STAIRS AT HOME AND BRUISED HIS LEG.
...AT LEAST, THAT'S WHAT HE TOLD LITERALLY EVERYONE WHO WOULD LISTEN...
...WHICH MADE NIKAIDOU COME ACROSS THAT MUCH CREEPIER.
ALL THE RUMORS ABOUT HIM STARTED TO GROW, LIKE THEY WERE BEING PASSED THROUGH A GAME OF TELEPHONE.
"IF YOU LOOK NIKAIDOU IN THE EYE, YOU'LL GET SLEEP PARALYSIS."
"IF YOU TOUCH NIKAIDOU, YOU'LL TURN INTO HIM TOO."
"IF NIKAIDOU TALKS TO YOU, YOUR ENTIRE ANSWER SHEET ON THE NEXT TEST WILL BE OFF BY ONE."
ANYWAY, EVERYONE JUST BECAME EVEN MORE SURE THAT THEY SHOULDN'T HAVE ANYTHING TO DO WITH HIM.

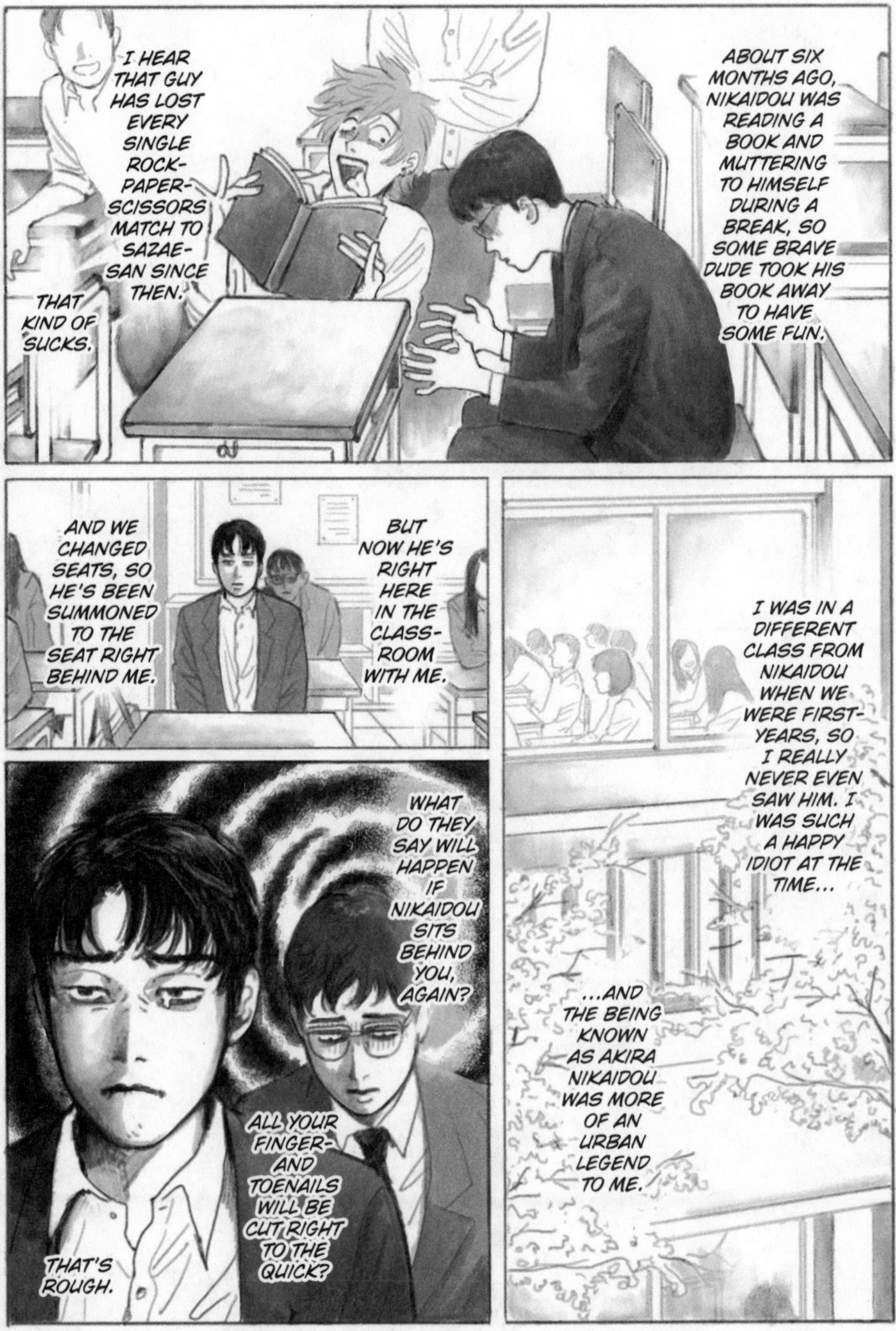
ABOUT SIX MONTHS AGO, NIKAIDOU WAS READING A BOOK AND MUTTERING TO HIMSELF DURING A BREAK, SO SOME BRAVE DUDE TOOK HIS BOOK AWAY TO HAVE SOME FUN.
I HEAR THAT GUY HAS LOST EVERY SINGLE ROCK-PAPER-SCISSORS MATCH TO SAZAE-SAN SINCE THEN.
THAT KIND OF SUCKS.
I WAS IN A DIFFERENT CLASS FROM NIKAIDOU WHEN WE WERE FIRST-YEARS, SO I REALLY NEVER EVEN SAW HIM. I WAS SUCH A HAPPY IDIOT AT THE TIME...
...AND THE BEING KNOWN AS AKIRA NIKAIDOU WAS MORE OF AN URBAN LEGEND TO ME.
BUT NOW HE'S RIGHT HERE IN THE CLASSROOM WITH ME.
AND WE CHANGED SEATS, SO HE'S BEEN SUMMONED TO THE SEAT RIGHT BEHIND ME.
WHAT DO THEY SAY WILL HAPPEN IF NIKAIDOU SITS BEHIND YOU, AGAIN?
ALL YOUR FINGER- AND TOENAILS WILL BE CUT RIGHT TO THE QUICK?
THAT'S ROUGH.

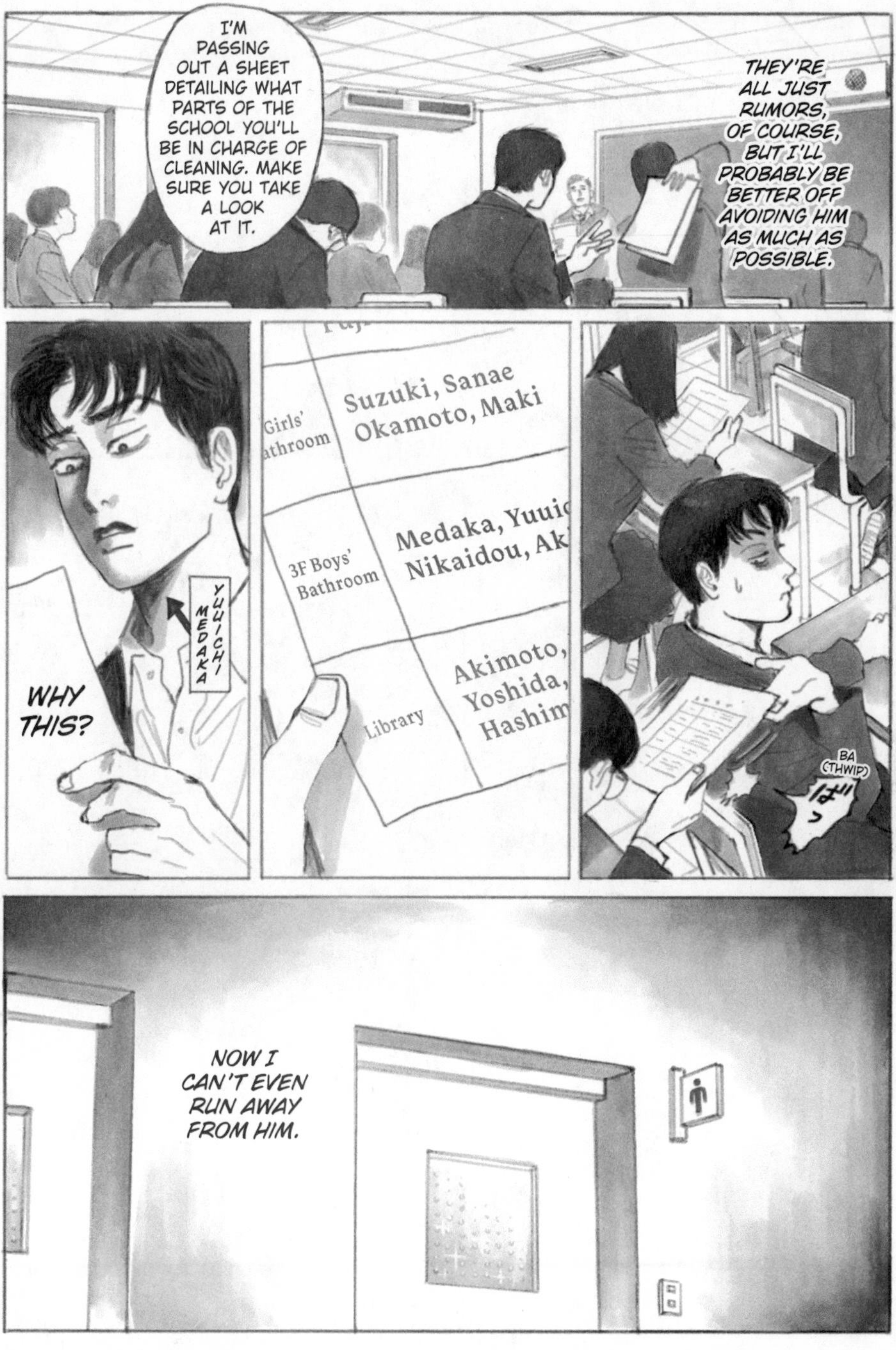
I'M PASSING OUT A SHEET DETAILING WHAT PARTS OF THE SCHOOL YOU'LL BE IN CHARGE OF CLEANING. MAKE SURE YOU TAKE A LOOK AT IT.
THEY'RE ALL JUST RUMORS, OF COURSE, BUT I'LL PROBABLY BE BETTER OFF AVOIDING HIM AS MUCH AS POSSIBLE.
BA (THWIP)
ぱっ
Girls' athroom
Suzuki, Sanae
Okamoto, Maki
3F Boys' Bathroom
Medaka, Yuuic
Nikaidou, Aki
Library
Akimoto,
Yoshida,
Hashim
YUUICHI MEDAKA
WHY THIS?
NOW I CAN'T EVEN RUN AWAY FROM HIM.

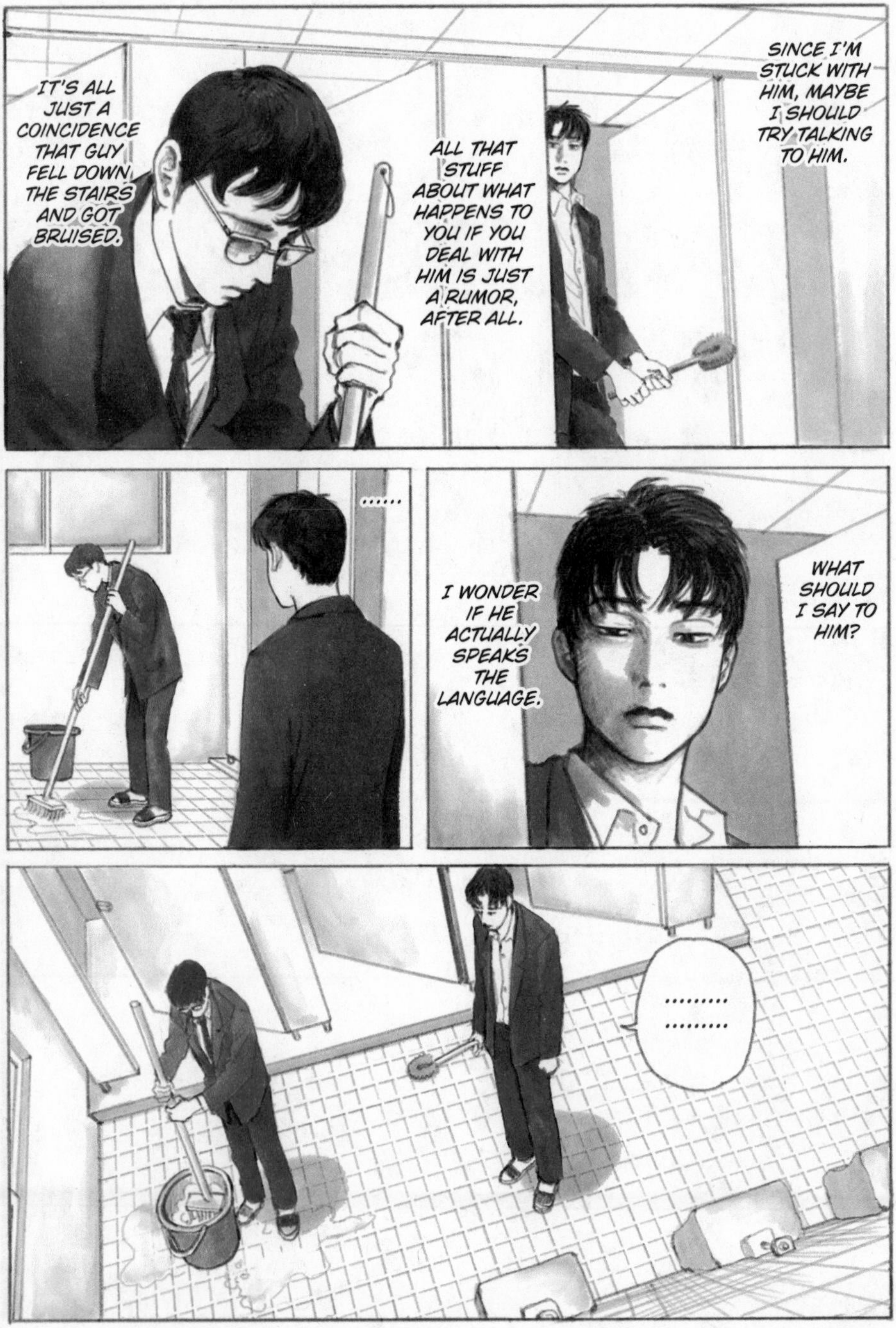
SINCE I'M STUCK WITH HIM, MAYBE I SHOULD TRY TALKING TO HIM.
ALL THAT STUFF ABOUT WHAT HAPPENS TO YOU IF YOU DEAL WITH HIM IS JUST A RUMOR, AFTER ALL.
IT'S ALL JUST A COINCIDENCE THAT GUY FELL DOWN THE STAIRS AND GOT BRUISED.
WHAT SHOULD I SAY TO HIM?
I WONDER IF HE ACTUALLY SPEAKS THE LANGUAGE.
......
....
....

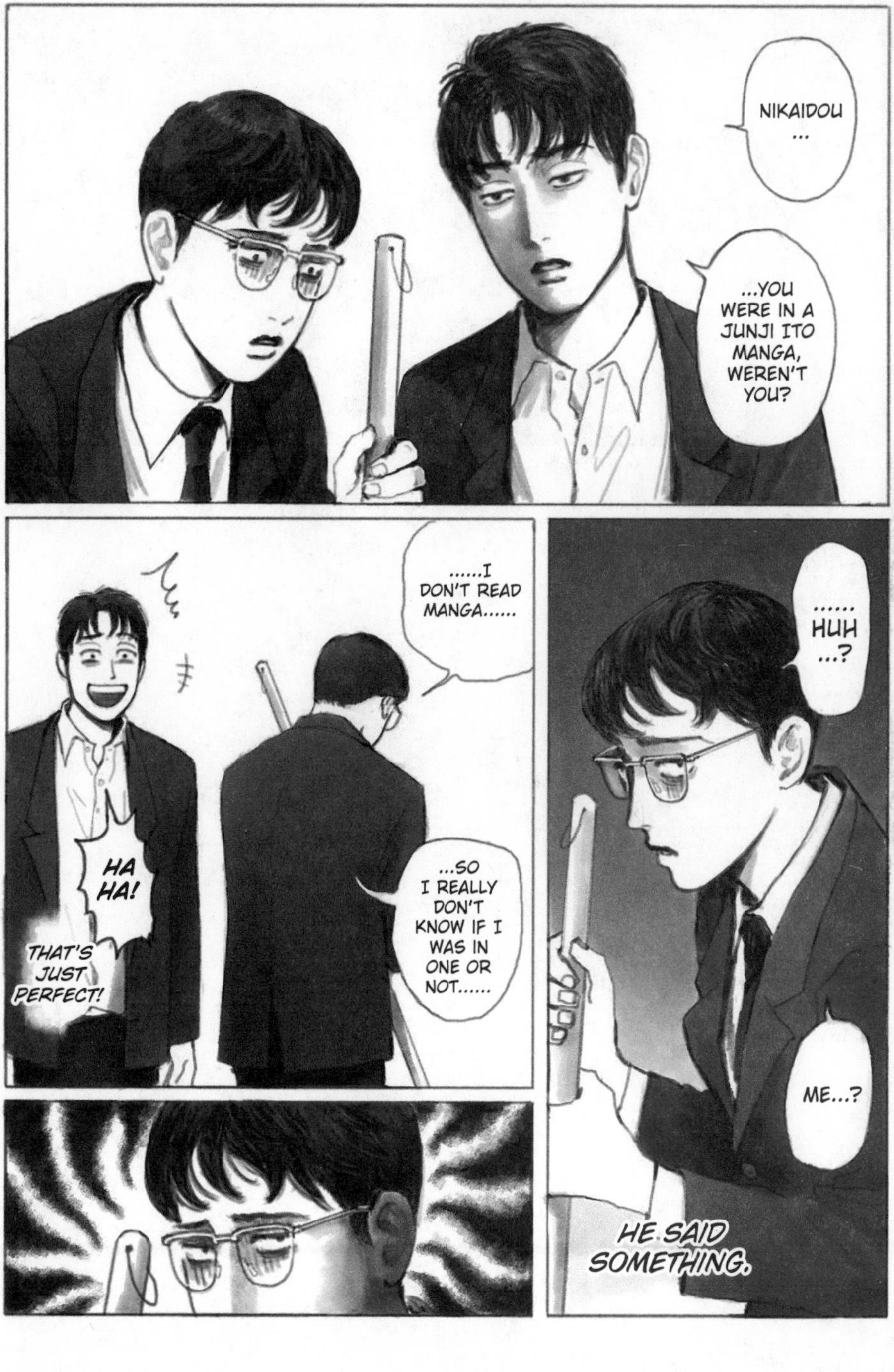
NIKAIDOU ...
...YOU WERE IN A JUNJI ITO MANGA, WEREN'T YOU?
...... HUH ...?
ME...?
HE SAID SOMETHING.
......I DON'T READ MANGA......
...SO I REALLY DON'T KNOW IF I WAS IN ONE OR NOT......
HA HA!
THAT'S JUST PERFECT!

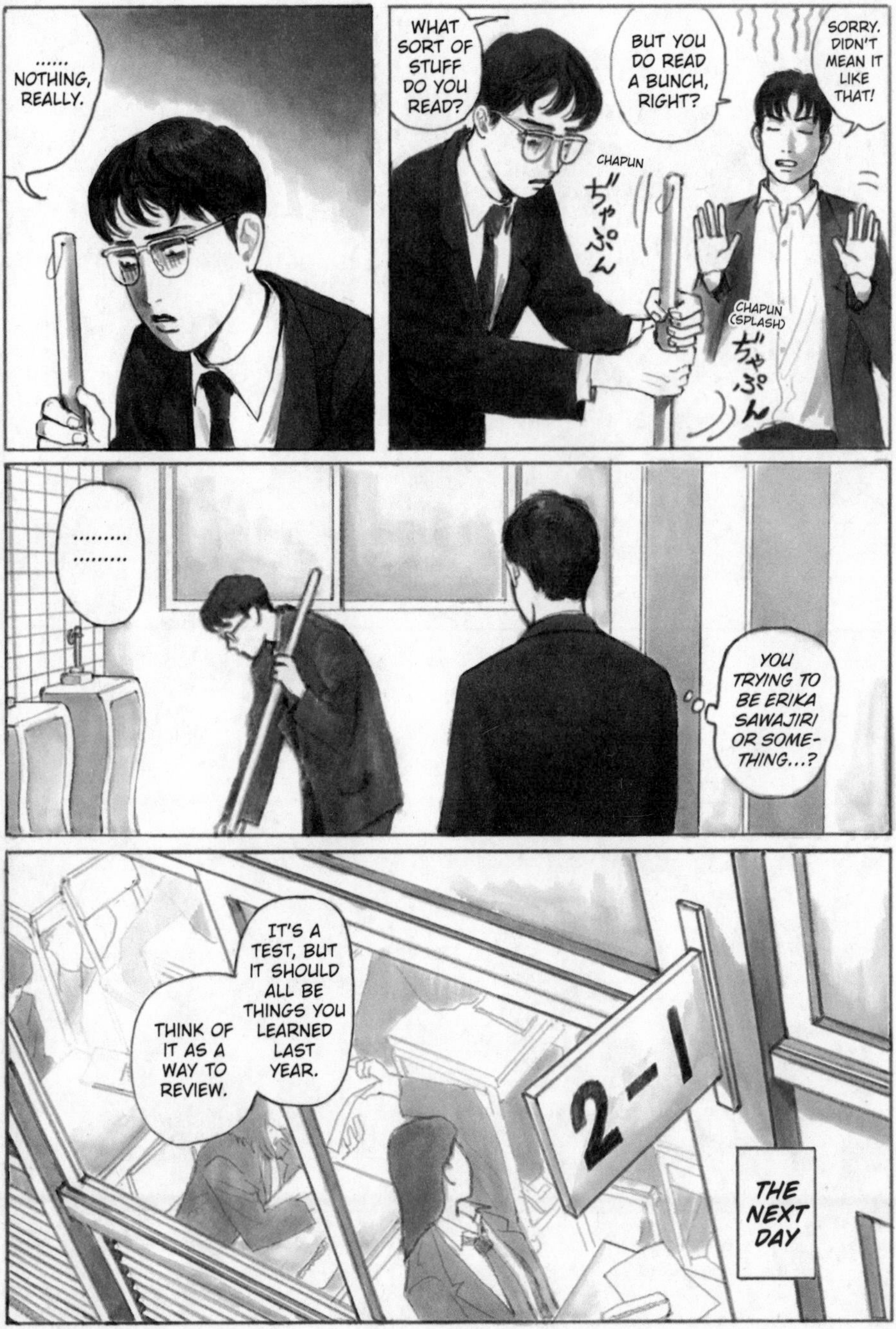
SORRY. DIDN'T MEAN IT LIKE THAT!
BUT YOU DO READ A BUNCH, RIGHT?
WHAT SORT OF STUFF DO YOU READ?
CHAPUN
ぢゃぷん
CHAPUN (SPLASH)
ぢゃぷん
...... NOTHING, REALLY.
YOU TRYING TO BE ERIKA SAWAJIRI OR SOMETHING...?
....
THE NEXT DAY
IT'S A TEST, BUT IT SHOULD ALL BE THINGS YOU LEARNED LAST YEAR.
THINK OF IT AS A WAY TO REVIEW.
2-1

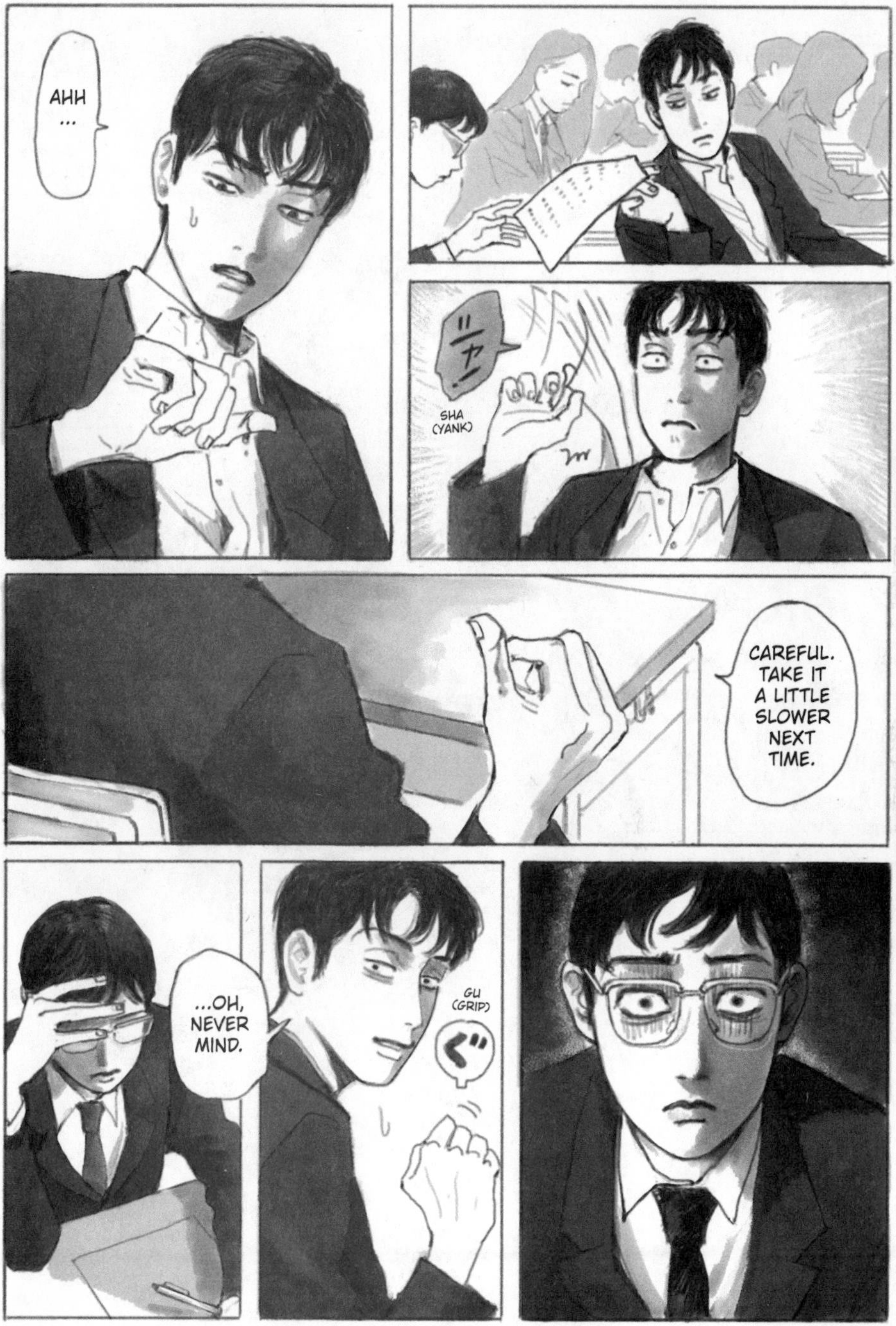
SHA
(YANK)
AHH
...
CAREFUL. TAKE IT A LITTLE SLOWER NEXT TIME.
GU
(GRIP)
ぐ
...OH, NEVER MIND.

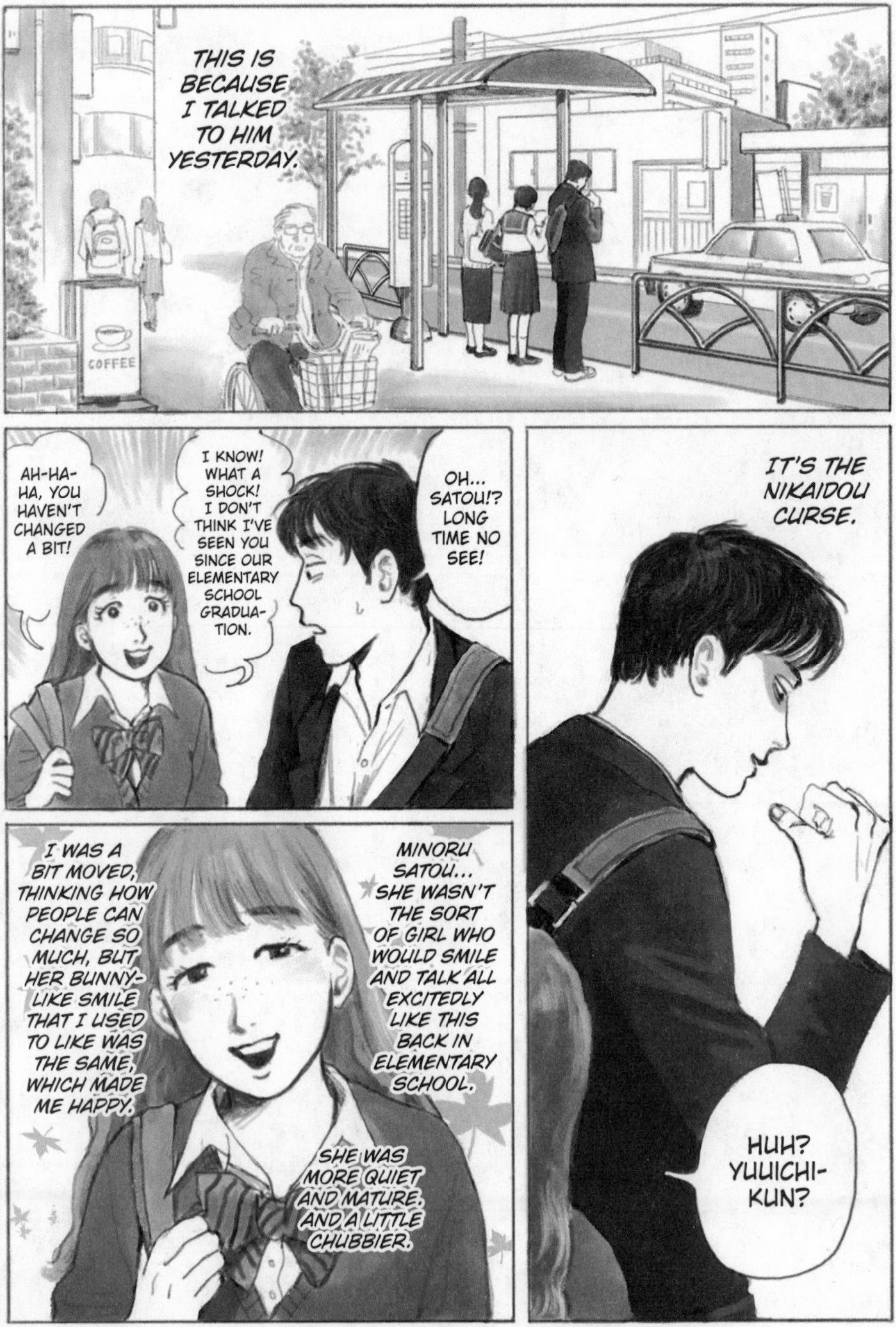
THIS IS BECAUSE I TALKED TO HIM YESTERDAY.
COFFEE
IT'S THE NIKAIDOU CURSE.
HUH? YUUICHI-KUN?
OH... SATOU!? LONG TIME NO SEE!
I KNOW! WHAT A SHOCK! I DON'T THINK I'VE SEEN YOU SINCE OUR ELEMENTARY SCHOOL GRADUA-TION.
AH-HA-HA, YOU HAVEN'T CHANGED A BIT!
MINORU SATOU... SHE WASN'T THE SORT OF GIRL WHO WOULD SMILE AND TALK ALL EXCITEDLY LIKE THIS BACK IN ELEMENTARY SCHOOL.
I WAS A BIT MOVED, THINKING HOW PEOPLE CAN CHANGE SO MUCH, BUT HER BUNNY-LIKE SMILE THAT I USED TO LIKE WAS THE SAME, WHICH MADE ME HAPPY.
SHE WAS MORE QUIET AND MATURE. AND A LITTLE CHUBBIER.

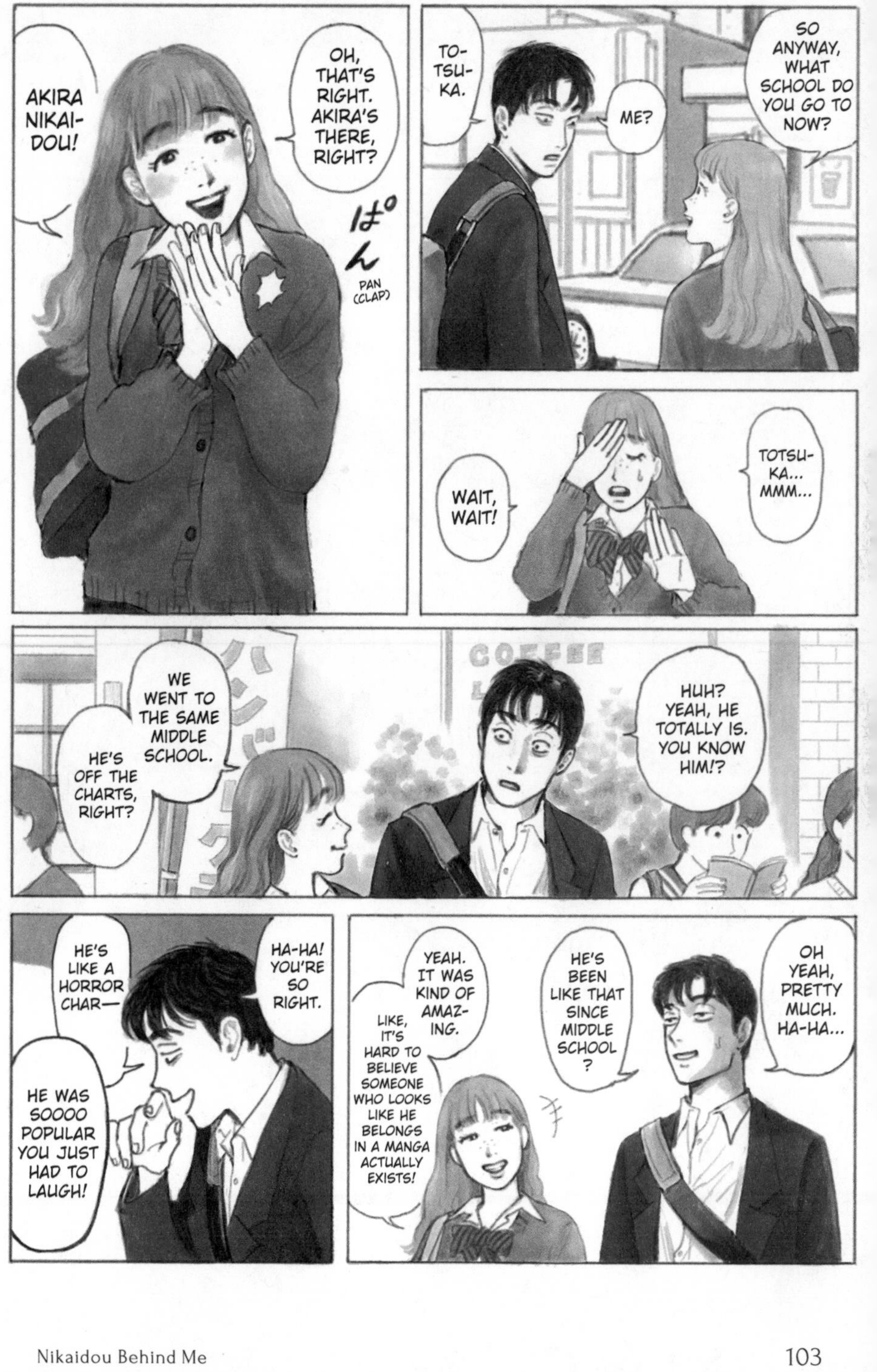
SO ANYWAY, WHAT SCHOOL DO YOU GO TO NOW?
ME?
TO-TSU-KA.
TOTSU-KA... MMM...
WAIT, WAIT!
OH, THAT'S RIGHT. AKIRA'S THERE, RIGHT?
ぱん
PAN (CLAP)
AKIRA NIKAI-DOU!
HUH? YEAH, HE TOTALLY IS. YOU KNOW HIM!?
WE WENT TO THE SAME MIDDLE SCHOOL.
HE'S OFF THE CHARTS, RIGHT?
OH YEAH, PRETTY MUCH. HA-HA...
HE'S BEEN LIKE THAT SINCE MIDDLE SCHOOL ?
YEAH. IT WAS KIND OF AMAZ-ING.
LIKE, IT'S HARD TO BELIEVE SOMEONE WHO LOOKS LIKE HE BELONGS IN A MANGA ACTUALLY EXISTS!
HA-HA! YOU'RE SO RIGHT.
HE'S LIKE A HORROR CHAR—
HE WAS SOOOO POPULAR YOU JUST HAD TO LAUGH!

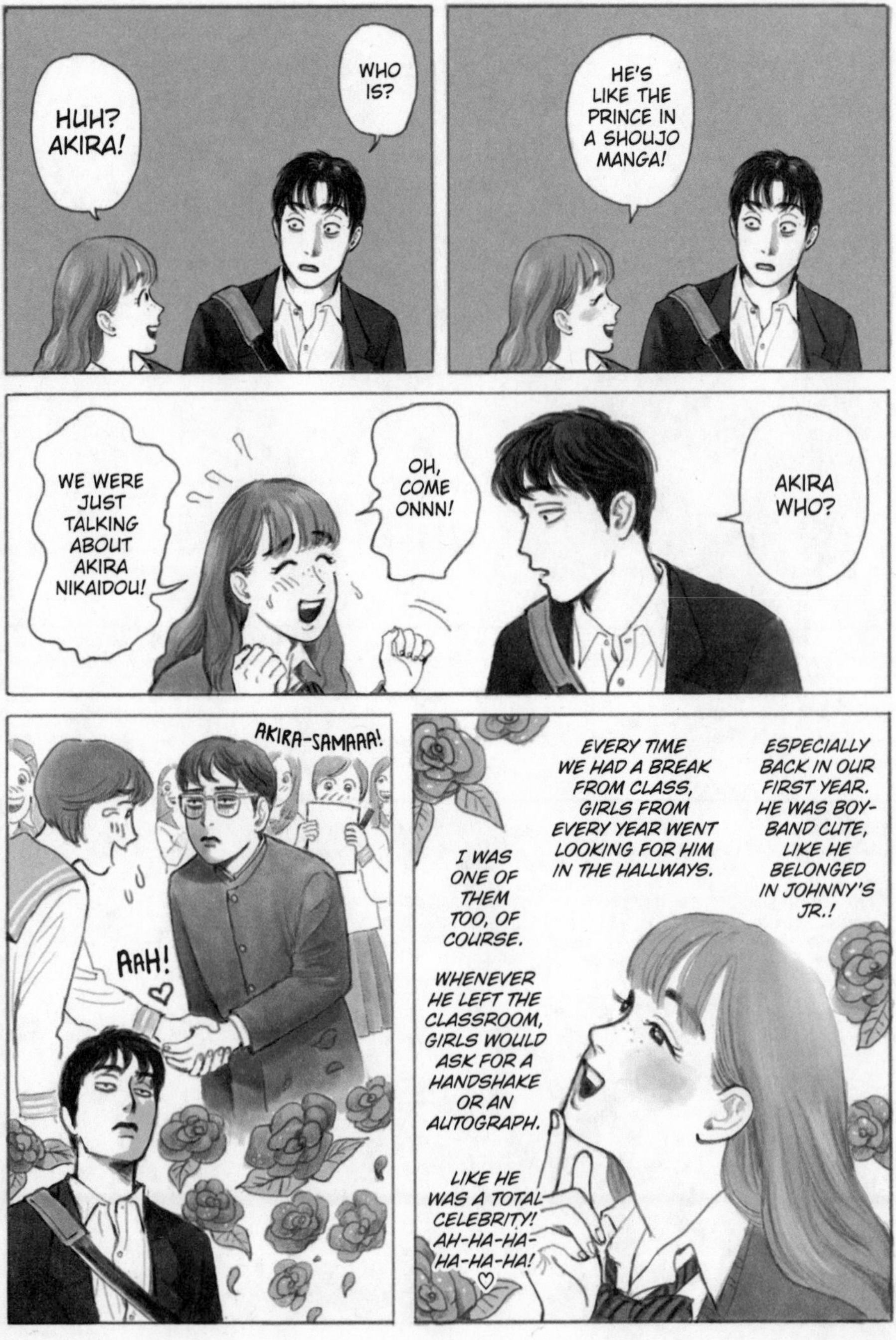
HUH? AKIRA!
WHO IS?
HE'S LIKE THE PRINCE IN A SHOUJO MANGA!
WE WERE JUST TALKING ABOUT AKIRA NIKAIDOU!
OH, COME ONNN!
AKIRA WHO?
AKIRA-SAMAAA!
AAH!
EVERY TIME WE HAD A BREAK FROM CLASS, GIRLS FROM EVERY YEAR WENT LOOKING FOR HIM IN THE HALLWAYS.
ESPECIALLY BACK IN OUR FIRST YEAR. HE WAS BOY-BAND CUTE, LIKE HE BELONGED IN JOHNNY'S JR.!
I WAS ONE OF THEM TOO, OF COURSE.
WHENEVER HE LEFT THE CLASSROOM, GIRLS WOULD ASK FOR A HANDSHAKE OR AN AUTOGRAPH.
LIKE HE WAS A TOTAL CELEBRITY! AH-HA-HA-HA-HA-HA!

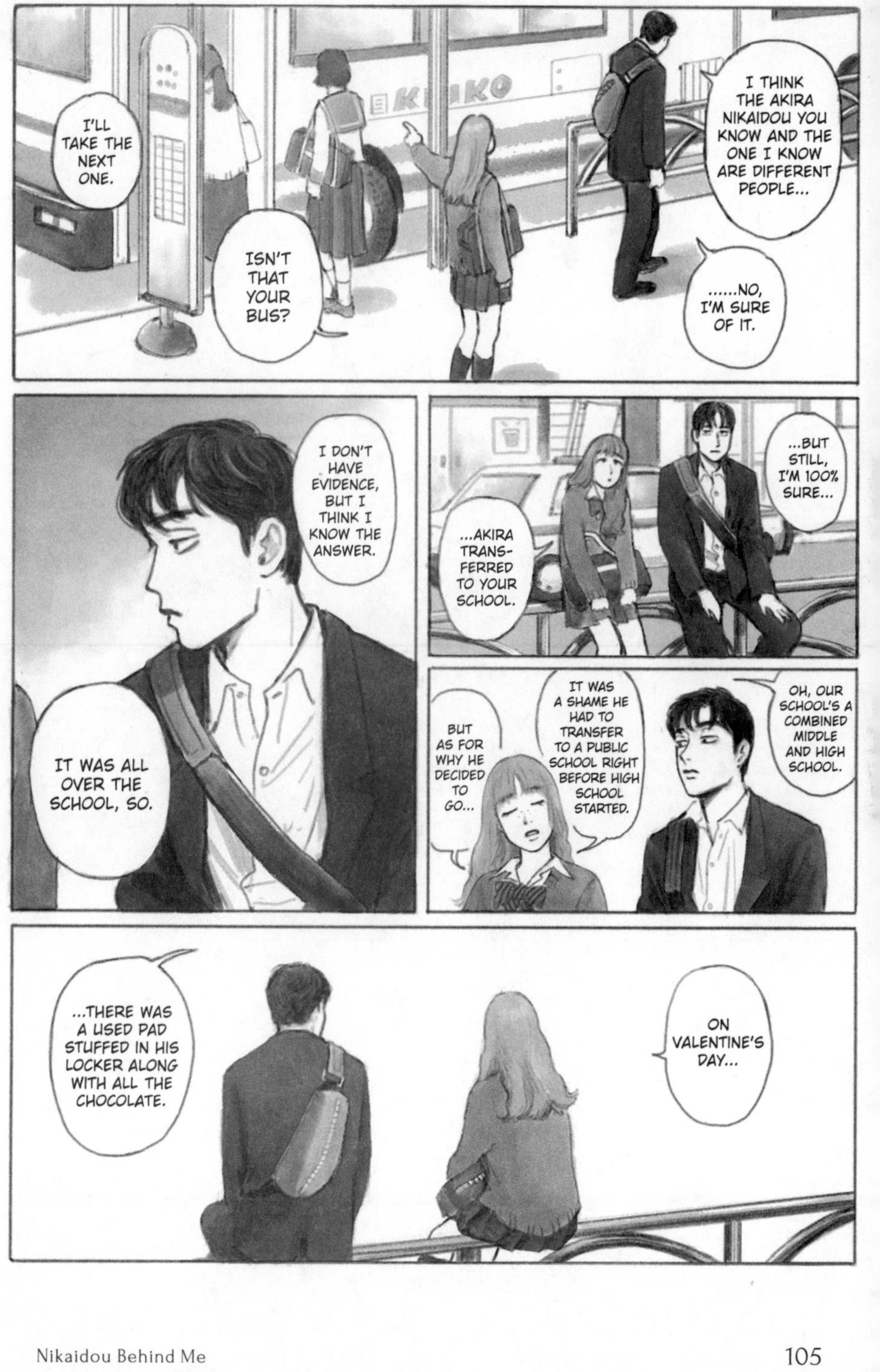
I THINK THE AKIRA NIKAIDOU YOU KNOW AND THE ONE I KNOW ARE DIFFERENT PEOPLE...
......NO, I'M SURE OF IT.
I'LL TAKE THE NEXT ONE.
ISN'T THAT YOUR BUS?
...BUT STILL, I'M 100% SURE...
...AKIRA TRANS-FERRED TO YOUR SCHOOL.
OH, OUR SCHOOL'S A COMBINED MIDDLE AND HIGH SCHOOL.
IT WAS A SHAME HE HAD TO TRANSFER TO A PUBLIC SCHOOL RIGHT BEFORE HIGH SCHOOL STARTED.
BUT AS FOR WHY HE DECIDED TO GO...
I DON'T HAVE EVIDENCE, BUT I THINK I KNOW THE ANSWER.
IT WAS ALL OVER THE SCHOOL, SO.
ON VALENTINE'S DAY...
...THERE WAS A USED PAD STUFFED IN HIS LOCKER ALONG WITH ALL THE CHOCOLATE.

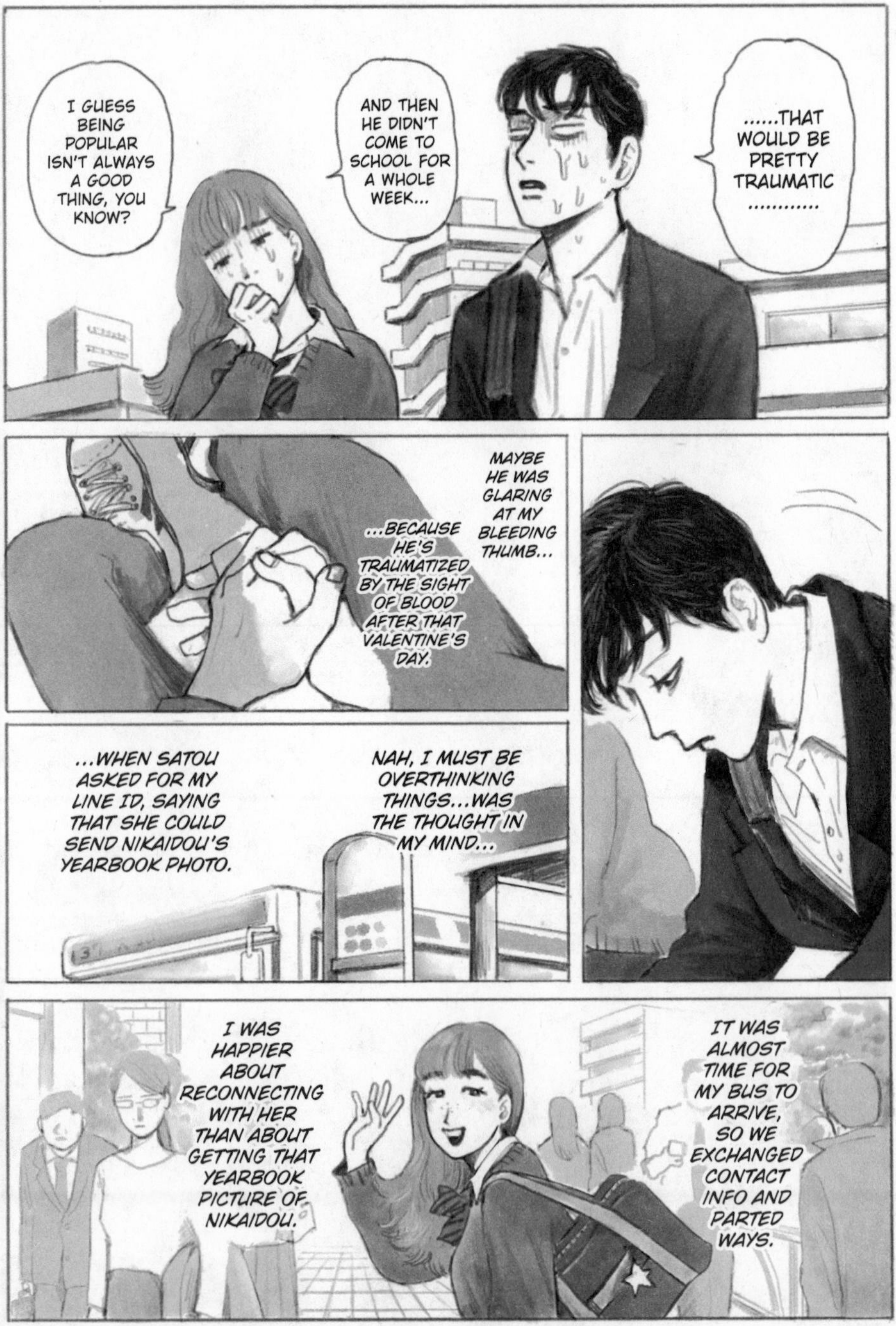
......THAT WOULD BE PRETTY TRAUMATIC ....
AND THEN HE DIDN'T COME TO SCHOOL FOR A WHOLE WEEK...
I GUESS BEING POPULAR ISN'T ALWAYS A GOOD THING, YOU KNOW?
MAYBE HE WAS GLARING AT MY BLEEDING THUMB...
...BECAUSE HE'S TRAUMATIZED BY THE SIGHT OF BLOOD AFTER THAT VALENTINE'S DAY.
NAH, I MUST BE OVERTHINKING THINGS...WAS THE THOUGHT IN MY MIND...
...WHEN SATOU ASKED FOR MY LINE ID, SAYING THAT SHE COULD SEND NIKAIDOU'S YEARBOOK PHOTO.
IT WAS ALMOST TIME FOR MY BUS TO ARRIVE, SO WE EXCHANGED CONTACT INFO AND PARTED WAYS.
I WAS HAPPIER ABOUT RECONNECTING WITH HER THAN ABOUT GETTING THAT YEARBOOK PICTURE OF NIKAIDOU.

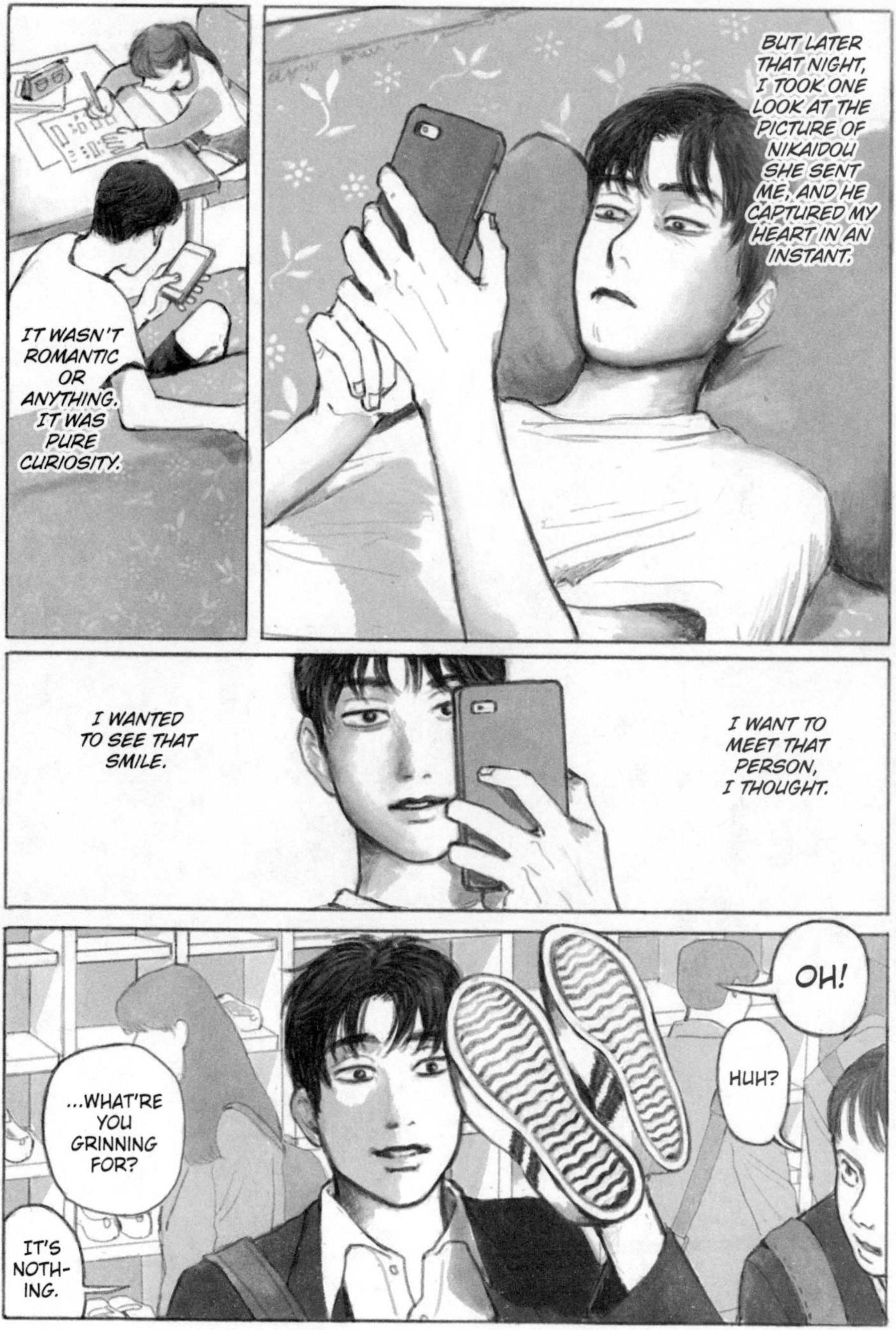
BUT LATER THAT NIGHT, I TOOK ONE LOOK AT THE PICTURE OF NIKAIDOU SHE SENT ME, AND HE CAPTURED MY HEART IN AN INSTANT.
IT WASN'T ROMANTIC OR ANYTHING. IT WAS PURE CURIOSITY.
I WANT TO MEET THAT PERSON, I THOUGHT.
I WANTED TO SEE THAT SMILE.
OH!
HUH?
...WHAT'RE YOU GRINNING FOR?
IT'S NOTH-ING.

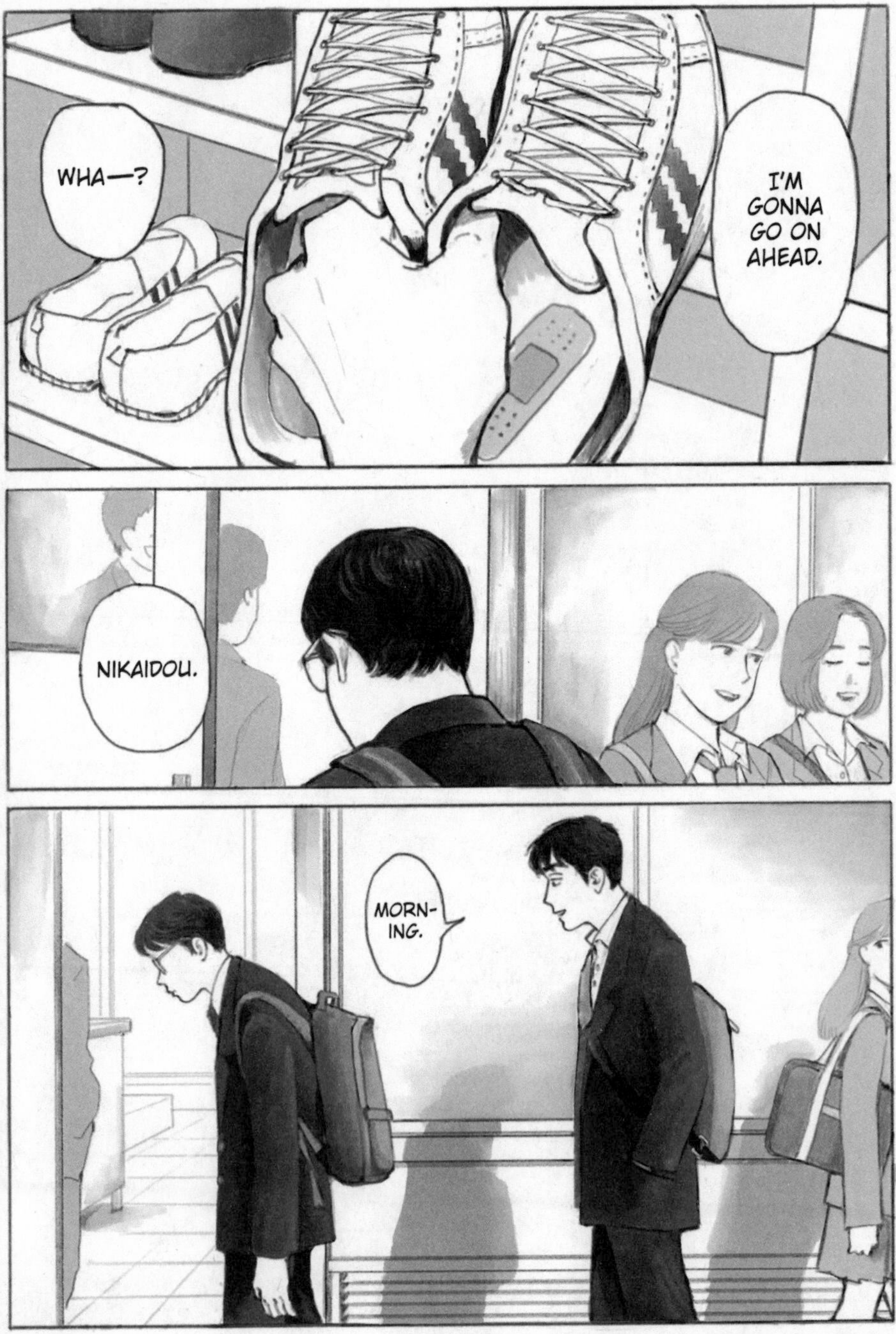
I'M GONNA GO ON AHEAD.
WHA—?
NIKAIDOU.
MORN-ING.

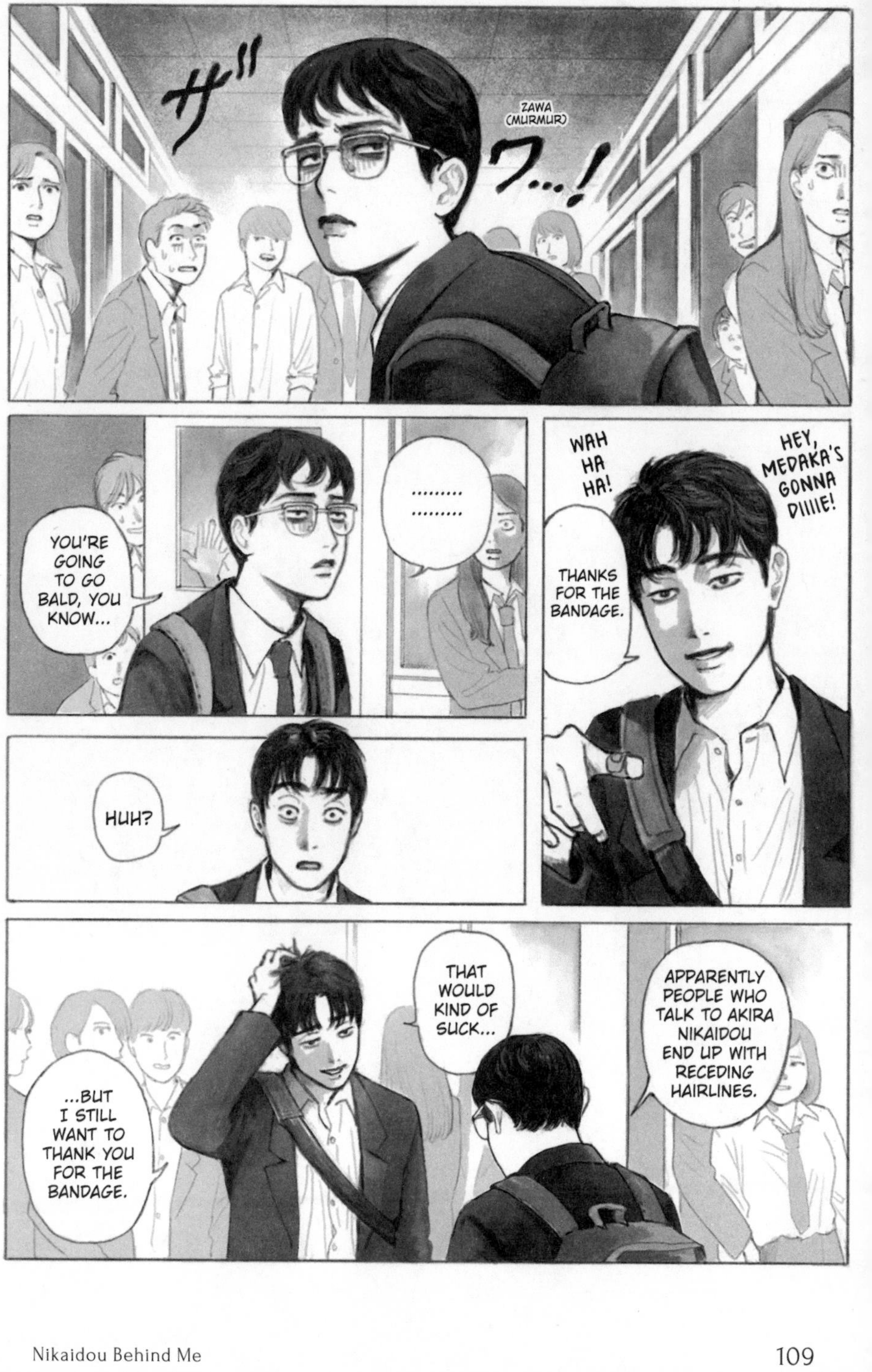
ザワ…!
ZAWA (MURMUR)
HEY, MEDAKA'S GONNA DIIIIE!
WAH HA HA!
THANKS FOR THE BANDAGE.
....
....
YOU'RE GOING TO GO BALD, YOU KNOW...
HUH?
APPARENTLY PEOPLE WHO TALK TO AKIRA NIKAIDOU END UP WITH RECEDING HAIRLINES.
THAT WOULD KIND OF SUCK...
...BUT I STILL WANT TO THANK YOU FOR THE BANDAGE.

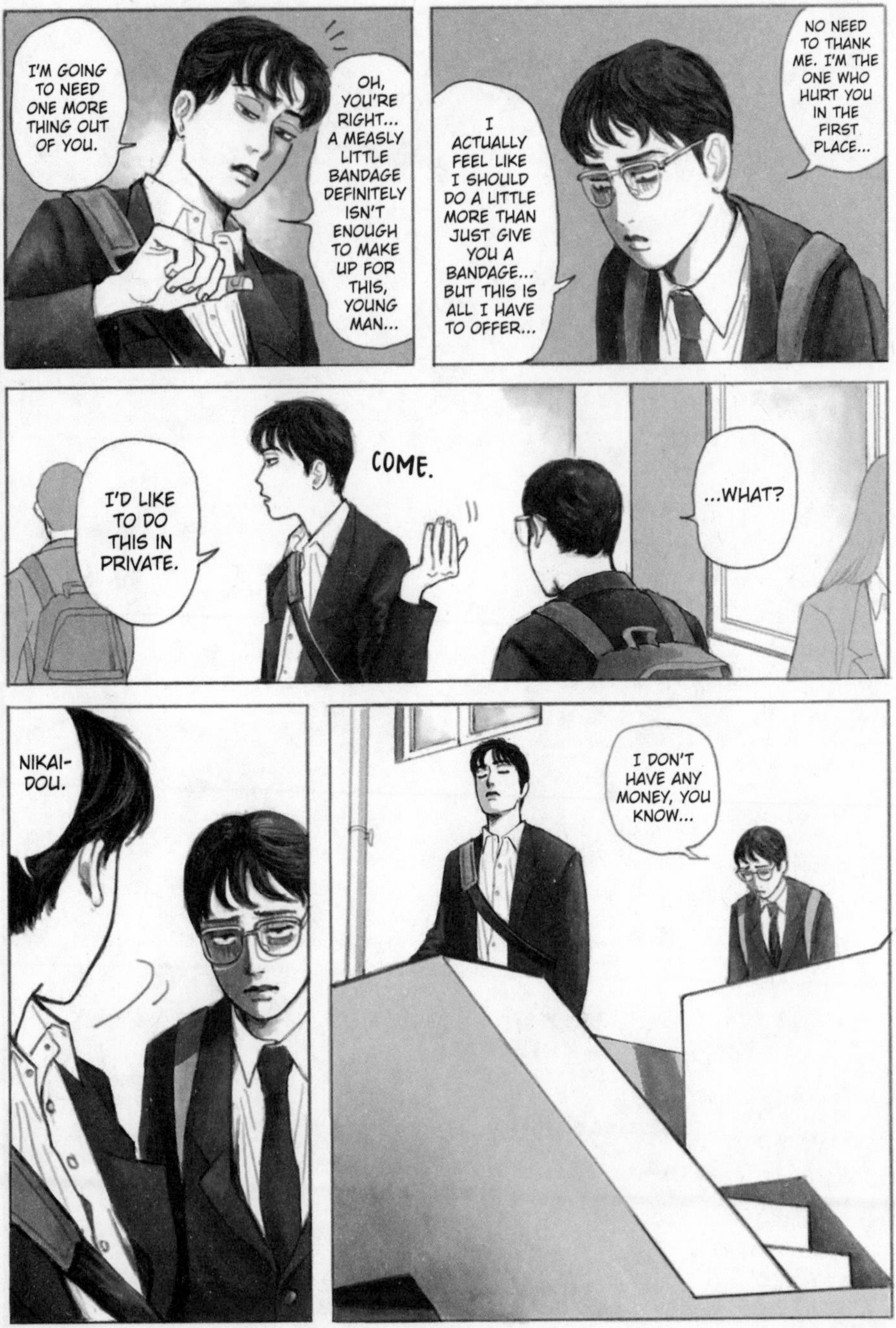
NO NEED TO THANK ME. I'M THE ONE WHO HURT YOU IN THE FIRST PLACE...
I ACTUALLY FEEL LIKE I SHOULD DO A LITTLE MORE THAN JUST GIVE YOU A BANDAGE... BUT THIS IS ALL I HAVE TO OFFER...
OH, YOU'RE RIGHT... A MEASLY LITTLE BANDAGE DEFINITELY ISN'T ENOUGH TO MAKE UP FOR THIS, YOUNG MAN...
I'M GOING TO NEED ONE MORE THING OUT OF YOU.
...WHAT?
COME.
I'D LIKE TO DO THIS IN PRIVATE.
I DON'T HAVE ANY MONEY, YOU KNOW...
NIKAI-DOU.

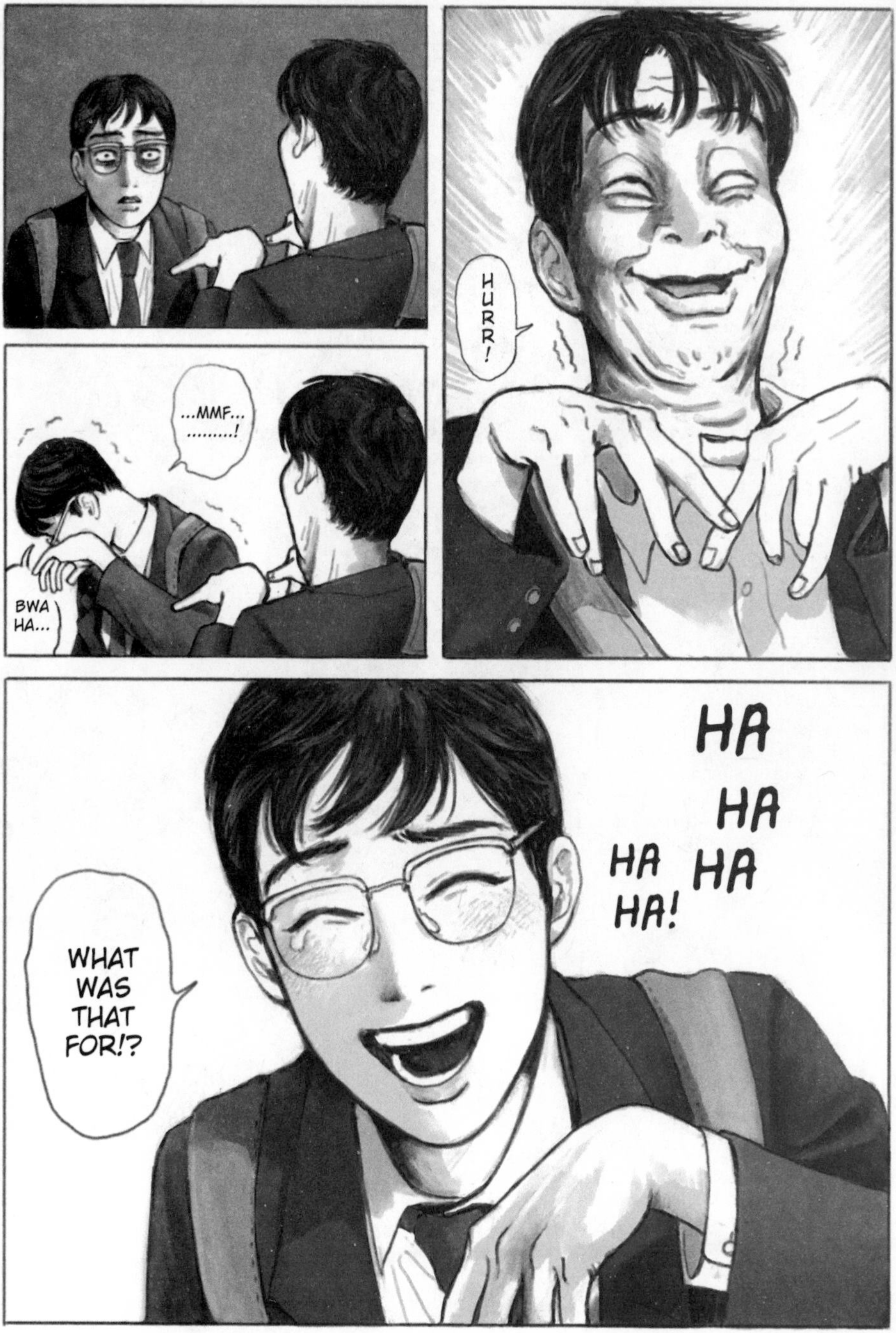
HURR!
...MMF... ....!
BWA HA...
HA HA HA HA HA!
WHAT WAS THAT FOR!?

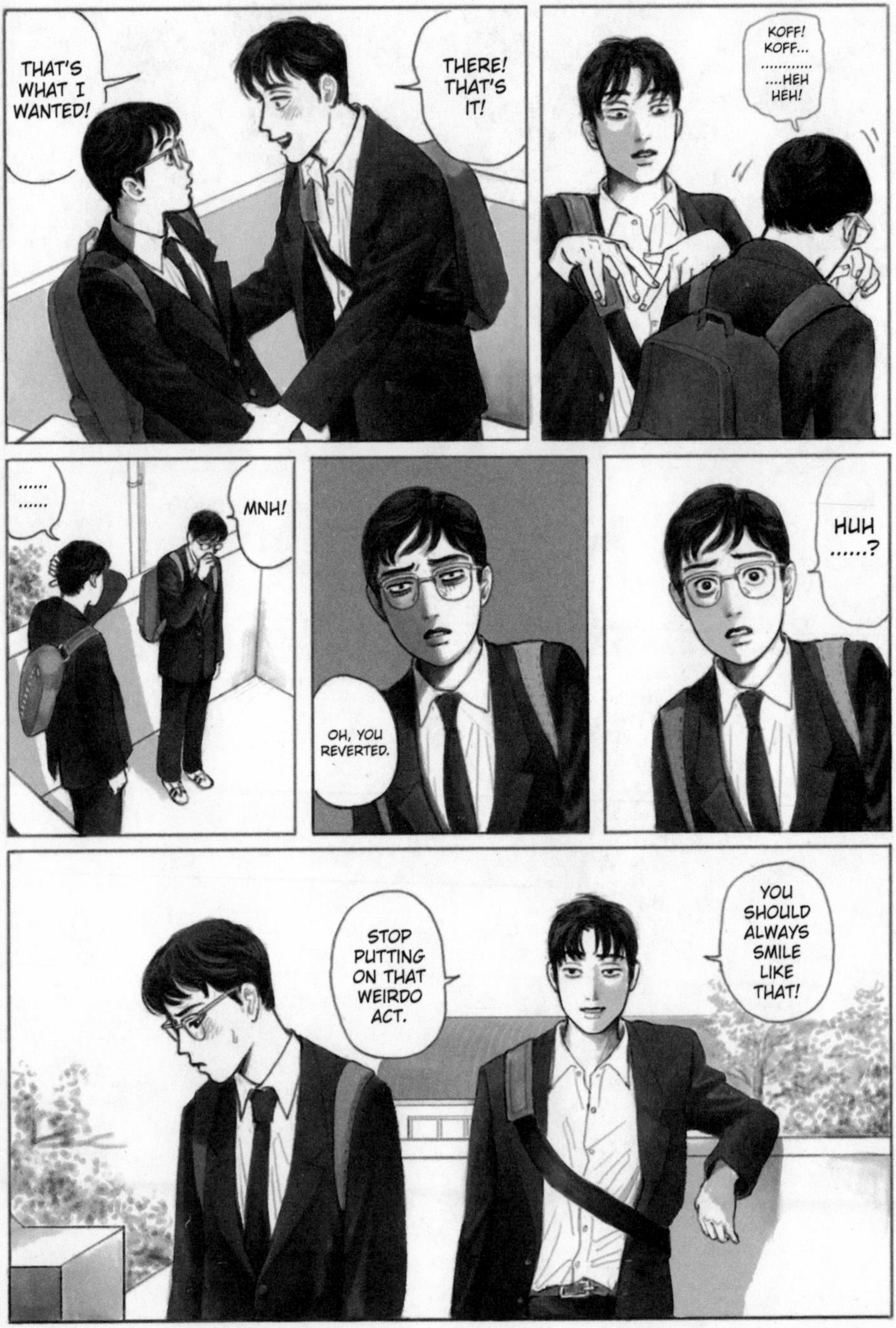
KOFF! KOFF... ....HEH HEH!
THERE! THAT'S IT!
THAT'S WHAT I WANTED!
HUH ......?
OH, YOU REVERTED.
MNH!
....
YOU SHOULD ALWAYS SMILE LIKE THAT!
STOP PUTTING ON THAT WEIRDO ACT.

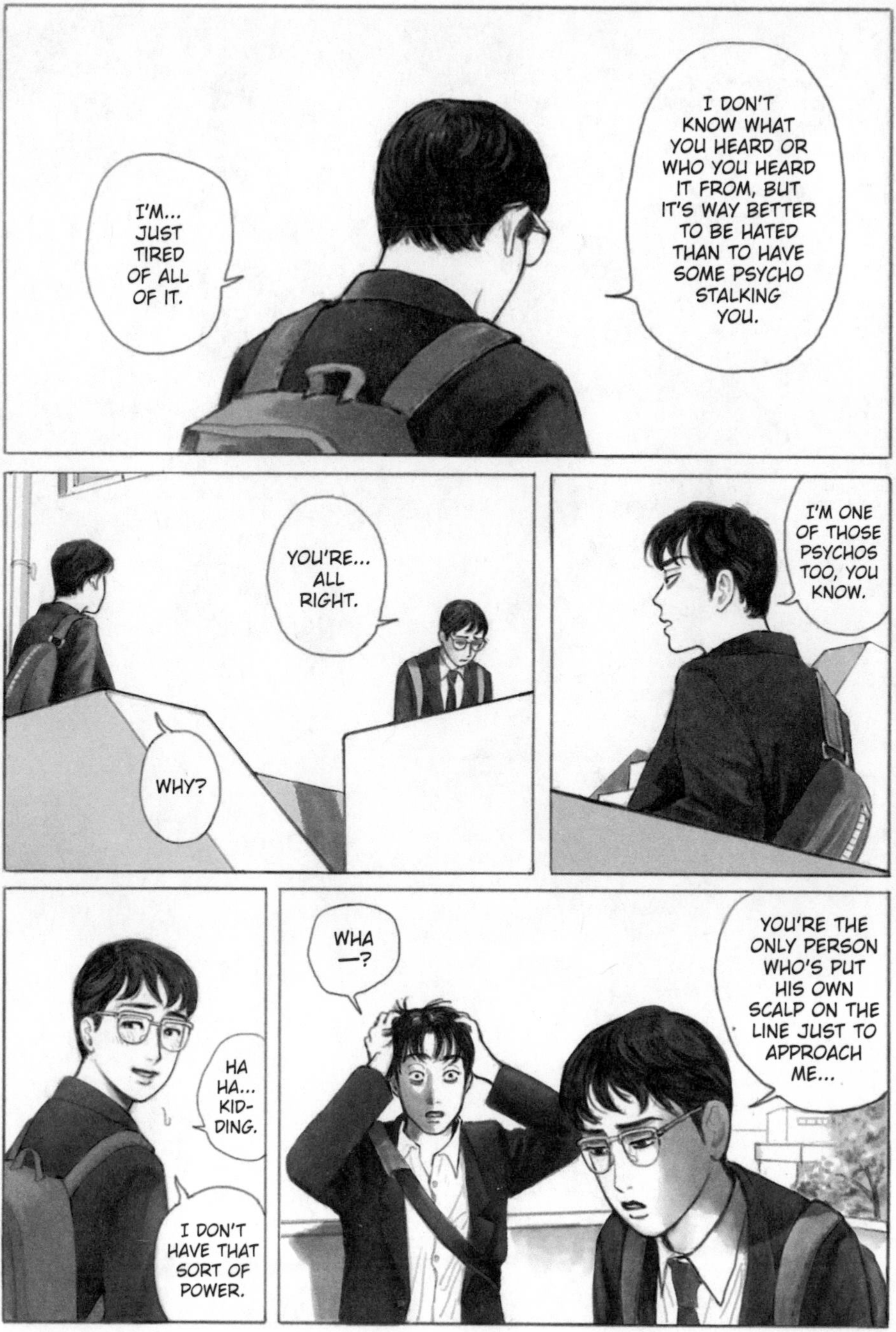
I DON'T KNOW WHAT YOU HEARD OR WHO YOU HEARD IT FROM, BUT IT'S WAY BETTER TO BE HATED THAN TO HAVE SOME PSYCHO STALKING YOU.
I'M... JUST TIRED OF ALL OF IT.
I'M ONE OF THOSE PSYCHOS TOO, YOU KNOW.
YOU'RE... ALL RIGHT.
WHY?
YOU'RE THE ONLY PERSON WHO'S PUT HIS OWN SCALP ON THE LINE JUST TO APPROACH ME...
WHA —?
HA HA... KID-DING.
I DON'T HAVE THAT SORT OF POWER.

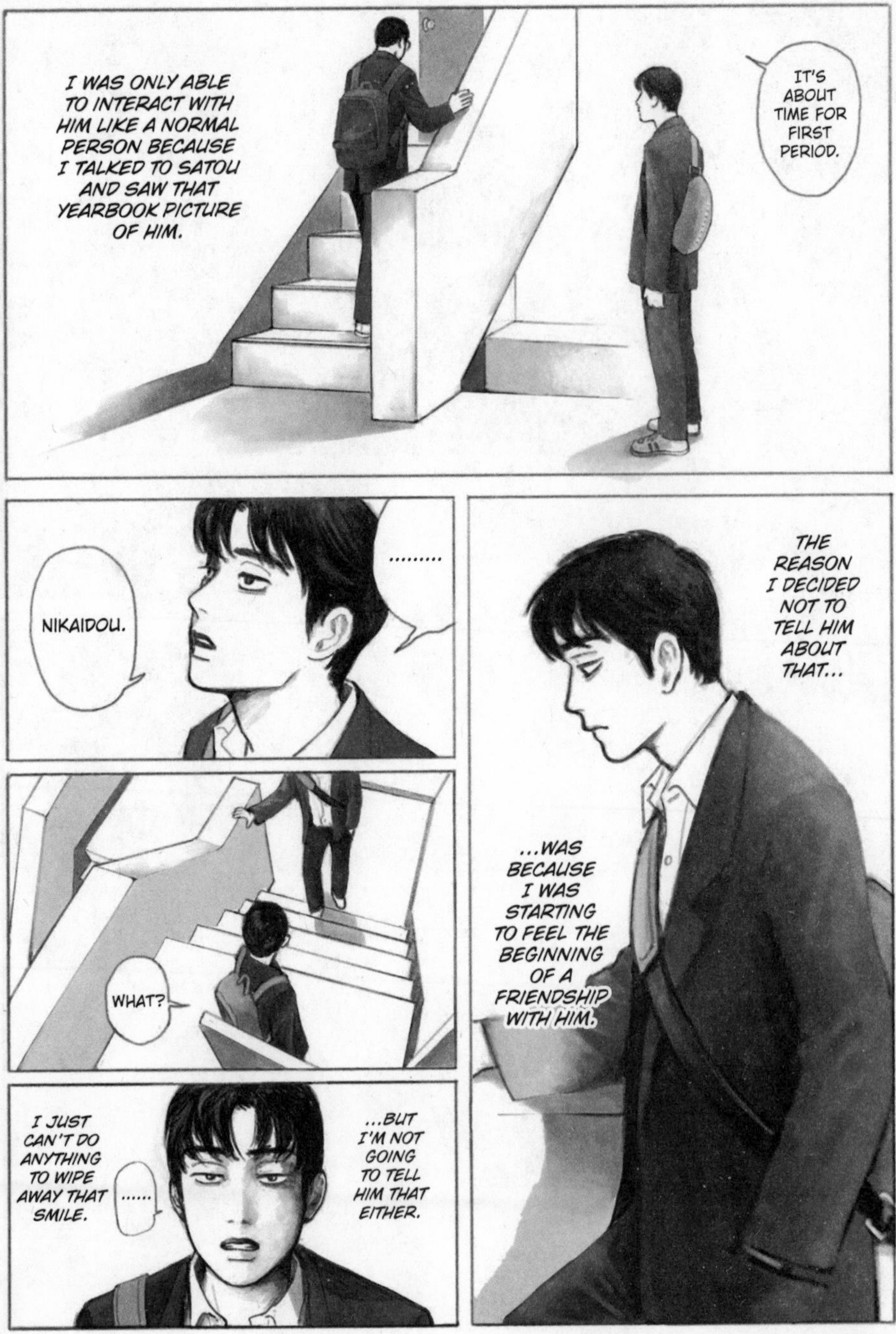
IT'S ABOUT TIME FOR FIRST PERIOD.
I WAS ONLY ABLE TO INTERACT WITH HIM LIKE A NORMAL PERSON BECAUSE I TALKED TO SATOU AND SAW THAT YEARBOOK PICTURE OF HIM.
THE REASON I DECIDED NOT TO TELL HIM ABOUT THAT...
...WAS BECAUSE I WAS STARTING TO FEEL THE BEGINNING OF A FRIENDSHIP WITH HIM.
....
NIKAIDOU.
WHAT?
...BUT I'M NOT GOING TO TELL HIM THAT EITHER.
......
I JUST CAN'T DO ANYTHING TO WIPE AWAY THAT SMILE.

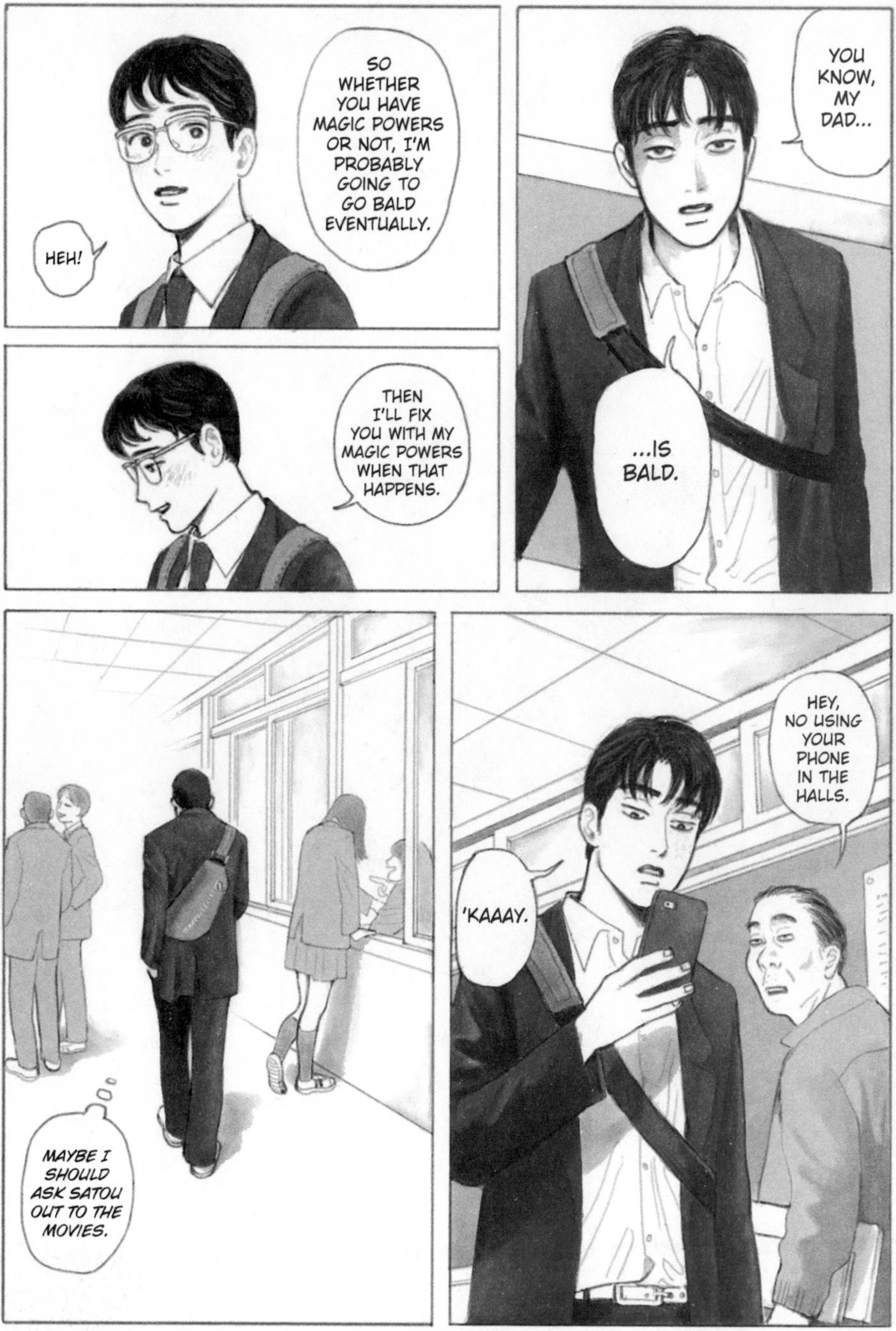
YOU KNOW, MY DAD...
...IS BALD.
SO WHETHER YOU HAVE MAGIC POWERS OR NOT, I'M PROBABLY GOING TO GO BALD EVENTUALLY.
HEH!
THEN I'LL FIX YOU WITH MY MAGIC POWERS WHEN THAT HAPPENS.
HEY, NO USING YOUR PHONE IN THE HALLS.
'KAAAY.
MAYBE I SHOULD ASK SATOU OUT TO THE MOVIES.

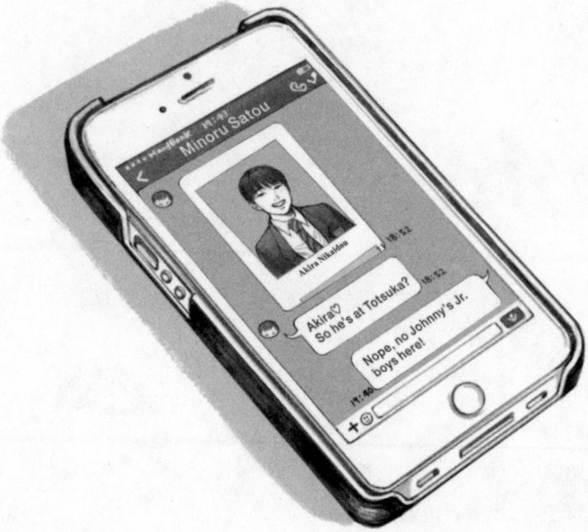
Minoru Satou
Akira Nikaidou
18:52
Akira♡
So he's at Totsuka?
18:52
Nope, no Johnny's Jr.
boys here!

[Nikaidou Extra]

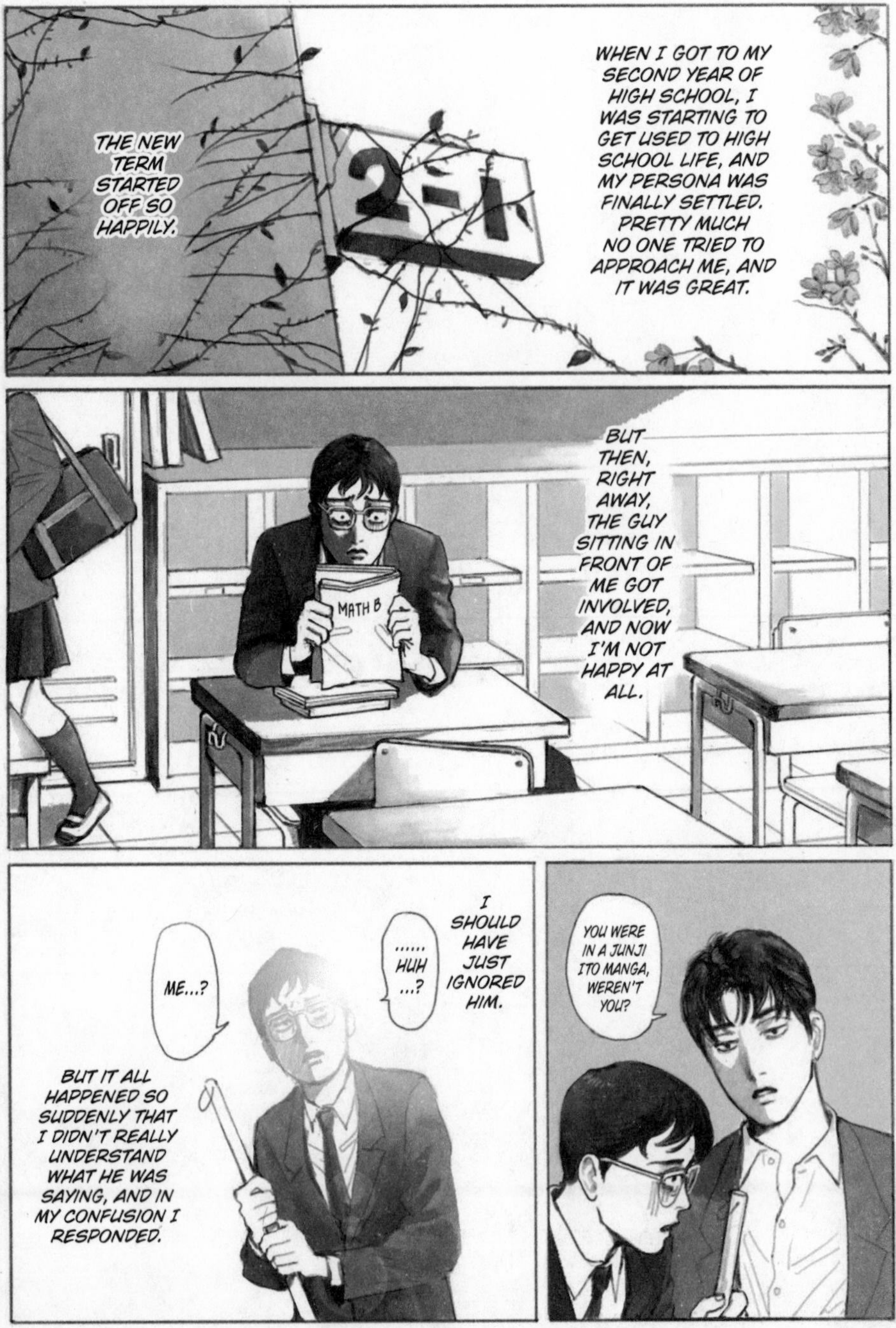
WHEN I GOT TO MY SECOND YEAR OF HIGH SCHOOL, I WAS STARTING TO GET USED TO HIGH SCHOOL LIFE, AND MY PERSONA WAS FINALLY SETTLED. PRETTY MUCH NO ONE TRIED TO APPROACH ME, AND IT WAS GREAT.
THE NEW TERM STARTED OFF SO HAPPILY.
2-1
BUT THEN, RIGHT AWAY, THE GUY SITTING IN FRONT OF ME GOT INVOLVED, AND NOW I'M NOT HAPPY AT ALL.
MATH B
YOU WERE IN A JUNJI ITO MANGA, WEREN'T YOU?
I SHOULD HAVE JUST IGNORED HIM.
......HUH...?
ME...?
BUT IT ALL HAPPENED SO SUDDENLY THAT I DIDN'T REALLY UNDERSTAND WHAT HE WAS SAYING, AND IN MY CONFUSION I RESPONDED.

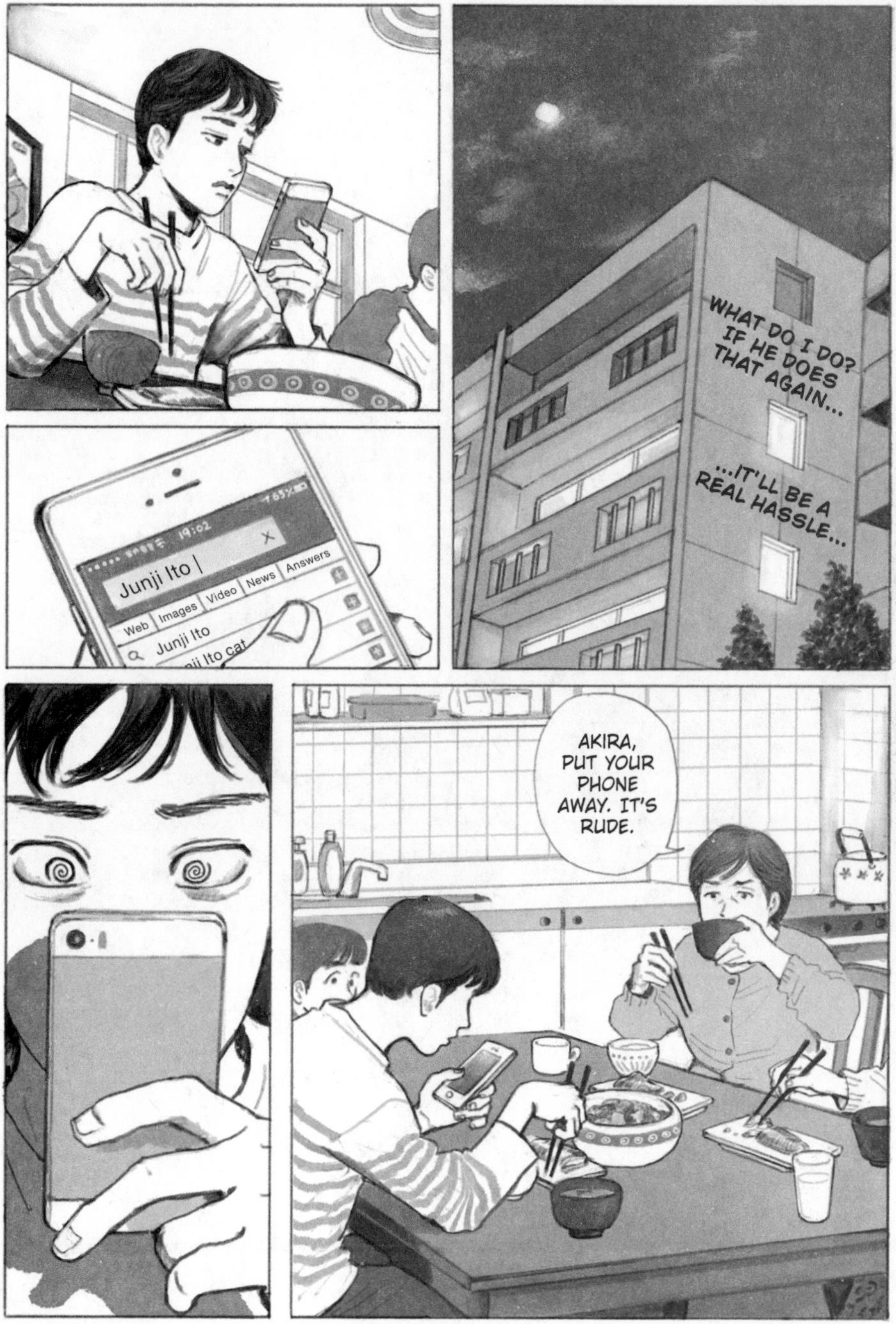
WHAT DO I DO? IF HE DOES THAT AGAIN...
...IT'LL BE A REAL HASSLE...
19:02
Junji Ito
Web
Images
Video
News
Answers
Junji Ito
AKIRA, PUT YOUR PHONE AWAY. IT'S RUDE.

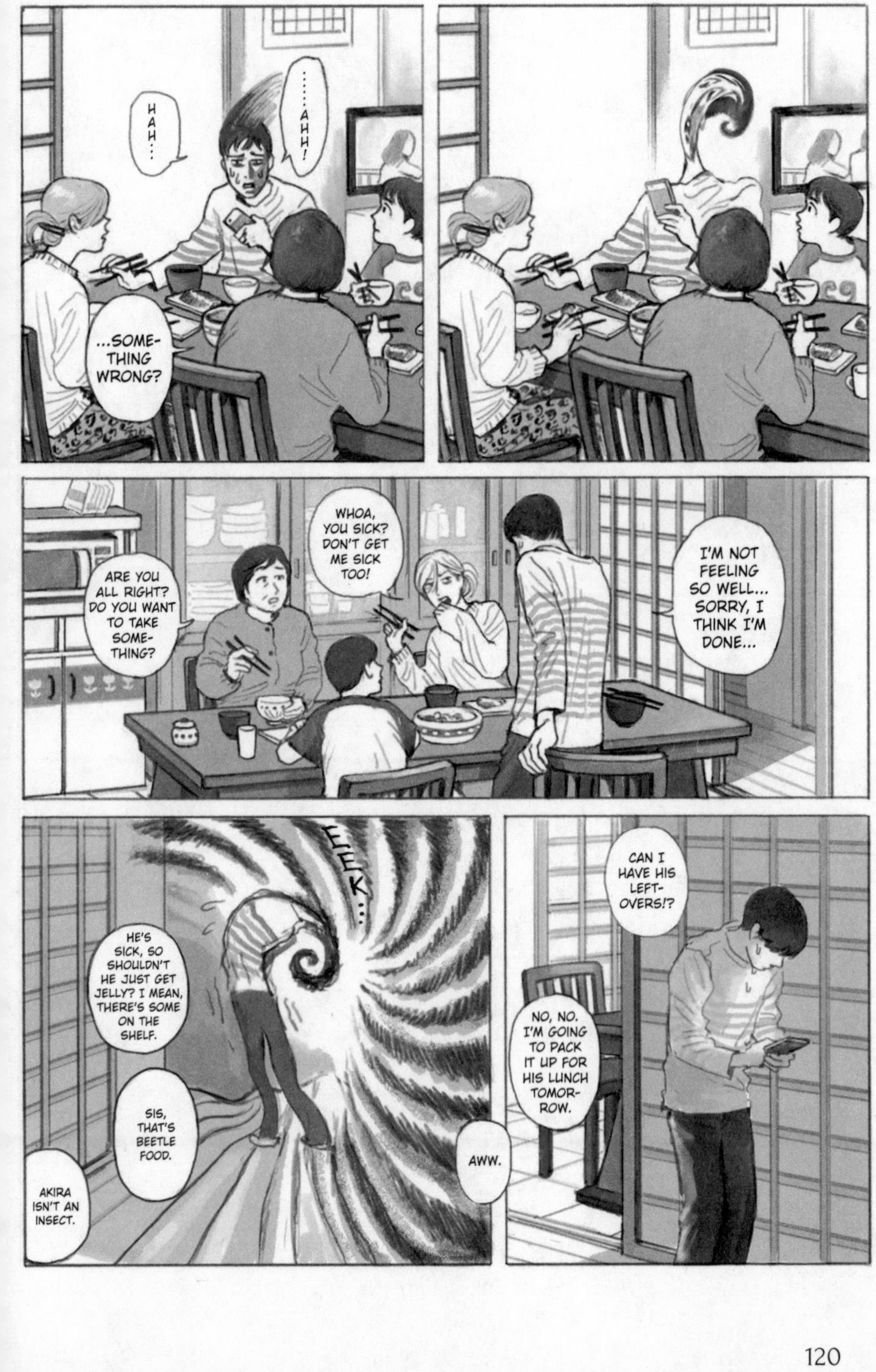
....AHH!
HAH...
...SOME-THING WRONG?
I'M NOT FEELING SO WELL... SORRY, I THINK I'M DONE...
WHOA, YOU SICK? DON'T GET ME SICK TOO!
ARE YOU ALL RIGHT? DO YOU WANT TO TAKE SOME-THING?
CAN I HAVE HIS LEFT-OVERS!?
NO, NO. I'M GOING TO PACK IT UP FOR HIS LUNCH TOMOR-ROW.
AWW.
EEEK...
HE'S SICK, SO SHOULDN'T HE JUST GET JELLY? I MEAN, THERE'S SOME ON THE SHELF.
SIS, THAT'S BEETLE FOOD.
AKIRA ISN'T AN INSECT.

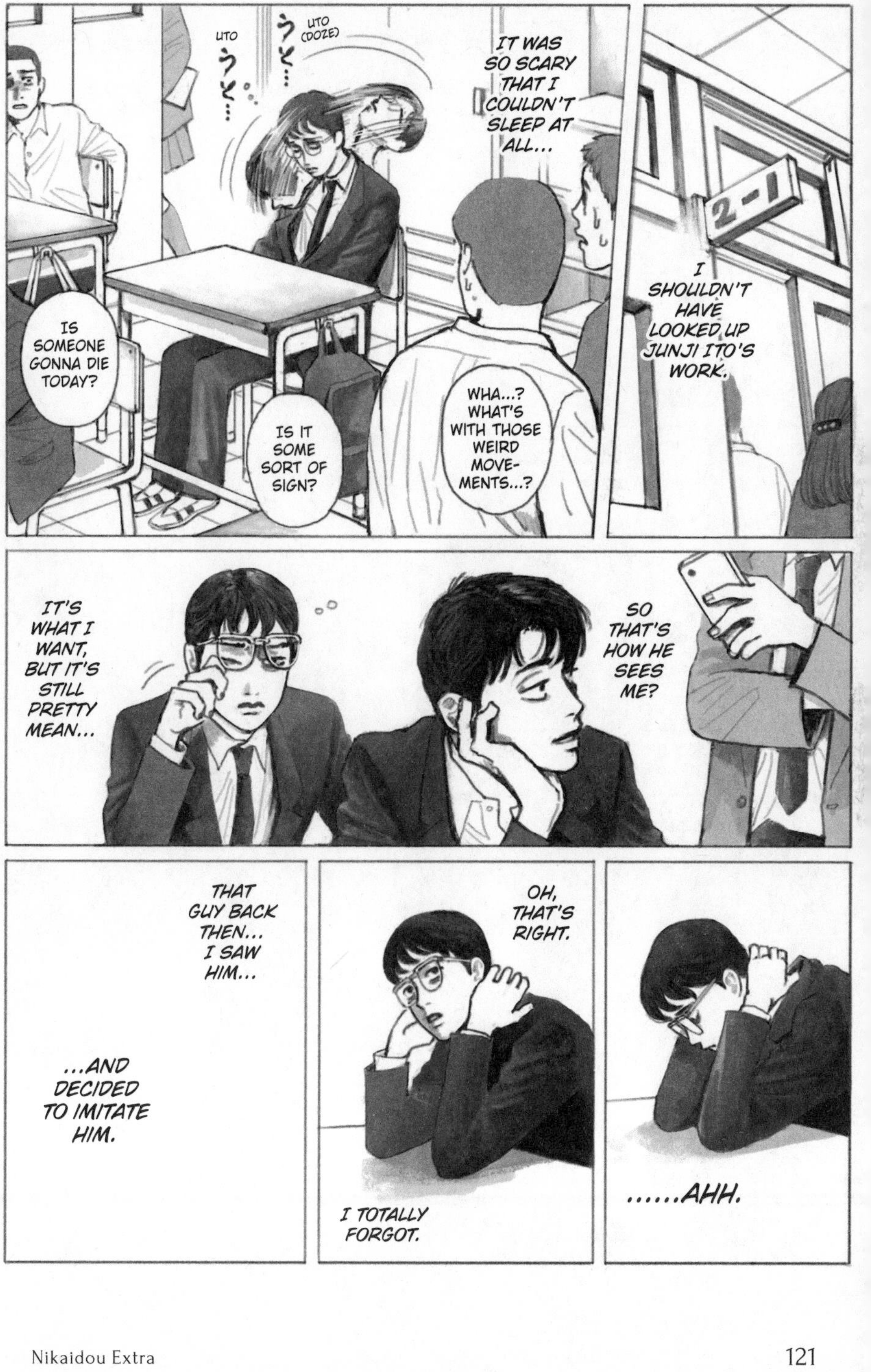
I SHOULDN'T HAVE LOOKED UP JUNJI ITO'S WORK.
IT WAS SO SCARY THAT I COULDN'T SLEEP AT ALL...
うと…
UTO (DOZE)
うと…
UTO
WHA...? WHAT'S WITH THOSE WEIRD MOVEMENTS...?
IS SOMEONE GONNA DIE TODAY?
IS IT SOME SORT OF SIGN?
2-1
SO THAT'S HOW HE SEES ME?
IT'S WHAT I WANT, BUT IT'S STILL PRETTY MEAN...
......AHH.
OH, THAT'S RIGHT.
I TOTALLY FORGOT.
THAT GUY BACK THEN... I SAW HIM...
...AND DECIDED TO IMITATE HIM.

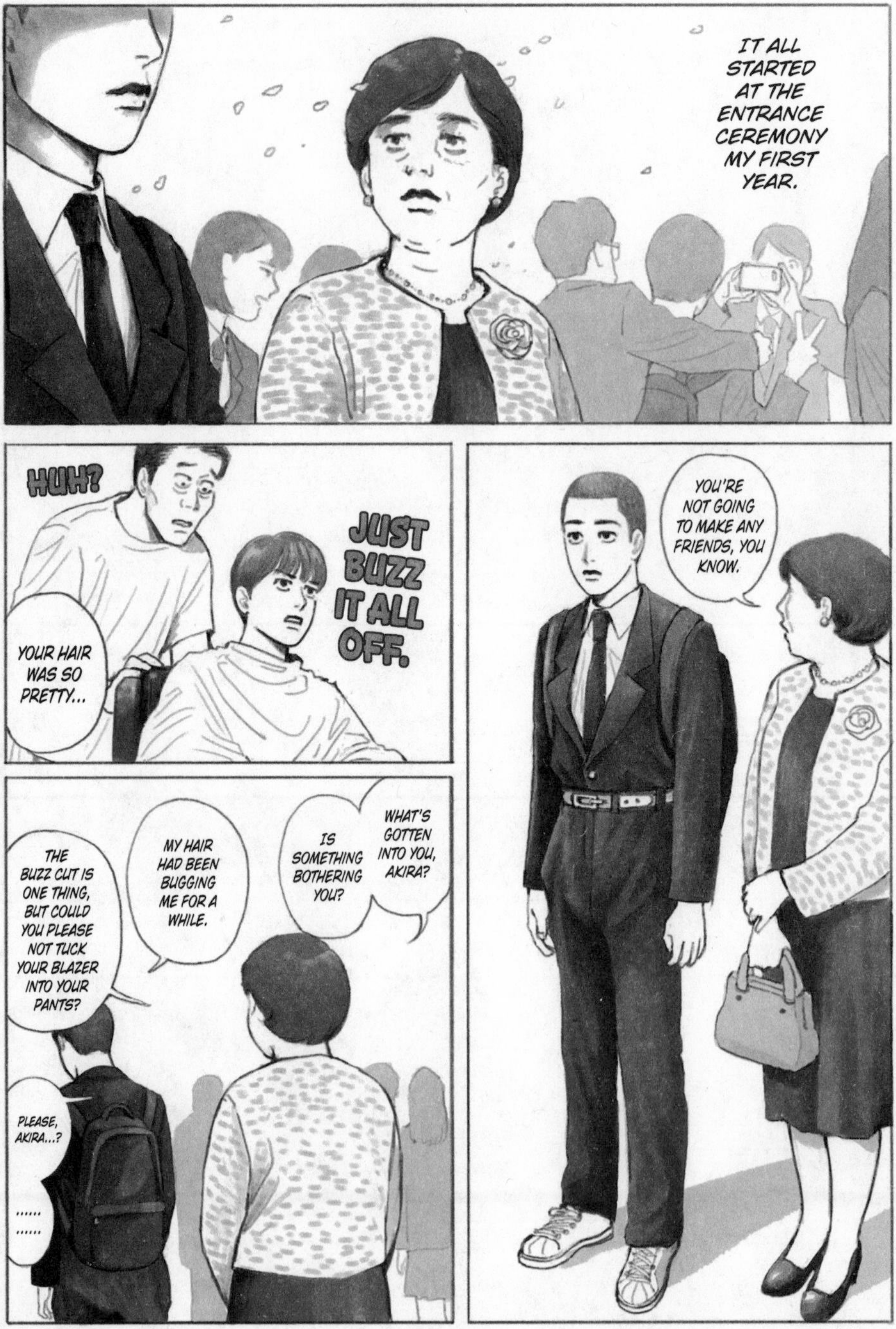
IT ALL STARTED AT THE ENTRANCE CEREMONY MY FIRST YEAR.
YOU'RE NOT GOING TO MAKE ANY FRIENDS, YOU KNOW.
JUST BUZZ IT ALL OFF.
HUH?
YOUR HAIR WAS SO PRETTY...
WHAT'S GOTTEN INTO YOU, AKIRA?
IS SOMETHING BOTHERING YOU?
MY HAIR HAD BEEN BUGGING ME FOR A WHILE.
THE BUZZ CUT IS ONE THING, BUT COULD YOU PLEASE NOT TUCK YOUR BLAZER INTO YOUR PANTS?
PLEASE, AKIRA...?
....

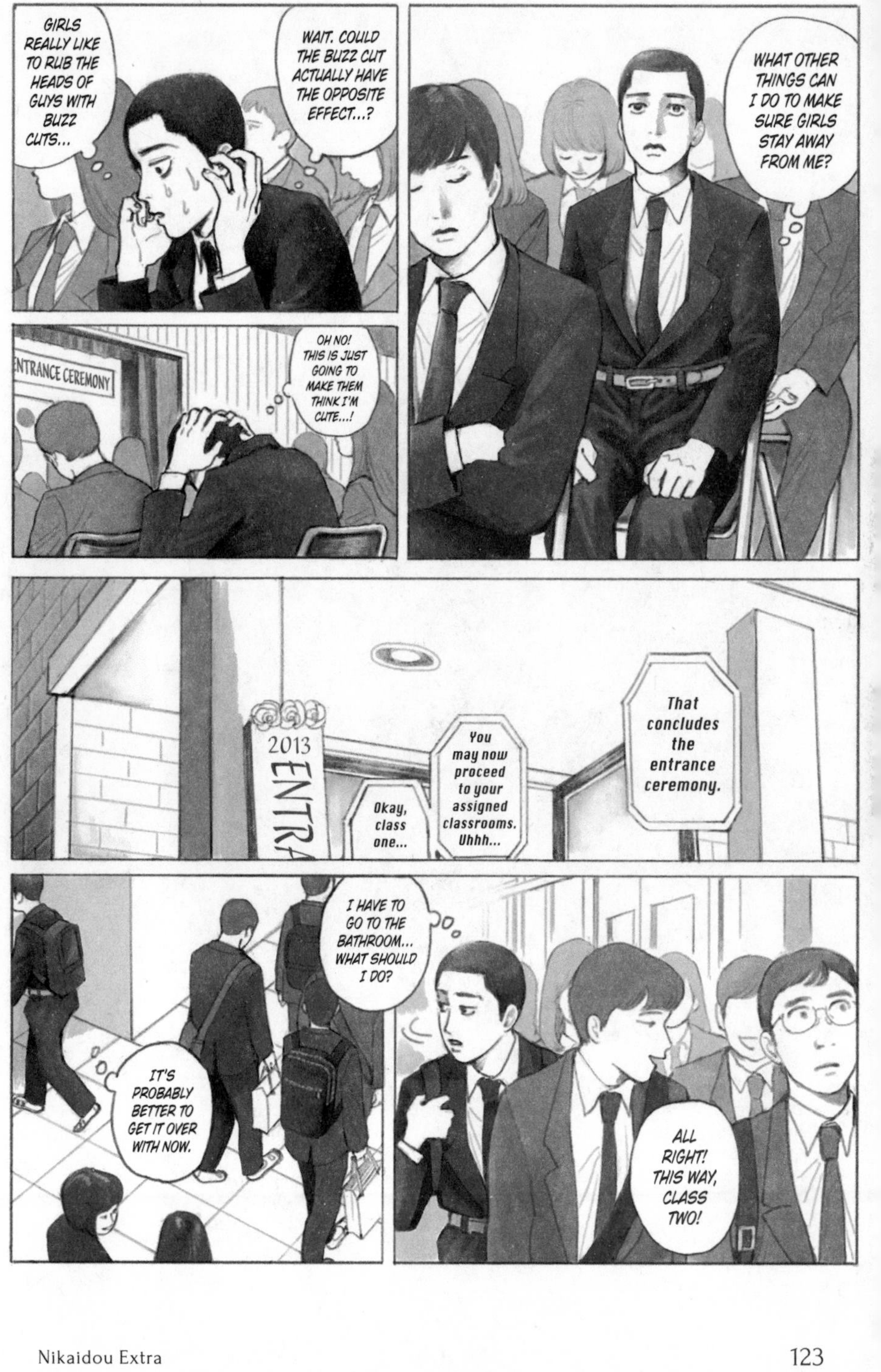
WHAT OTHER THINGS CAN I DO TO MAKE SURE GIRLS STAY AWAY FROM ME?
GIRLS REALLY LIKE TO RUB THE HEADS OF GUYS WITH BUZZ CUTS...
WAIT. COULD THE BUZZ CUT ACTUALLY HAVE THE OPPOSITE EFFECT...?
NTRANCE CEREMONY
OH NO! THIS IS JUST GOING TO MAKE THEM THINK I'M CUTE...!
That concludes the entrance ceremony.
You may now proceed to your assigned classrooms. Uhhh...
Okay, class one...
2013
ENTR
I HAVE TO GO TO THE BATHROOM... WHAT SHOULD I DO?
ALL RIGHT! THIS WAY, CLASS TWO!
IT'S PROBABLY BETTER TO GET IT OVER WITH NOW.

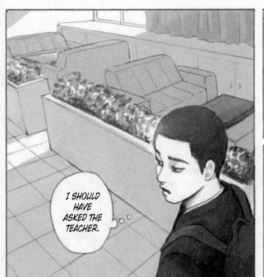

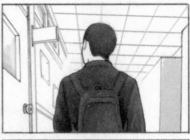

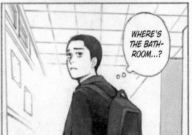

WHERE'S THE BATH-ROOM...?
I SHOULD HAVE ASKED THE TEACHER.
BATAN (SHUT)
バタン
ビクッ
BIKU (FLINCH)
HFF!
HAFF...
HAAH...

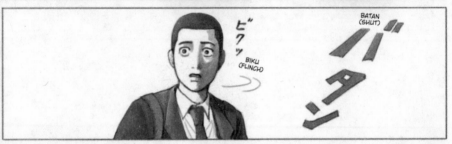

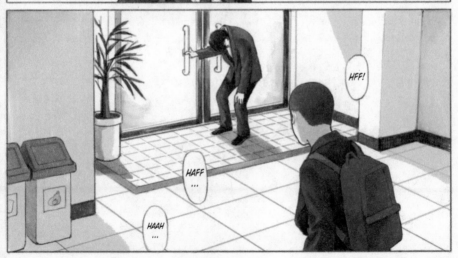

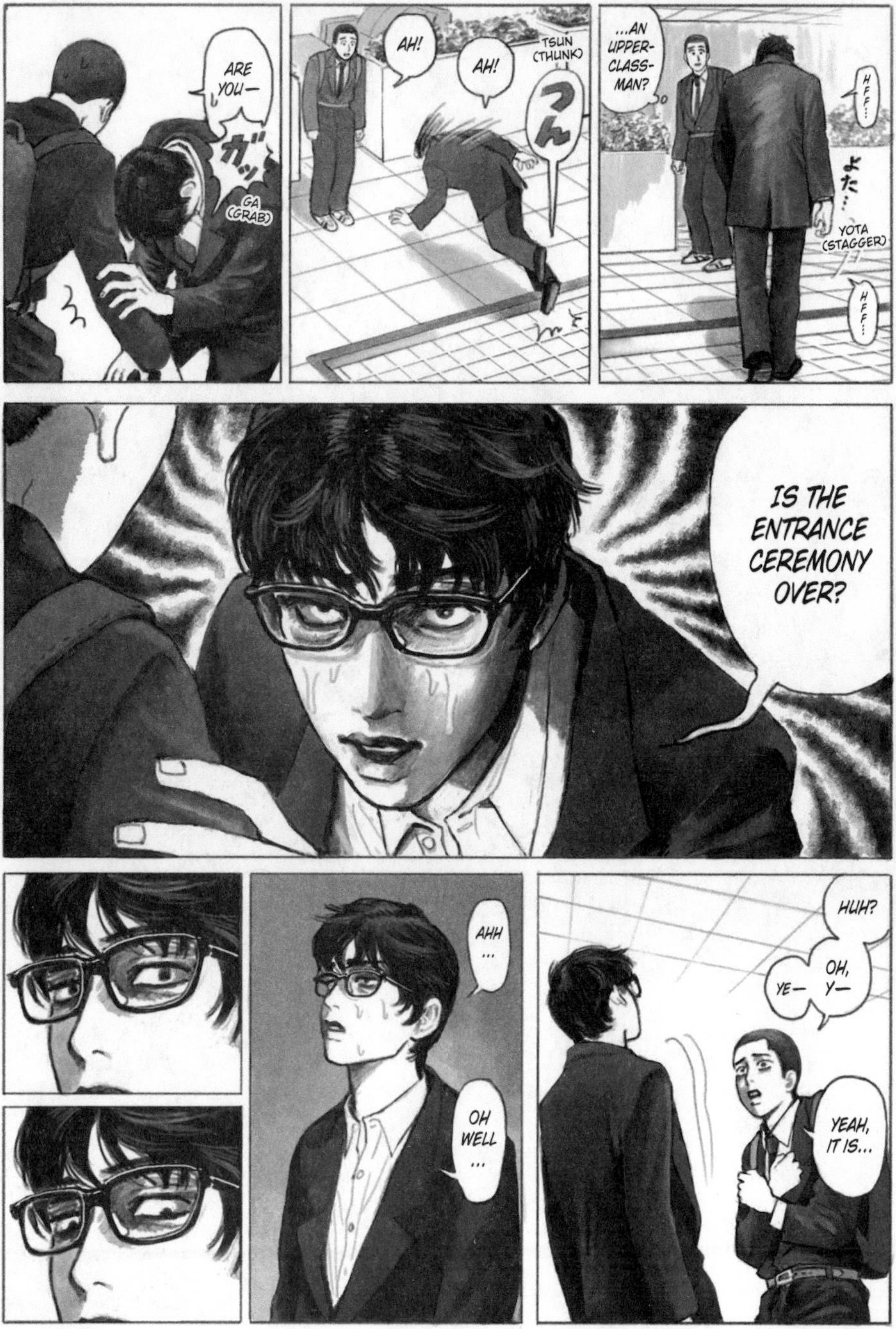
...AN UPPER-CLASSMAN?
HFF...
よた…
YOTA (STAGGER)
HFF...
AH!
AH!
TSUN (THUNK)
つん
ARE YOU—
ガッ
GA (GRAB)
IS THE ENTRANCE CEREMONY OVER?
HUH?
OH, Y—
YE—
YEAH, IT IS...
AHH ...
OH WELL ...

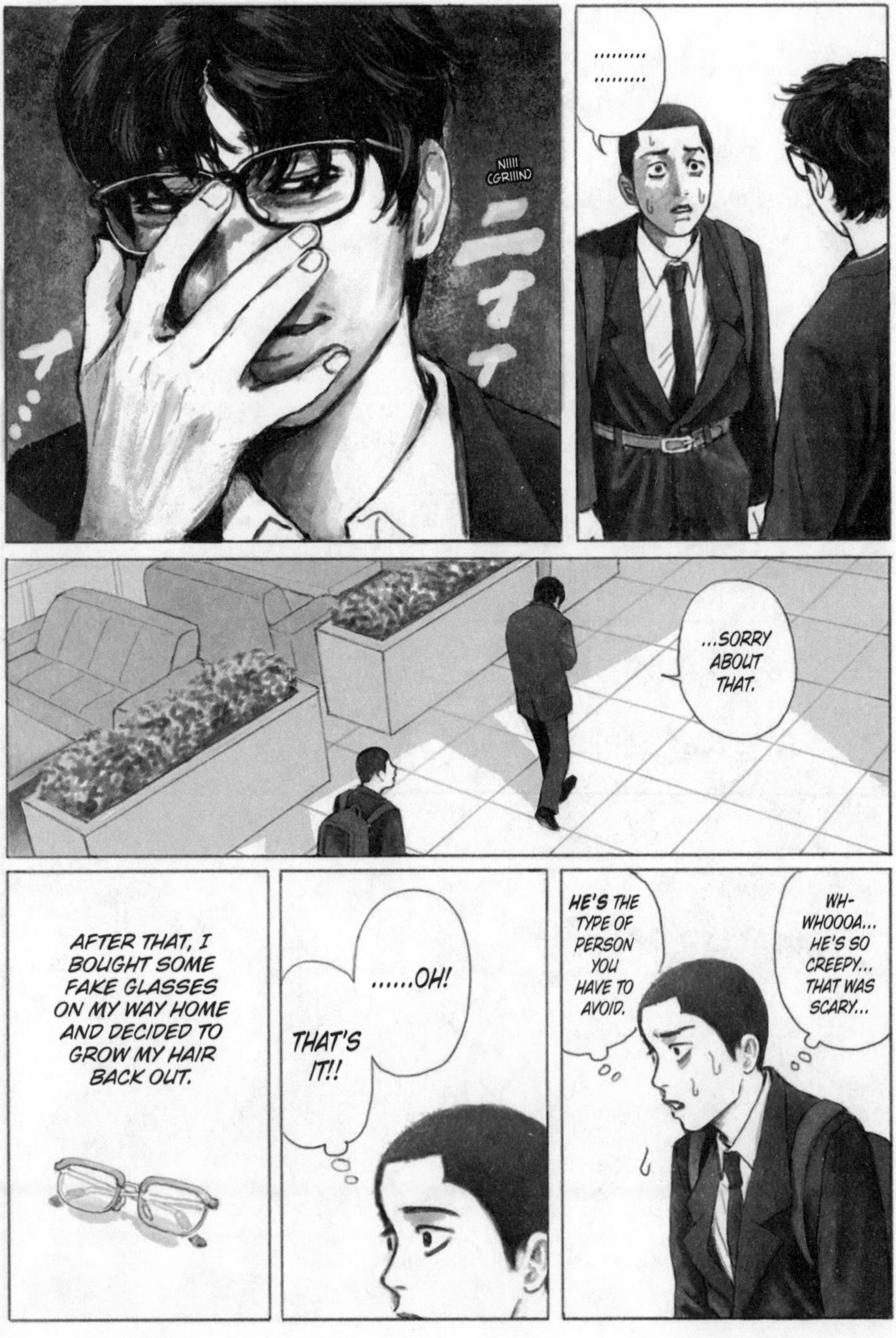
....
....
NIIII (GRIIIN)
...SORRY ABOUT THAT.
WH-WHOOOA... HE'S SO CREEPY... THAT WAS SCARY...
HE'S THE TYPE OF PERSON YOU HAVE TO AVOID.
......OH!
THAT'S IT!!
AFTER THAT, I BOUGHT SOME FAKE GLASSES ON MY WAY HOME AND DECIDED TO GROW MY HAIR BACK OUT.

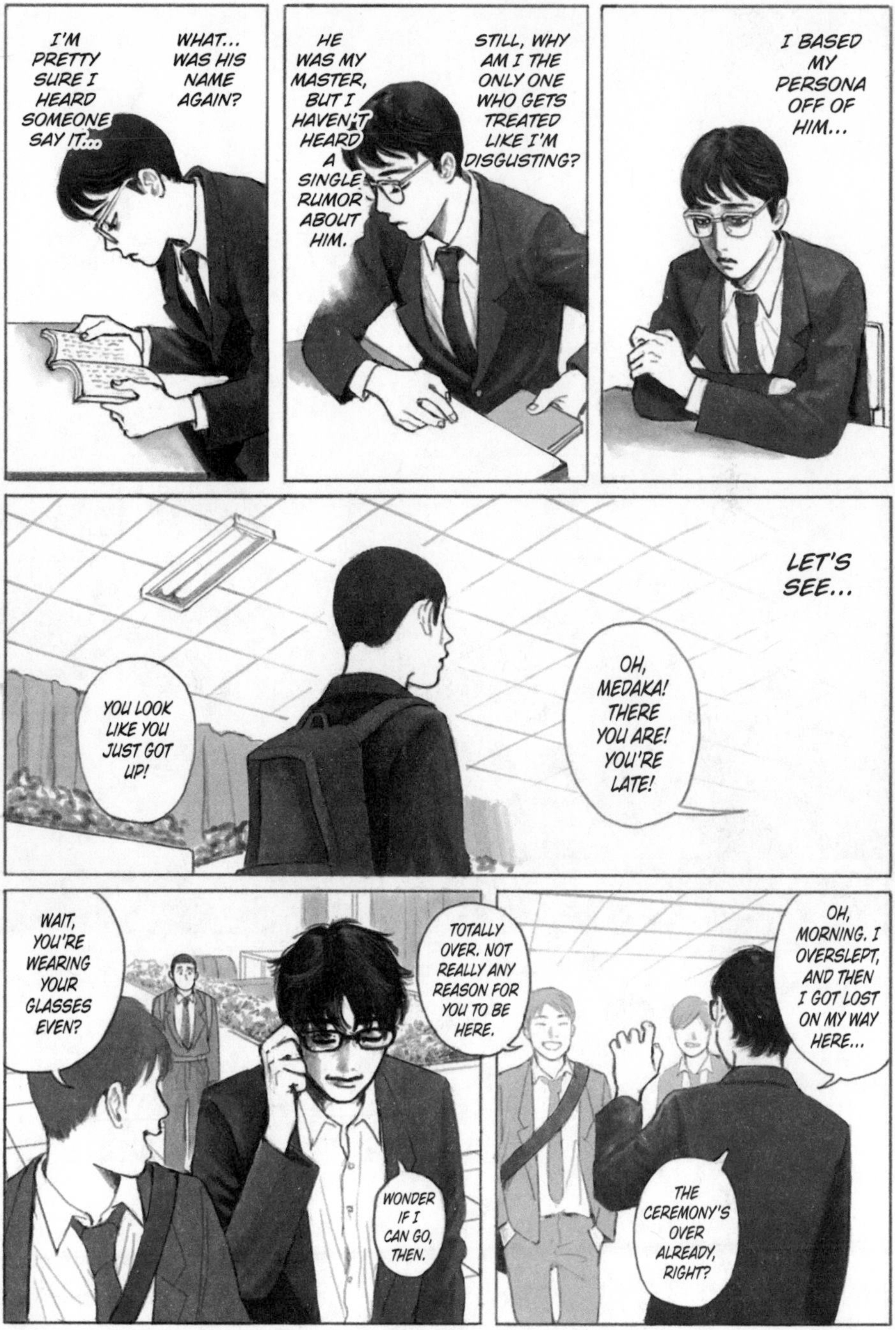
I BASED MY PERSONA OFF OF HIM...
STILL, WHY AM I THE ONLY ONE WHO GETS TREATED LIKE I'M DISGUSTING?
HE WAS MY MASTER, BUT I HAVEN'T HEARD A SINGLE RUMOR ABOUT HIM.
WHAT... WAS HIS NAME AGAIN?
I'M PRETTY SURE I HEARD SOMEONE SAY IT...
LET'S SEE...
OH, MEDAKA! THERE YOU ARE! YOU'RE LATE!
YOU LOOK LIKE YOU JUST GOT UP!
OH, MORNING. I OVERSLEPT, AND THEN I GOT LOST ON MY WAY HERE...
THE CEREMONY'S OVER ALREADY, RIGHT?
TOTALLY OVER. NOT REALLY ANY REASON FOR YOU TO BE HERE.
WAIT, YOU'RE WEARING YOUR GLASSES EVEN?
WONDER IF I CAN GO, THEN.

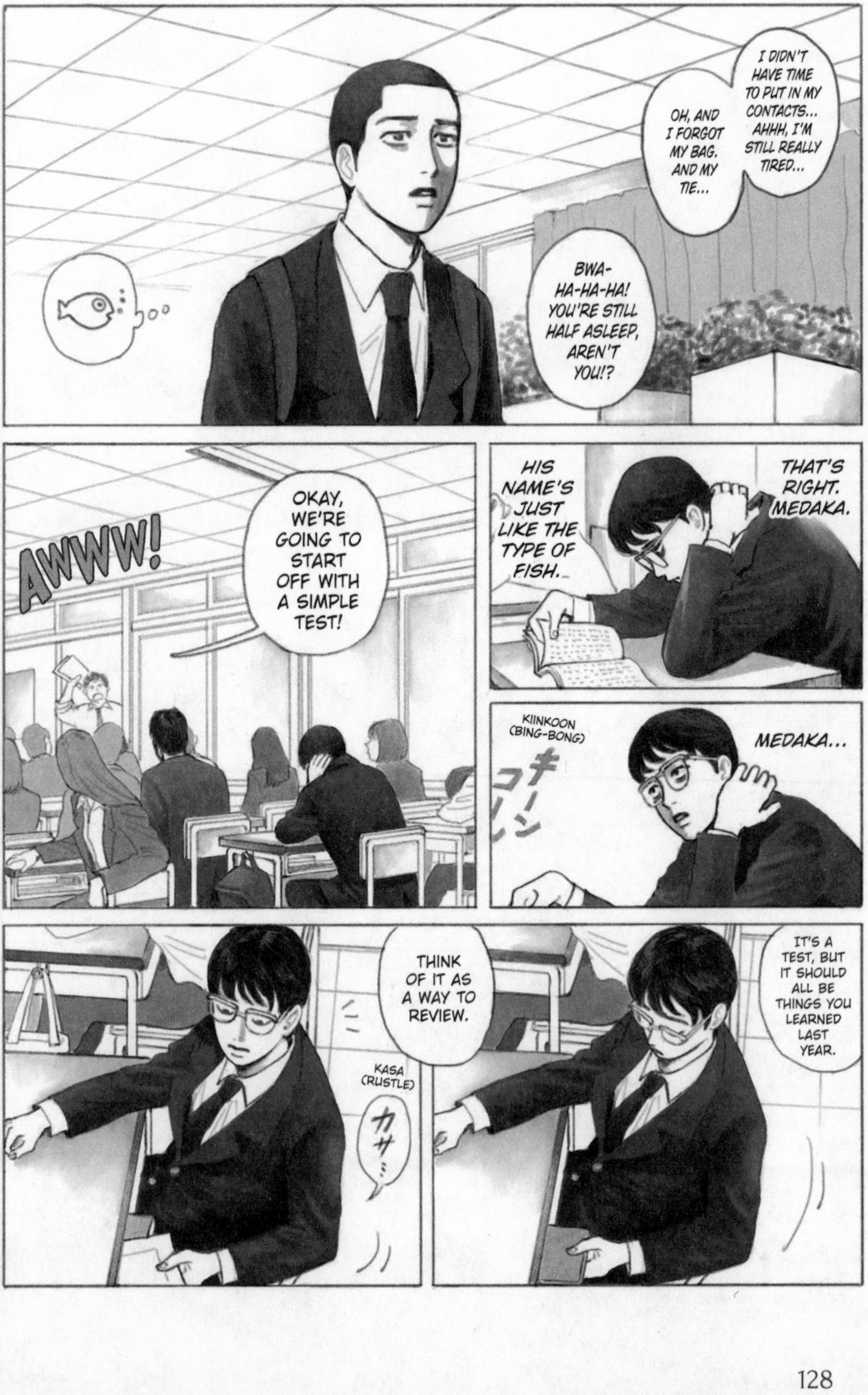
I DIDN'T HAVE TIME TO PUT IN MY CONTACTS... AHHH, I'M STILL REALLY TIRED...
OH, AND I FORGOT MY BAG. AND MY TIE...
BWA-HA-HA-HA! YOU'RE STILL HALF ASLEEP, AREN'T YOU!?
THAT'S RIGHT. MEDAKA.
HIS NAME'S JUST LIKE THE TYPE OF FISH.
MEDAKA...
KIINKOON (BING-BONG)
キーンコーン
OKAY, WE'RE GOING TO START OFF WITH A SIMPLE TEST!
AWWW!
IT'S A TEST, BUT IT SHOULD ALL BE THINGS YOU LEARNED LAST YEAR.
THINK OF IT AS A WAY TO REVIEW.
KASA (RUSTLE)
カサ…

OH!

....

....
....

Computer Lab	Fujiwa...
3F Girls' Bathroom	Suzuki, Sanae Okamoto, Mak...
3F Boys' Bathroom	**Medaka, Yuuic...** **Nikaidou, Akir...**
...rary	Akimoto, Nats... Yoshida, Teruy... Hashimoto, Sh...

!

PIRI
(SLICE)

SHA
(YANK)

....
....
....

...HM?

...MEDA
....

YUUICHI
MEDAKA...

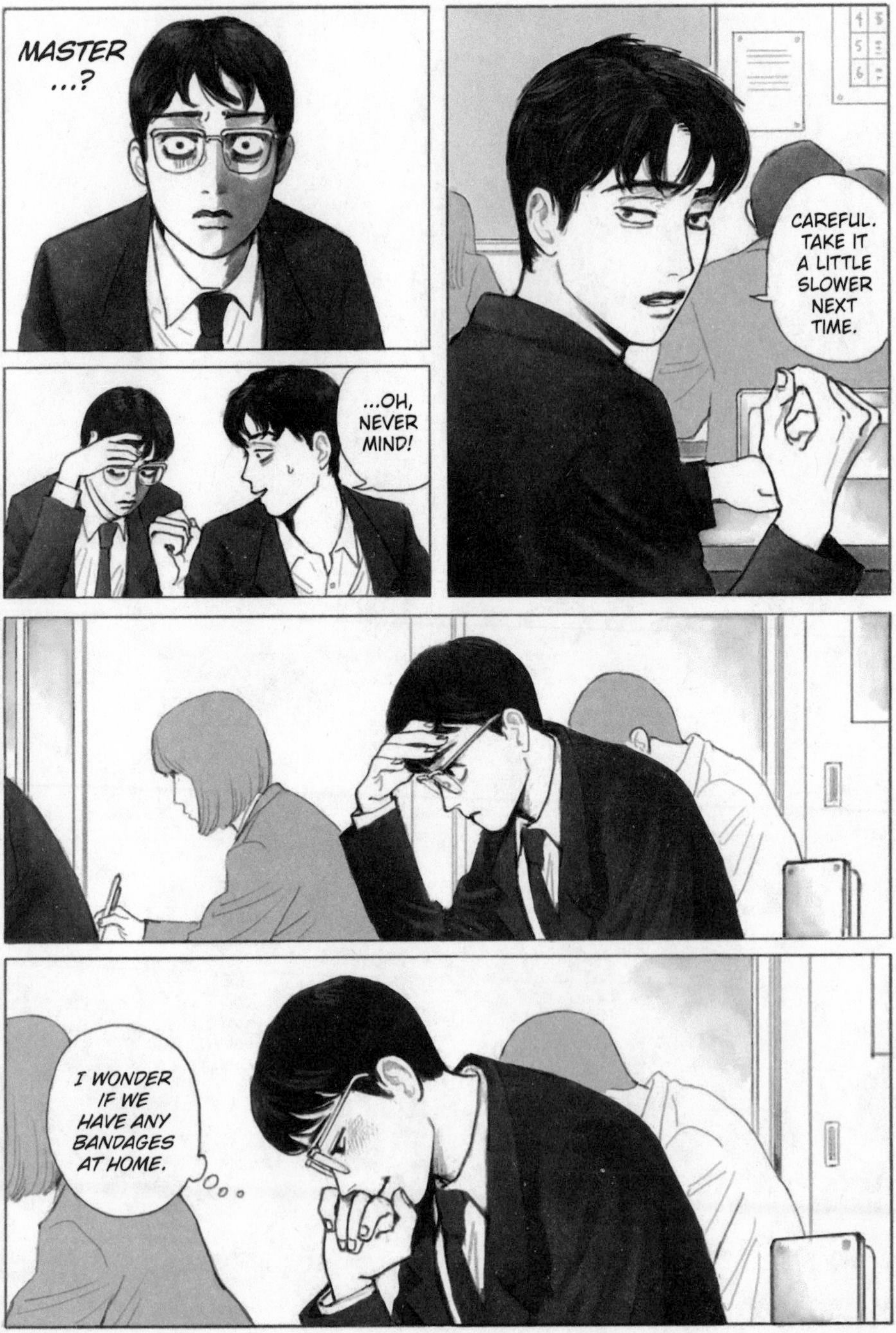
CAREFUL. TAKE IT A LITTLE SLOWER NEXT TIME.
MASTER ...?
...OH, NEVER MIND!
I WONDER IF WE HAVE ANY BANDAGES AT HOME.

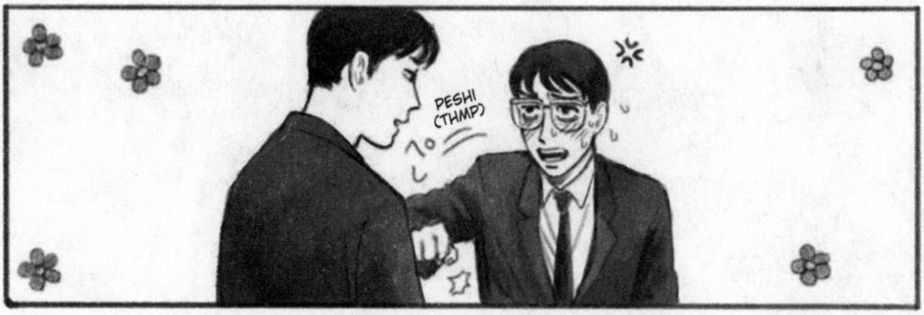
PESHI
(THMP)

[Nikaidou Behind Me: Angry Class Ver.]

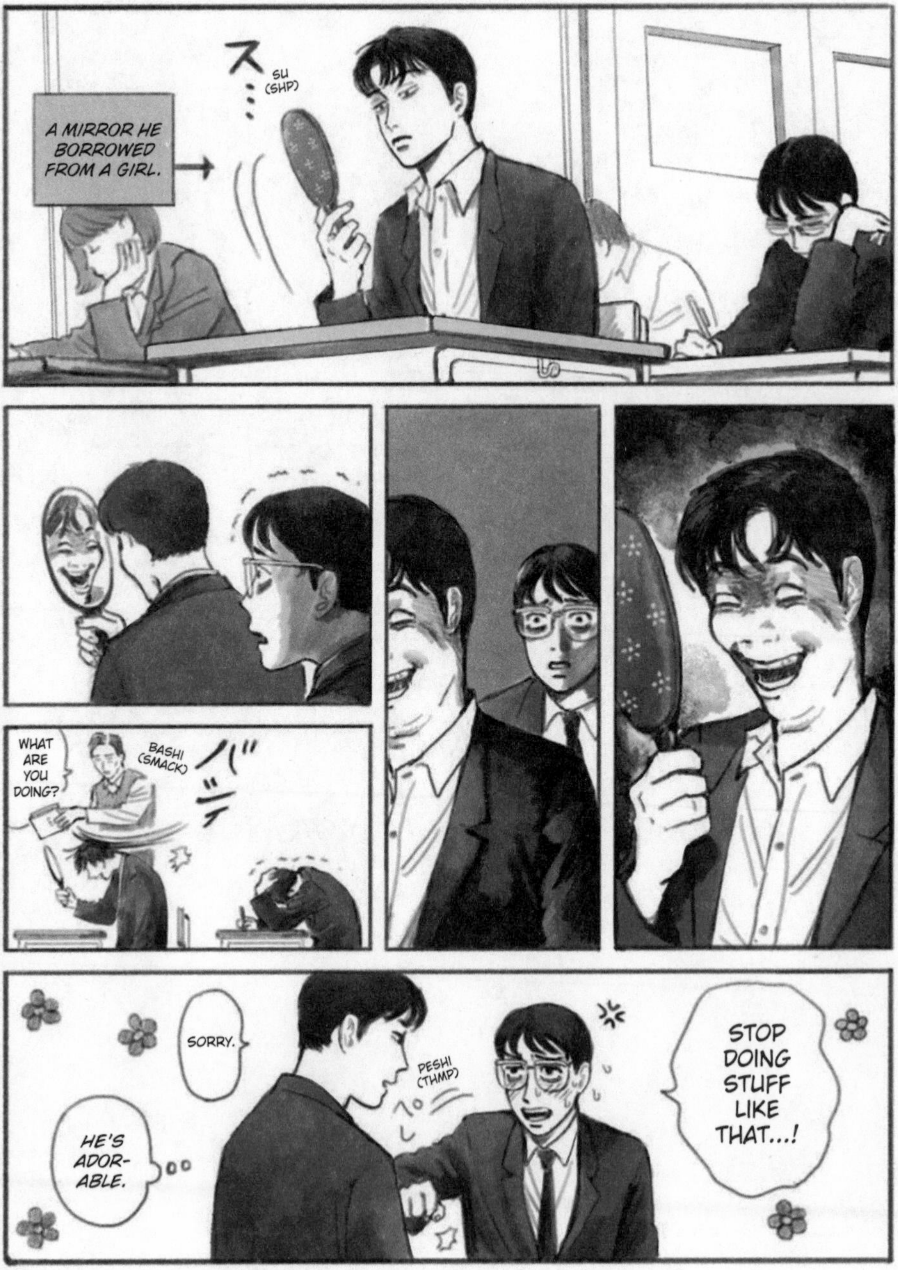
ス
SU (SHP)
A MIRROR HE BORROWED FROM A GIRL.
バシ
BASHI (SMACK)
WHAT ARE YOU DOING?
STOP DOING STUFF LIKE THAT...!
ぺし
PESHI (THMP)
SORRY.
HE'S ADORABLE.

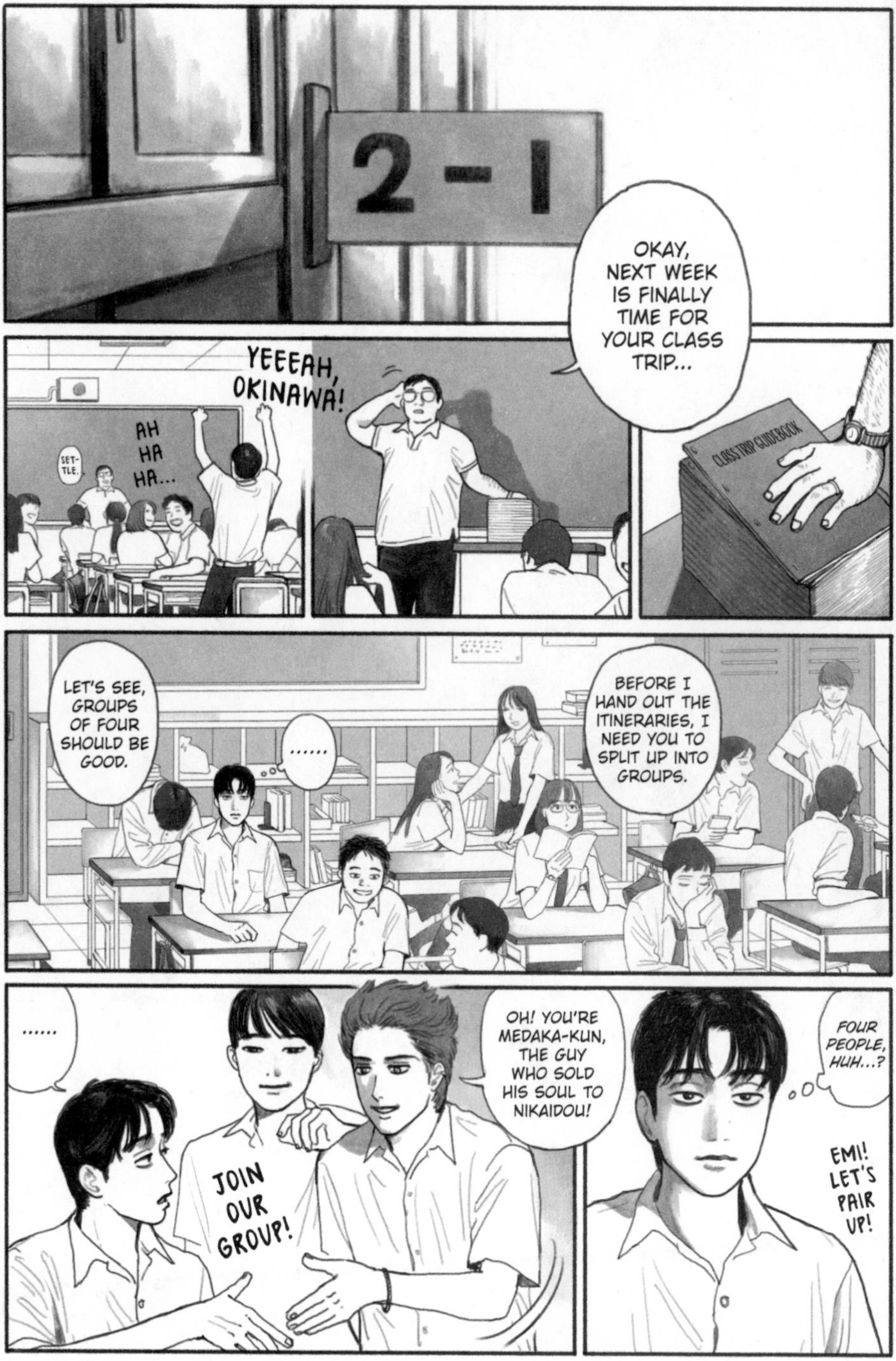

2-1
OKAY, NEXT WEEK IS FINALLY TIME FOR YOUR CLASS TRIP...
CLASS TRIP GUIDEBOOK
YEEEAH, OKINAWA!
AH HA HA...
SET-TLE.
BEFORE I HAND OUT THE ITINERARIES, I NEED YOU TO SPLIT UP INTO GROUPS.
......
LET'S SEE, GROUPS OF FOUR SHOULD BE GOOD.
FOUR PEOPLE, HUH...?
EMI! LET'S PAIR UP!
OH! YOU'RE MEDAKA-KUN, THE GUY WHO SOLD HIS SOUL TO NIKAIDOU!
JOIN OUR GROUP!
......

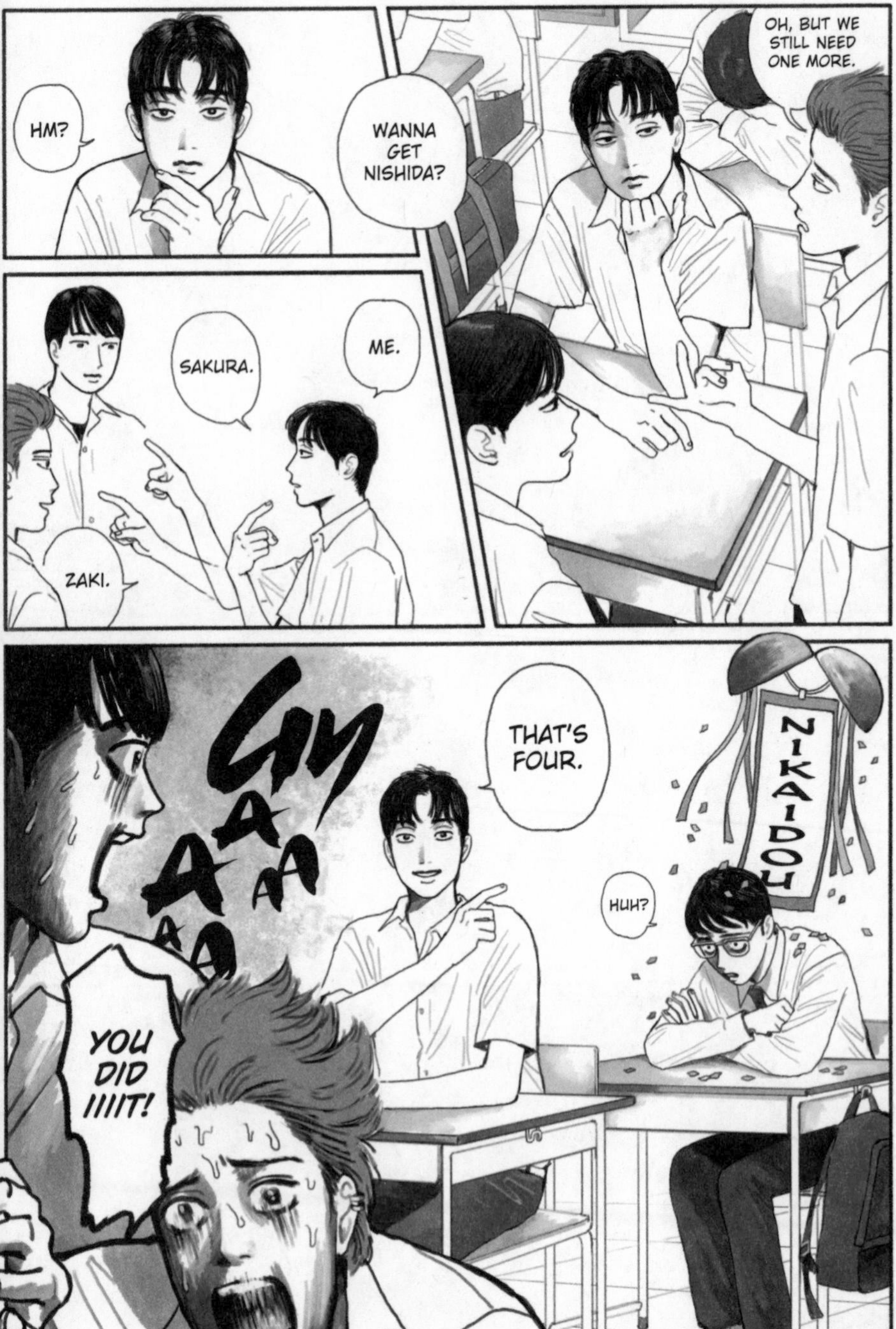
OH, BUT WE STILL NEED ONE MORE.
WANNA GET NISHIDA?
HM?
ME.
SAKURA.
ZAKI.
THAT'S FOUR.
NIKAIDOU
HUH?
GYAAAAAA
YOU DID IIIIT!

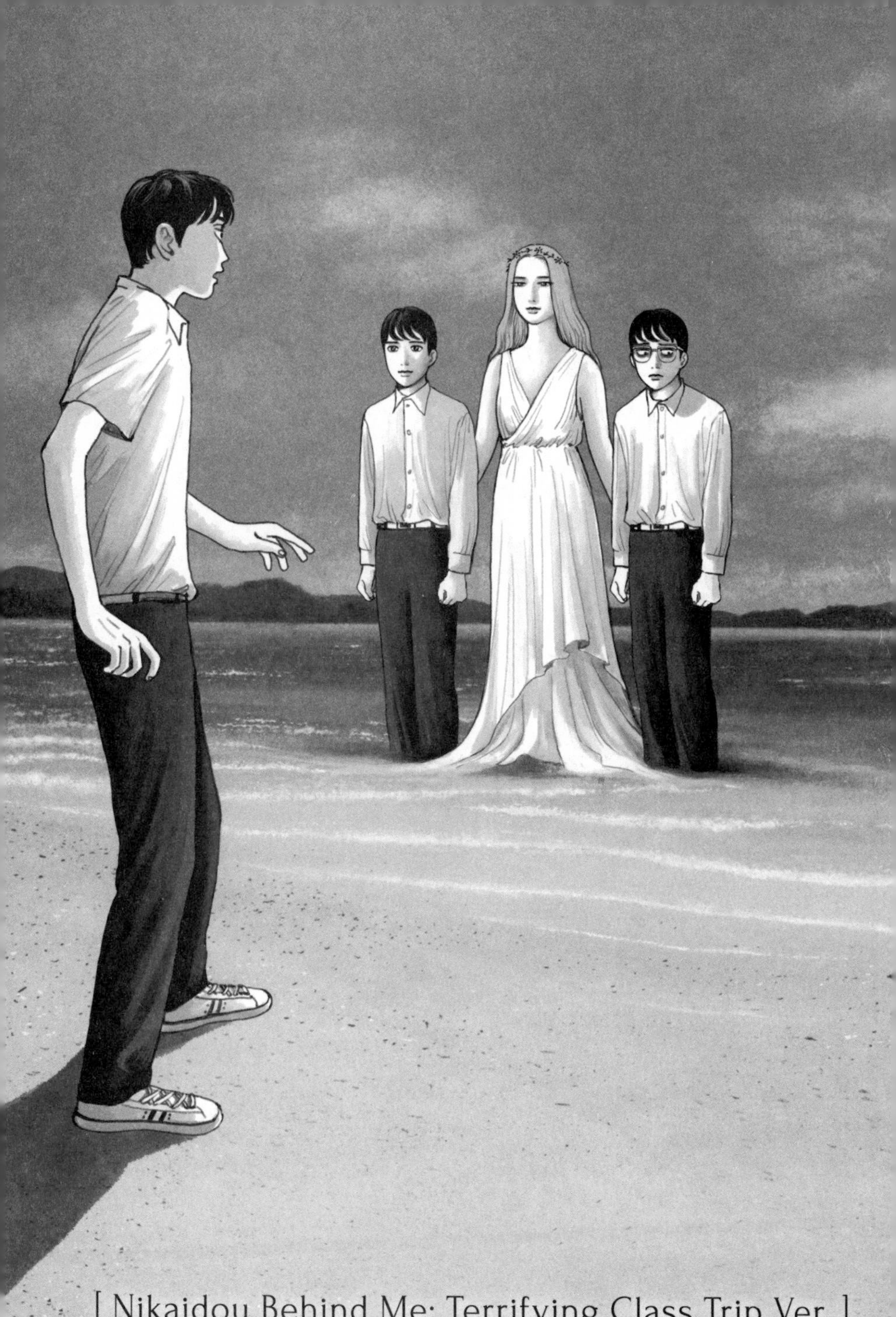

[Nikaidou Behind Me: Terrifying Class Trip Ver.]

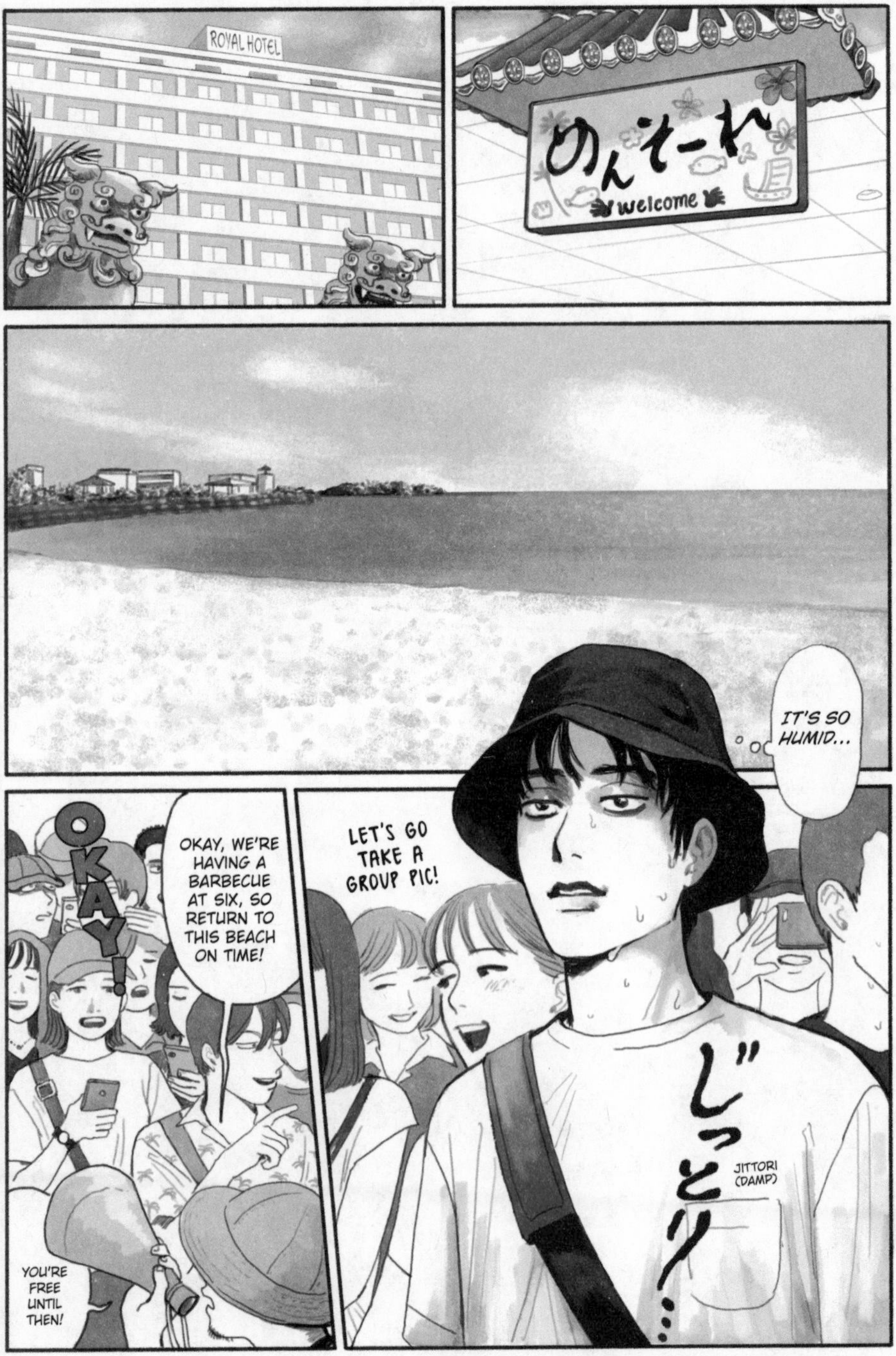
めんそーれ
welcome
ROYAL HOTEL
IT'S SO HUMID...
LET'S GO TAKE A GROUP PIC!
じっとり…
JITTORI (DAMP)
OKAY, WE'RE HAVING A BARBECUE AT SIX, SO RETURN TO THIS BEACH ON TIME!
OKAY!
YOU'RE FREE UNTIL THEN!

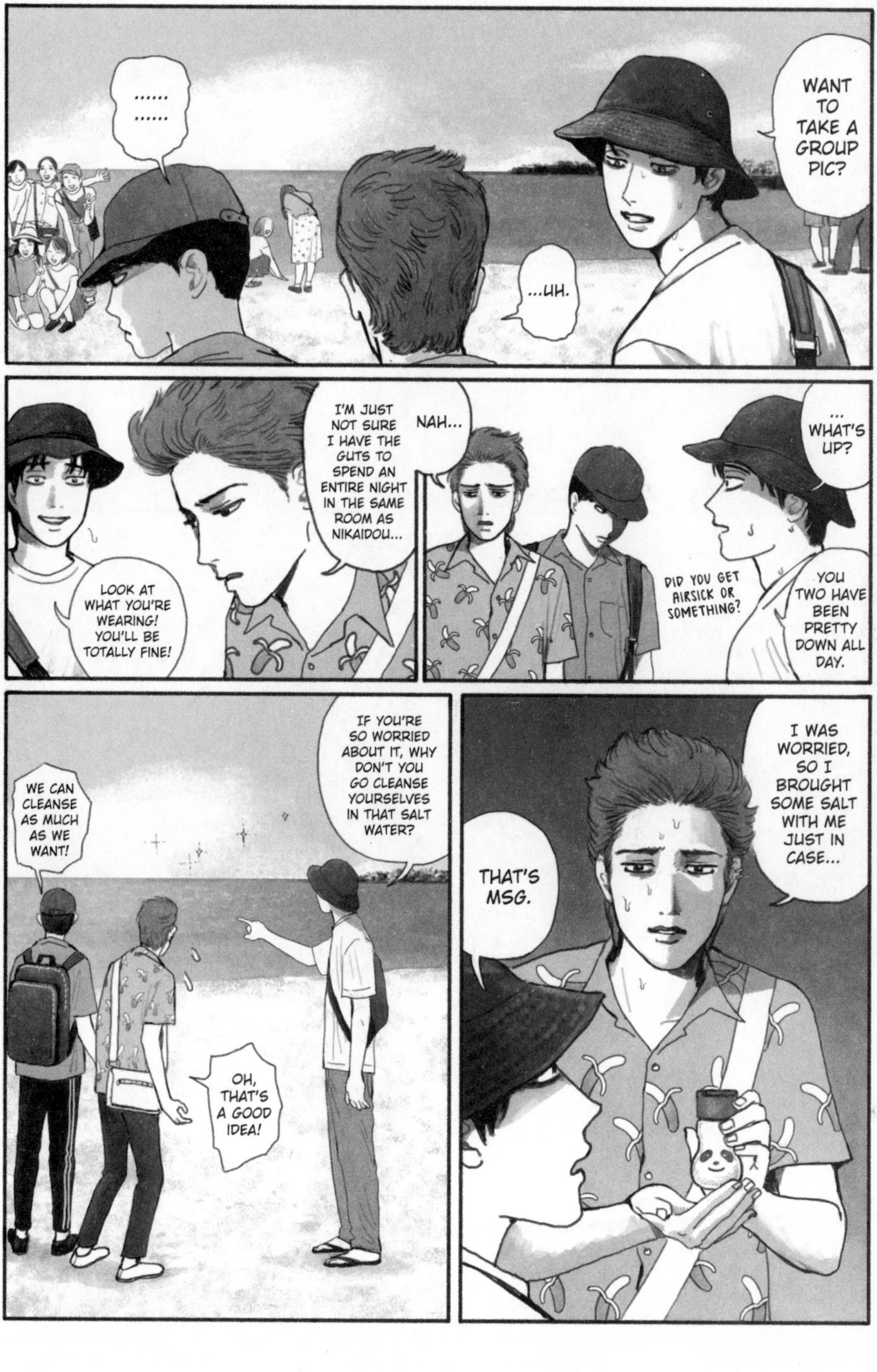
WANT TO TAKE A GROUP PIC?
...UH.
....
... WHAT'S UP?
YOU TWO HAVE BEEN PRETTY DOWN ALL DAY.
DID YOU GET AIRSICK OR SOMETHING?
NAH...
I'M JUST NOT SURE I HAVE THE GUTS TO SPEND AN ENTIRE NIGHT IN THE SAME ROOM AS NIKAIDOU...
LOOK AT WHAT YOU'RE WEARING! YOU'LL BE TOTALLY FINE!
I WAS WORRIED, SO I BROUGHT SOME SALT WITH ME JUST IN CASE...
THAT'S MSG.
IF YOU'RE SO WORRIED ABOUT IT, WHY DON'T YOU GO CLEANSE YOURSELVES IN THAT SALT WATER?
WE CAN CLEANSE AS MUCH AS WE WANT!
OH, THAT'S A GOOD IDEA!

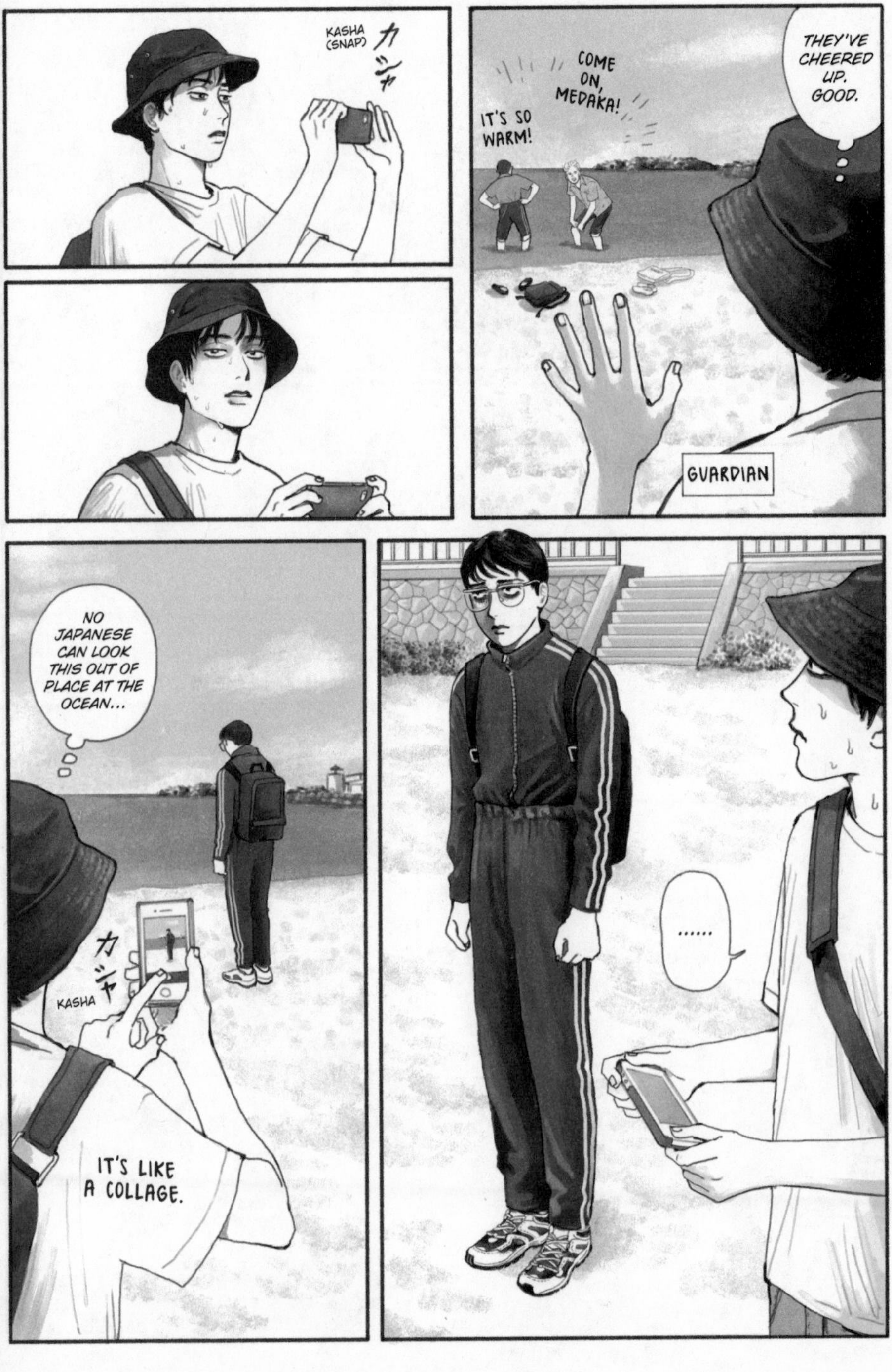
THEY'VE CHEERED UP. GOOD.
COME ON, MEDAKA!
IT'S SO WARM!
GUARDIAN
カシャ
KASHA (SNAP)
......
NO JAPANESE CAN LOOK THIS OUT OF PLACE AT THE OCEAN...
カシャ
KASHA
IT'S LIKE A COLLAGE.

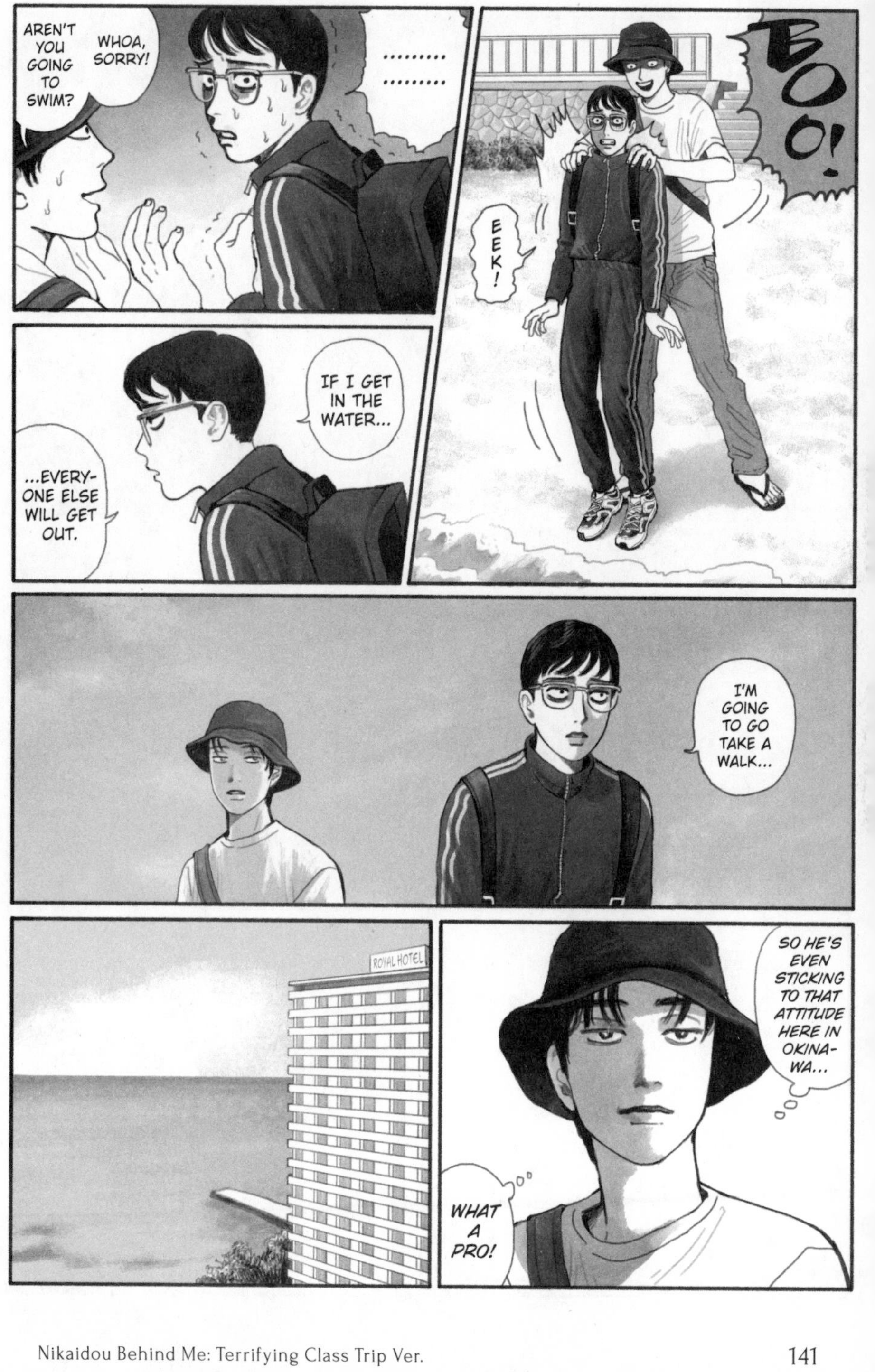
BOO!
EEK!
....
....
WHOA, SORRY!
AREN'T YOU GOING TO SWIM?
IF I GET IN THE WATER...
...EVERYONE ELSE WILL GET OUT.
I'M GOING TO GO TAKE A WALK...
SO HE'S EVEN STICKING TO THAT ATTITUDE HERE IN OKINAWA...
WHAT A PRO!
ROYAL HOTEL

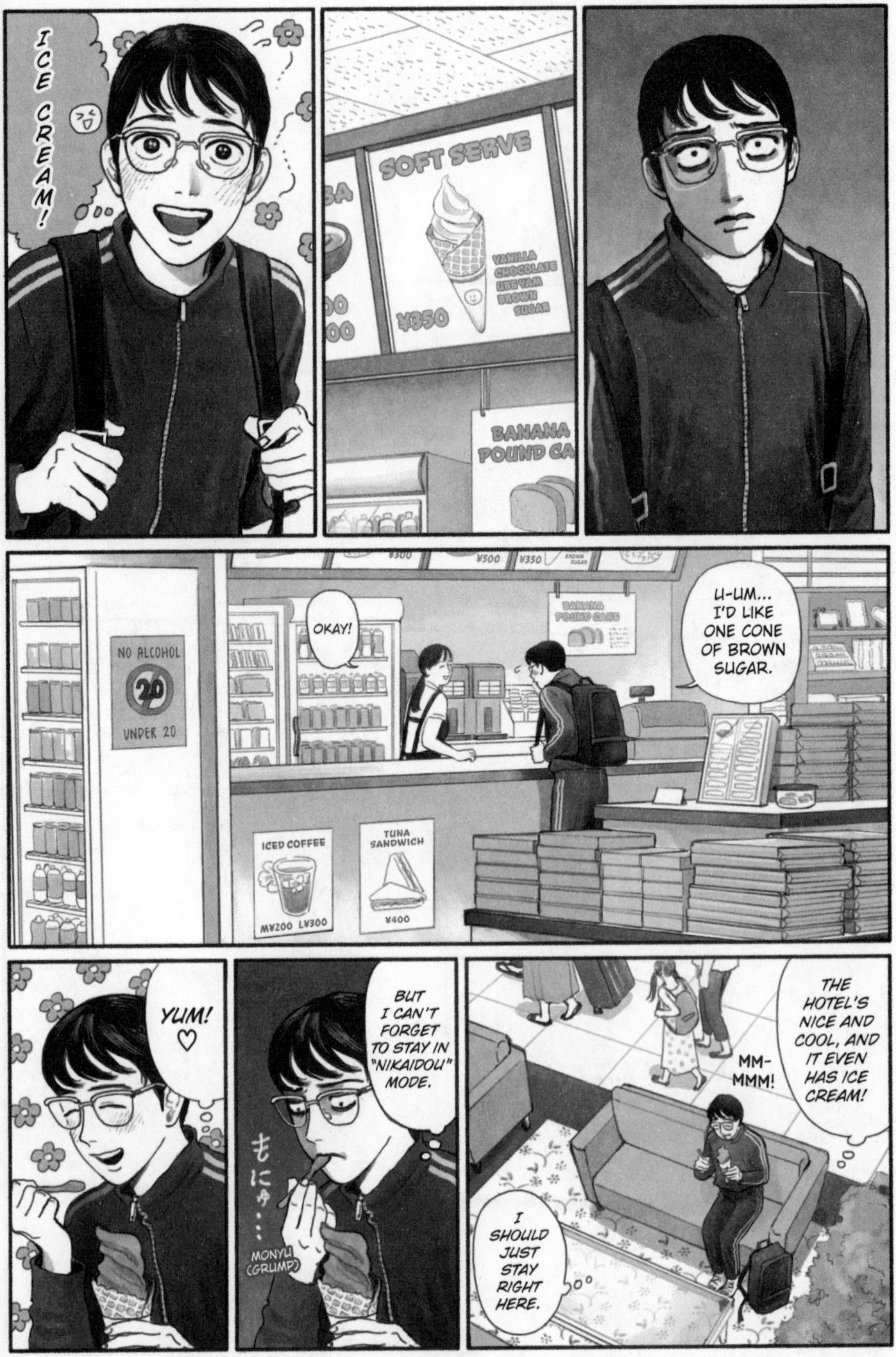
SOFT SERVE
VANILLA CHOCOLATE UBE YAM BROWN SUGAR
¥350
BANANA POUND CA
ICE CREAM!
U-UM... I'D LIKE ONE CONE OF BROWN SUGAR.
OKAY!
BANANA POUND CAKE
NO ALCOHOL 20 UNDER 20
ICED COFFEE M¥200 L¥300
TUNA SANDWICH ¥400
THE HOTEL'S NICE AND COOL, AND IT EVEN HAS ICE CREAM!
MM-MMM!
I SHOULD JUST STAY RIGHT HERE.
BUT I CAN'T FORGET TO STAY IN "NIKAIDOU" MODE.
もにゅ…
MONYU (GRUMP)
YUM! ♡

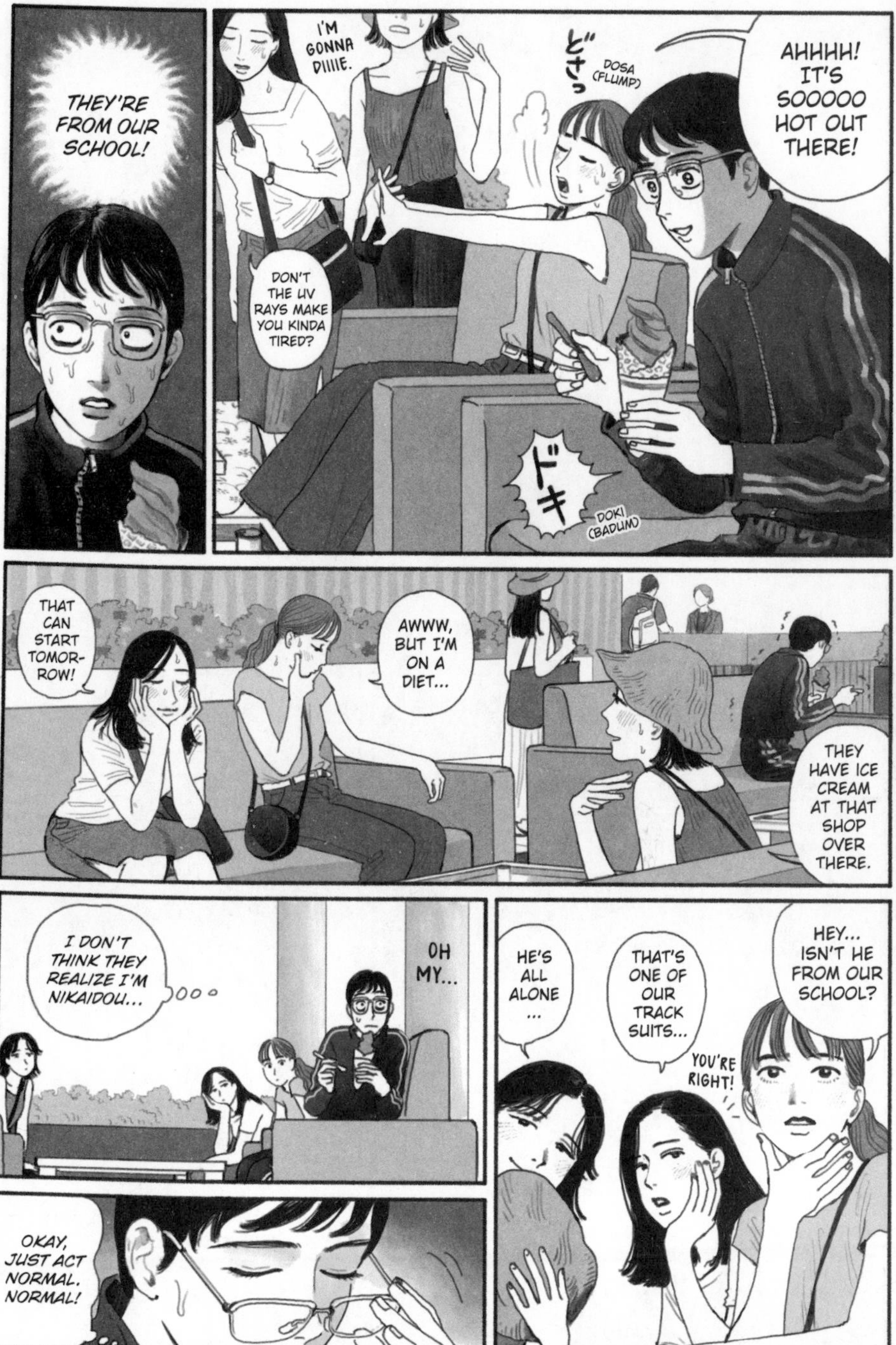
AHHHH! IT'S SOOOOO HOT OUT THERE!
どさっ
DOSA (FLUMP)
I'M GONNA DIIIIE.
DON'T THE UV RAYS MAKE YOU KINDA TIRED?
ドキ
DOKI (BADUM)
THEY'RE FROM OUR SCHOOL!
THEY HAVE ICE CREAM AT THAT SHOP OVER THERE.
AWWW, BUT I'M ON A DIET...
THAT CAN START TOMORROW!
HEY... ISN'T HE FROM OUR SCHOOL?
THAT'S ONE OF OUR TRACK SUITS...
YOU'RE RIGHT!
HE'S ALL ALONE ...
OH MY...
I DON'T THINK THEY REALIZE I'M NIKAIDOU...
OKAY, JUST ACT NORMAL. NORMAL!

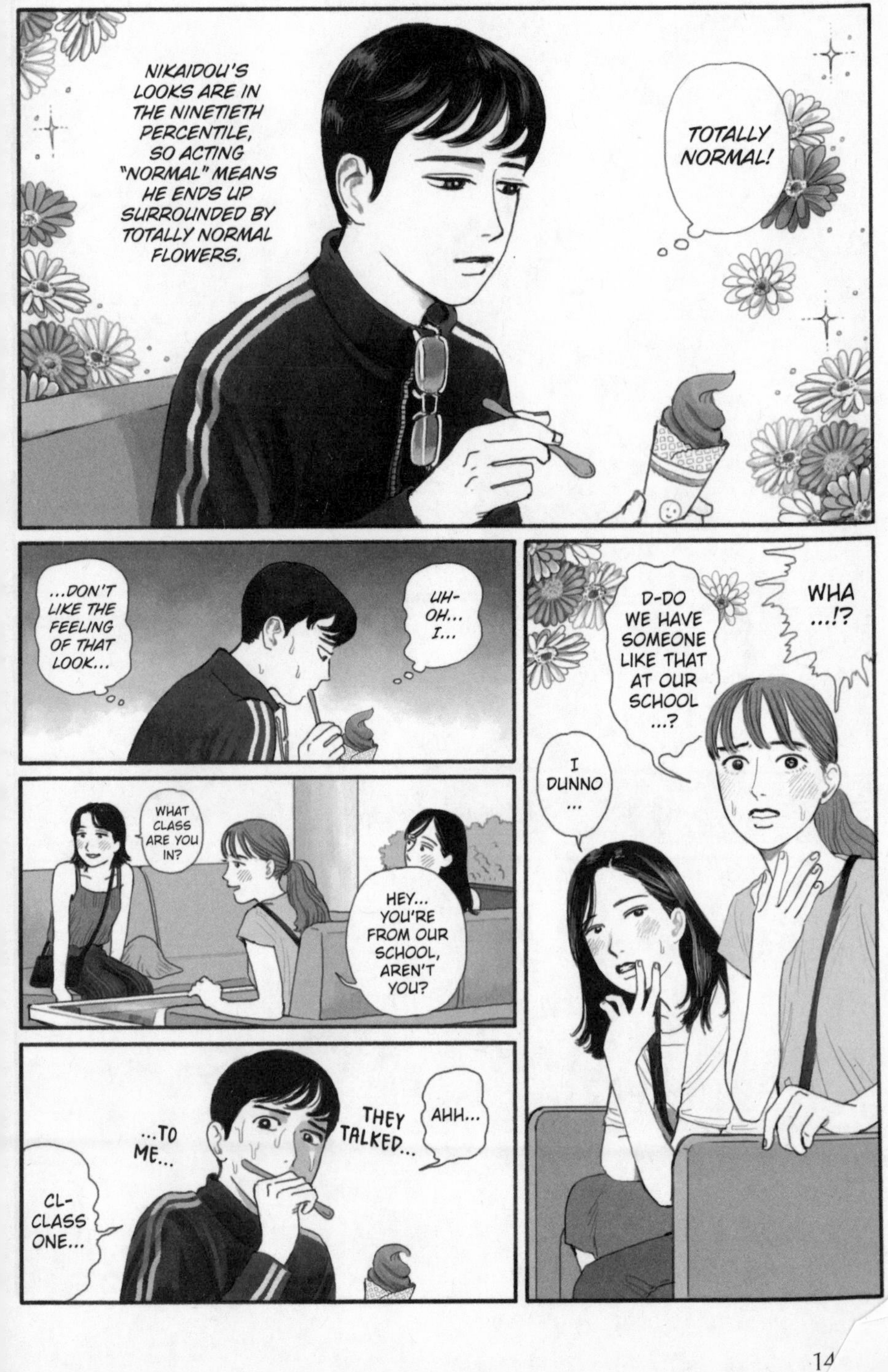
TOTALLY NORMAL!
NIKAIDOU'S LOOKS ARE IN THE NINETIETH PERCENTILE, SO ACTING "NORMAL" MEANS HE ENDS UP SURROUNDED BY TOTALLY NORMAL FLOWERS.
WHA ...!?
D-DO WE HAVE SOMEONE LIKE THAT AT OUR SCHOOL ...?
I DUNNO ...
UH-OH... I...
...DON'T LIKE THE FEELING OF THAT LOOK...
HEY... YOU'RE FROM OUR SCHOOL, AREN'T YOU?
WHAT CLASS ARE YOU IN?
AHH...
THEY TALKED...
...TO ME...
CL- CLASS ONE...

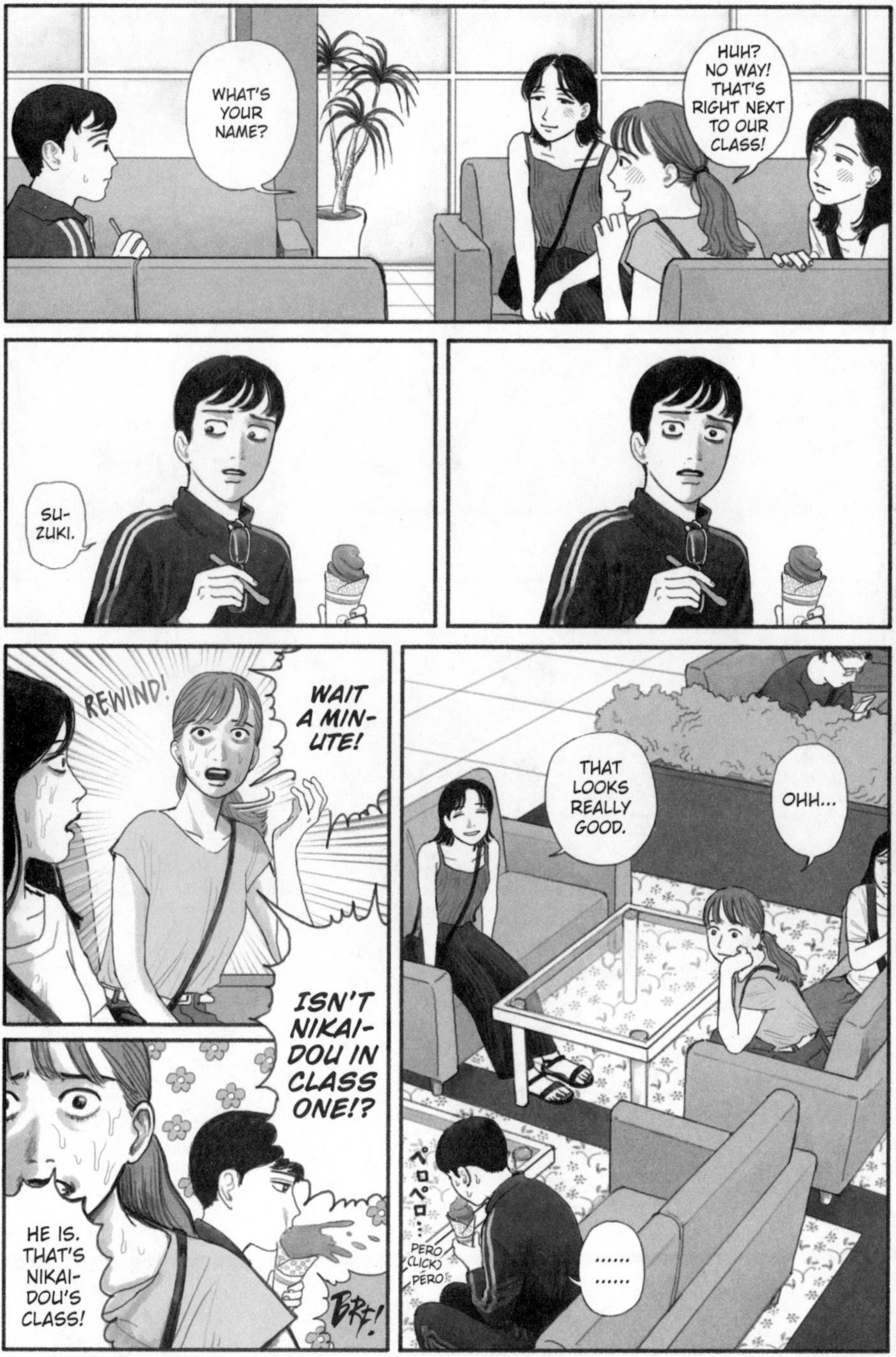
HUH? NO WAY! THAT'S RIGHT NEXT TO OUR CLASS!
WHAT'S YOUR NAME?
SU-ZUKI.
OHH...
THAT LOOKS REALLY GOOD.
ペロペロ…
PERO (CLICK) PERO
......
......
WAIT A MIN-UTE!
REWIND!
ISN'T NIKAIDOU IN CLASS ONE!?
HE IS. THAT'S NIKAIDOU'S CLASS!
BRE!

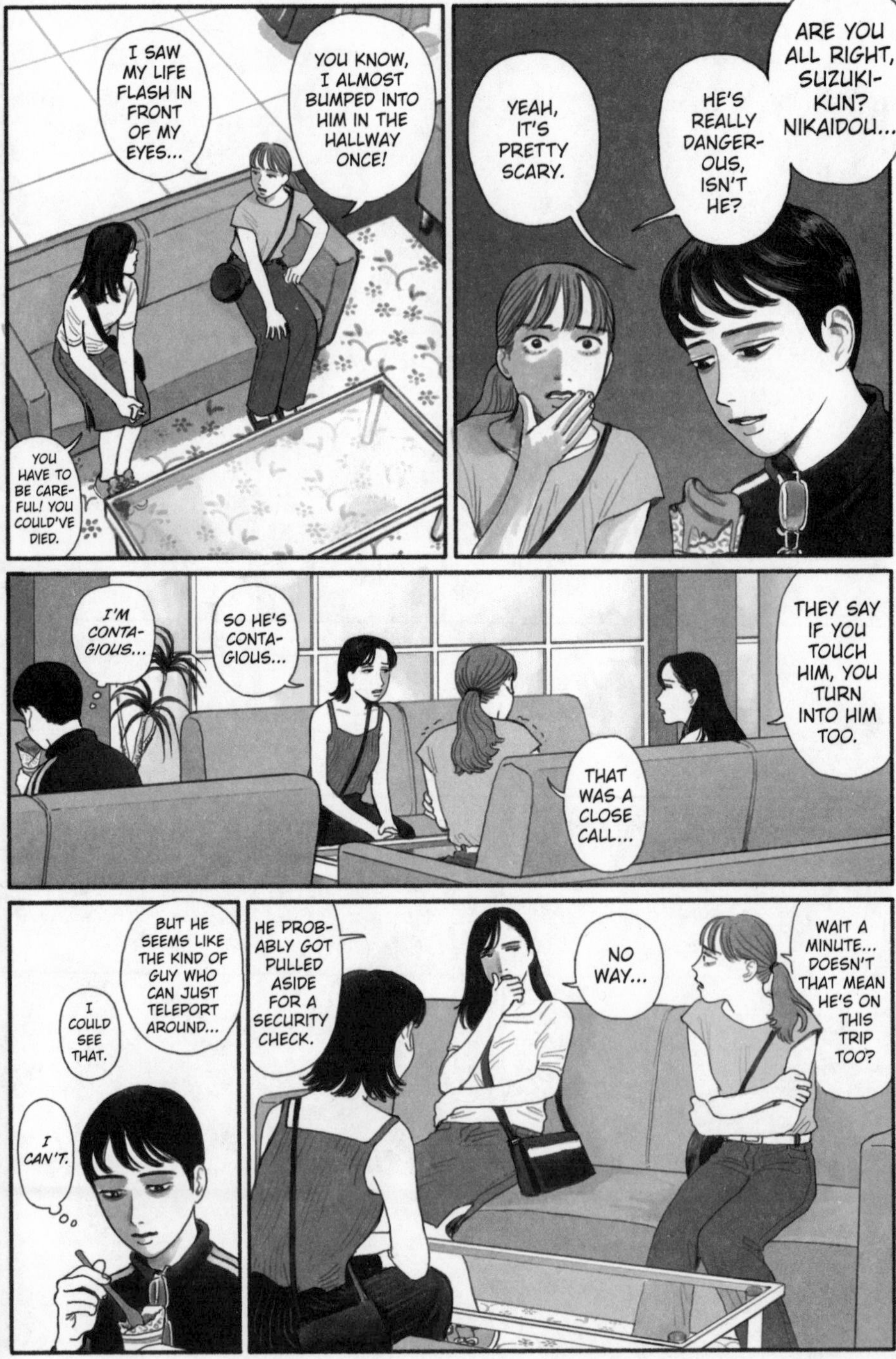
ARE YOU ALL RIGHT, SUZUKI-KUN? NIKAIDOU...
HE'S REALLY DANGER-OUS, ISN'T HE?
YEAH, IT'S PRETTY SCARY.
YOU KNOW, I ALMOST BUMPED INTO HIM IN THE HALLWAY ONCE!
I SAW MY LIFE FLASH IN FRONT OF MY EYES...
YOU HAVE TO BE CARE-FUL! YOU COULD'VE DIED.
THEY SAY IF YOU TOUCH HIM, YOU TURN INTO HIM TOO.
THAT WAS A CLOSE CALL...
SO HE'S CONTA-GIOUS...
I'M CONTA-GIOUS...
WAIT A MINUTE... DOESN'T THAT MEAN HE'S ON THIS TRIP TOO?
NO WAY...
HE PROB-ABLY GOT PULLED ASIDE FOR A SECURITY CHECK.
BUT HE SEEMS LIKE THE KIND OF GUY WHO CAN JUST TELEPORT AROUND...
I COULD SEE THAT.
I CAN'T.

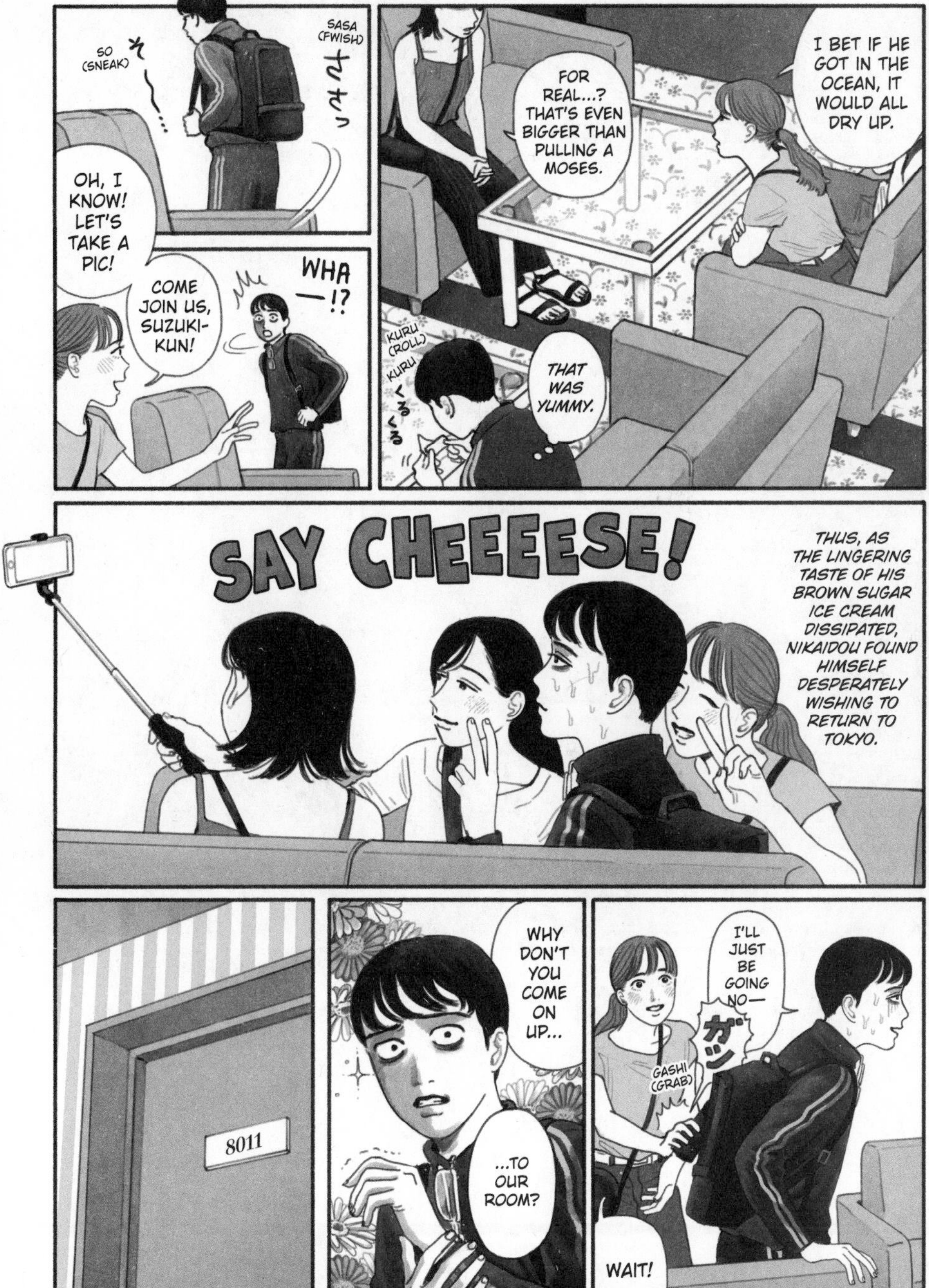
I BET IF HE GOT IN THE OCEAN, IT WOULD ALL DRY UP.
FOR REAL...? THAT'S EVEN BIGGER THAN PULLING A MOSES.
THAT WAS YUMMY.
KURU (ROLL) KURU くるくる
SASA (FWISH) ささっ
SO (SNEAK) そ〜…
OH, I KNOW! LET'S TAKE A PIC!
WHA—!?
COME JOIN US, SUZUKI-KUN!
THUS, AS THE LINGERING TASTE OF HIS BROWN SUGAR ICE CREAM DISSIPATED, NIKAIDOU FOUND HIMSELF DESPERATELY WISHING TO RETURN TO TOKYO.
SAY CHEEEESE!
I'LL JUST BE GOING NO—
ガシ
GASHI (GRAB)
WAIT!
WHY DON'T YOU COME ON UP...
...TO OUR ROOM?
8011

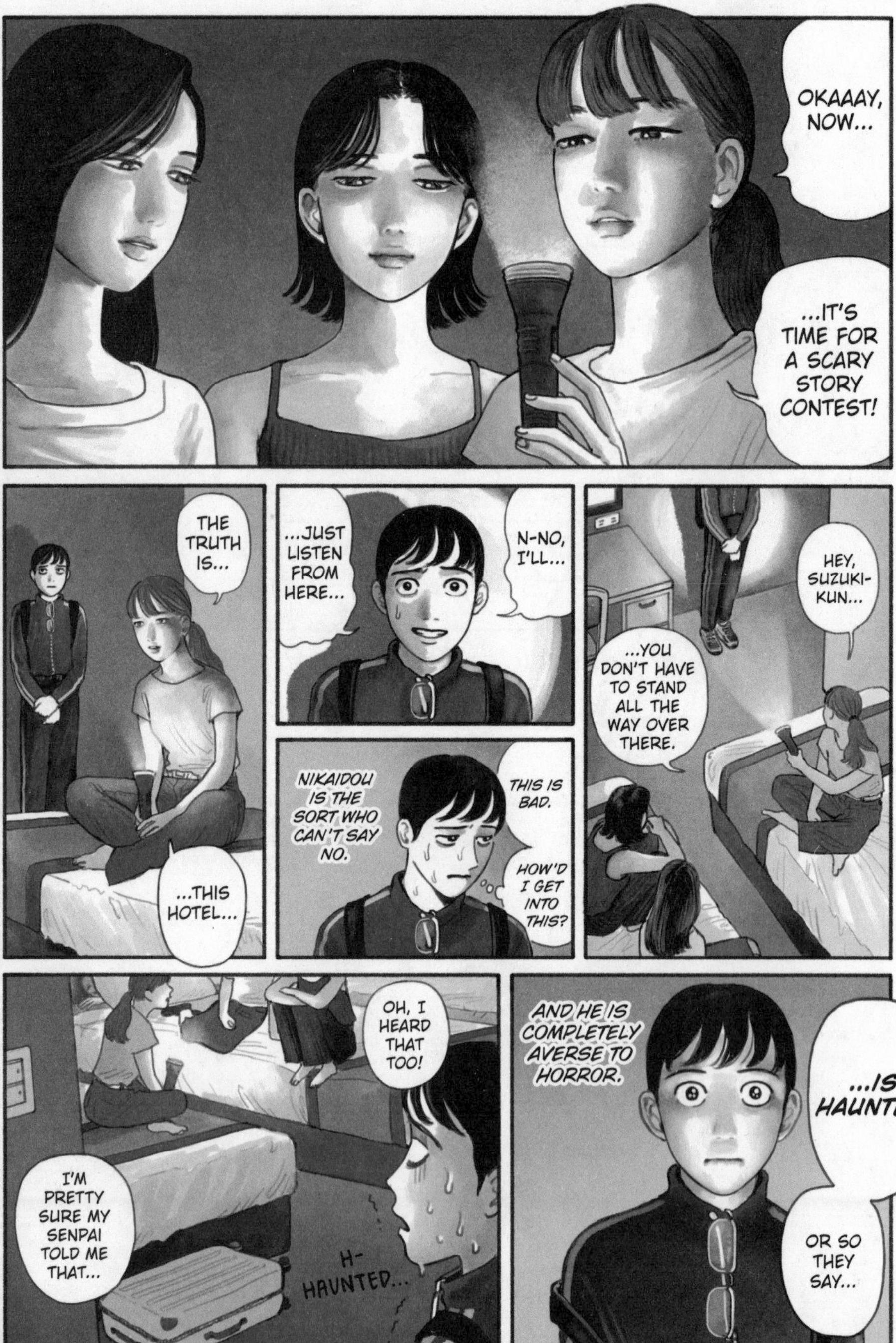
OKAAAY, NOW...
...IT'S TIME FOR A SCARY STORY CONTEST!
HEY, SUZUKI-KUN...
...YOU DON'T HAVE TO STAND ALL THE WAY OVER THERE.
N-NO, I'LL...
...JUST LISTEN FROM HERE...
THIS IS BAD.
HOW'D I GET INTO THIS?
NIKAIDOU IS THE SORT WHO CAN'T SAY NO.
THE TRUTH IS...
...THIS HOTEL...
...IS HAUNTED.
AND HE IS COMPLETELY AVERSE TO HORROR.
OR SO THEY SAY...
OH, I HEARD THAT TOO!
I'M PRETTY SURE MY SENPAI TOLD ME THAT...
H-HAUNTED...

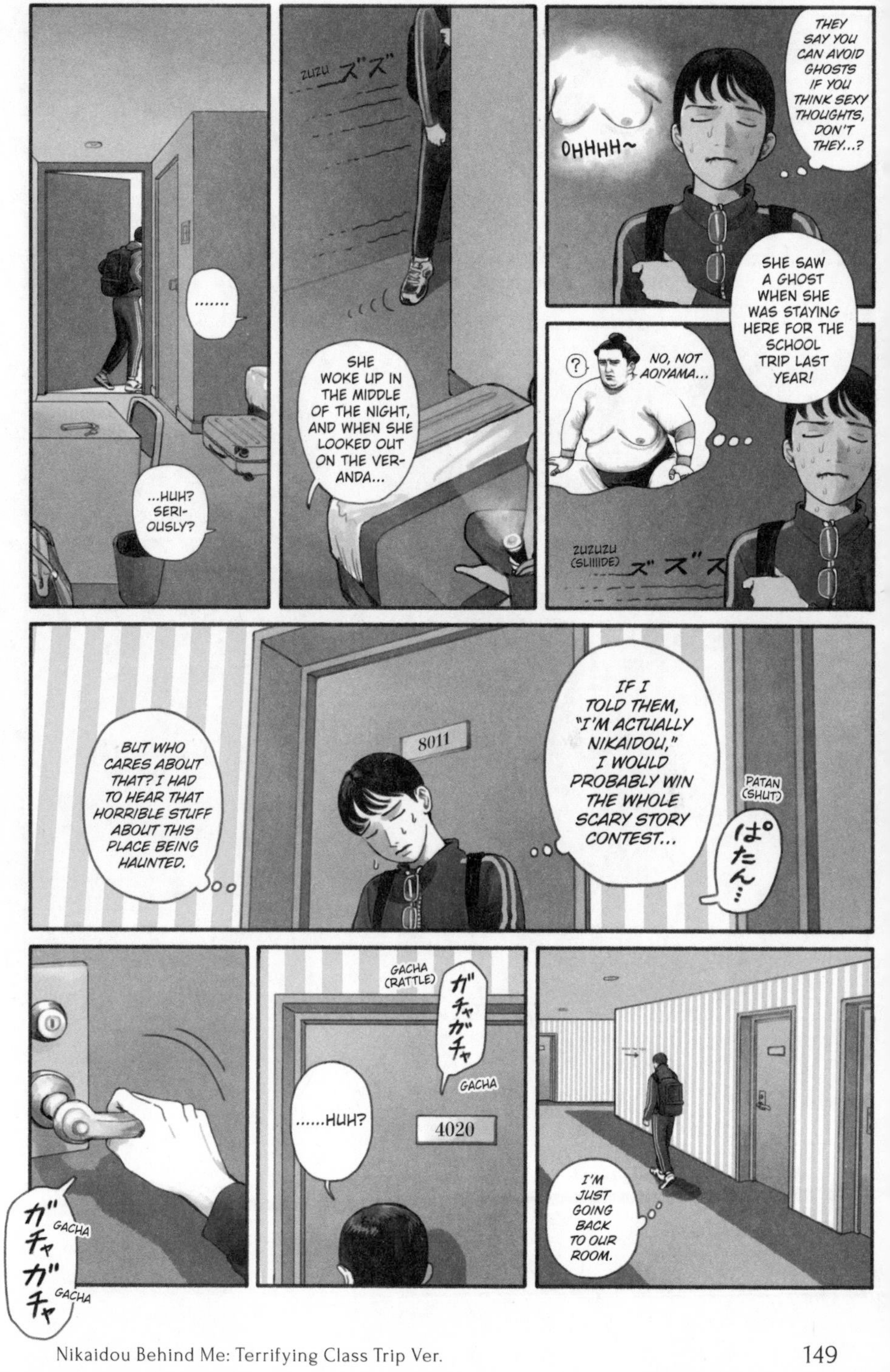

THEY SAY YOU CAN AVOID GHOSTS IF YOU THINK SEXY THOUGHTS, DON'T THEY...?
OHHHH~
SHE SAW A GHOST WHEN SHE WAS STAYING HERE FOR THE SCHOOL TRIP LAST YEAR!
?
NO, NOT AOIYAMA...
ZUZUZU (SLIIIIDE) ズズズ
ZUZU ズズ
SHE WOKE UP IN THE MIDDLE OF THE NIGHT, AND WHEN SHE LOOKED OUT ON THE VER-ANDA...
....
...HUH? SERI-OUSLY?
IF I TOLD THEM, "I'M ACTUALLY NIKAIDOU," I WOULD PROBABLY WIN THE WHOLE SCARY STORY CONTEST...
PATAN (SHUT) ぱたん…
8011
BUT WHO CARES ABOUT THAT? I HAD TO HEAR THAT HORRIBLE STUFF ABOUT THIS PLACE BEING HAUNTED.
I'M JUST GOING BACK TO OUR ROOM.
GACHA (RATTLE) ガチャガチャ GACHA
......HUH?
4020
ガチャ GACHA ガチャ GACHA

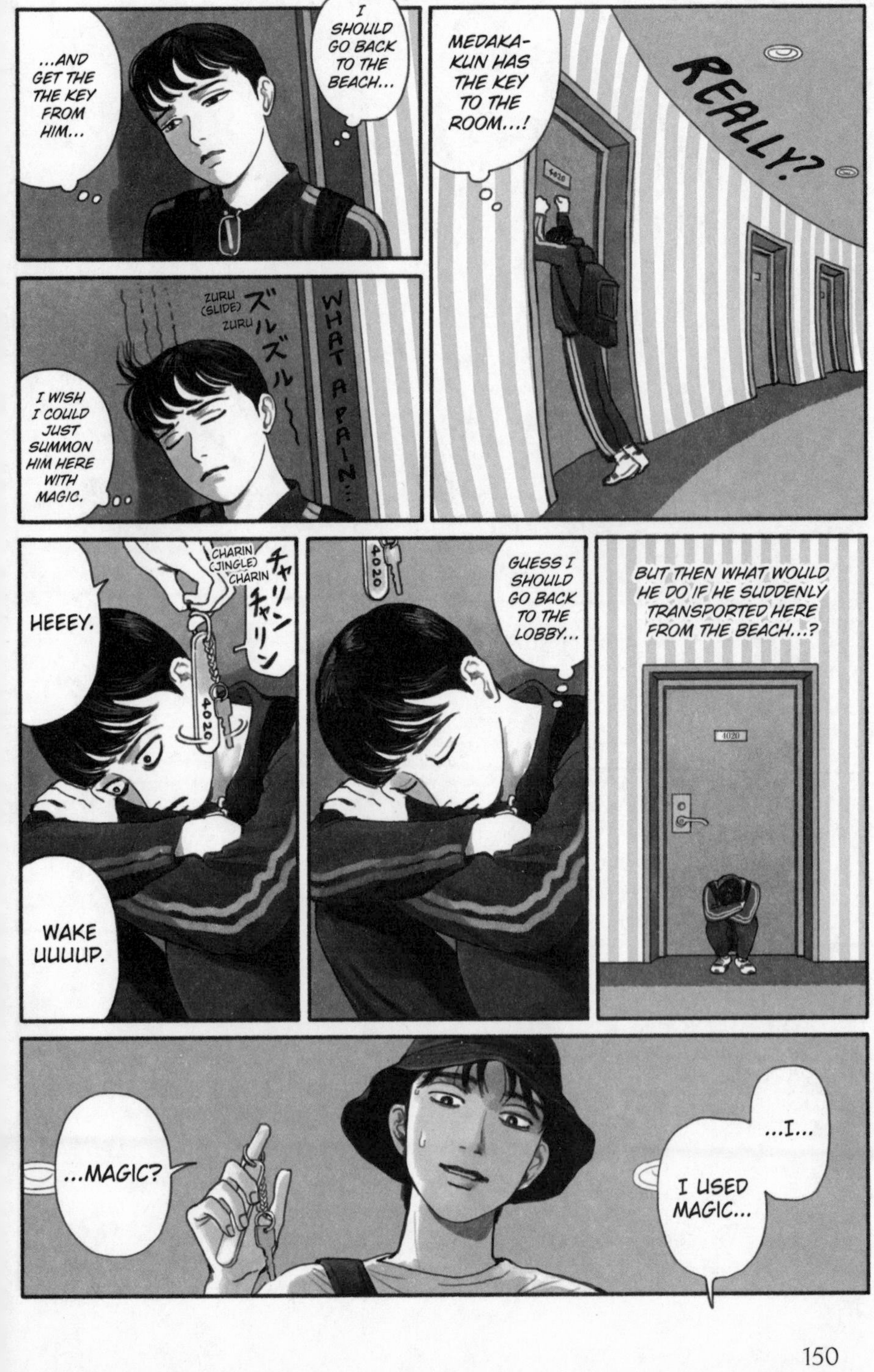
MEDAKA-KUN HAS THE KEY TO THE ROOM...!
REALLY?
I SHOULD GO BACK TO THE BEACH...
...AND GET THE THE KEY FROM HIM...
ズルズル～
ZURU (SLIDE) ZURU
WHAT A PAIN...
I WISH I COULD JUST SUMMON HIM HERE WITH MAGIC.
BUT THEN WHAT WOULD HE DO IF HE SUDDENLY TRANSPORTED HERE FROM THE BEACH...?
GUESS I SHOULD GO BACK TO THE LOBBY...
チャリンチャリン
CHARIN (JINGLE) CHARIN
HEEEY.
WAKE UUUUP.
...I...
I USED MAGIC...
...MAGIC?

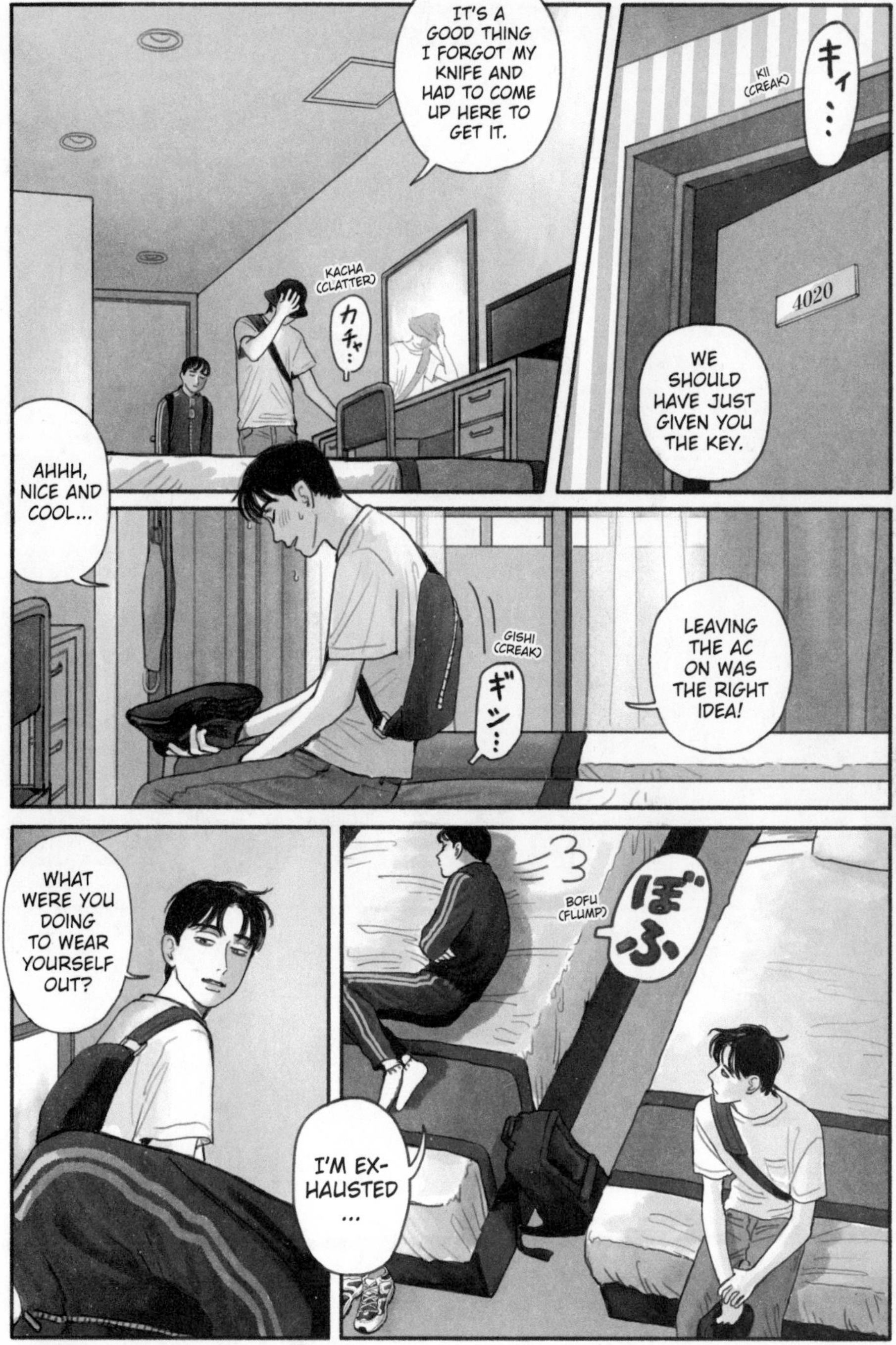
キィ…
KII (CREAK)
WE SHOULD HAVE JUST GIVEN YOU THE KEY.
IT'S A GOOD THING I FORGOT MY KNIFE AND HAD TO COME UP HERE TO GET IT.
KACHA (CLATTER)
カチャ…
LEAVING THE AC ON WAS THE RIGHT IDEA!
GISHI (CREAK)
ギッ…
AHHH, NICE AND COOL…
ぼふ
BOFU (FLUMP)
I'M EX-HAUSTED…
WHAT WERE YOU DOING TO WEAR YOURSELF OUT?

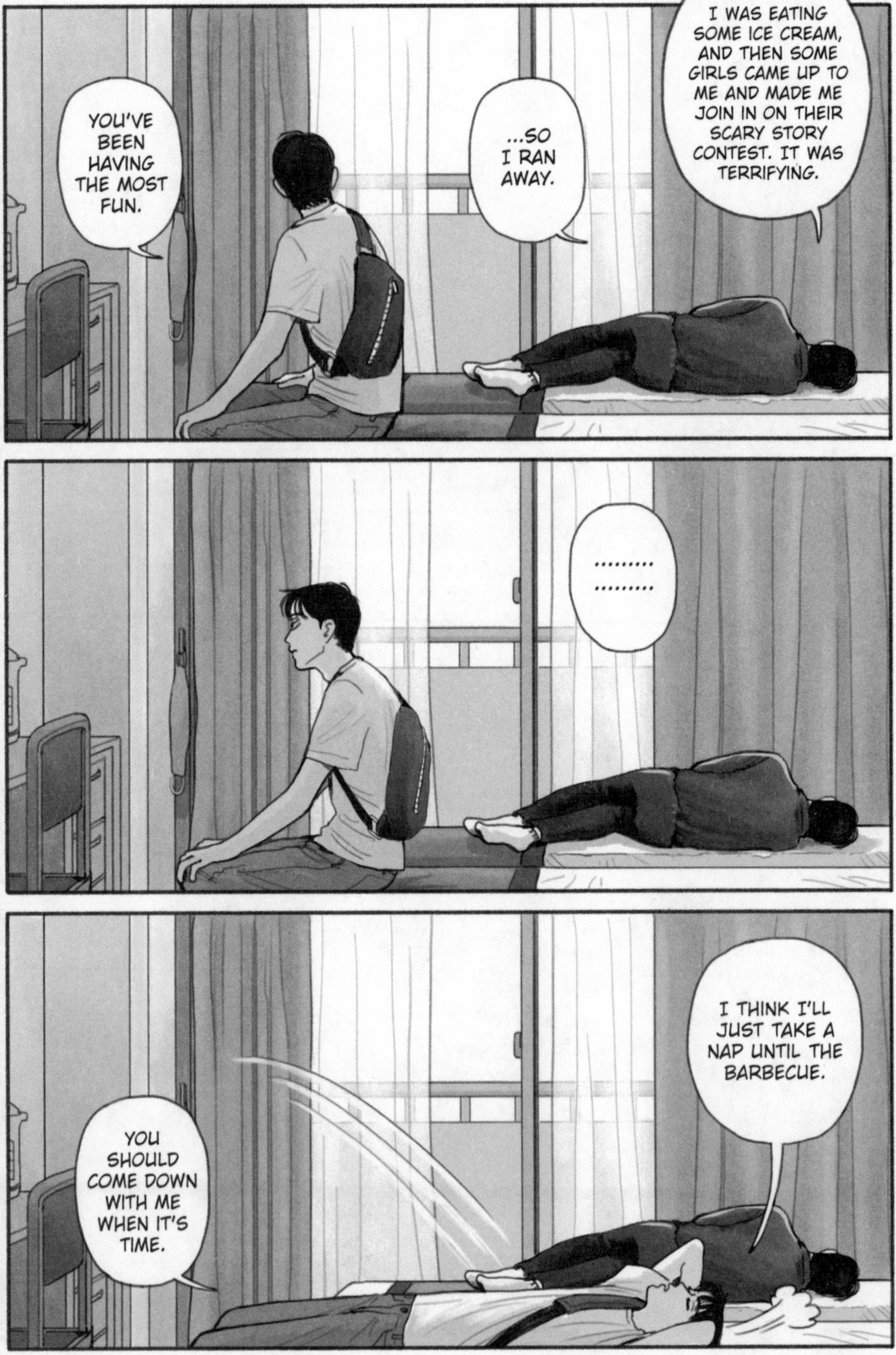
I WAS EATING SOME ICE CREAM, AND THEN SOME GIRLS CAME UP TO ME AND MADE ME JOIN IN ON THEIR SCARY STORY CONTEST. IT WAS TERRIFYING.
...SO I RAN AWAY.
YOU'VE BEEN HAVING THE MOST FUN.
....
....
I THINK I'LL JUST TAKE A NAP UNTIL THE BARBECUE.
YOU SHOULD COME DOWN WITH ME WHEN IT'S TIME.

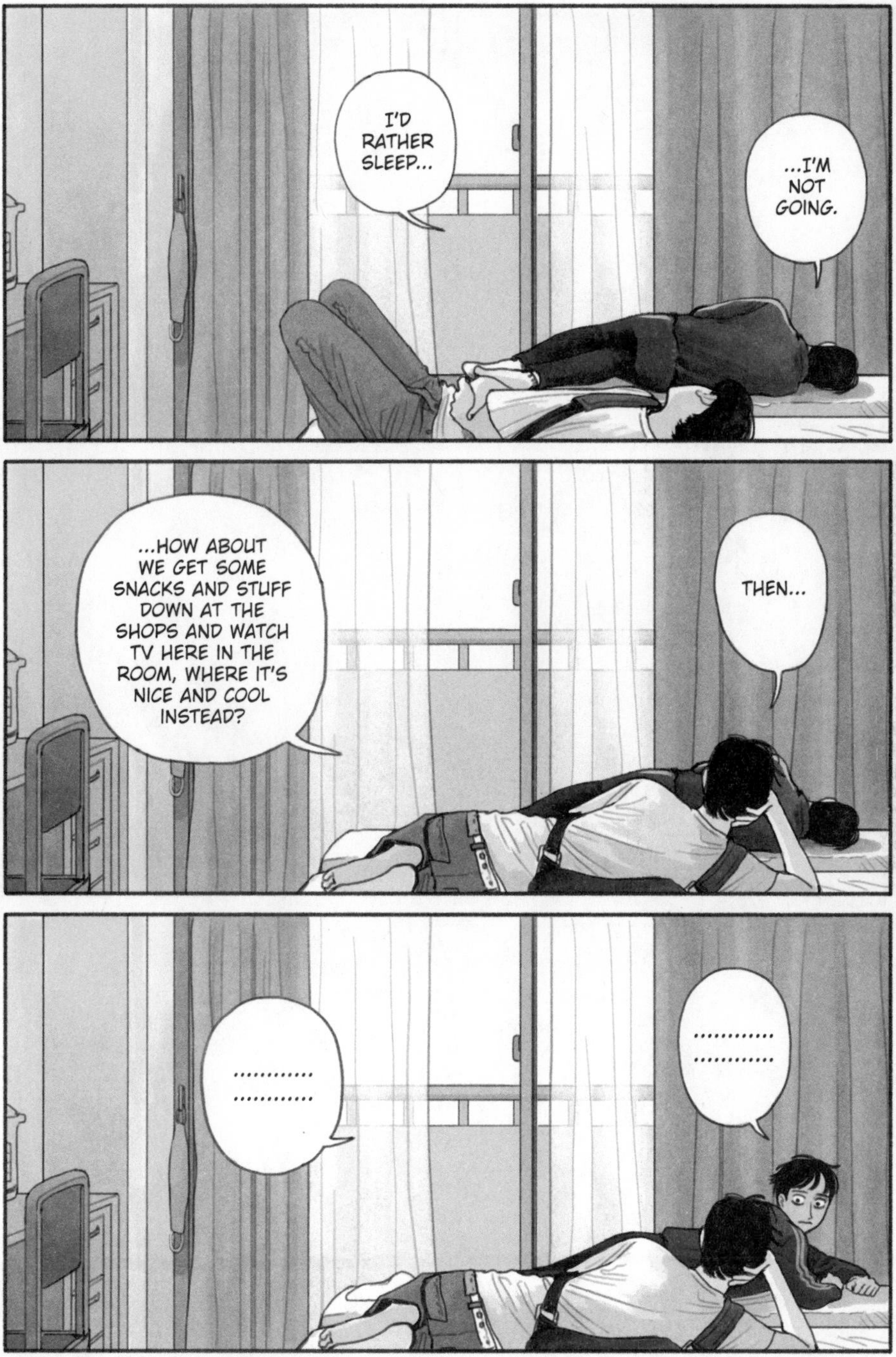
...I'M NOT GOING.
I'D RATHER SLEEP...
THEN...
...HOW ABOUT WE GET SOME SNACKS AND STUFF DOWN AT THE SHOPS AND WATCH TV HERE IN THE ROOM, WHERE IT'S NICE AND COOL INSTEAD?
....
....

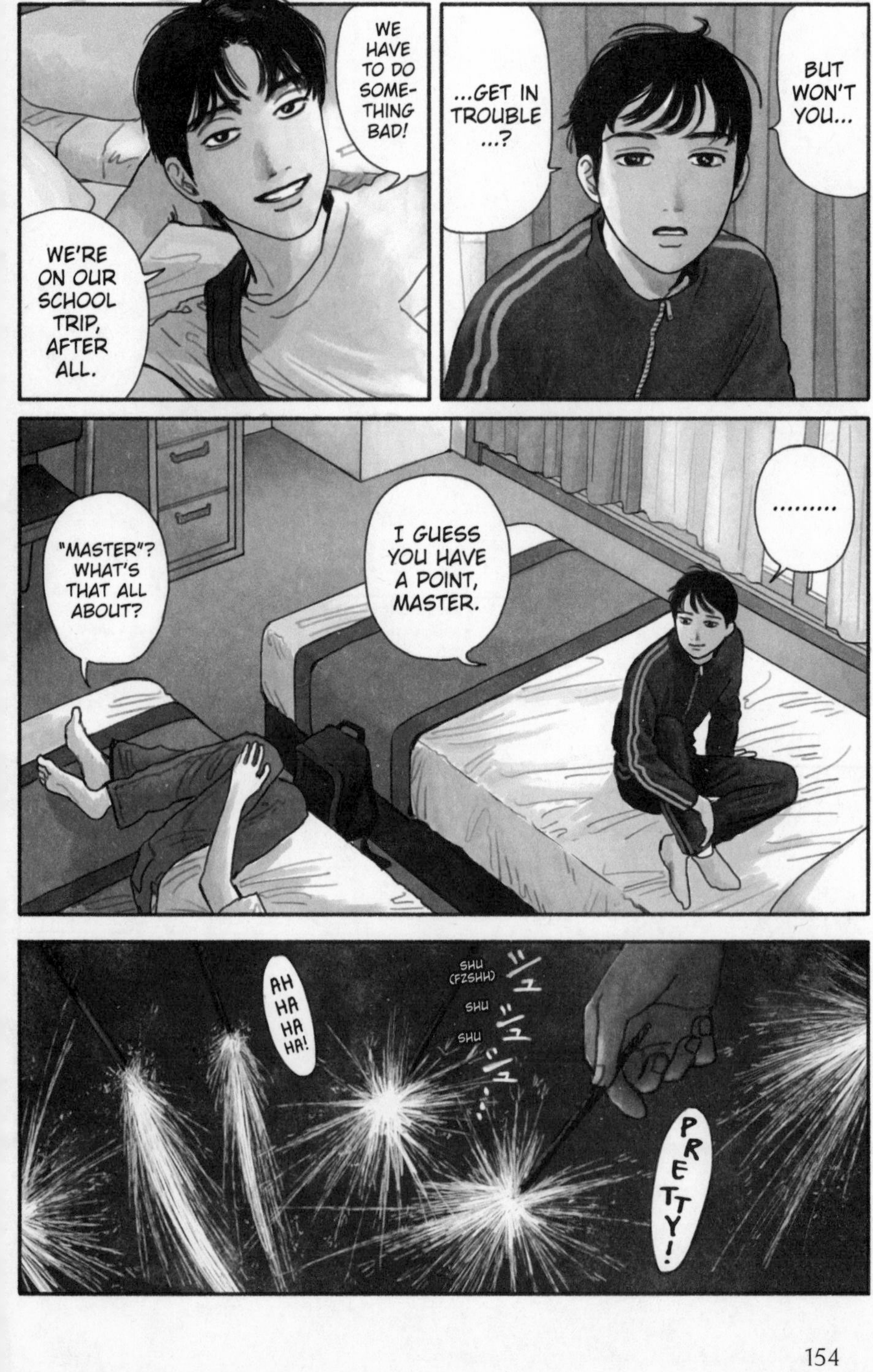
BUT WON'T YOU...
...GET IN TROUBLE ...?
WE HAVE TO DO SOME-THING BAD!
WE'RE ON OUR SCHOOL TRIP, AFTER ALL.
....
I GUESS YOU HAVE A POINT, MASTER.
"MASTER"? WHAT'S THAT ALL ABOUT?
PRETTY!
シュ
シュ
シュ...
SHU (FZSHH)
SHU
SHU
AH HA HA HA!

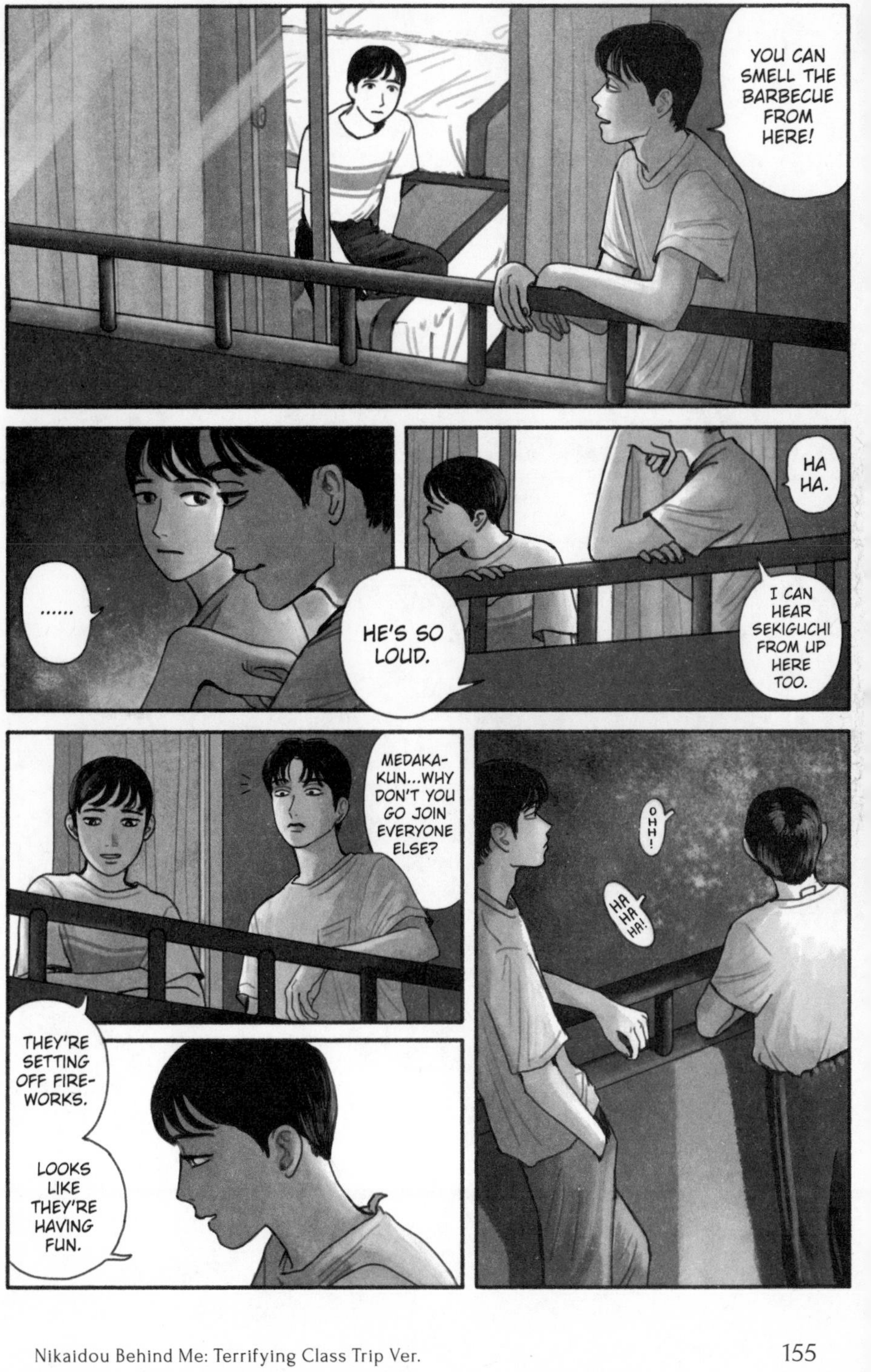
YOU CAN SMELL THE BARBECUE FROM HERE!
HA HA.
I CAN HEAR SEKIGUCHI FROM UP HERE TOO.
HE'S SO LOUD.
......
OHH!
HA HA HA!
MEDAKA-KUN...WHY DON'T YOU GO JOIN EVERYONE ELSE?
THEY'RE SETTING OFF FIRE-WORKS.
LOOKS LIKE THEY'RE HAVING FUN.

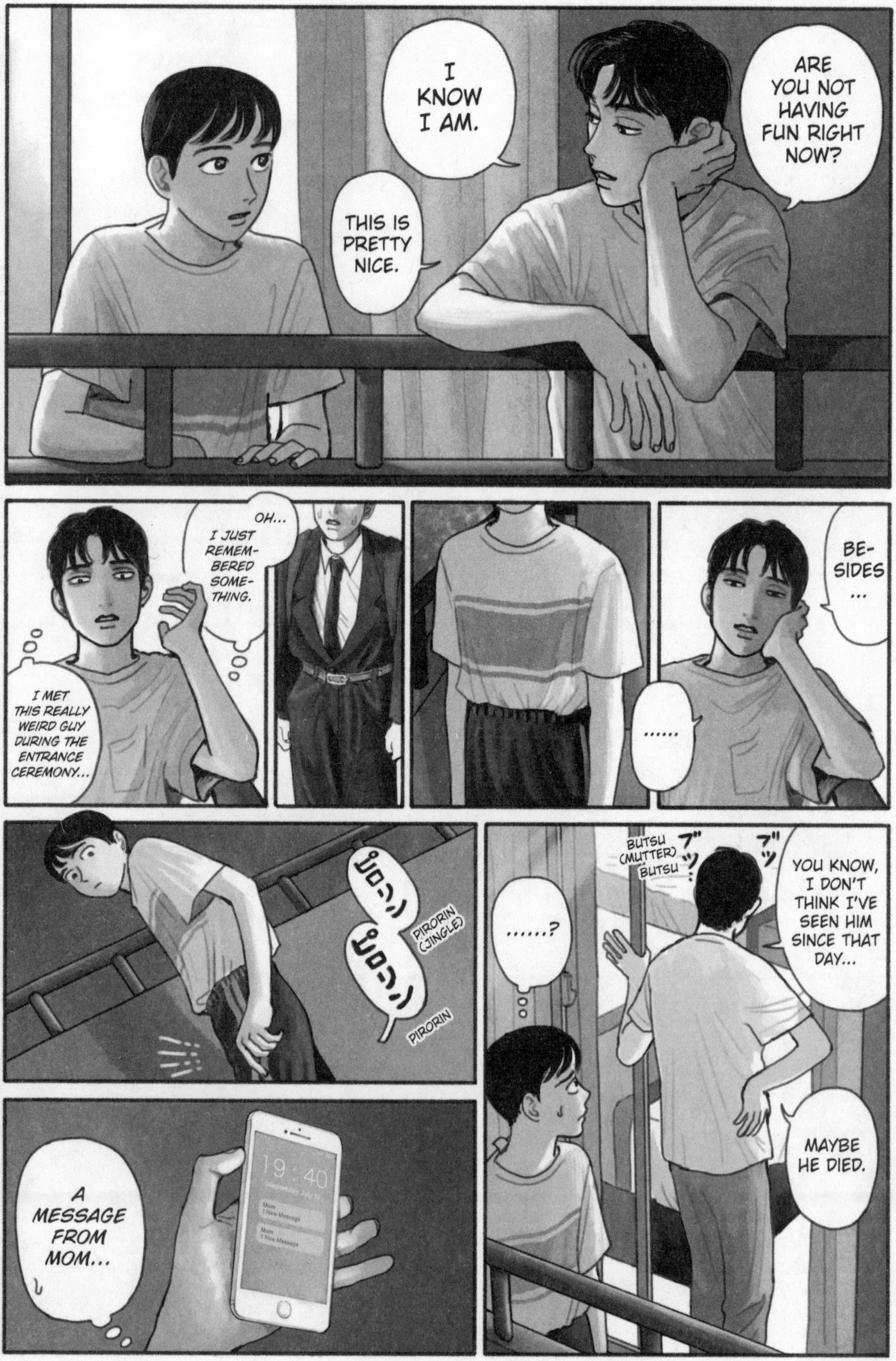
ARE YOU NOT HAVING FUN RIGHT NOW?
I KNOW I AM.
THIS IS PRETTY NICE.
BE-SIDES...
......
OH... I JUST REMEMB-BERED SOME-THING.
I MET THIS REALLY WEIRD GUY DURING THE ENTRANCE CEREMONY...
ブツ BUTSU (MUTTER)
ブツ BUTSU
YOU KNOW, I DON'T THINK I'VE SEEN HIM SINCE THAT DAY...
......?
MAYBE HE DIED.
ピロリン PIRORIN (JINGLE)
ピロリン PIRORIN
A MESSAGE FROM MOM...

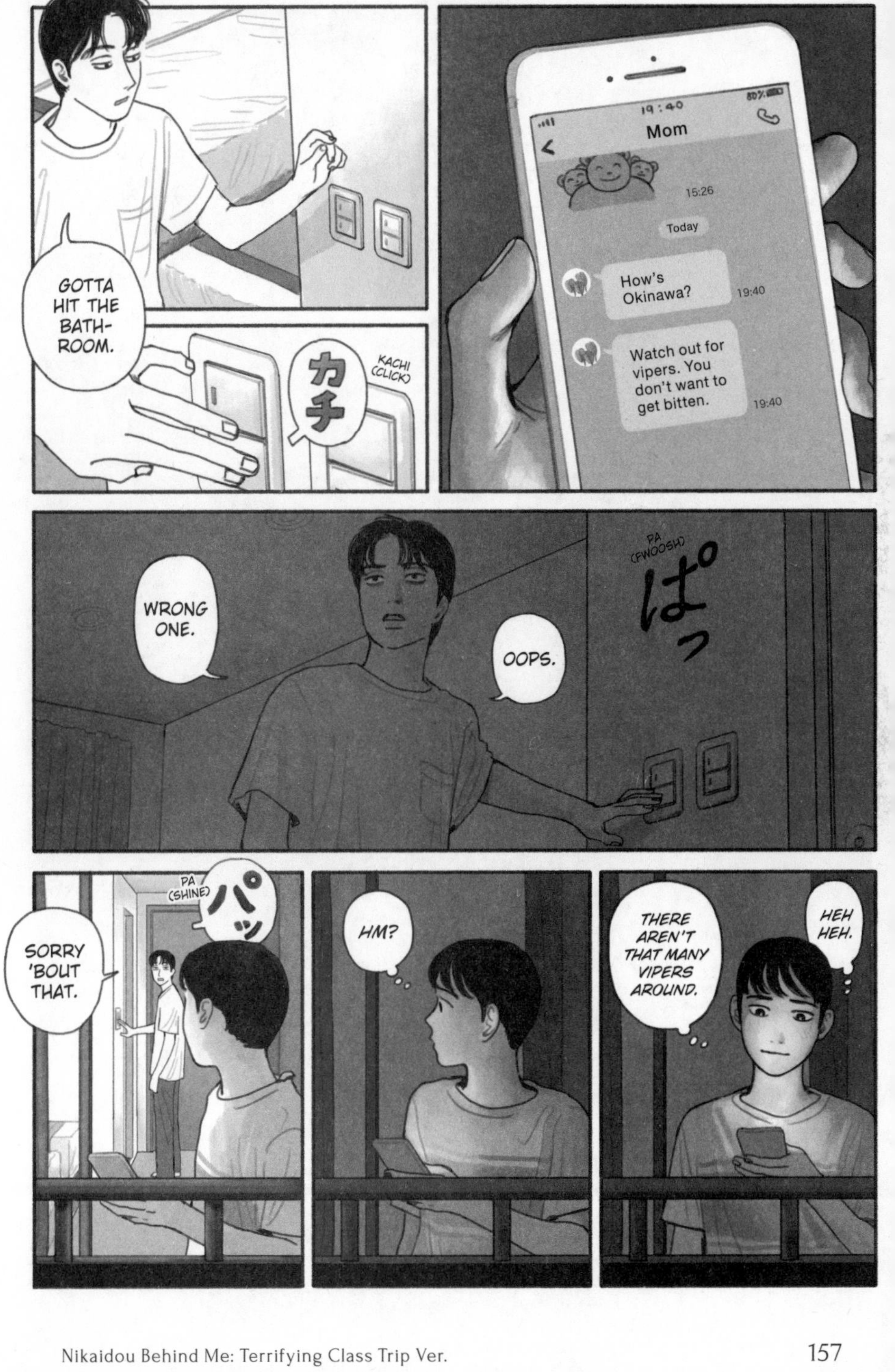
19:40
80%
Mom
15:26
Today
How's Okinawa?
19:40
Watch out for vipers. You don't want to get bitten.
19:40
GOTTA HIT THE BATH-ROOM.
カチ
KACHI (CLICK)
PA (FWOOSH)
ぱっ
OOPS.
WRONG ONE.
HEH HEH.
THERE AREN'T THAT MANY VIPERS AROUND.
HM?
パッ
PA (SHINE)
SORRY 'BOUT THAT.

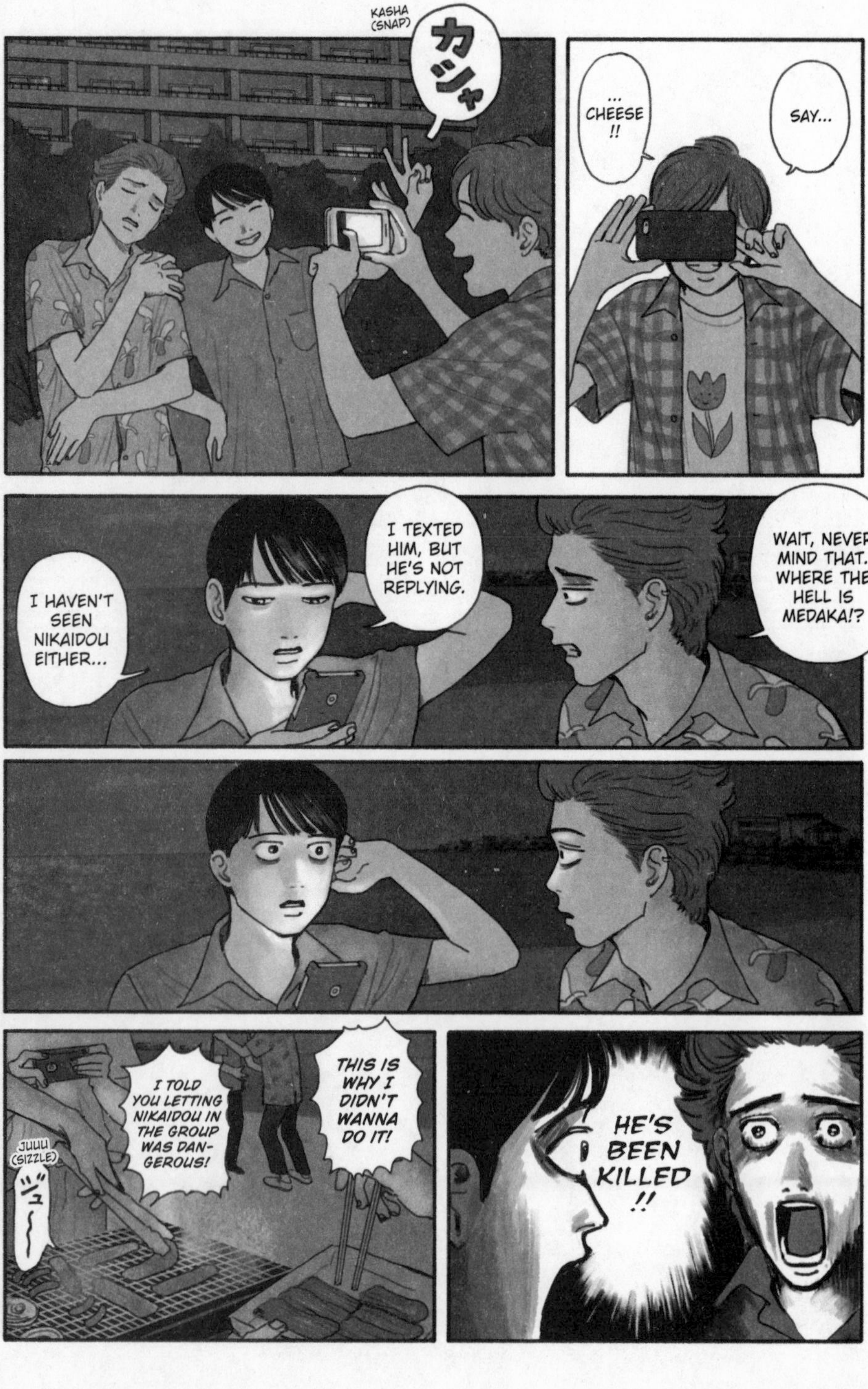
SAY...
... CHEESE !!
KASHA (SNAP)
カシャ
WAIT, NEVER MIND THAT. WHERE THE HELL IS MEDAKA!?
I TEXTED HIM, BUT HE'S NOT REPLYING.
I HAVEN'T SEEN NIKAIDOU EITHER...
HE'S BEEN KILLED !!
THIS IS WHY I DIDN'T WANNA DO IT!
I TOLD YOU LETTING NIKAIDOU IN THE GROUP WAS DAN-GEROUS!
JUUU (SIZZLE)
ジュ～～

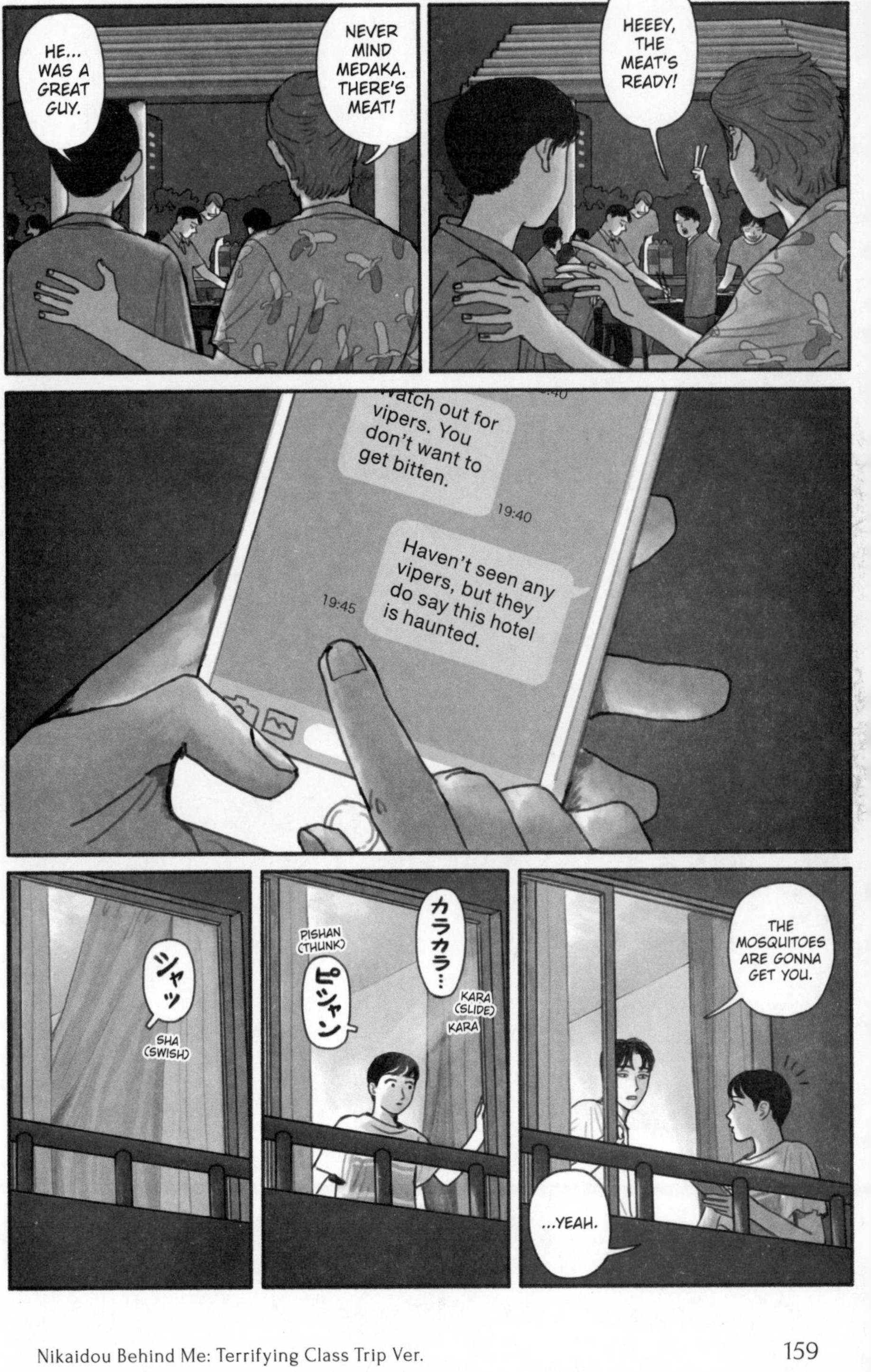
HEEEY, THE MEAT'S READY!
NEVER MIND MEDAKA. THERE'S MEAT!
HE... WAS A GREAT GUY.
Watch out for vipers. You don't want to get bitten.
19:40
Haven't seen any vipers, but they do say this hotel is haunted.
19:45
THE MOSQUITOES ARE GONNA GET YOU.
...YEAH.
カラカラ…
KARA (SLIDE) KARA
ピシャン
PISHAN (THUNK)
シャッ
SHA (SWISH)

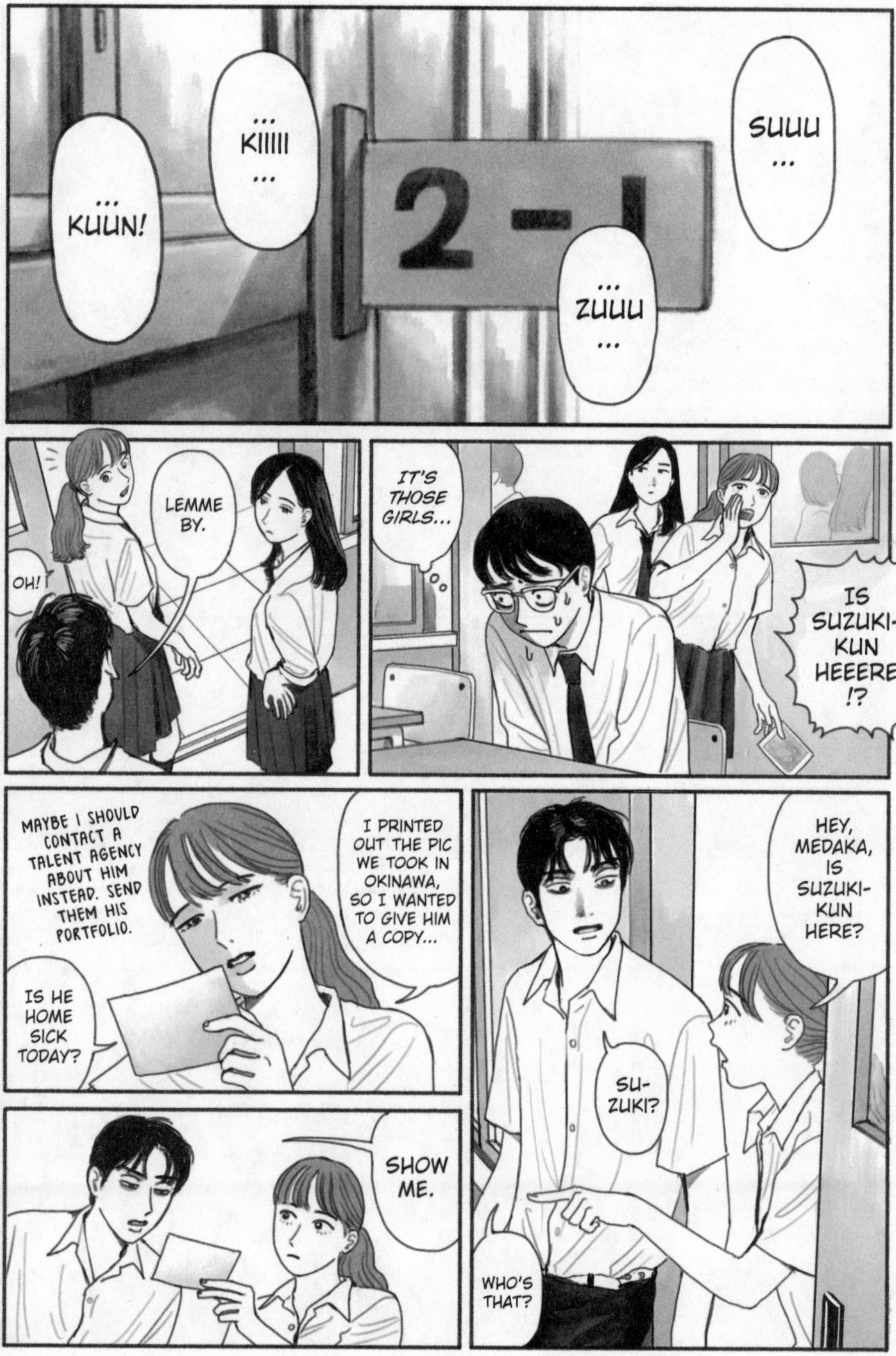
SUUU ...
... ZUUU ...
... KIIIII ...
... KUUN!
IS SUZUKI-KUN HEEERE!?
IT'S THOSE GIRLS...
LEMME BY.
OH!
HEY, MEDAKA, IS SUZUKI-KUN HERE?
SU-ZUKI?
WHO'S THAT?
I PRINTED OUT THE PIC WE TOOK IN OKINAWA, SO I WANTED TO GIVE HIM A COPY...
MAYBE I SHOULD CONTACT A TALENT AGENCY ABOUT HIM INSTEAD. SEND THEM HIS PORTFOLIO.
IS HE HOME SICK TODAY?
SHOW ME.

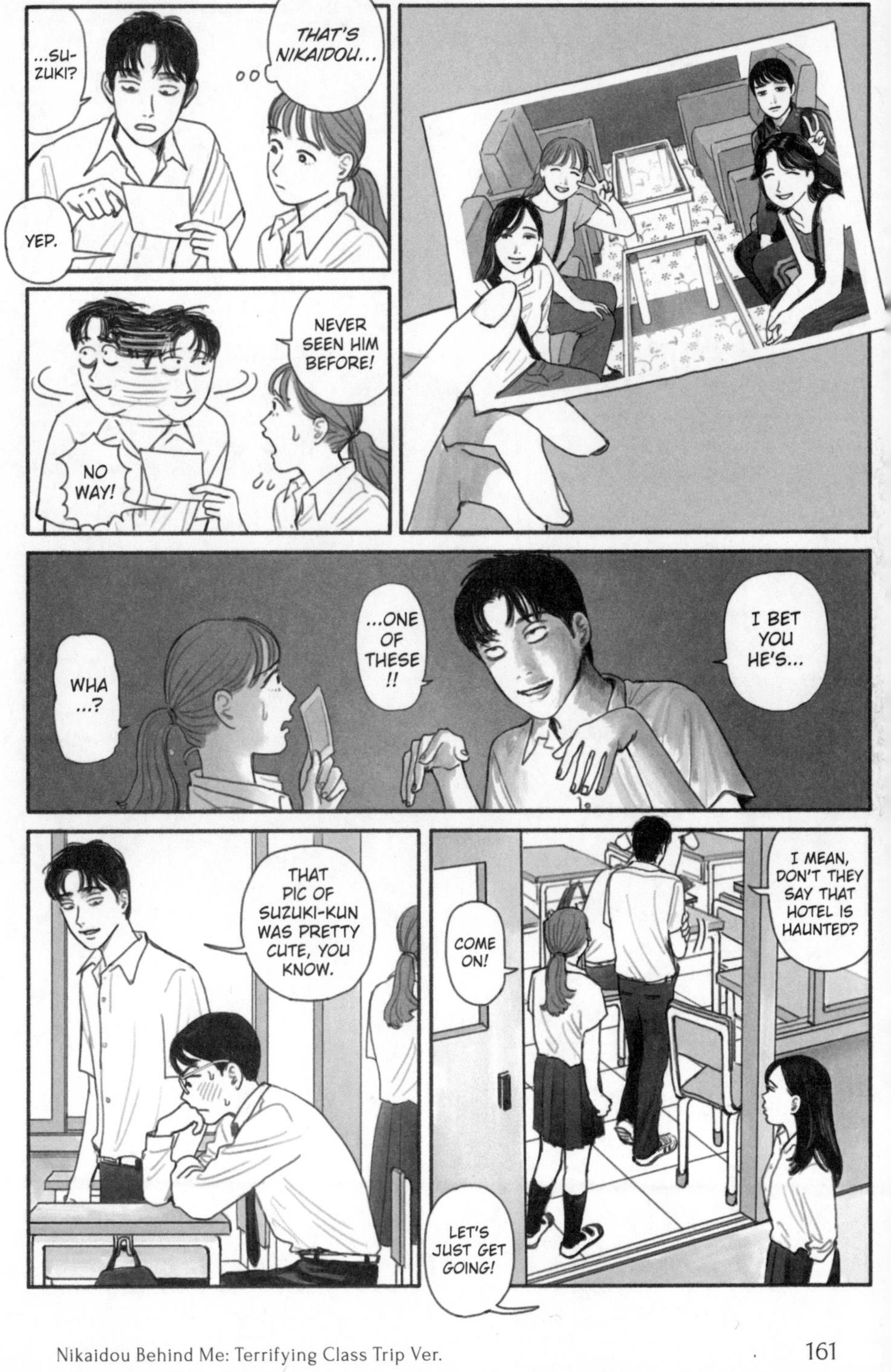
THAT'S NIKAIDOU...
...SU-ZUKI?
YEP.
NEVER SEEN HIM BEFORE!
NO WAY!
I BET YOU HE'S...
...ONE OF THESE !!
WHA ...?
I MEAN, DON'T THEY SAY THAT HOTEL IS HAUNTED?
COME ON!
LET'S JUST GET GOING!
THAT PIC OF SUZUKI-KUN WAS PRETTY CUTE, YOU KNOW.

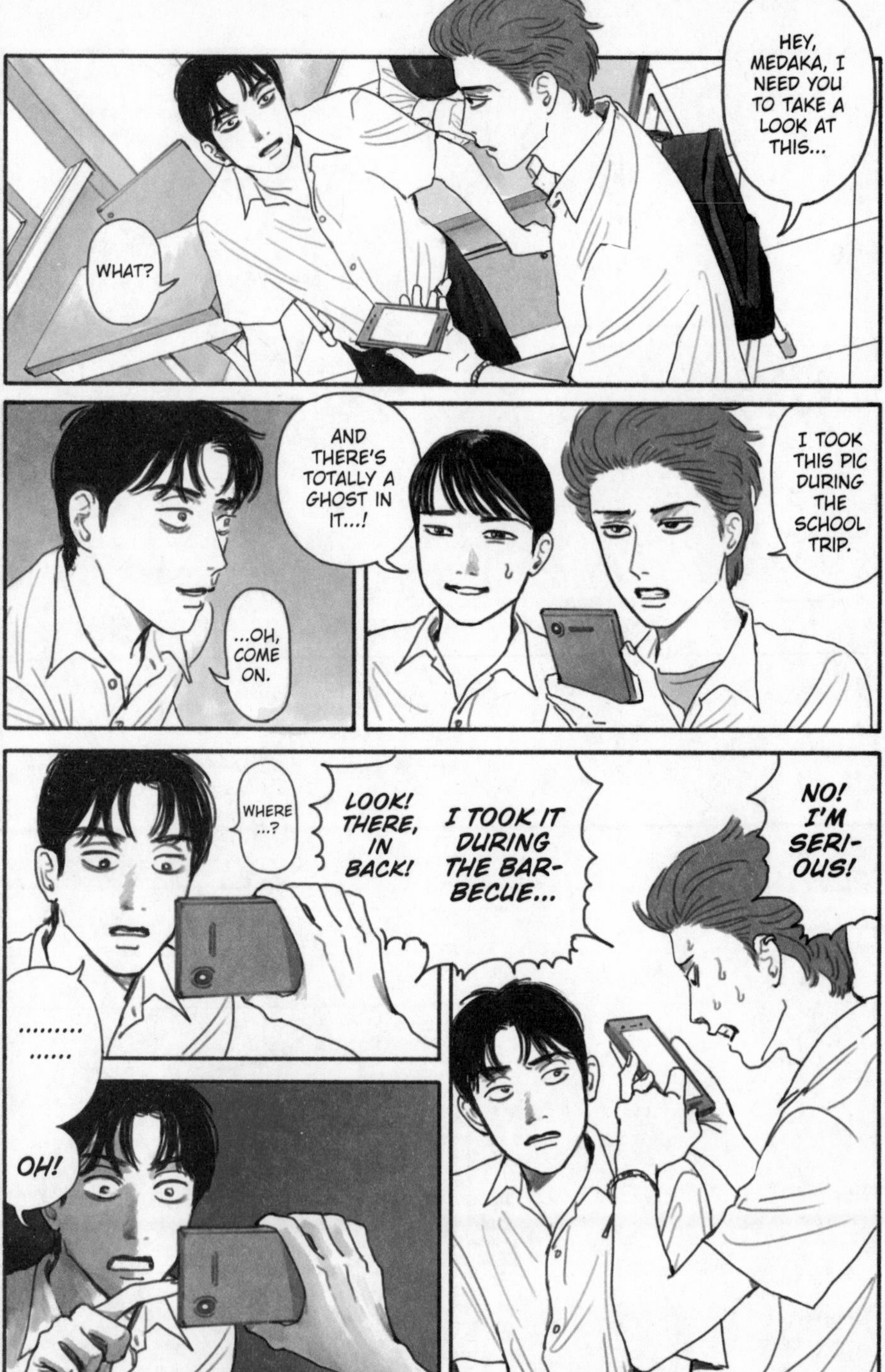
HEY, MEDAKA, I NEED YOU TO TAKE A LOOK AT THIS...
WHAT?
I TOOK THIS PIC DURING THE SCHOOL TRIP.
AND THERE'S TOTALLY A GHOST IN IT...!
...OH, COME ON.
NO! I'M SERI-OUS!
I TOOK IT DURING THE BAR-BECUE...
LOOK! THERE, IN BACK!
WHERE ...?
....
OH!

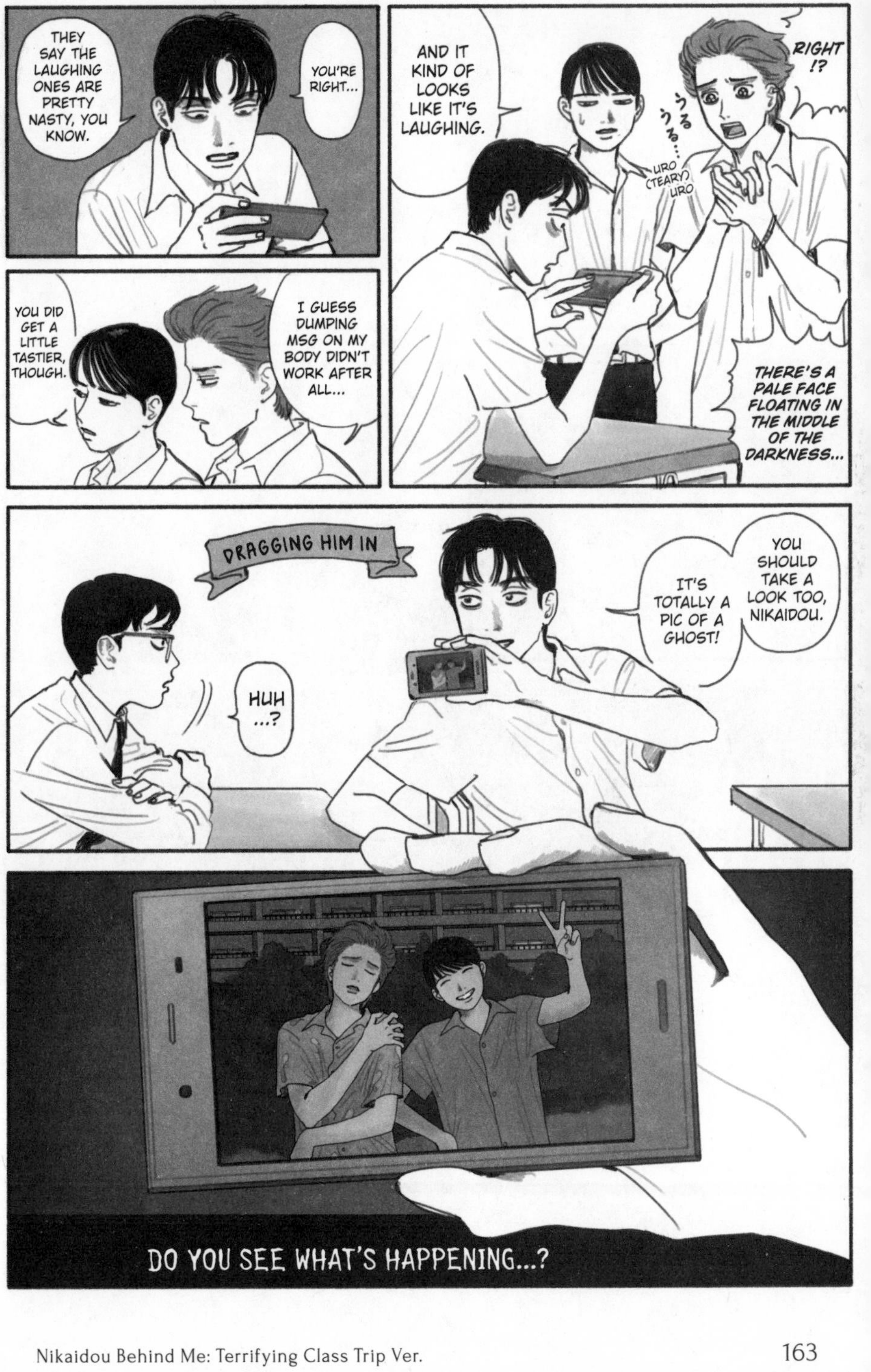
RIGHT!?
うるうる…
URO (TEARY) URO
AND IT KIND OF LOOKS LIKE IT'S LAUGHING.
THERE'S A PALE FACE FLOATING IN THE MIDDLE OF THE DARKNESS...
YOU'RE RIGHT...
THEY SAY THE LAUGHING ONES ARE PRETTY NASTY, YOU KNOW.
I GUESS DUMPING MSG ON MY BODY DIDN'T WORK AFTER ALL...
YOU DID GET A LITTLE TASTIER, THOUGH.
YOU SHOULD TAKE A LOOK TOO, NIKAIDOU.
IT'S TOTALLY A PIC OF A GHOST!
DRAGGING HIM IN
HUH ...?
DO YOU SEE WHAT'S HAPPENING...?

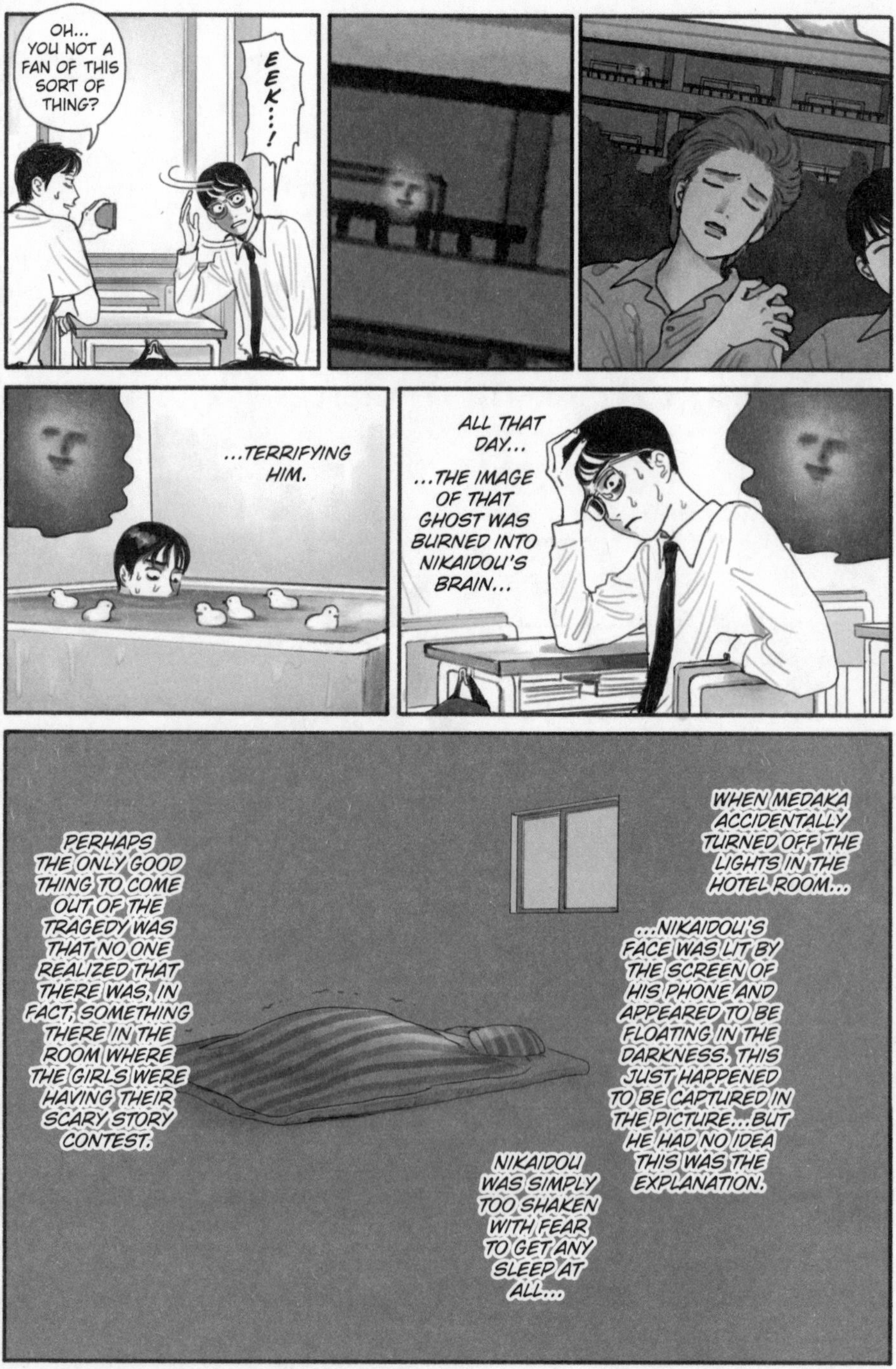
EEK...!
OH... YOU NOT A FAN OF THIS SORT OF THING?
ALL THAT DAY...
...THE IMAGE OF THAT GHOST WAS BURNED INTO NIKAIDOU'S BRAIN...
...TERRIFYING HIM.
WHEN MEDAKA ACCIDENTALLY TURNED OFF THE LIGHTS IN THE HOTEL ROOM...
...NIKAIDOU'S FACE WAS LIT BY THE SCREEN OF HIS PHONE AND APPEARED TO BE FLOATING IN THE DARKNESS. THIS JUST HAPPENED TO BE CAPTURED IN THE PICTURE...BUT HE HAD NO IDEA THIS WAS THE EXPLANATION.
NIKAIDOU WAS SIMPLY TOO SHAKEN WITH FEAR TO GET ANY SLEEP AT ALL...
PERHAPS THE ONLY GOOD THING TO COME OUT OF THE TRAGEDY WAS THAT NO ONE REALIZED THAT THERE WAS, IN FACT, SOMETHING THERE IN THE ROOM WHERE THE GIRLS WERE HAVING THEIR SCARY STORY CONTEST.

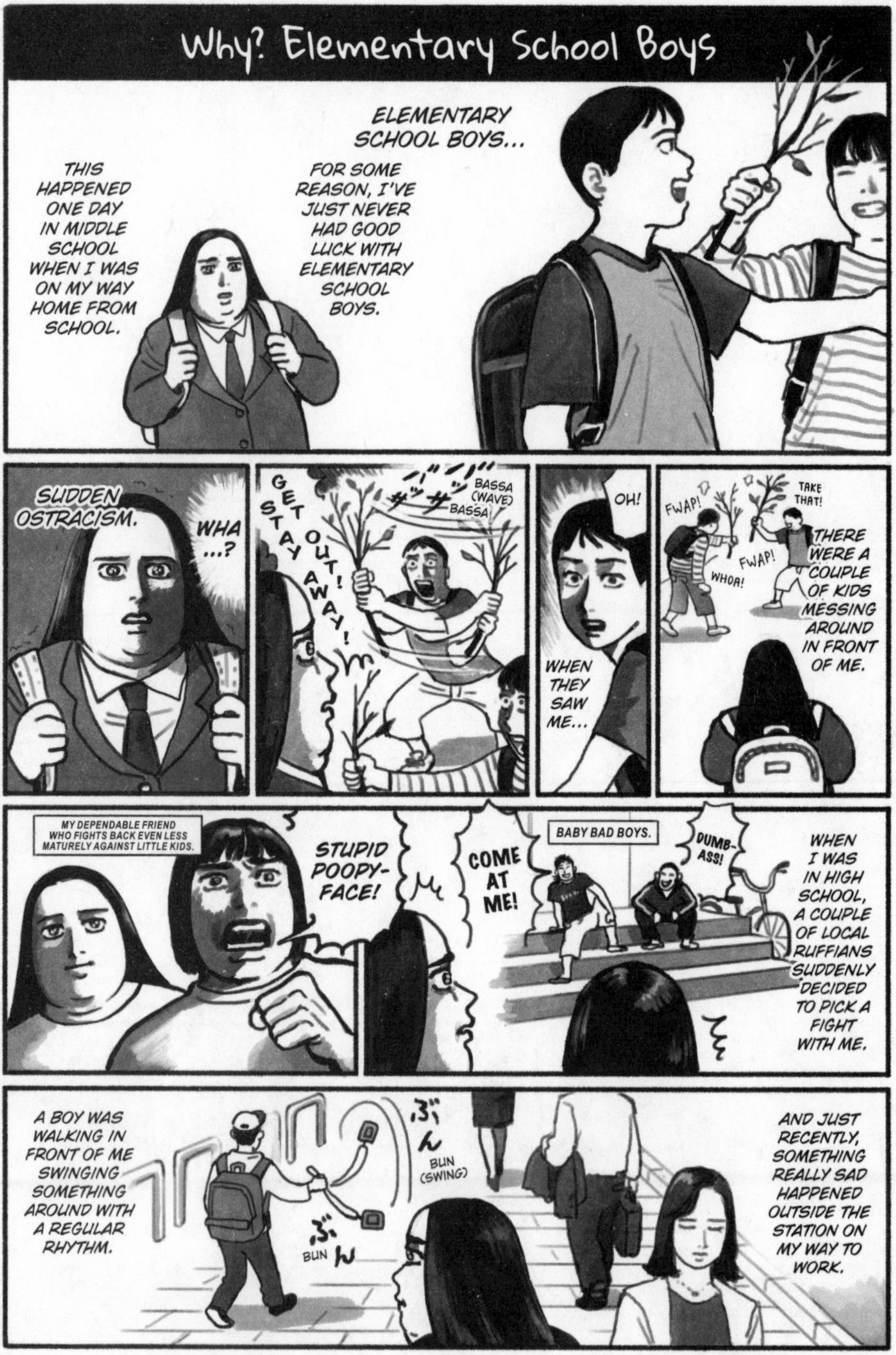

Why? Elementary School Boys
ELEMENTARY SCHOOL BOYS...
FOR SOME REASON, I'VE JUST NEVER HAD GOOD LUCK WITH ELEMENTARY SCHOOL BOYS.
THIS HAPPENED ONE DAY IN MIDDLE SCHOOL WHEN I WAS ON MY WAY HOME FROM SCHOOL.
TAKE THAT!
FWAP!
THERE WERE A COUPLE OF KIDS MESSING AROUND IN FRONT OF ME.
WHOA!
FWAP!
OH!
WHEN THEY SAW ME...
BASSA (WAVE) BASSA
GET OUT!
STAY AWAY!
WHA ...?
SUDDEN OSTRACISM.
WHEN I WAS IN HIGH SCHOOL, A COUPLE OF LOCAL RUFFIANS SUDDENLY DECIDED TO PICK A FIGHT WITH ME.
DUMB-ASS!
BABY BAD BOYS.
COME AT ME!
STUPID POOPY-FACE!
MY DEPENDABLE FRIEND WHO FIGHTS BACK EVEN LESS MATURELY AGAINST LITTLE KIDS.
AND JUST RECENTLY, SOMETHING REALLY SAD HAPPENED OUTSIDE THE STATION ON MY WAY TO WORK.
ぶん
BUN (SWING)
ぶん
BUN
A BOY WAS WALKING IN FRONT OF ME SWINGING SOMETHING AROUND WITH A REGULAR RHYTHM.

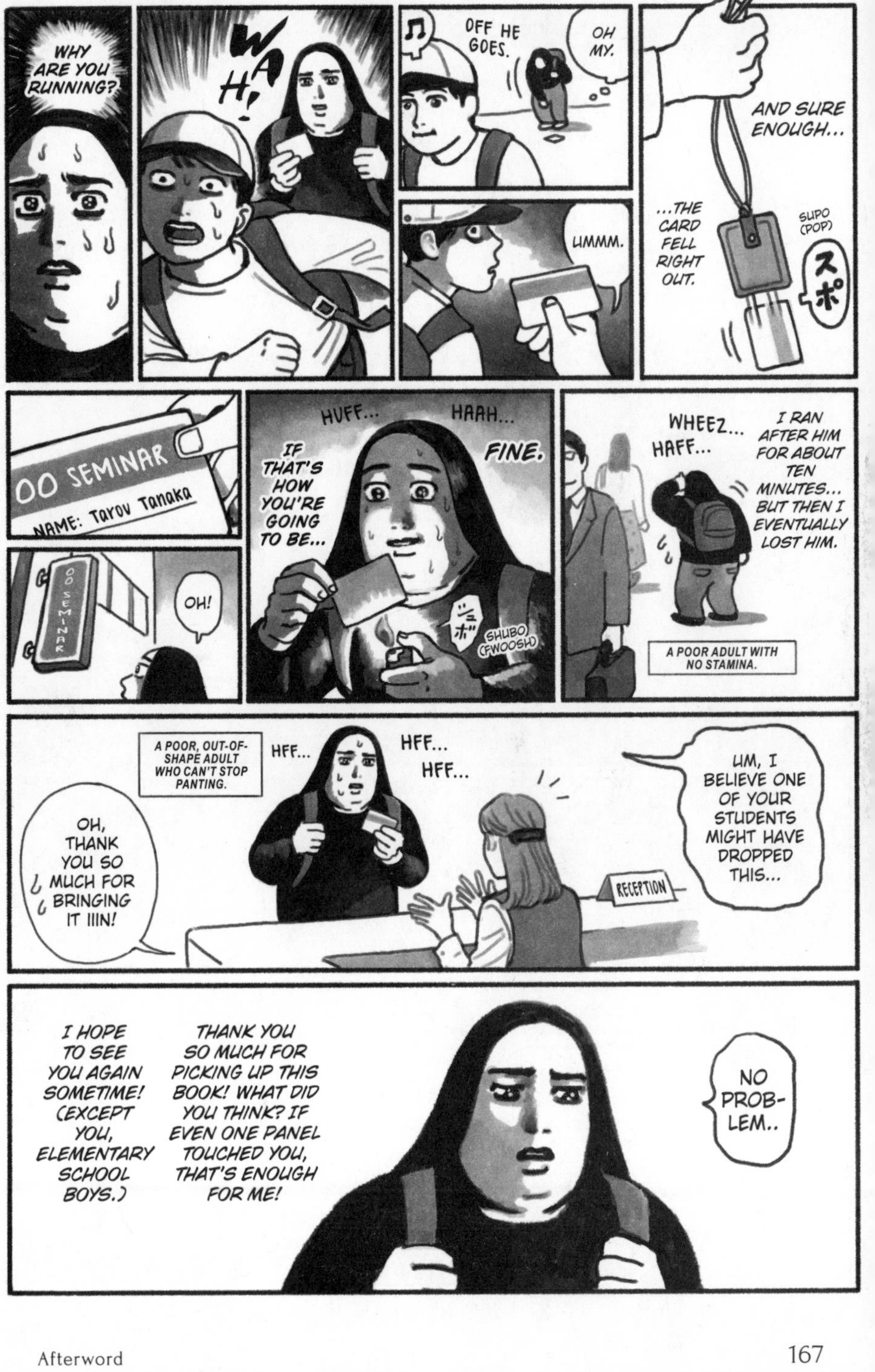
AND SURE ENOUGH...
...THE CARD FELL RIGHT OUT.
SUPO (POP)
スポ
OH MY.
OFF HE GOES.
♫
UMMM.
WAH!
WHY ARE YOU RUNNING?
I RAN AFTER HIM FOR ABOUT TEN MINUTES... BUT THEN I EVENTUALLY LOST HIM.
WHEEZ...
HAFF...
A POOR ADULT WITH NO STAMINA.
HAAH...
FINE.
HUFF...
IF THAT'S HOW YOU'RE GOING TO BE...
シュボ
SHUBO (FWOOSH)
OO SEMINAR
NAME: Tarou Tanaka
OO SEMINAR
OH!
UM, I BELIEVE ONE OF YOUR STUDENTS MIGHT HAVE DROPPED THIS...
HFF...
HFF...
HFF...
A POOR, OUT-OF-SHAPE ADULT WHO CAN'T STOP PANTING.
RECEPTION
OH, THANK YOU SO MUCH FOR BRINGING IT IIIN!
NO PROBLEM..
THANK YOU SO MUCH FOR PICKING UP THIS BOOK! WHAT DID YOU THINK? IF EVEN ONE PANEL TOUCHED YOU, THAT'S ENOUGH FOR ME!
I HOPE TO SEE YOU AGAIN SOMETIME! (EXCEPT YOU, ELEMENTARY SCHOOL BOYS.)

[Translation Notes]

COMMON HONORIFICS
no honorific: Indicates familiarity or closeness; if used without permission or reason, addressing someone in this manner would constitute an insult.
-san: The Japanese equivalent of Mr./Mrs./Ms. The fail-safe honorific if politeness is required.
-kun: Used most often when referring to boys, this honorific indicates affection or familiarity. Occasionally used by older men among their peers, but it may also be used by anyone referring to a person of lower standing.
-chan: Affectionate honorific indicating familiarity used mostly in reference to girls; also used in reference to cute persons or animals of any gender.
-sensei: A respectful term for teachers, artists, or high-level professionals.
-sama: An honorific conveying great respect.

CURRENCY CONVERSION
While exchange rates fluctuate daily, a good approximation is 100 JPY to 1 USD.

PAGE 7
Kanna Hashimoto is a singer and actor who first rose to prominence as part of the singing group Rev. from DVL. Photos taken at one of these early performances earned her viral praise and attention for her cuteness, and she was later named the Cutest Idol in a student survey.

PAGE 8
Yonesuke is the host of the Japanese reality show *Totsugeki! Tonari no Bangohan* (literally, "*Break In! On the Neighbor's Dinner*"). In each episode, Yonesuke appears unannounced on various families' doorsteps and joins them for dinner.

PAGE 22
Jinbocho is a district of Tokyo known to be a hub of bookstores, used bookstores, and publishing companies.

PAGE 23
Warren Cromartie is a former baseball player who played professionally from 1974 to 1991. After ten years in the with the Montreal Expos, Cromartie sought opportunities in Japan and played for the Yomiuri Giants from 1984 to 1990.

PAGE 24
Shiritori is a popular Japanese word game. Players take turns saying a word that begins with the last character of the preceding word. In Parolee's feed, the words are: *Kuromat**i*** (Cromartie) and ***i**kihaji* (living in disgrace), and later **u**n**ko** (poop), ***ko**mesoudo**u*** (rice riots, referencing post-WWI protests over the rising price of rice), and ***u**uroncha* (oolong tea).

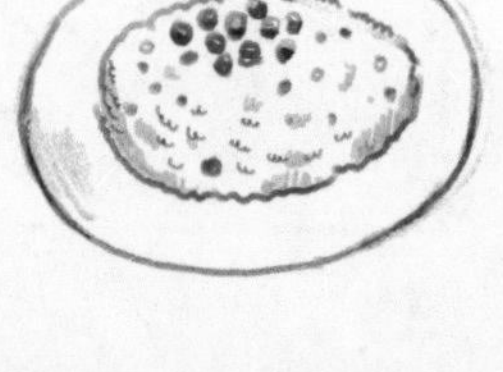

PAGE 33
Both **Yoshinoya** and **Matsuya** are names of popular Japanese chain restaurants.

PAGE 49
There's a casual pun on "**drawing**" here, with the class and Hayashi asking, "Eh?" (meaning "Huh?" or "Wha—?") and Komatsu emphasizing the "*e*" (meaning "drawing") in his response.

PAGE 51
The name of Hayashi's family's restaurant, **Fukuraku**, is made up of the characters for "good fortune" and "peace and comfort."

PAGE 58
Tien Shinhan is a character from the *Dragon Ball* manga and anime who has a shaved head.

PAGE 64
Osamu Dazai's short story "**Run, Melos!**" is a classic work of literature read in many Japanese schools and based on the ancient Greek legend of Damon and Pythias.

PAGE 67
The opposite of "*senpai*," the term "***kouhai***" refers to a junior classmate or coworker.

PAGE 96
Sazae-san is a classic newspaper comic that ran from 1946 to 1974 and describes the experiences of the titular Sazae in a post-war world, particularly in redefining women's traditional roles. The animated adaptation of the series began in 1969 and continues today. Since 1991, each show ends with a rock-paper-scissors match between Sazae and the viewers, with Sazae holding up a sign to indicate her choice.

PAGE 99
Junji Ito is a popular horror manga artist. In addition to numerous short stories, his series include *Uzumaki* (literally, "spiral"), the tale of a town that is cursed by various supernatural events involving spirals. One of the characters, Shuichi Saito, looks not unlike Nikaidou.

PAGE 100
Erika Sawajiri is an actor who went viral for her curt response to reporters during a press event, using the same phrase Nikaidou uses here.

PAGE 104
Johnny's Jr. is a part of the Johnny & Associates talent agency, which trains and promotes male idols and idol groups. The Jr. branch focuses on training up younger boys before they go on to debut as part of a group or solo act.

PAGE 149
Aoiyama Kousuke is a top-tier sumo wrestler from Bulgaria.

This book is a collection of the artist's self-published doujinshi, online stories, and newly drawn pieces.

Captivated, by you

Yama Wayama

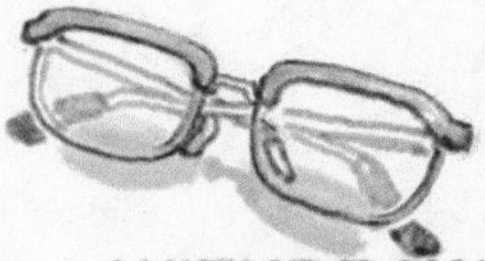

TRANSLATION: Leighann Harvey

LETTERING: Abigail Blackman

MUCHU SA, KIMI NI.
©Yama Wayama 2019
First published in Japan in 2019 by KADOKAWA CORPORATION, Tokyo.
English translation rights arranged with KADOKAWA CORPORATION, Tokyo, through Tuttle-Mori Agency, Inc.

English translation © 2021 by Yen Press, LLC

Yen Press
150 West 30th Street,
19th Floor
New York, NY 10001

Visit us at yenpress.com • facebook.com/yenpress • twitter.com/yenpress • yenpress.tumblr.com • instagram.com/yenpress

First Yen Press Edition: July 2021

Yen Press is an imprint of Yen Press, LLC. The Yen Press name and logo are trademarks of Yen Press, LLC.

The publisher is not responsible for websites (or their content) that are not owned by the publisher.

Library of Congress Control Number: 2021935586

ISBNs: 978-1-9753-2398-1 (hardcover)
978-1-9753-2399-8 (ebook)

10 9 8 7 6 5 4 3 2 1

WOR

Printed in the United States of America